The Essential

Writings of

Machiavelli

THE ESSENTIAL WRITINGS OF MACHIAVELLI

Edited and translated by
Peter Constantine

Introduction by
Albert Russell Ascoli

THE MODERN LIBRARY

NEW YORK

2007 Modern Library Paperback Edition

Copyright © 2007 by Random House, Inc.
Introduction copyright © 2007 by Albert R. Ascoli

Published in the United States by Modern Library,
an imprint of The Random House Publishing Group,
a division of Random House, Inc., New York.

MODERN LIBRARY and the TORCHBEARER Design are registered
trademarks of Random House, Inc.

LIBRARY OF CONGRESS CATALOGING-IN-PUBLICATION DATA

The essential writings of Machiavelli / edited and translated by Peter Constantine;
with an introduction by Albert R. Ascoli.—Modern Library pbk. ed.
p.   cm.
Includes bibliographical references.
ISBN 978-0-8129-7423-2 (alk. paper)
1. Political science—Early works to 1800. 2. Political ethics—Early works to 1800.
3. Machiavelli, Niccolò, 1469-1527—Political and social views. I. Constantine, Peter

JC143.M146M1469 2007
320.1   dc22   2006046902

Printed in the United States of America

www.modernlibrary.com

6 8 9 7 5

MACHIAVELLI

Niccolò Machiavelli was born on May 3, 1469, to the notary Bernardo
Machiavelli and his wife, Bartolomea de' Nelli. The father's meager
salary was supplemented by income from renting out his land near San
Casciano, a small village south of Florence. (Machiavelli was to write
his major political and literary works there while in exile.) Machiavelli
grew up in Florence's Santo Spirito district, where in his short story
"Belfagor" the archdevil took residence. Machiavelli's father kept a
diary for fourteen years, from 1474, when Niccolò turned five, which
provides us with the only information about Machiavelli's early years.
The diary underlines the straitened circumstances of the family, but
also provides an interesting insight into Machiavelli's literary education. We learn that he studied Latin and that the family had an unusually large selection of books for the time: among them volumes by
Livy, Cicero, Aristotle, Julián—books that Machiavelli would analyze
and comment on in his later works.

Machiavelli emerges from obscurity in 1498, when he was nomi-
nated Secretary of the Second Chancery, an office that handled matters relating to Florence's territories and external affairs. His fortunes
rose over the next decade, when he acted as diplomat, ambassador, and
negotiator for Florence's high-level relations with other Italian states
and foreign powers. His analytical reports and discourses from these

diplomatic missions give testimony to his political acumen and the extent of his experience.

At what seemed the height of his political career—he had become the foremost adviser to Piero Soderini, Gonfalonier of Florence—Machiavelli's fortunes changed. In 1512 Soderini was ousted from office, the Medici returned to power in Florence, and Machiavelli's illustrious political career came to an abrupt end. He came under suspicion of conspiracy against the Medici, and was imprisoned and tortured. He was subsequently exiled from Florence and sought refuge on the farm near San Casciano that he had inherited from his father.

As Machiavelli's letters from this period attest, he lived in misery. But these years of exile were to be a period of incredible productivity. This period—1512–20—produced the works for which he is remembered today: *The Prince, The Discourses, The Art of War,* and his plays *The Woman of Andros* and *The Mandrake.*

In 1520 Machiavelli grasped at the first real opportunity to reinstate himself as a central figure in Florentine politics. Lorenzo de' Medici had just died, and his cousin Giulio de' Medici (who was to become Pope Clement VII in 1523) became virtual ruler of Florence. Giulio de' Medici, aware of Machiavelli's expertise, sent him on a minor diplomatic mission to the city of Lucca. There Machiavelli wrote an astute analysis of Lucca's political system and also the famous *Life of Castruccio Castracani of Lucca.* Giulio de' Medici was impressed and offered Machiavelli a position at the University of Florence as the city's official historiographer. The product of this appointment was Machiavelli's last great work, *Florentine Histories.*

His career was showing every sign of reaching its former glory when the Medici government fell, and Machiavelli, in the final months of his life, found himself again out of favor. He died on June 21, 1527.

Contents

Biographical Note   v

Introduction *by Albert Russell Ascoli*   ix

Editor's Note   xvii

THE ESSENTIAL WRITINGS OF MACHIAVELLI

Political Works

The Prince   3

Selections from The Discourses   101

Selections from The Art of War   289

Selections from Florentine Histories   315

Political Essays and Treatises

Discourse on Pisa   349

On Pistoian Matters   351

On the Nature of the French   355

On How to Treat the Populace of
    Valdichiana After Their Rebellion   359

How Duke Valentino Killed the Generals Who
    Conspired Against Him   365

Discourse on the Affairs of Germany
    and Its Emperor   373
A Caution to the Medici   375

LITERATURE

Rules for an Elegant Social Circle   381
The Persecution of Africa   387
Belfagor   393
The Life of Castruccio Castracani of Lucca   403
The Mandrake   433

LETTERS

    483

INTRODUCTION

Albert Russell Ascoli

In his second and lesser known play, *Clizia,* Niccolò Machiavelli imagines history, following the late Greek historian Polybius and ultimately Plato, as a cyclical process: "If in the world the same men were to return, as the same events recur, a hundred years would not pass before we would find ourselves once more together, doing the same things as we do today."[1] Machiavelli, who believed strongly in the utility of reading the past in order to understand, and to shape, the present, nonetheless speaks in the verbal mode of "condition-contrary-to-fact," suggesting the improbability of his hypothesis and ironically undermining his claims even as he makes them. It is this voice—wise, self-critical, sometimes quite bitter, and often very funny—that the present volume offers up to be heard, as it rarely is by an English-language public, in something very near its full range, power, and beauty.

We no longer believe that history moves in cycles, and we are beginning to lose faith in the model of relentless forward progress—technological, economic, sociopolitical—that has predominated, at least in the imperial West, since the Enlightenment. And we have responded to this loss of our principal models of historical understand-

---

1. *Clizia,* Preface; see also *The Discourses,* Book II, Preface and chapters 39 and 43, and Book III, chapter 1, and the *Florentine Histories* Book III, chapter 1, and Book V, chapter 1; cf. *The Prince,* chapter 6.

ing by forgetting the past—or chopping it into postmodern fragments—
or turning it into grotesque fantasies of hermetic codes that unlock a
violently repressed past (which, oddly enough, then looks very like the
present). If there is an idea of history we have not forgotten, it is
the Christian, or Marxian, idea of history's end—of the Apocalypse, or
of "the withering away of the state." Under such conditions, Machiavelli still has much to offer, whether he is seen as constituting the origins of our current circumstances, as "the father of modern politics"
and a sponsor of what is known in some quarters as secular humanism,
or instead viewed as someone experiencing, and recording, a crisis in
world order and sociopolitical institutions not entirely unlike the one
we ourselves now face.

Unlike his contemporaries Michelangelo, Leonardo da Vinci, and
the epic poet Ludovico Ariosto, Niccolò Machiavelli (1469–1527)
does not tempt us with the possibility of flight into a past both simpler
and more beautiful than our own world. Rather, he has consistently
been figured as the originator of ideas and practices that have led directly to the present state of things. On the one hand, his exaltation of
the Roman Republic (as against the later Empire), his links to the last
stirrings of anti-Medicean Florentine republicanism, and his violent
critique of the Catholic Church's role in Italian politics have been
understood as throwing open the gates to a secularization of the political that led to English parliamentary government and thence to the
American and French revolutions.[2] And this view finds real support in
his work, particularly on the pages of his long commentary on Livy's
Roman *Histories, The Discourses,* where, for example, he exposes Julius
Caesar's power grab (and the literary propaganda machine that legit-
imized it) and argues, against all received wisdom of the time, that the
"people" understand the world better than the "Prince."

On the other hand, he has been linked, and not without reason, to
the degradation and delegitimization of a politics decoupled from
moral imperatives and transcendent religious principles. Already in
Elizabethan England he is "the murderous Machiavel" dramatized in
the diabolical shenanigans of Shakespeare's Richard III, not to mention Iago, and frequently tied—ironically—to the Protestant demoni-

2. As J.G.A. Pocock argues in *The Machiavellian Moment* (Princeton University Press, 1975).

zation of the corrupt papacy. For Hannah Arendt, and even more for Leo Strauss, he is the patron saint not of modern democracy, but rather of demagogic totalitarianisms, from Fascism and Nazism to Stalin's Soviet Union. Here also, and more obviously, there is a great deal of supporting evidence: for example, in the famous dicta from *The Prince* that "all armed prophets were successful, while unarmed prophets came to ruin"; "a man is quicker to forget the death of his father than the loss of his patrimony"; "a wise [prince] will not keep his word"; and so on. Or in the exemplary role conferred on the bloody state-building of Cesare Borgia, son of Pope Alexander VI. Or in the mockery of Roman Lucretia's chastity and suicide—out of which Livy says the Roman Republic arose—via the adulterous seduction and corruption of Florentine Lucrezia in his darkly comic play, *The Mandrake.*

What these two apparently contradictory views share is the notion that in Machiavelli can be found the first stirrings of modernity—of secularization, of dispassionately scientific thought, of human agency and foresight ("prudence"), rather than divine providence, as the driving engines of politics and society. What they share as well is a strong tendency to wrench Machiavelli's words and works out of their original historical context and to turn his always qualified, always historically grounded precepts into abstract, universal rules of conduct. Moreover, both views identify Machiavelli with one text—usually *The Prince,* sometimes *The Discourses*—when in fact he wrote across a broad spectrum ranging from diplomatic reports, to political-historical treatises, to a dialogic primer in *The Art of War,* to a collection of fascinating personal letters, to poetry and drama, and even to a treatise on the Tuscan language (in which he stages a dialogue between himself and his illustrious precursor Dante Alighieri, whose work he both loved and mocked). There is a strong case, then, for looking at Machiavelli's oeuvre as a whole and for reading it in the flickering light of his personal biography and of the turbulent era which gave rise to him, and which he, as much as anyone, is responsible for blazoning in the historical imagination of the West. In particular, there is a case to be made for seeing his experience of a radical historical and ideological crisis as analogous to the unsettled world that we now confront.

Niccolò Machiavelli was born in 1469, the same year that Lorenzo

de' Medici (called the Magnificent) assumed unofficial control of Florence, following in the footsteps of his father and especially his grandfather, Cosimo the elder.[3] Machiavelli was a member of the oligarchic
elite that ruled Florence, but not of its upper echelon (unlike his friends
Francesco Vettori and especially Francesco Guicciardini, author of the
first great *History of Italy*). He came of age, politically speaking, between 1494 and 1500, when, in rapid succession, (1) the vulnerability
of the Italian peninsula—divided into small, independent, fractious
states—was exposed by the invasion of Charles VIII, King of France;
(2) the Medici family—now headed by Lorenzo's feckless son, Piero—
was unseated from power and temporarily exiled from Florence by a
combination of religious zeal (centered on the "unarmed prophet"
himself, Girolamo Savonarola), of anti-Medicean, pro-republican sentiment, and of King Charles's almost unwitting collaboration; (3) Savonarola rose to power and then fell, burned at the stake, in 1498,
having failed in his utopian quest for religious and political reform;
and (4) a new, moderate republican government was instituted under
the leadership of one Piero Soderini, with Machiavelli assuming the
role of second secretary to the ruling council, ultimately becoming
Soderini's chief political, diplomatic, and military adviser.

Machiavelli's vocation—his true calling, as he himself understood
it—was in the role of active participant in the world of Florentine and
Italian politics. His writings from the period when he served the re-
founded republic (from 1498 to its fall in 1512) are largely confined to
official dispatches, reports, and briefings; his only serious literary endeavors were two chronicles of Florentine political life over two
decades, written in the rhyme scheme *terza rima*, invented by Dante for
the *Divine Comedy* (ca. 1320). Only with the ignominious collapse of the
republic—provoked by an invasion by troops of the other European
superpower, Spain, and with the collaboration of Pope Julius II
(Michelangelo's patron)—and the triumphant return of the Medici,
whose head, Giovanni de' Medici, would shortly be crowned Pope
Leo X, did Machiavelli's career as "Machiavelli" begin in earnest. In
a justly famous—caustic, pathetic, and brilliant—letter of Decem-

---

3. This Lorenzo is not to be confused with his grandson of the same name, to whom *The
Prince* is dedicated.

ber 10, 1513, Machiavelli, from his exile on the fringes of Florence, speaks of writing what would become *The Prince*—declaring its content to be the fruit of his private colloquies with the (books of the) ancient philosophers, historians, and poets, and its purpose to be that of acquiring favor with the Medici (who were, reasonably enough, deeply suspicious of this counselor to their enemies, whom they had recently arrested and briefly tortured before banishing him) and thus regaining active employment.

That purpose was never fully realized, though his relations with the Medici gradually improved to the point of his receiving a commission from Leo's Medicean successor as pope, Clement VII, to write the *Florentine Histories*. Instead, in the fifteen years between his exclusion from the precincts of power and his untimely death (in 1527, at the age of fifty-eight), Machiavelli would write *The Prince, The Discourses, The Art of War,* the *Histories,* and his two plays, along with various poems, a misogynistic short story ("Belfagor"), essays, a biography, and many, many letters. In these, he offers an inside view, at once melancholy and incisive, poignant and satirical, of the daily life of Renaissance Florence, revealing what for us today has become a kind of museum—an architectural and artistic monument, a memorial to the great artists and writers of its past (from Dante and Giotto to Alberti, Donatello, and Lorenzo, to Michelangelo and Machiavelli himself)—as a raw, raunchy, vital, profoundly human place. At the same time, he invents (or so it is claimed) the scientific study of politics, takes lengthy strides toward modern ideas of the writing of history, and makes a crucial contribution to the refounding of a secular dramatic theater, which would reach its zenith less than a hundred years later, in the England of Shakespeare.

All of these works, most of which are represented in this collection in whole or in part, deserve their own, separate consideration, which, alas, they cannot receive in an introduction of this kind. Together they represent a powerful, anguished response to a crisis not only in Machiavelli's own life and in the life of his beloved Florence, but in that of the Italian peninsula and of Europe generally. The elements of that crisis are well known: the rise of the nation-state (France, Spain, England), which would soon render the independent states of Italy obsolete; the discovery of an unknown world that both unsettled traditional understandings of human society and unleashed a frenzied pursuit of imperial dominion and economic hegemony; the fragmentation of Christianity with the Lutheran-Protestant revolt (whose first warning shot—the Lutheran theses—was directed at the gaudy, worldly papacy of Leo and was heard in the same year we believe Machiavelli completed *The Prince,* 1517); and so on and on. Machiavelli's writings, especially the ones on politics and history, represent an extreme response to an extreme situation—and they betray the angry, if often bitingly funny, awareness that traditional theocentric ways of thinking and established institutions (whether Florentine republicanism or the Catholic Church itself) were incapable of coping with a menacing tide of drastic changes.

It is tempting to find in this experience, Machiavelli's experience, an allegory of our recent history and present state: the decay and evident inadequacy of protodemocratic institutions; wars between superpowers that carry along the rest of the world in their wake; globalization driven by economic exploitation and the exportation of an imperial culture; fierce, at times violent, attacks motivated by religious intolerance (most obviously between Protestants and Catholics, but the expanding Muslim world, in the form of the Ottoman Empire, was an increasingly present worry for Europe); a world in which terror is a weapon of first resort. No doubt, Machiavelli would tell us if he could, such parallels have their limitations, but also their uses.

Which brings me to a last point, one that encapsulates my own admiration of and wariness about this courageous, dangerous, ever-innovative author: Machiavelli's political thought places us at the very top of the intellectual and ethical "slippery slope" one hears so much about—that is, in a world of politics, society, and culture no longer grounded in sacred truths or moral imperatives, no longer able to count on long-cherished principles of order and understanding. But, we should ask ourselves—as Machiavelli's best readers have asked themselves since his own time—does he invent this slippery slope, or does he simply reveal that it has been the uncertain ground beneath our feet all along? Does he create or does he expose the perils of a historical world of contingency where our neighbors' (and perhaps even our own) intentions are frequently bad, where justice is often an empty, crowd-pleasing spectacle, where human rights and freedom are not di-

vinely given and "unalienable" but, if they exist as such at all, hard won
and easily lost?

There is no easy answer to this question—which is in some ways *the*
question we face today—but the reading of Machiavelli in all of his
many facets, in the complexity of his thought and of his imagination,
demands of us that we address it before it is too late.

—

ALBERT RUSSELL ASCOLI is Gladys Arata Terrill Distinguished Professor of Italian Studies at the University of California, Berkeley. He has
held research fellowships from the NEH and ACLS, and was awarded
the Rome Prize for study at the American Academy in Rome in
2004–5. His publications include *Ariosto's Bitter Harmony: Crisis and
Evasion in the Italian Renaissance* (Princeton, 1987) and *Dante and the
Making of a Modern Author* (forthcoming from Cambridge University
Press, 2007). With Victoria Kahn he co-edited *Machiavelli and the Discourse of Literature* (Cornell, 1993), which includes his essay "Machiavelli's Gift of Counsel."

EDITOR'S NOTE

Born in a city which more than any other spoke in a way
that was ideal for expressing itself in verse and prose.

NICCOLÒ MACHIAVELLI

When Machiavelli set out to write his final great work, *Florentine Histories,* his contract with Cardinal Giulio de' Medici stipulated that Machiavelli would compile "the annals and chronicles of Florence" but also specified that it was up to him in what tongue he chose to do so, "Latin or Tuscan." In the early 1500s Latin was the language of intellectual discourse and high literature. Machiavelli, throughout his life as a literary and political writer, championed a new and vibrant Italian idiom based on the Tuscan speech of Florence, an idiom which the great Florentine writers of his time who chose not to write in Latin could bolster with Latin or Latinate words.

The contract to write *Florentine Histories* was drawn up in 1520. At that time Machiavelli had been exiled from Florentine political life for eight years and was living on his farm in straitened circumstances after a decade of being in the center of Florentine politics as the foremost adviser to the Gonfalonier Piero Soderini. But in 1520, when Soderini offered him a prestigious and profitable position in Ragusa (present-day Dubrovnik), Machiavelli made a surprising choice: After years of desperate attempts to return to political life, he now declined Soderini's offer. He opted instead to become Florence's official historiographer at about half the salary he had earned a decade earlier as Soderini's right-hand man. To Machiavelli, being a literary figure was of greater importance.

This interest in elegant writing manifested itself throughout Machiavelli's career. Judging by what has come down to us, his prose first came to notice when he was thirty. We have discourses written in an official capacity, pieces such as "Discourse on Pisa" and "On Pistoian Matters," which are incisive analyses of urgent political problems that Florence was facing. They are remarkable not only for their immediate sizing up of issues, but also for their clear and beautiful prose. In a piece believed to be from that time, "How Duke Valentino Killed the Generals Who Conspired Against Him," Machiavelli describes the brutal and cunning means by which Cesare Borgia (Duke Valentino) eliminated rivals who crossed him. The controlled prose describing the mounting menace of Borgia's murderous tactics is given a touch of lyricism as Machiavelli describes the landscape, retarding the action:

> Whoever approaches Senigallia has on his right the mountains, with foothills that come so close to the sea that there is often only a narrow strip of land between them and the waves. Even in those places where the foothills are further inland, the strip is never more than two miles wide. Senigallia lies a bow's shot from these foothills, and less than a mile away from the shore. There is a little river by the city that washes the walls facing toward Fano.

Machiavelli's manuscripts reveal how carefully he edited his own work: words crossed-out, sentences chiseled down for concision, a lofty Latin word replaced by a simpler and more direct Italian one. The slightly hyperbolic and pompous *redundando in utilità* (literally: "redounding in benefit") of a first draft is changed into the simpler *retornando utilità* ("returning benefit").

The translator must keep in mind that words change their meanings and nuances over the centuries: *Virtù*, for instance, in modern Italian, primarily means "virtue" in the modern English sense, but in Machiavelli's Italian it had a range of meaning depending on the context. It principally reflected the Latin *virtus*—excellence, manliness, strength, vigor, bravery, and courage. In Renaissance Italian it also took on shades of "skill," "competence," and "virtue" in the modern sense. Machiavelli uses the word in many forms throughout his works: *virtuoso, virtude, virtutis, virtuosissimo, virtuosissimamente. Religione* is another word that has different shades of meaning in Machiavelli's Italian. Mostly it means "religion" in the modern sense, but it can also reflect the Latin original *religio:* conscientiousness, moral obligation, duty.

Throughout his works Machiavelli was refracting ancient texts, particularly in *The Discourses on Livy.* Where he was specifically responding to Latin and ancient Greek texts, I have translated the passages from the original in the footnotes.

—

Machiavelli took himself seriously as an important literary figure of his time. When in *Orlando Furioso* his contemporary Ludovico Ariosto has the poet return from the sea of writing to the shore of reading, he encounters a crowd of literary figures of the day—but not Machiavelli.[*] He was angry at being omitted.

Today, Machiavelli's most widely read work is *The Prince,* and the three books of *The Discourses on Livy* has a more limited readership. But the vast body of Machiavelli's important and compelling works is unjustly neglected. This volume presents a wider panorama of Machiavelli's many guises as a political philosopher and literary figure. His work has been clouded by centuries of controversy, but as you read through *The Prince, The Discourses on Livy,* and his historical and literary masterpieces, a clearer sense of their powerful, multilayered texture emerges—precisely the texture that has led to so much debate and disagreement.

What has perplexed readers for the past five centuries is that Machiavelli's most popular work, *The Prince,* seems to espouse the ruthless acquisition and maintenance of power by a single ruler, while his significantly more far-reaching book, *The Discourses on Livy,* advocates republican forms of government. How can these two incompatible sides of Machiavelli be reconciled? It is widely believed that *The Discourses on Livy* corresponds to his fundamental beliefs: he interprets the great Roman historian's *History of Rome* as offering viable models to be emulated in his own time. *The Prince,* on the other hand, is seen as offering viable classical models to a single ruler. Machiavelli hoped that this ruler would be one of the Medici, who in appreciation might restore him to his former high position in politics.

The Essential Writings of Machiavelli is divided into four parts. The

---

[*]Albert Russell Ascoli and Victoria Kahn, in *Machiavelli and the Discourse of Literature* (Ithaca, N.Y.: Cornell University Press, 1993), p. 1.

first presents the major political works: *The Prince,* and selections from *The Discourses on Livy, The Art of War,* and *Florentine Histories.* The second part contains Machiavelli's political essays and treatises. These lesser-known pieces are from the period when Machiavelli was at the height of his political career. They range from strategic analyses of urgent and critical issues that Florence was facing beyond its borders during the first decade of the 1500s to lighter pieces, such as Machiavelli's irreverent "On the Nature of the French." The selection of fiction, social satire, historical prose, and theater in the third part shows perhaps the greatest range of Machiavelli's literary talent. *The Mandrake* is considered one of the most well-crafted theatrical pieces of the Italian Renaissance. It is the only play of the period that is still widely performed in our time. The final part is a brief selection of Machiavelli's letters to friends and family. They reveal Machiavelli as a caring, witty, sensitive man, and contain some of his most beautiful writing.

ACKNOWLEDGMENTS

I would like to thank Burton Pike for his encouragement, support, and knowledgeable editorial advice throughout this project. I am also grateful to Albert Russell Ascoli for his encouragement: I benefited from both his advice and his extensive publications over the years on Machiavelli and the Italian Renaissance. I am also grateful to Daniel Javitch for his editorial recommendations, to Nelson Moe, and to Beth Hadas for her insights into Machiavelli's comic prose. I am especially thankful to Judy Sternlight, my editor at Modern Library, for her tireless support and helpful knowledge of the Renaissance, to Vincent La Scala, and to Jessica Wainwright.

I am particularly grateful to Columbia University's libraries and the help of Karen Green, the Librarian of Ancient and Medieval History and Religion. Columbia's substantial Italian Renaissance collection was of great help for the annotation and interpretation of the texts.

—*Peter Constantine*

POLITICAL

WORKS

THE PRINCE

The Prince *is the first modern treatise of political philosophy, and over the centuries it has remained one of the most influential and most widely read works. It is of outspoken clarity, and yet is one of the most enigmatic works in history. It tells in clear terms how to gain power, how to keep it, and how to wield it, and has often been seen as the product of cold cynicism. Despite its clarity, however, centuries of readers have not been able to agree on what its principles actually are.*

The Prince *was written around 1513 while Machiavelli was in exile from Florence, after the republican government of Piero Soderini was ousted by the Medici. He wrote* The Prince *in the hope of gaining favor with the Medici, but unfortunately did not succeed.*

During Machiavelli's lifetime The Prince *circulated in manuscript form and was only published posthumously, in 1532.*

NICCOLÒ MACHIAVELLI TO HIS MAGNIFICENCE LORENZO DE' MEDICI[1]

Those who wish to win the favor of a prince will generally approach him with gifts of what they value most or what they believe will most delight him. Hence we see princes being offered horses, arms, vestments of gold, precious stones, and similar accoutrements worthy of their grandeur. Wishing to present myself to Your Magnificence with a token of my deepest respect, I have found among my possessions nothing that I value or esteem higher than my knowledge of the deeds of great men. I have acquired this knowledge through my long experience of modern affairs and a lifelong study of ancient times, all of which I have weighed and examined with great diligence and brought together into this small volume, which I am now offering to Your Magnificence. Though I deem this work unworthy of being in Your illustrious presence, my confidence in Your benevolence persuades me that it will be accepted, and that Your Magnificence will recognize that I cannot offer You a greater gift than the prospect of Your understanding in the shortest period all that I have experienced and learned over so many years and with so much danger and hardship. I have not filled this volume with pompous rhetoric, with bombast and magnificent words, or with the unnecessary artifice with which so many writers gild their work. I wanted nothing extraneous to ornament my writing,

1. Lorenzo de' Medici (1492–1519) was the grandson of Lorenzo the Magnificent.

for it has been my purpose that only the range of material and the gravity of the subject should make it pleasing. Nor do I wish it to be thought presumptuous that a man of low and humble condition like myself should presume to map out and direct the government of princes. But just as a cartographer will descend into the plains in order to study the nature of the mountains, and will then climb the highest peaks in order to study the low-lying land, so, too, only an exalted prince can grasp the nature of the people, and only a lesser man can perceive the nature of a prince.

I hope therefore that Your Magnificence will accept this humble gift in the spirit in which it is offered. Should You condescend to read and consider it carefully, You will perceive in its pages my profound desire that Your Magnificence will rise to the greatness that Fortune and Your qualities promise. And should Your Magnificence deign to look down from the lofty summit of Your eminence to these lowly depths, You will see how I have suffered undeservedly Fortune's great and continuing malignity.

CHAPTER ONE

OF THE KINDS OF PRINCIPALITIES THAT EXIST, AND HOW THEY CAN BE ACQUIRED

All states, all dominions that rule or have ruled over men, are or have been either republics or principalities. Principalities are either hereditary, with a long-established bloodline, or new. And the new principalities are either entirely new, as Milan was to Francesco Sforza,[2] or are like limbs added to the hereditary state of the prince who acquires them, as the Kingdom of Naples was to the King of Spain.[3] States obtained in this way are accustomed either to living under a prince, or to being free. They are acquired either with the arms of others, or with one's own, either by chance or by skill.

---

2. Francesco Sforza (1401–66) was a soldier of fortune who became Duke of Milan in 1450.
3. Ferdinand the Catholic (1452–1516), King of Aragon, also became Ferdinand III of Naples in 1504.

CHAPTER TWO

OF HEREDITARY PRINCIPALITIES

I will not discuss republics, as I have already done so at some length elsewhere. I shall only concentrate on principalities, and shall weave together the threads I have already laid out. I will show how these principalities can be governed and maintained.

First, states that are hereditary and tied to the bloodline of their prince are easier to maintain than new ones. It is enough not to diverge from the practices of one's forebears, and to handle unforeseen issues as they arise. If such a prince is of at least average ability he can retain his position of power, so long as no extraordinary or excessive force deprive him of it. If this prince is deprived of his state, he will find he can reacquire it if any misfortune befalls the usurper.

In Italy we have the example of the Duke of Ferrara, who resisted the assaults of the Venetians in 1484 and of Pope Julius II in 1510, for the simple reason that he had inherited an ancient principality.[4] A hereditary prince has less cause to mistreat his subjects, and so is more loved by them. If unusual vices do not make him hated, it is to be expected that he will be loved by his people.

The long continuum of the dominion obliterates the memories and issues that make men yearn for innovation, for one change will inevitably forge a link to another.

4. In fact, Duke Ercole d'Este of Ferrara managed to end the war with Venetians in 1484, while his son Duke Alfonso managed to stay in power despite excommunication and an ongoing war with the papal forces.

CHAPTER THREE

Of mixed principalities

It is in the new principality that the difficulties lie. First, if the principality is not completely new, but is like a limb or extension added to another principality (in which case we could almost call the whole state a mixed principality), its volatility stems mainly from a difficulty inherent in all new principalities. This is that men will willingly change their ruler in the hope that they will fare better, a hope that leads them to take up arms against their old ruler. But in this they are deceived, because, as they invariably discover, their lot under a new ruler is inevitably worse. This is the result of another natural and basic inevitability: that you cannot avoid offending those whose new ruler you are, both with your armed soldiers and with innumerable other provocations that come in the wake of a conquest. You end up making enemies of all those you have offended during your conquest of the principality, and you find that you cannot keep the friendship of those who helped you to power, since you cannot satisfy them in the way they had envisioned. Furthermore, you cannot take strong measures against them, as you are indebted to them. Even with the most powerful army, if you want to invade a state, you need the support of the people. It was for these reasons that King Louis XII of France was quick to occupy Milan, and just as quick to lose it. Duke Ludovico's own forces were enough to win Milan back the first time, because the same masses that had opened the gates for Louis, finding themselves misled in their hopes for a better future, could not endure the new prince's offenses.[5]

It is a fact that once a prince acquires a rebellious state for the second time, it also proves harder to lose that state a second time.[6] This is because the prince who seizes the opportunity of the rebellion has fewer scruples about securing his position by punishing offenders, flushing out suspects, and strengthening all the places where he is weakest. In this sense, it was enough for a Duke Ludovico to make a little noise along the borders for Louis XII to lose Milan the first time. But for him to lose Milan a second time the whole world had to unite against him, defeat his army, and chase it out of Italy.[7] This followed from the causes I have already laid out. Nonetheless, both the first and second time, Milan was taken from him.

The general reasons for the first loss have been discussed. It now remains to discuss the second, and to see what recourse someone in Louis's position could have taken to maintain himself more securely in his new acquisition. I must stress that the states a prince acquires and adds to his own are either of the same country and language, or are not. If they are it is much easier to retain them, particularly if they are not used to freedom. To hold them securely, it is enough to extinguish the line of the previous prince who ruled them. As for the rest, if the new acquisition's former state of affairs is kept and there is no difference in customs, men will live quite peacefully, as we have seen in Burgundy, Brittany, Gascony, and Normandy, which for a long time now have all belonged to France. Although there is some difference in language, their customs are similar, and their people get along with one another quite easily. He who acquires such states and wishes to retain them has to make sure of two things: that the bloodline of their former princes is extinguished, and that their laws and taxes remain the same. This way, the prince's new state merges with the old, quickly becoming a single body.

But difficulties arise when you acquire states in a land with differ-

5. Louis XII occupied Milan in September 1499, but was ousted in February 1500 by Ludovico Sforza. Louis, however, managed to recapture Milan within two months.
6. Once Louis XII recaptured Milan, it remained under his rule until 1512.
7. The Holy League of 1511, organized by Pope Julius II, was an anti-French coalition that included Spain, Venice, the Holy Roman Empire, England, and the Swiss. The League managed to drive the French out of Milan in May 1512.

ing languages, customs, and laws. To keep these states, you need good fortune and much diligence. One of the best and quickest solutions is for the new prince to go and live in his new state. This makes the possession more durable and secure. The Turk did this in Greece.[8] With all the other measures he took to keep Greece in his possession, had he not gone to live there he would not have succeeded, because once the prince is established within his new state he is able to see problems as they arise and can remedy them. If he is not there, problems become obvious only once they are dire and can no longer be remedied. Furthermore, if he is present, his new state will not be looted by his officials, and his new subjects can enjoy immediate access to their prince. This will give them more reason to love him if they are on his side, and to fear him if they are not, and foreign powers wishing to attack his state will respect him more. Hence, if the prince lives in his new state, it is difficult for him to lose it.

Another efficient remedy is to set up colonies in one or two places that will act as the shackles of your new state. If you do not set up colonies, you will have to send a great number of troops to secure it, while a colony can be established and maintained at negligible cost. The only subjects who will be affronted are those whose fields and houses will be confiscated to be given to the new colonists. But these dispossessed subjects make up only a small part of the state and will end up poor and dispersed, and so can do no harm. The rest of your new subjects will not be affronted (and hence will be acquiescent), but will also be frightened of transgressing, worried that they too might be dispossessed. I conclude that colonies do not cost much, are loyal, and will cause less trouble. And as I have already mentioned, those you dispossess cannot harm you, as they will be poor and dispersed. In short, men must either be flattered or eliminated, because a man will readily avenge a slight grievance, but not one that is truly severe. Hence, the offense done a man must be of the kind that cannot incur vengeance.

If you choose armed forces instead of colonies, you will spend more and will have to squander all the income from the new state in order to pay the army. This will turn the acquisition into a loss, and all your

8. The Turks occupied Constantinople in 1453, and in 1457 transferred the capital of the Ottoman Empire from Edirne to Constantinople.

new subjects will end up offended, since an army, constantly on the move and constantly requartered, hurts the whole state. Everyone feels the pain, and everyone becomes your enemy. And these are enemies who can harm you, because though they have been defeated, they remain on their own ground. So in every sense, using armed forces is as useless as setting up colonies is useful.

It is also important when a prince has conquered a foreign state that he become the protector of the surrounding weaker powers, and do all he can to weaken the stronger ones. He must take precautions so that no foreigner equal in power manages to enter his new state. If he should enter, it will be because he was brought in by discontented factions driven by ambition or fear. We saw this in the case of the Aetolians who introduced the Romans into Greece;[9] and in every other province in which the Romans set foot, it was with the help of some of the inhabitants. The order of things is that the moment a powerful invader takes over a state, all the weaker factions within it join forces with him, spurred on by their envy of the ruler who had wielded power over them before. In other words, the new prince has no trouble winning the weaker factions over, because they will willingly become part of his new state. He has only to see to it that they do not gain too much power and authority. With his forces and their favor, he can easily bring down those who are powerful so that he will remain the only arbiter in the land. He who does not follow this course will quickly lose all he has gained, and will be plagued by infinite difficulties while he holds power.

The Romans were careful to follow these principles in the provinces they conquered, establishing colonies, supporting the less powerful without increasing their strength, undercutting the strong, and not letting powerful foreigners gain standing there. Greece serves as a perfect example. The Romans supported the Achaeans and the Aetolians, weakened the Kingdom of Macedonia, and chased out Antiochus.[10] Yet despite the help that the Achaeans and the Aetolians

9. The Aetolian League, a federation of cities north of the Gulf of Corinth, had become one of the leading military powers in Greece by the fourth century BCE. In 211 and 200–197 BCE the Aetolians joined Rome in its war against Philip V of Macedon.

10. The Achaean League, a federation of cities in the Peloponnesus, entered an alliance with Rome in 198 BCE against Philip V of Macedon, at the time the most powerful ruler in Greece. The alliance temporarily gave the Achaeans and the Aetolians (see previous footnote) domi-

provided, the Romans did not permit them to expand their territories. Nor did Philip's subtle persuasions induce the Romans to become his friends without undercutting him. And all of Antiochus's power still did not persuade the Romans to consent to his ruling over any state within their territories. The Romans did what every wise prince must do: They kept their eyes trained not only on present problems but also future ones, which must be anticipated with great care, because when one sees these problems approaching they can still be remedied, whereas if one waits for them to arrive it will be too late to administer medicine. The illness will have become incurable. As physicians say of consumption: In the first stages it is easy to cure though hard to detect, but with the progress of time, if not detected or treated, consumption becomes easy to detect but hard to cure. This can also be said of the affairs of state. If one recognizes evolving ills in advance (for which one must be farsighted), one can cure them quickly. But if they are left to develop until they are plain for all to see, it will be too late for remedies.

The Romans recognized potential difficulties in advance and always remedied them in time. They never let problems develop just so they could escape a war, for they knew that such wars cannot be avoided, only postponed to the advantage of others. Consequently, the Romans chose to wage war on Philip and Antiochus in Greece so that they would not have to do so in Italy, even though they could have avoided war with either of them for a while. But they chose not to. The Romans never liked the dictum we constantly hear from the wise men of our day, that time will take care of things. The Romans preferred to take care of things by means of their own skill and prudence, because time will sweep everything before it and can bring good things as well as bad, bad things as well as good.

But let us return to France, and see if her king did any of the things we have discussed. I shall speak of Louis XII, not of Charles, as Louis held his acquisitions in Italy for a longer period, which gives us the opportunity to evaluate his progress with greater clarity. We will see how he did the exact opposite of what one must do to maintain a foreign state one has acquired.

---

nance in Greece. But within a few decades they were degraded to weak protectorates of Rome. Antiochus the Great (242–187) created a vast empire in Asia Minor and the East, but was finally defeated by Rome in the Battle of Magnesia in 190 BCE.

Louis XII managed to enter Italy through the ambition of the Venetians, who wanted to acquire half the state of Lombardy by his coming. I do not wish to censure the king's course of action: He wanted to gain a footing in Italy, and did not have any friends there. In fact, as all doors were shut to him on account of King Charles's actions,[11] Louis XII had to make friends wherever he could, and he would have succeeded in this course had he not made a number of mistakes elsewhere. Once he had acquired Lombardy, King Louis quickly regained the reputation that Charles had cost him. Genoa yielded, and the Florentines rushed to become his friends, as did the Marquis of Mantua, the Duke of Ferrara, Bentivoglo, the Countess of Forlì, the Lords of Faenza, Pesaro, Rimini, Camerino, Piombino, and the men of Lucca, Pisa, and Siena. The Venetians quickly realized the rashness of the course they had chosen: In order to gain two holdings in Lombardy, they had helped King Louis gain dominion over two-thirds of Italy.

Let us consider how easily Louis could have maintained his reputation in Italy if he had observed the aforementioned rules. He could have remained secure had he stood by his friends, who, because they were many, weak, and afraid (some of the Church, some of the Venetians), would have been forced to remain at his side. With their help he could have kept in check those who remained powerful. But no sooner did he set foot in Milan than he did the exact opposite, helping Pope Alexander to occupy the province of the Romagna. What Louis did not realize was that with this move he weakened himself, alienating his allies and those who would readily have rushed into his arms, and strengthened the Church, adding to its spiritual power, which gives it such authority, a prodigious amount of temporal power.

Having made this initial mistake, Louis was forced to continue making mistakes, so that in the end, in order to curb Pope Alexander's ambitions and stop him from becoming the ruler of Tuscany, he was forced to invade Italy. It was not enough that Louis strengthened the Church and pushed away his friends, but because he coveted the Kingdom of Naples, he decided to share it with the King of Spain. The result was that, whereas he had been the only authority in Italy, he now

11. Charles VIII of France had marched through Italy in 1494 to occupy Naples, which he had inherited from the Angevins. He was crowned King of Naples in 1495, but was ousted in the Battle of Fornovo that same year by Ludovico Sforza, Emperor Maximilian I, the pope, and King Ferdinand II of Aragon, who formed the League of Venice.

introduced a powerful companion to whom ambitious and dissatisfied men could turn. Instead of leaving a king in Naples who would be a puppet, he drove him out and brought in a king who was powerful enough to drive Louis out.[12]

The wish to acquire is a most natural thing, and men who manage to acquire are always applauded (or at least not blamed) when they succeed. What is an error and worthy of blame is when a man cannot acquire something, but desires to obtain it in any way he can. If Louis, for instance, could have conquered Naples with his own forces, he should have done so. If he could not, he should have desisted, and not opted for sharing Naples with another power. It is excusable that he shared Lombardy with the Venetians, because that was how he managed to secure a foothold in Italy, but that he shared Naples merits blame, because it cannot be excused by any such necessity.

In other words, Louis XII made the following five mistakes: He destroyed the smaller powers; he helped a single power in Italy to gain strength;[13] he brought a powerful foreigner into Italy;[14] he did not go to live there; and he did not establish colonies. These errors would not have redounded on him in his lifetime had he not committed a sixth error by depriving the Venetians of their state. Had he not strengthened the Church or brought Spain into Italy, undercutting the Venetians would have been necessary in order to weaken them. But having made the first moves, Louis should never have consented to Venice's ruin. A strong Venice would have kept the others out of Lombardy, either because Venice would not have allowed anyone but itself to become Lombardy's ruler, or because the others would not have wanted to take Lombardy from France simply in order to hand it over to Venice. Furthermore, they would not have had the spirit to fight both France and Venice. Were someone to argue that King Louis ceded the Romagna to Pope Alexander and the Kingdom of Naples to Spain in order to avoid war, I would respond with the point I have already made: You must never allow disorder to develop in an attempt to avoid war, as this way you are not escaping war, but simply postponing it

---

12. In 1500, Louis XII signed the Treaty of Granada with Ferdinand II for a partition of the Kingdom of Naples. But tensions soon grew between Louis and Ferdinand over the partition, and by 1504 Louis had been ousted from Naples.

13. Pope Alexander.

14. King Ferdinand.

to your own disadvantage. And if others were to allege that Louis had pledged his support in the pope's campaign in gratitude for the Church's annulment of his marriage and the hat of Rouen,[15] I will counter that with some later points concerning the pledges of princes and how they should be regarded.

In short, Louis lost Lombardy because he did not observe some of the principles followed by others who have taken territories and managed to keep them. Nor is any of this a miracle, but quite ordinary and reasonable. I spoke to the Cardinal of Rouen about this matter at Nantes, when Valentino (that was how Cesare Borgia, the son of Pope Alexander, was known to his friends) was occupying the Romagna. When the cardinal declared that the Italians did not understand warfare, I replied that the French did not understand the state; because had they understood the state, they would not have let the Church rise to such power. And experience has shown that the strength of the Church and of Spain in Italy was brought about by France, and that France's ruin was brought about by them. From this one can draw a general rule that is almost always true: He who helps another man to power is setting himself up for ruin, because that power has been brought about by either diligence or force, both of which are suspect to the man who has newly become powerful.

15. Louis XII had been granted an annulment of his marriage to Jeanne de Valois, and a cardinalate for his minister, Georges d'Amboise, Archbishop of Rouen.

CHAPTER FOUR

WHY DARIUS'S[16] KINGDOM, WHICH ALEXANDER HAD OCCUPIED, DID NOT REBEL AGAINST ALEXANDER'S SUCCESSORS AFTER HIS DEATH

Considering the difficulties of retaining a newly acquired state, one marvels at how in a few years Alexander the Great managed to become the ruler of Asia and, having occupied it, died.[17] It would seem reasonable that after his death the territories he had acquired would have rebelled. And yet Alexander's successors did retain these territories, and had no difficulties other than those that arose among themselves, difficulties sparked by their own ambition. My point is that all the principalities in history have been governed in two ways: either by a prince and his servants, in which case the ministers who help him govern do so by his favor and concession, or by a prince and a group of barons, who hold their rank not by his favor but by the rights of their bloodline. These barons have their own states and subjects, who recognize them as their lords and have a natural affection for them.

In those states where a prince and his servants govern, the prince has more authority, as in all his territory there is no man who is considered superior to him. And if subjects obey a minister, they obey him as an official of the prince, and not out of particular affection.

Examples of these two kinds of government in our times are the

16. Darius III (d. 330 BCE) was the last king of Persia's Achaemenid dynasty. His empire was conquered by Alexander the Great in a series of battles from 334 to 331 BCE.
17. Alexander the Great (356–23 BCE), King of Macedonia, had within a decade conquered the Persian Empire and parts of northern India by the time he died at the age of thirty-four.

Turk and the King of France. The Turk's monarchy is governed by a single ruler, and everyone else is his servant. Dividing his kingdom into *sanjaks,* or provinces, he sends out governors, changing them at his pleasure. But the King of France is at the center of an ancient multitude of lords, recognized by their subjects and loved by them. These lords have their own dominions, which the king can take from them only at his peril.

If one considers these two states, one finds it difficult to acquire that of the Turk, but easy to keep once it is won. It is difficult to conquer because there are no barons who can be called on to help the conqueror, nor is there hope for a rebellion of the Turk's entourage. This springs from the reasons I have mentioned previously. As all the Turk's men are dependents and bondsmen it is harder to corrupt them; and if they are corrupted, they prove of little use, as they do not have the populace behind them for the reasons I have mentioned. Consequently, whoever attacks the Turk should expect to find a united front, and must rely more on his own power than on the disorder of others. But once the Turk has been utterly defeated on the battlefield so that he cannot regroup, there is nothing left to fear but his own bloodline. Once that is extinguished, nobody remains to be feared, as there is no one who has credit with the people. Just as the victor could not expect anything from the Turk's men before the victory, he has nothing to fear from them afterward.

The opposite happens in kingdoms like France, which you can conquer with ease by winning over some baron of the realm, because there are always those who are dissatisfied and desire change. They can open the way for you and help you to victory. But afterward, when you try to maintain yourself in your new acquisition, you will face infinite difficulties both from those who helped you and from those you oppressed. Nor is it enough for you to extinguish the bloodline of the former prince, because there remain those lords who aspire to be leaders of a new regime. And as you will be unable either to please them or destroy them, you will lose the state whenever the opportunity to seize it from you arises.

If we look at Darius's kingdom, we find that its government was similar to that of the Turk. Therefore, Alexander needed first to strike at it in full force and achieve a decisive victory, after which, with Darius dead, the state, for the reasons I have already mentioned, stayed firmly in Alexander's grip. And Alexander's successors, had they been united, could have enjoyed this state in complete idleness. No turmoil broke out in their territories except for the turmoil they themselves provoked. But states organized like France cannot be possessed with such ease. This was also the reason for the frequent rebellions against the Romans in Spain, France, and Greece, because of the many old principalities in those territories. While the memory of those principalities lasted, the Romans were always tenuous in their possession. But ultimately, with the power and continuum of the empire, the memory died out and they became secure possessions. Later, when the Roman governors began fighting among themselves, each could take back part of the provinces according to how much power he had acquired in these territories. And since the bloodline of their old princes had been extinguished, the Roman governors were the only rulers these states recognized.

Considering all these issues, one should not be surprised at the ease with which Alexander kept his acquisitions in Asia, and the difficulty others had in conserving theirs (like Pyrrhus,[18] to name one of many). This is not a matter of the victor's skill, but of the different characteristics of the state he conquers.

---

18. King Pyrrhus of Epirus (319–272 BCE) fought energetically to expand his empire, seizing territories from Macedonia and Rome. His costly military accomplishments, however, resulted in his inability to hold on to his new acquisitions, giving rise to the modern phrase "Pyrrhic victory": a victory at too great a cost.

CHAPTER FIVE

How one should govern cities or principalities which lived under their own laws before being conquered

When an acquired state has been accustomed to living in freedom under its own laws, there are three ways of securing it. The first is to destroy it; the second, to move there oneself; the third, to let it live with its own laws, exacting a tribute and creating within it a regime of a selected few who will keep it friendly toward you. As the regime of the state has been created by the new prince, it knows it cannot exist without his goodwill and power, and must do everything to maintain him. The best way to keep a city accustomed to living freely is through its citizens.

Consider, for example, the Spartans and the Romans. The Spartans occupied Athens and Thebes, creating a state governed by a few (though they lost this state again). The Romans, on the other hand, destroyed Capua, Carthage, and Numantia, and therefore did not lose them. They also wanted to occupy Greece in almost the same way the Spartans had occupied Athens and Thebes, making it free and with its own laws. This did not work, and the Romans ended up having to destroy many of Greece's cities in order to keep the province. In fact, the only secure way of keeping such a city is to destroy it. And whoever becomes the ruler of a city that is used to living free without destroying it can expect to be destroyed by the city. Because when such a city rebels, it always waves the banners of liberty and its former government, which are not forgotten with the passage of time or through any benefits bestowed by the new ruler. Notwithstanding what a new prince does or anticipates, if the inhabitants are not dispersed or driven into quarreling factions, they will never forget the former government or order of things, and will quickly revert to it at every opportunity (as did Pisa after a hundred years of servitude to the Florentines). It is a different matter when cities or states are accustomed to living under a prince and his bloodline is extinguished, as on one hand they are used to obeying, and on the other they do not have their former prince. They will not be capable of uniting to elect a prince from among themselves, and they do not know how to live in freedom without a prince. Consequently, they are slower at taking up arms, and a new prince can win and secure them with greater ease. But in republics there is more vitality, more hatred, and more desire for revenge. The memory of former freedom simply will not leave the people in peace. In this case the safest course is for the prince either to destroy them or to go and live there himself.

CHAPTER SIX

Of new principalities acquired
through arms and skill

No one will be surprised if I cite a few eminent examples in speaking of principalities that are completely new in both prince and government. Men will always follow paths beaten by others, and proceed in their actions by imitation. But as they are rarely able to keep to these paths, or to match the skill of those they imitate, a prudent man should always set out on paths beaten by those who are truly great and worthy of imitation. This way, even if his own skill does not attain the same heights, he can at least expect to achieve some of the effect. A wise archer, for instance, will perceive that the distance of the target he intends to hit is too far off, and, knowing the extent of his bow's capacity, will aim quite a bit higher, not so that he will reach that height with his arrow, but so that he will gain his objective by aiming above it. The point I wish to make is that maintaining a principality that is entirely new, where there is a new prince, depends entirely on the skill of that prince. And because turning from a private citizen to a prince presupposes skill or good fortune, it would seem that either of these two factors will alleviate many of the difficulties. And yet he who has relied less on good fortune to acquire his principality has a better prospect of keeping it. Things also become much easier when the new prince does not have another state, and is obliged to live in his new acquisition.

But to come to those who have become princes through their own skill and not through chance, I would say that foremost among them are Moses, Cyrus, Romulus, and Theseus.[19] One ought perhaps not to count Moses, as he was a mere executor of the will of God; he must nevertheless be admired, if only for the grace that made him worthy of speaking to God. But let us consider Cyrus, and the others who acquired or founded kingdoms. They are all most admirable. If one weighs their actions and the measures they took, it is clear that they are not very different from those of Moses, who had such a great preceptor watching over him. If we examine their actions and lives, we see that the only gift that Fortune accorded them was the opportunity that gave them the substance they could mold into any form they pleased. Without that opportunity, their skill would not have flourished, and without that skill, the opportunity would have presented itself in vain. In other words, it was essential for Moses to find the people of Israel pining under the Egyptian yoke, so that they could emerge from slavery and be willing to follow him. It was vital for Romulus not to remain in Alba but to be exposed at birth,[20] so that he would become King of Rome and founder of the nation. It was crucial for Cyrus to find the Persians unhappy under the Empire of the Medes, and for the Medes to have grown soft and effeminate from a long period of peace. Theseus could not have demonstrated his skill had he not found the Athenians dispersed. Consequently, those opportunities favored these men, and with their skill they seized the opportunity, with the result that their nations were ennobled and prospered.

Those who become princes through such skill acquire their principality with difficulty, but retain it with ease. The difficulties they have in acquiring the principality arise in part from the new order they are forced to introduce to set up their state and ensure their own security. Nothing is harder to do, more dubious to succeed at, or more dangerous to manage, than making oneself a ruler and introducing a new order. This is because he who introduces the new order makes enemies of all those who have done well under the old, and finds only halfhearted defenders in the men who would do well under the new. This halfheartedness arises in part from these men's fear of adversaries who

19. Machiavelli often uses these historical figures as examples of princely skill and ability. (See *The Prince,* chapters 16 and 26, and *Discourses,* Book II, chapter 13.)
20. Romulus, one of the legendary founders of Rome, had been ordered to be exposed to death as an infant by his uncle, King Amulius of Alba. According to legend, Romulus and his brother, Remus, were then raised by a wolf.

have the law on their side, and in part from the incredulity of man. Men intrinsically do not trust new things that they have not experienced themselves. Consequently, when enemies of the new order find any chance to attack the prince, they will attack him in full force, while men who benefit from the new order will defend him halfheartedly. Hence the prince is in a precarious position.

It is therefore necessary when examining this matter to ascertain whether the prince introducing the new order can act alone or must depend on others. In other words, he must seek help or use force to achieve his innovations. If he seeks help, he will always end up badly and accomplish nothing. But if he relies on his own skill and can use force, the innovator will rarely be in harm's way. This is why all armed prophets were successful, while unarmed prophets came to ruin. Another factor that must be considered is that a populace is always erratic. It is easy enough to win the people over, but difficult to keep their allegiance. Therefore, matters must be arranged in such a way that when the populace no longer believes, a prince can compel them to believe by force. Moses, Cyrus, Theseus, and Romulus would not have been able to make their people observe their laws for long without the force of arms, as we have seen in our own times with Girolamo Savonarola,[21] who came to ruin with his new order when the multitude lost belief in him. Savonarola did not have a system for holding on to those who had believed in him, nor did he have a system for making those believe who did not. Therefore, rulers like Savonarola have great difficulty in proceeding; their path is strewn with difficulties that they must overcome through prowess. Once they overcome these difficulties, the populace begins to venerate them. And once these rulers have eliminated those who resent their achievement, they remain powerful, secure, honored, and content.

To these illustrious examples I would like to add a less eminent one, but one that is to some extent comparable, which might suffice for all other similar cases. It is the example of Hiero of Syracuse, who from private citizen became Prince of Syracuse.[22] In his case, Fortune did not accord him more than an opportunity. The people of Syracuse

---

21. Girolamo Savonarola (1452–98) was a charismatic Christian preacher who, after the fall of the Medici in Florence in 1494, ruled Florence as the leader of a strict and sober republican government until he was executed in 1498. See Machiavelli's letter to Riccardo Bechi.
22. Hiero II of Syracuse (d. 216 BCE).

were oppressed, and so elected him their general, after which he proved himself worthy of being made their prince. He had so much skill, even as a private citizen, that someone who wrote about him says: *Quod nihil illi deerat ad regnandum praeter regnum* (He lacked nothing to make him a ruler except a kingdom).[23] Hiero eliminated the old army and set up a new one, abandoned old friendships for new ones, and on the foundation of these new soldiers and friends realized that he could build any edifice. It took much effort for him to acquire his state, but little to keep it.

23. Machiavelli quotes an altered line from Justin's *Epitome of the Philippic History of Pompeius Trogus* (Book XXIII, chapter 4): *Prorsus ut nihil ei regium deesse praeter regnum uideretur.*

CHAPTER SEVEN

OF NEW PRINCIPALITIES
ACQUIRED BY THE ARMS AND BY
THE GOOD FORTUNE OF OTHERS

Private citizens who become princes by good fortune alone do so with little effort, but maintaining their position requires a great deal of effort. They have no difficulty in getting there, because their way is easy; the difficulties arise once they arrive. These are rulers who acquire a principality through money or by favor of a grantor. This was the case with many rulers in the cities of Ionia and the Hellespont in Greece, where Darius, in order to ensure his security and glory, created princes who would hold these lands.[24] There were also private citizens who became rulers by bribing soldiers. Such men depend on the will and good fortune of whoever has granted them their rule, two factors that are extremely unreliable. In general, a ruler of this kind is neither capable of maintaining nor successful in maintaining his position. He is not capable, because unless he is a man of the greatest intelligence and skill, he cannot be expected, as a mere former private citizen, to know how to command; and he is not able to maintain his position because he does not have loyal forces that will support him. Furthermore, states that spring up suddenly, like all things in nature that sprout and grow quickly, cannot develop the necessary roots and connections, and hence they expire with the first bad weather. As I have

---

24. Darius I (550–486 BCE), King of Persia, also known as Darius the Great, attempted to conquer Greece but was ultimately defeated by the Athenians at Marathon in 490 BCE.

mentioned, the only exceptions are princes who, though they have become princes suddenly, have so much skill that they instantly know how to use and conserve what Fortune has dropped in their laps. Once they have their principality, they are quick to lay the foundations that others have had to lay before becoming princes.

I would like to illustrate with two examples from our recent history the two ways—by skill or by Fortune—of becoming prince: those of Francesco Sforza and Cesare Borgia. Sforza, through well-chosen means and great skill, began as a private citizen and became the Duke of Milan. What he gained with a thousand toils, he maintained with little effort. On the other hand, Cesare Borgia, called Duke Valentino by the people, acquired his state through his father's good fortune, and through his father's subsequent bad fortune lost it; this though Borgia used every means in his power and did all that a prudent and skillful man must do in order to establish himself in those states which the arms and good fortune of another have granted him. Because, as I have already stated, he who does not lay foundations first, must do so with prodigious skill later, even if this entails hardship for the architect and danger to the edifice. If one considers the system that Cesare Borgia applied, it is clear that he had laid strong foundations for his future power. In my view he is an important example, as I know not what better precept to give a new prince. If in the end Borgia did not prevail, it was not his fault, but the result of the extreme malignity of Fortune.

Pope Alexander VI wanted to make his son Cesare Borgia great, but he encountered many difficulties. He could not find a way of making him prince of a state that did not belong to the Church, and he knew that if he attempted to give his son a state that did belong to the Church, the Duke of Milan and the Venetians would intervene; Faenza and Rimini already stood under the protection of Venice. Furthermore, the Italian mercenary armies, particularly those the pope would most need, were in the hands of rulers who had reason to fear his growing power. He could not trust them, as they all belonged to the Orsini and Colonna clans and their allies. He had to disrupt the existing order and create turmoil in those rulers' states in order to gain control of part of them. This proved easy enough, because he found that the Venetians, for their own motives, intended to bring the French back into Italy. Not only did the pope not oppose this, but he facilitated it by obliging King Louis with an annulment of his former marriage. So Louis entered Italy with the help of the Venetians and the blessing of the pope, and no sooner had Louis set foot in Milan than he supplied the pope with men for the latter's campaign in the Romagna, which the pope conquered unhindered as he had the support and backing of the king.[25]

So after Cesare Borgia had acquired the Romagna and defeated the Colonna family, he intended to maintain the Romagna and expand further. But Borgia faced two impediments: his army, which did not seem loyal, and the designs of France. He sensed that the army of the Orsini, which he had been using, could not be relied upon. He feared that it would not only interfere with his further conquests, but take from him what he had already acquired, and that the King of France would follow suit. Borgia was confirmed in this when, after the conquest of Faenza, he attacked Bologna and saw how halfheartedly the Orsini went into battle. King Louis's intentions also became clear when Borgia attacked Tuscany after successfully taking the Duchy of Urbino, and Louis forced him to retreat. Consequently, Borgia decided to depend no longer on the army and goodwill of another. The first thing he did was to weaken the Orsini and Colonna factions in Rome by winning over all the noblemen who supported them, making them his own noblemen and granting them large stipends. He bestowed upon them, according to their rank, army commands and government positions. The result was that within a few months their affection for their former leaders was transferred to Borgia. He now waited for an opportunity to destroy the Orsini, having already dispersed the house of Colonna. An excellent opportunity presented itself, and he made excellent use of it. The Orsini had realized too late that the power of Borgia and the Church meant their ruin; they assembled at Magione, in Perugino, and fomented rebellions in Urbino and throughout the Romagna, which put Borgia in a very precarious position. He managed to overcome these dangers with the help of the French, but once he regained power, he did not trust France or any other outside force. So that he would not have to put their allegiance to him to the test, he turned to deception. He was such a master of dissimulation that the Orsini, through the mediation of Signor Paolo Orsini, 'were prepared to reach a reconciliation. Borgia showered

25. Pope Alexander's son, Cesare Borgia, was appointed commander of the papal armies.

Paolo Orsini with every courtesy in order to reassure him, giving him money, precious garments, and horses. Then Borgia set a trap for the Orsini at Sinigallia, and they foolishly walked right into it.[26] By eliminating the leaders and turning their followers into his allies, Borgia laid a solid foundation for his power, having the whole of the Romagna and the Duchy of Urbino in his grip. What is more important, it was clear that he had gained the friendship of the Romagna and all its people, who had begun to experience the benefits of his rule.

I would also like to mention the following, because it is noteworthy and merits imitation: When Cesare Borgia took over the Romagna, he found it to have been ruled by weak princes who would sooner rob their subjects than govern them, causing dissension rather than unity. Robbery, intrigue, and every kind of evil had been rampant throughout the province, and Borgia found it essential to set up a strong government in order to pacify it and make it submit to his rule. He put in charge a resolute and ruthless man, Ramiro de Lorqua, giving him complete authority, and within the shortest time de Lorqua brought peace and unity to the Romagna, gaining much power and influence in the process. But Borgia judged that such excessive authority over the people could have dangerous consequences, as it might arouse their hatred, so he set up a civil court in the center of the province, with an excellent presiding judge, every city having its own advocate. Borgia was aware that de Lorqua's rigor had created hatred among the people, and in order to purge their minds and win them over, he decided to make it clear that if there had been any cruelty it had been triggered by his minister's abrasive nature. At the first opportunity, he had de Lorqua cut in two on the main square in Cesena, with a piece of wood and a bloody knife at his side. The brutality of this spectacle left the people both stunned and appeased.

But to return from our digression. Cesare Borgia now found himself powerful and to some extent secure, being well armed and having to a great extent destroyed neighboring armies that might have put him in harm's way. If he wanted to continue expanding his acquisitions, he now had to take the King of France into account. For Borgia knew that Louis, who had realized his mistake too late, would not allow him to expand his territories. So Borgia began seeking new allies, and vacillat-

---

26. See "How Duke Valentino Killed the Generals Who Conspired Against Him."

ing with France in its campaign against the Kingdom of Naples and the Spaniards who were besieging Gaeta.[27] His intention was to secure himself against the French, which he could have done with ease had Pope Alexander lived. This was how Borgia handled the problems at hand. As for his future problems, his main fear was that the next pope might be ill disposed toward him and attempt to take away what Pope Alexander had given him.

Cesare Borgia set out to secure his position vis-à-vis the Church in four ways: First, to extinguish the bloodlines of the lords he had dispossessed, in order to take away a future pope's opportunity of using them; second, to win over all the noblemen of Rome, in order to keep the pope in check; third, to gain as much influence as he could within the College of Cardinals; and fourth, to acquire as large an empire as possible before Pope Alexander died so that he could resist an initial attack from any enemy without assistance from others. Of these four schemes, he had accomplished only three by the time Pope Alexander died;[28] the fourth he had almost achieved. He had killed as many of the lords he had dispossessed as he could get his hands on (only a few managed to escape), he won over the Roman noblemen, and he controlled the largest faction in the College of Cardinals. As for his further conquests, he already owned Perugia and Piombino, held Pisa under his protection, and had designs on Tuscany. As he no longer had to defer to France (the Spaniards had already robbed France of the Kingdom of Naples, with the result that both the French and the Spaniards were compelled to buy Borgia's friendship), he would have conquered Pisa. After this, Lucca and Siena would have been quick to capitulate, partly out of fear and partly to spite the Florentines, and the Florentines could have done nothing about it. Had Borgia succeeded— and he was on the point of success the very year Pope Alexander died—he would have amassed so many forces and so much influence that he could have imposed his own will, depending on his own power and skill and not on the Fortune or arms of others.

But Pope Alexander died five years after Borgia had first drawn his

---

27. Naples was claimed by the French king Charles VIII, who held it briefly in 1495, but it was taken by the Spanish in 1503. Borgia had initially supported the French claim, but by 1503 proved to be "vacillating" in his support when he did not send troops as expected to help the town of Gaeta, which the Spanish army was besieging.

28. August 18, 1504.

sword, leaving him with nothing secured but the province of the Romagna (all the other possessions being up in the air). Borgia was now
caught between two powerful enemy armies, and deathly ill. But he
had great ferocity and skill, and was acutely aware of how men were to
be won or lost. The foundations he had laid in such a short time were
so sturdy that he could have stood firm against any difficulty, if [the
French and Spanish] armies had not been bearing down on him and
had he not been so very ill. The sturdiness of these foundations was
clear, for his province waited more than a month for him. In Rome, although barely alive, he remained secure. And though the Ballioni,
Vitelli, and Orsini came to Rome, they could not raise a following
against him. Even if Borgia could not dictate the selection of the new
pope, at least he managed to prevent a choice of which he did not approve. Had he not been ill when Pope Alexander died, he would have
had no difficulty. Borgia himself told me on the day Pope Julius II was
elected that he, Borgia, had carefully weighed everything that might
happen after his father, Pope Alexander, died, and had found a solution
for everything. There was only one thing he had not anticipated: the
possibility that he himself might be at death's door.

Having laid out all the actions Borgia took, I can find nothing to reproach him with. I would even say, as I already have, that he serves as
an excellent example of a prince who rose to power through Fortune
and by means of the arms of others. He had great courage and lofty aspirations, and could not have conducted himself in any other way. The
only things that foiled his designs were the brevity of Pope Alexander's life and his own illness. Hence, a prince wishing to secure himself
against enemies in his new principality cannot find a more compelling
example than Cesare Borgia of how to gain friends, how to win by
force or deception, how to make the populace love and fear him, how
to gain the loyalty and respect of his soldiers, the necessity of eliminating those who can or will harm him, and the importance of substitut-
ing new laws for old. Borgia was exemplary in both his severity and his
kindness. He was magnanimous and liberal, eliminated disloyal troops
and marshaled new ones, and cultivated friendships with kings and
princes so that they had to either help him with favors or confront him
with caution. Borgia's only error was to allow Julius to become the
next pope. This was a bad decision because, as I have already stated,
even if he could not make the man he wanted pope, he could at least

have prevented the accession of a pope he did not want. He should never have agreed to the papacy of any of the cardinals he had harmed, or who would have cause to fear him once they became pope, since men will attack you out of fear or hatred. Among the men Borgia had harmed were San Piero ad Vincula,[29] Colonna, San Giorgio, and Ascanio. All the other claimants to the papacy would have had to fear him, except for Rouen and the Spaniards—Rouen because of his connection to the King of France, the Spaniards because of kinship and obligation. Therefore, Borgia's first choice for pope should have been a Spaniard, and if not a Spaniard, then Rouen. But he should not have chosen San Piero ad Vincula. For whoever believes that great advancement and new benefits make men forget old injuries is mistaken. Hence Borgia made a bad decision. And it was this decision that ultimately brought about his ruin.

29. Pope Julius II, who was Cardinal of San Piero ad Vincula before being elected to the pontificate.

CHAPTER EIGHT

OF THOSE WHO BECOME
PRINCES THROUGH EVIL

I must mention two other ways for a private citizen to become a prince that cannot be attributed to Fortune or skill, though I shall discuss one of them at greater length when I speak of republics. These are when a man obtains a principality in an evil or nefarious way, or when a private citizen, by the favor of his fellow citizens, becomes the prince of his state. Speaking of the first way, I shall offer two examples, one ancient, the other from our times, and shall leave it at that, as these examples will be enough for anyone constrained to imitate them.

When Agathocles the Sicilian became King of Syracuse, he did so not only as a private citizen, but as one who came from the lowliest and most humble circumstances. He was the son of a potter, and led a wicked life from first to last.[30] And yet he combined his wickedness with such skill of mind and body that when he joined the army, he rose through the ranks to become Praetor of Syracuse. Once established in that position, he set about becoming prince and retaining his principality by means of violence, without depending on others for that

---

30. Justin writes in *Epitome of the Philippic History of Pompeius Trogus*, Book XXII, chapter 1: "[Agathocles] rose to royal power from a birth that was humble and base. In fact, he was born in Sicily to a potter. His youth was no more honorable than his birth, for being remarkable for his beauty and physical charm, he lived for a long time by submitting himself to being ravished. Emerging from puberty, he transferred his lust from men to women. Having thus become notorious with both sexes, he changed his way of life to that of a mercenary."

which he had originally been granted by his fellow citizens. He conspired with Hamilcar the Carthaginian,[31] who was waging war in Sicily with his army, and one morning Agathocles called together the people and the senate of Syracuse as if to discuss important issues concerning the republic, and then at a signal to his soldiers had them kill all the senators and the richest men of the city.[32] Then he became the unchallenged prince of that city. And though the Carthaginians defeated him twice and finally besieged Syracuse, he managed to defend the city, and, leaving a part of his army to withstand the siege, left on a campaign with the rest to assault Africa. Within a short time he freed Syracuse from the siege and brought Carthage to its knees, forcing it to reach an agreement with him and to content itself with the possession of Africa, leaving Sicily to Agathocles.

If one weighs Agathocles's actions and skill, there is not much that can be attributed to Fortune. As I have pointed out, he did not gain his principality through anyone's favor, but rose to it through the ranks of the army with a thousand privations and dangers, and then kept possession of the principality through many bold and dangerous feats. And yet we cannot define as skillful killing one's fellow citizens, betraying one's friends, and showing no loyalty, mercy, or moral obligation. These means can lead to power, but not glory. Because if one considers Agathocles's skill at plunging into and out of danger, and the greatness of his spirit in enduring and overcoming adversity, he cannot be judged inferior to the most excellent leaders. In other words, one cannot attribute to Fortune or skill what he attained without either of them.

In our own times, during the reign of Pope Alexander VI, we have the example of Oliverotto da Fermo. He had been orphaned as a child and raised by his maternal uncle, Giovanni Fogliani, and in his early years had been sent to serve under Paolo Vitelli to master the military

31. A Carthaginian general fighting in Sicily, not to be confused with Hannibal's father, Hamilcar (d. 229 BCE), also a general in Sicily.

32. Justin writes in *Epitome of the Philippic History of Pompeius Trogus,* Book XXII, chapter 2: "Having received from him [Hamilcar] five thousand African soldiers, he put to death the most powerful among the foremost citizens. Then he ordered the populace to assemble in the theater, feigning that he wished to redraw the constitution of the state, also calling together the senate in the Gymnasium, under the guise of laying the groundwork. Having set this up, he sent his troops to besiege the people, had all the senators slaughtered, and then proceeded to kill all the wealthiest and most prominent plebeians."

arts, so that he might attain a high rank in the army. When Paolo died, Oliverotto fought under Paolo's brother Vitellozzo, and very quickly, being resourceful and vigorous in body and mind, became commander of Vitellozzo's army. But he felt that serving under others was unbecoming. He decided to seize the town of Fermo with the support of Vitellozzo and the help of some of Fermo's citizens, who preferred servitude to freedom for their city. Oliverotto wrote to his uncle Giovanni Fogliani that, having been away from home for many years, he wanted to return to see him and his town and reacquaint himself with his patrimony. He wrote that in all these years he had fought in order to acquire honor, and now he wanted his fellow citizens to see that he had not spent his time in vain. He wanted to return with honor, accompanied by a hundred friends and servants on horseback, and asked his uncle to ensure that the citizens of Fermo would receive him with ceremony, which would also reflect well on his uncle as his guardian. And Giovanni did not fail to show his nephew every courtesy. Having him received with honor by the citizens of Fermo, he quartered him and his men in his houses. After a few days, having waited to put into place what was necessary for his future wickedness, Oliverotto ordered a great feast, to which he invited Giovanni Fogliani and all the foremost men of Fermo. After the courses had been eaten and the usual entertainments were over, Oliverotto artfully introduced delicate subjects, speaking of the greatness of Pope Alexander and his son Cesare and of their campaigns. Giovanni and the others responded, and Oliverotto suggested that such delicate matters should be discussed in a more private place. He retired to a chamber with Giovanni and the other citizens, and no sooner had they seated themselves than soldiers emerged from a hiding place and slaughtered Giovanni and the rest. After the slaughter, Oliverotto mounted a horse and took over the town, besieging the supreme magistrate in his palace. The citizens were forced to obey him out of fear, and he made them form a new government with himself as prince. As everyone who would have opposed him was dead, they could not harm him, and Oliverotto reinforced his position with new civil and military laws. Within a year, he was secure in the town of Fermo and had become a source of fear for its neighbors. It would have been as hard to defeat him as to defeat Agathocles, had Oliverotto not let himself be deceived by Cesare Borgia, who, as I have mentioned, trapped the Orsini and the Vitelli in Sinigallia. It was in Sinigallia, a year after Oliverotto had murdered his uncle, that he was strangled along with Vitellozzo, who had been his tutor in skill and wickedness.

One might wonder how Agathocles and others like him, after countless betrayals and so much cruelty, could live so long and securely in their states and defend themselves from outside enemies, and why they were never conspired against by their citizens, whereas many others could not retain their states through cruelty, either in times of peace or in the uncertain times of war. I believe this depends upon whether cruelty is used well or badly. Cruelty can be called well used (if it is even permitted to use the word "well" in connection with evil) if it is executed at a single stroke out of the necessity to secure one's power, and is then not continued but converted into the greatest possible benefit for one's subjects. Badly used cruelty is cruelty that, even if initially limited, increases with time rather than subsiding. Those who follow the first path can maintain their position in their state with the blessing of God and man, as Agathocles did. The others cannot possibly survive.

A prince can conclude from this that when he conquers a state, he must weigh all the acts of cruelty that are necessary, and execute them all at a single stroke so they will not have to be repeated every day, and by not repeating them assure the people and win them over by subsequently benefiting them. Whoever proceeds otherwise, through fear or bad judgment, must always keep a knife at hand. He can never rely on his subjects, as they cannot feel secure under him. Therefore any cruelty has to be executed at once, so that the less it is tasted, the less it offends; while benefits must be dispensed little by little, so that they will be savored all the more. Primarily, a prince must live with his subjects in such a way that no incident, either good or bad, should make him change his course, because when bad times cause him to employ more stringent methods, it will be too late, nor will the good he does benefit him, because it will be judged to have been forced.

CHAPTER NINE

OF THE CIVIL PRINCIPALITY

But let us consider the other alternative, when a private citizen becomes prince of his native state through the favor of his fellow citizens, and not through wickedness or some violence that proves intolerable to the citizens. Such a principality can be called a civil principality, since to acquire it the prince does not have to depend entirely on skill or Fortune, but rather on a fortunate astuteness. One acquires this principality through the favor of either the people or the nobles, because in every city there are two opposing humors. This arises from the fact that the nobles want to command and oppress the people, but the people do not want to be commanded or oppressed by the nobles.[33] These two opposing impulses within a city will result in one of three outcomes: a principality, liberty, or anarchy.

The principality is brought about by the people or the nobility, depending on which has the opportunity. When the nobles see that they cannot stand up to the people, they put all their support behind one of their own, making him prince so they can satisfy their ambition in the safety of his shadow. And the people, finding that they cannot stand up to the nobility, put all their support behind one man and make him prince, in the hope that his authority will shield them.

33. See *Discourses*, Book I, chapter 5: "For without doubt, if one considers the respective aims of the nobles and the populace, one sees in the former a strong desire to dominate, and in the latter merely a desire not to be dominated."

A prince who obtains a state with the help of the people maintains his position with less difficulty than a prince who acquires it with the help of the nobility, because in the latter case he is surrounded by men who consider themselves his equals and whom he therefore cannot command or govern as he pleases. But a prince who acquires a principality through the favor of the people is unhampered: Only a few in his circle are unready to obey him. Furthermore, one cannot satisfy the nobles in a manner that is just and does not harm the people, but one can so satisfy the people, because their aspirations are more just than those of the nobles: The nobles want to oppress them, but the people want only not to be oppressed. Moreover, a prince cannot shield himself against a populace that is hostile toward him, because there are too many of them; but he can shield himself against the nobles, as they are few in number.[34] The worst that a prince can expect from a hostile populace is for them to abandon him, but from hostile noblemen he has also to fear their conspiring against him. Noblemen, having more foresight and cunning, tend to act in time to save themselves, and are quick to seek out those who they hope will prevail. The prince is constrained always to live with that same populace, but he can do well enough without those same noblemen, as he is able to make and unmake them at will, giving and taking away their power as he pleases.

To clarify this point, I propose that noblemen must be considered in two ways: Either they link themselves entirely to your destiny, or they do not. Those who link themselves to you and are not greedy should be honored and loved. Those who do not are acting out of pusillanimity and a natural lack of courage. You should make use of those among them who offer good counsel, because in prosperity they will bring you honor, while in difficult times you need not fear them. But if out of malicious design and ambition they do not align themselves with you, it is a sign that they are thinking more of themselves than of you. A prince must be on his guard against them. He should fear them as if they were declared enemies, because in adversity they will inevitably help to bring about his ruin.

34. See *Discourses*, Book I, chapter 16: "In fact, I consider those princes unfortunate who are compelled to resort to exceptional means to secure their state because the populace is their enemy, for he who has as his enemy the few can secure himself easily and without much turmoil, but he who has the whole populace as his enemy can never secure himself."

And yet he who becomes prince through the favor of the people must keep the people on his side. This should be simple enough, as all they ask of him is that he not oppress them. But he who becomes prince through the favor of the nobility against the will of the people must make it a priority to win over the people, which is easy enough if he becomes their protector. Because men, when they encounter benevolence where they expected harm, show greater gratitude to their benefactor, and the populace becomes even more supportive than if the prince had acquired the state through their favor. And the prince can earn this favor in many ways, but as these vary greatly depending on the circumstances, one cannot lay down a fixed rule. I will only conclude that a prince must have the people on his side, otherwise he will not have support in adverse times.

Prince Nabis of Sparta fended off a siege led by the whole of Greece and an illustrious Roman army, managing to save the state and city of his birth.[35] He overcame the danger, having to protect himself against only a few of his subjects, an endeavor that would have failed had the populace been against him.

And let nobody respond with the trite proverb that he who builds upon the masses builds upon sand, because this proverb holds only when a private citizen builds a foundation on the populace in the hope that they will come to his rescue when he is in trouble with magistrates or his enemies. In this case he might find himself disabused, as were the Gracchi in Rome and Giorgio Scali in Florence.[36]

But if a prince builds a foundation on the populace and can command, and is a man of courage unruffled in adversity who has taken his precautions, a man who has made himself popular with the people

---

35. Nabis (d. 192 BCE), the last king of an independent Sparta, managed to maintain his power despite the wars between Rome and Philip V of Macedon and their allies that were destabilizing the territories of all the Greek states.

36. The Gracchi brothers were influential Roman statesmen whose reforms acted as a catalyst to end the Roman Republic. Giorgio Scali was one of the Florentine political figures who came to power after the popular Revolt of the Ciompi in 1378. Machiavelli writes in *Florentine Histories* (Book III, chapter 21) that as Scali was being executed by the populace he had championed, he "blamed himself for having set too much stock in the populace, which can be moved and corrupted by every voice, every act, every suspicion." The fifteenth-century chronicler Piero Vagliente attributed to Giorgio Scali the "trite proverb" that Machiavelli quotes: "Giorgio Scali, who said that he who builds upon deferring to the masses builds upon shit."

through his spirit and government, he will never be abandoned by the populace. Principalities tend to be vulnerable when they move from civil to absolute order, because princes command either directly or through magistrates. In the latter case, the prince finds his position weaker and more dangerous because he is at the mercy of citizens who have become magistrates. They can, particularly in adverse times, easily take the state away from him, either by abandoning him or by opposing him. Once this happens, the prince no longer has time to establish his absolute authority, because the populace are used to following the orders of the magistrates, and will not obey the prince's orders during difficult times. In adversity, he will find that there is a lack of people he can trust, because a prince in his position cannot rely on his experience during times of peace, when citizens are in need of the state and fall all over each other with promises, eagerly proclaiming that they are willing to die for him when death is at a safe distance. But in adverse times, when the state needs its citizens, only a few are to be found. This experience is all the more dangerous in that it can be experienced only once. Therefore, a wise prince must find a way in which his citizens will consider him and the state to be indispensable in every circumstance and at all times. Then his citizens will be always faithful.

CHAPTER TEN

HOW THE STRENGTH OF
PRINCIPALITIES IS TO BE MEASURED

In examining the characteristics of all these types of principalities I have mentioned, it is important to keep another consideration in mind: whether a prince rules a state strong enough to enable him to stand on his own or whether he will always need the protection of others. To clarify this point, I judge a prince capable of standing on his own when he has enough men or money to gather an army capable of engaging in battle anyone who comes to attack him; and I judge a prince as needing the assistance of others when he is not strong enough to engage an enemy on the battlefield and is compelled to seek refuge behind his walls, which he then has to defend. I have already discussed the first case and will discuss it further;[37] as for the second, one can only urge such a prince to stock up on provisions and fortify his city but disregard the surrounding area. Whoever sufficiently fortifies his city and has looked after his subjects (which I have already touched on and will do so again later),[38] will not be attacked without great hesitation, because men are always wary of enterprises in which the difficulties are obvious. And it is quite clear that attacking a prince whose

---

37. See chapter 6 and chapters 12–14.
38. Machiavelli touched on this matter in the previous chapter when he discussed the importance of "the favor of the people" to the prince. He makes mention of it again in the following chapters.

city is well fortified and who is not hated by his people is not an easy matter.

The cities of Germany are very free. They own but little of the land that surrounds them, obey the emperor when it suits them, and fear neither him nor any neighboring king. This is because they are well enough fortified so that anyone who intends to invade them would see it as a strenuous and difficult endeavor, as the cities have enough ditches and walls and sufficient artillery and keep themselves stocked with a year's supply of food, drink, and firewood. Furthermore, these cities have the means of keeping their citizens fed by providing them with enough work for a year, occupying them in activities that are the lifeblood of the city and that yield the products that sustain the people. In this way, municipal funds are not depleted either. The German cities also hold military exercises in high esteem and have many ordinances that maintain them.[39]

Therefore a prince who has organized his city in this way and has not given his people cause to hate him will not be attacked. (And if he should be, the enemy will withdraw in shame, because the affairs of this world are so changeable that one cannot sit idly and wait outside a city with a besieging army.) Some might argue that the populace could lose heart if it sees its possessions outside the walls in flames, and that a long siege and self-interest will result in the people's forgetting their love for their prince. To this I reply that a prudent and spirited prince can overcome these difficulties. At times he must inspire his people with the hope that the evil will be short-lived; at other times he must instill in them a fear of the enemy's cruelty and, when necessary, cleverly shield himself from those individuals among his subjects who might pose a threat. It is also to be expected that the enemy, as soon as it appears, will ravage and burn the area outside the city at a time when the populace is still ardent to defend itself. Therefore the prince should not hesitate, because within a few days, once the people's spirits have flagged, the harm will have been done, the wounds inflicted, and it will be too late for remedy.

The populace will have all the more reason to unite behind their

39. See also Machiavelli's discussion of German cities in *Discourses,* Book I, chapter 55.

prince when they see that he is obligated to them, as their houses have been burned and their possessions ruined in his defense. (It is man's nature to obligate himself as much for the benefits he gives as for the benefits he receives.) Therefore, all things considered, it is not difficult for a prudent prince to bolster the spirits of his people throughout a siege as long as there is no lack of provisions or ammunition.

CHAPTER ELEVEN

OF ECCLESIASTICAL PRINCIPALITIES

All that remains now is to consider ecclesiastical principalities. The difficulties they present all occur before they are acquired, for while they are acquired either by skill or by Fortune, they are maintained without the one or the other. This is because ecclesiastical principalities are sustained by age-old religious institutions, which are so strong and efficacious that these principalities will maintain their princes in power regardless of how they live or what they do. Their princes are the only ones who have states they do not defend, and subjects they do not govern. Although such states are undefended, they are not taken away from these princes, and the subjects, although they are ungoverned, remain unconcerned, and neither think of, nor are able to estrange themselves from, these princes. Thus these are the only principalities that are secure and successful. But since they are under the guidance of a superior power that the mind of man cannot fathom, I will not discuss them. For, as they are exalted and maintained by God, it would be the act of a presumptuous and audacious man to do so. Nevertheless, one might ask how it is that the Church has gained so much temporal power, since up to the time of Pope Alexander VI, Italian rulers (and here I include every baron and lord, however minor) had little regard for the pope's temporal power, though now, even the King of France trembles before it since it managed to expel him from

Italy and ruin the Venetians. In this sense, it does not seem to me redundant to commit the essentials of this situation to memory.

Italy, before King Charles of France[40] arrived, was under the power of the pope, the Venetians, the King of Naples, the Duke of Milan, and the Florentines. These rulers had two primary concerns: to prevent a foreigner from entering Italy with an army, and to prevent any single ruler among them from growing in strength by occupying more states. The pope and the Venetians worried the others most. In order to keep the Venetians in check, all the other rulers united (as happened in the defense of Ferrara),[41] and to keep the pope in check, they manipulated the barons of Rome, who were divided into the Orsini and Colonna factions, which were always fighting each other. Eyeing the pope with weapons drawn, they kept him weak and on unsteady ground. From time to time a spirited pope did emerge—like Sixtus IV—but neither Fortune nor ingenuity could free him from these warring factions. The brevity of a pope's tenure in office was also a factor, because in the ten years that his pontificate might last, he could not be expected to subdue either faction. If, for instance, one pope managed to crush the Colonna, another pope, who might be an enemy of the Orsini, would see to it that the Colonna resurged, but he in turn would not hold office long enough to see the Orsini crushed. As a result, the pope's temporal power was not held in high esteem in Italy.

Then came Pope Alexander VI, who of all the popes in history demonstrated the extent to which a pope could succeed with the help of money and arms. By way of his son, Cesare Borgia, and the invasion of the French, Alexander did all the things I have already discussed.[42] And though his intent was to make Cesare Borgia great and not the Church, his actions ultimately resulted in the greatness of the Church, which, after his and Cesare's deaths, became the beneficiary of all his efforts. Then came Pope Julius. He found the Church powerful and in possession of the whole of the Romagna, with the barons of Rome destroyed and their factions crushed by Pope Alexander. He also found the way open to accumulating money in ways that had never before

40. Charles VIII invaded Italy in 1494.
41. Duke Ercole d'Este of Ferrara fought an alliance of the Republic of Venice and Pope Sixtus IV from 1482 to 1484.
42. See chapter 7.

been possible. Pope Julius not only took advantage of these opportunities but added to them. He set out to gain Bologna, destroy the Venetians, and drive the French out of Italy. In all this he succeeded, and he is worthy of even more praise since he did everything in order to strengthen the Church and not any of his own people. He also kept the Orsini and Colonna factions in the weakened condition in which he found them. Though there were leaders among these families ready to cause trouble, two factors kept them in check: the power of the Church, and the fact that they no longer had any cardinals in the College of Cardinals, which is where many of the troubles in the past had begun. Neither faction would have remained subdued had they had their cardinals in place, because it is these cardinals who incite the different factions, and the barons of the Orsini and the Colonna families are then forced to defend themselves. It is from the ambitions of the prelates of the Church that discord and tumult has always arisen among the barons.

Hence, His Holiness Pope Leo has found the pontificate in a most powerful condition, which leads one to hope that whereas the other popes made it great with the help of arms, he will make it even greater and more revered through his goodness and his many other virtues.

CHAPTER TWELVE

OF THE DIFFERENT TYPES OF ARMIES, AND OF MERCENARIES

I have now laid out in detail all the qualities of the principalities that I proposed to discuss at the beginning of this work; I have weighed the reasons for their successes and failures and shown the ways in which many men tried to acquire and keep these principalities. It remains for me to discuss the means of attack and defense that can be applied to each of the previously mentioned cases.

We have already discussed how a prince needs a good foundation[43] if he wants to avoid failure. The primary foundation of all states—new, old, or mixed—is good laws and a good army. And as there cannot be good laws where there is not a good army, and where there is a good army there have to be good laws, I will omit any discussion of laws and speak only of armies.

The army with which a prince defends his state is either his own, a mercenary army, an auxiliary army,[44] or one that is a mix of these. The mercenary and auxiliary armies are useless and dangerous. A prince who holds a state that is founded on the strength of mercenary armies will never be firm or secure, since such armies are divided, ambitious, without discipline, and fickle—brave in the face of friends, cowardly in

43. Chapters 7 and 9.
44. As Machiavelli explains in *Discourses,* Book II, chapter 20: "Auxiliary troops are those which another prince or republic sends to help you, and which are paid and commanded by them."

the face of enemies. Such soldiers have neither fear of God nor dependability with men, and one's ruin can be held off only as long as an assault can be deferred. In peace one is despoiled by the mercenaries, in war by one's enemies. The reason for this is that all that keeps mercenaries on the battlefield are the negligible wages you pay them, which are not sufficient to make them want to die for you. They are eager to be your soldiers as long as you are not at war. The moment there is a war, they either take flight or desert. It is easy enough for me to make my case since the present ruin of Italy has been brought about by a reliance on mercenary armies over a period of many years.[45] There have been mercenaries who were effective and did well fighting other mercenaries, but as soon as foreign forces invaded, they showed their true colors. As a result, King Charles of France was able to conquer Italy with a piece of chalk,[46] and he who said that our sins were responsible was speaking the truth,[47] though they were not the sins that he had in mind but the ones I have laid out. As these were sins committed by the Italian princes, it was they who had to pay the price.

I would like to demonstrate more fully the inadequacy of mercenary armies. Mercenary generals are either excellent or not. If they are, one cannot rely on them because they will inevitably aspire to their own greatness, either by oppressing the prince they are working for, or by oppressing others whom the prince does not intend to oppress. If the mercenary general is not adroit, he will ruin the prince by losing his battles. If someone were to argue that this is true regardless of whose hand—mercenary or not—carries the weapon, I maintain that the weapons must be wielded by a prince or by a republic. The prince should personally take on the role of general.[48] The republic

---

45. Machiavelli was writing during the period of the Italian Wars, which had begun in 1494 with the invasion of Charles VIII of France. All sides relied heavily on foreign mercenaries.
46. Philippe de Commynes (1447–1511), a noted historian and diplomat of the French court, wrote in *Mémoirs* (Book VII, chapter 14): "As Pope Alexander who reigns today has said, 'The French have come with wooden spurs, their quartermasters, quite unhindered, carrying bits of chalk to mark the doors of houses where they are to be quartered.' ".
47. Machiavelli is referring to Savonarola, who in his fiery sermons blamed the affliction of Florence on the Florentines' luxuriant ways.
48. See *Discourses*, Book I, chapter 30, which opens with the line: "To escape the need of living in constant suspicion or being ungrateful, a prince must himself go out on military expeditions, as the Roman emperors initially did and as the Turk does in our times."

should send out one of its citizens as general, and if he does not turn out to be valiant, he must be replaced. If he is valiant, he must be held in check by laws that do not let him overstep the mark. Experience has shown that only princes and republics that have their own army make great progress, while mercenary armies do nothing but harm. A republic that has its own army is much less likely to come under the sway of one of its own citizens than one that relies on foreign mercenaries.

Both Rome and Sparta were for many centuries armed and free. The Swiss are well armed and very free. [49] As for mercenary armies in ancient times, we have the example of the Carthaginians, who were almost overwhelmed by their mercenary soldiers after the first war with the Romans, even though the Carthaginians had their own citizens as generals. The Thebans had made Philip of Macedon their general after the death of Epaminondas, but once Philip was victorious in battle he took away the Thebans' liberty.[50] The Milanese, after the death of Duke Filippo Visconti, hired Francesco Sforza to fight the Venetians: After Sforza vanquished them at Caravaggio he joined the Venetians to oppress the Milanese, his patrons. Francesco Sforza's father, a mercenary to Queen Giovanna of Naples, left her defenseless, and she was forced to throw herself on the mercy of the King of Aragon so as not to lose her realm.

In the past the Venetians and the Florentines managed to expand their empires with the help of mercenaries, and the mercenary generals did not make themselves princes but stood by them. This, however, in the case of the Florentines was only because they were favored by Fortune. They had employed some illustrious generals whom they had cause to fear, but some of these happened to lose battles, others ran into staunch opposition, and still others turned their ambitions elsewhere. Giovanni Aucut was one of the mercenary generals who did not win, so we do not know where his loyalty would ultimately have lain.[51] But it will be admitted that had he been victorious, the Florentines would have been at his mercy. Francesco Sforza always had the Brac-

49. See *Discourses,* Book I, chapter 12.
50. Epaminondas (c. 410–362 BCE) was a Theban statesman and general who made Thebes the foremost military power in Greece from 370 to 362 BCE. After his death, Thebes declined into civil strife, and in 346 was forced to admit Philip of Macedon's garrisons.
51. The English condottiere Sir John Hawkwood.

cio faction against him—each side watching the other. Sforza turned his ambition to Lombardy, and Braccio marched against the Church and the Kingdom of Naples.

But let us consider our times. The Florentines hired as their general Paolo Vitelli, a most astute man who had risen from private citizen to a position of great prominence. Had he conquered Pisa for them, the Florentines would have been forced to keep him, for they would have been in grave danger had he gone over to the Pisans. But had the Florentines kept him, they would have ended up under his thumb.

In the case of the Venetians, if one weighs their successes it is clear that they acted wisely and bravely as long as they used their own soldiers to fight their wars, which they did before they began to expand from Venice onto the mainland. Both their noblemen and armed plebeians had always fought most valiantly. But the moment the Venetians stepped on terra firma they lost their skill and resorted to mercenaries, as was common throughout Italy. At the beginning of their expansion they had a small state but a substantial reputation, and so did not have much to fear from their mercenary generals. But as they expanded, which they did under General Carmignola, they received ample proof of their error.[52] Carmignola had shown his skill in battle, having defeated the Duke of Milan, but subsequently the Venetians saw his ardor for battle cool. They saw that they could not expect any further victories from him but were not willing or able to relieve him of his duties, since they did not want to lose what they had gained if he switched allegiance. So for their own security they were compelled to execute him. After Carmignola, the Venetians hired mercenaries like Bartolomeo da Bergamo, Roberto da San Severino, and the Count of Pitigliano, from whom they had more reason to fear defeat than victory (as happened at the Battle of Vailà, where in one day Venice lost all that it had laboriously gained over eight hundred years). Mercenary armies afford only slow, laborious, and insubstantial victories, while the losses they bring are sudden and spectacular.

As these examples have brought me to Italy, which has been ruled for so many years by mercenary armies, I would like to discuss them in greater depth, so that by tracing their origin and development it will

---

52. Francesco Bussone da Carmignola, c. 1380–1432, commanded Florentine and Venetian forces against Milan. His irresolute conduct of the war led the Venetians to suspect treason, and he was tried and executed.

be easier to remedy the problem. It must be kept in mind how, in recent times since the empire was driven out of Italy and the pope has gained in temporal power, Italy has split into more states; for many of the great cities took up arms against their nobles who had been favored by the emperor and had oppressed them, while the Church favored the oppressed cities in order to gain temporal power. In many other cities, their own citizens became princes. As a result, Italy fell into the hands of the Church and of several republics. Since these new rulers were priests and private citizens, they knew nothing about armies and turned to foreign mercenaries. The first to give a mercenary army prominence was Alberigo da Conio from the Romagna. From his school came, among others, Braccio and Sforza, who in their day were the arbiters of Italy. After them came all the others, who up until the present day have led these mercenary armies. The result: Italy was overrun by Charles, pillaged by Louis, ravished by Ferrando, and disgraced by the Swiss.

The mercenaries moved quickly to take away the standing of the infantry and appropriate it to themselves. They did this because, not having a state of their own and living by their profession, too few soldiers would not afford them the standing they needed, while they could not support and feed as many soldiers as they did need. So they limited themselves to the cavalry, where the force was smaller and could be fed and paid. As a result, in an army of twenty thousand you could not find two thousand infantrymen. Furthermore, the mercenary generals did their utmost to keep themselves and their soldiers out of the way of fatigue and danger, and did not kill the enemy in the fray but took prisoners, and that without ransom. They did not attack cities at night, nor did those defending the cities attack the encampments outside. They did not build stockades or ditches around their camps, and they did not go on campaigns during the winter. All these things were consistent with their military conventions and, as I have pointed out, enabled them to escape fatigue and danger. They have driven Italy into slavery and disgrace.

CHAPTER THIRTEEN

THE AUXILIARY ARMY, THE CITIZEN ARMY, AND THE ARMY THAT COMBINES THE TWO

An auxiliary army is also a worthless army. It is the kind that a powerful figure brings with him when you call upon to help defend you. Pope Julius did this in our times. In the campaign of Ferrara, the pope witnessed the miserable performance of his mercenary army and turned to an auxiliary one, reaching an agreement with King Ferdinand of Spain to come to his aid with troops. Such troops can be useful and good in themselves, but will almost always prove harmful to him who summons them. If this army loses, he ends up dissatisfied, and if it wins, he ends up its prisoner. Even though history is full of examples, I prefer to cite the contemporary example of Pope Julius II, whose decision to turn to Ferdinand of Spain for help could not have been more ill advised. The pope was so eager to gain Ferrara that he threw himself into the arms of a foreigner. But Fortune happened to be on the pope's side, and hence he was not compelled to taste the bitter fruit of his decision, for after his auxiliary army was defeated at Ravenna[53] the Swiss routed the victorious French, much to his surprise and everyone else's. The pope was not taken prisoner by the enemy, since they had fled, nor by his auxiliary troops, since his ultimate vic-

---

53. In April 1512, the French army fought a battle with the Spanish, Venetian, and papal troops outside Ravenna. The French were victorious, but were then forced by the Swiss (then the pope's main allies) to evacuate Milan. In 1513 the Swiss routed the French at Novara.

tory had been gained not by them but by another army. The Florentines, having no army at all, had engaged ten thousand Frenchmen to conquer Pisa, which exposed them to more danger than they had ever faced before. The Emperor of Constantinople, in order to fend off his neighbors, had brought ten thousand Turks into Greece, and once the war was over these Turks did not want to leave. This was the beginning of Greece's enslavement to the Infidel.

In short, anyone ready to lose battles should avail himself of such troops, because they are far more dangerous than mercenaries. For if you use auxiliary troops the cards are stacked against you, since they are united under the command of an outsider. But for mercenary troops to harm you, even if they are victorious, takes a certain amount of time and the right opportunity. Mercenary troops are not a single body, as it is you who assemble them and pay them. An outsider whom you appoint as their commander cannot establish his authority quickly enough to do you harm. In essence, the most dangerous aspect of mercenaries is their indolence, while that of auxiliary troops is their prowess. Wise princes have always avoided auxiliary troops and relied on their own. They have preferred defeat with their own army rather than victory with that of another, judging that a victory won with another's army is not a true victory.

I shall never hesitate to cite Cesare Borgia and his actions. He entered the Romagna at the head of an auxiliary army made up entirely of Frenchmen, and with it took Imola and Forlì. But the moment he felt that this army was not reliable, he turned to mercenaries, considering them less dangerous, and hired the Orsini and the Vitelli. When he subsequently saw that they too were unreliable, disloyal, and dangerous, he destroyed them[54] and went back to using his own men. It is easy to see the difference between these types of armies, considering Cesare Borgia's standing when he had only the French, when he had the Orsini and Vitelli, and when he was self-sufficient with his own soldiers. Then his standing increased. His reputation was at its height when men saw him in every way as the master of his own army.

Though I intended to focus on recent Italian examples, I do not wish to pass over Hiero of Syracuse, as I have already mentioned

---

54. At Sinigallia in 1502. See "How Duke Valentino Killed the Generals Who Conspired Against Him."

him.[55] The Syracusans had made him general of their army, and he was quick to see that the mercenary troops, much like our own Italian condottieri, were useless. As he felt that he could neither keep them nor dismiss them, he had them slashed to pieces.[56] After that, he made war using his own troops and not those of others. I also wish to cite an example from the Old Testament. David stepped forward to fight Goliath, the Philistine challenger. Saul offered him his own armor to give him courage, but no sooner had David put it on than he cast it off again, saying that he could not make use of his own strength with another's armor. He wanted to face the enemy with his own slingshot and knife. In short, the arms of another will either fall off your back, weigh you down, or hamper you.

Louis XI's father, King Charles VII, who freed France from the English[57] with the help of Fortune and his skill, recognized the importance of having his own army. He issued a decree in his kingdom to enlist an infantry and a cavalry. After him, his son Louis disbanded the infantry and began hiring Swiss mercenaries. This mistake, followed by others, has led, as we have seen, to the many dangers France has had to face. Having given power to the Swiss, Louis undermined his own, because he disbanded his infantry and made his cavalry dependent on the mercenaries' skill. And the cavalry, once accustomed to fighting alongside the Swiss, felt it could not win without them. As a result, the French cannot stand up to the Swiss, but neither are they willing to face others on the battlefield without them. Hence the French army has become mixed—in part mercenary, in part French citizens—which is still better than an army that is entirely auxiliary or mercenary, but far inferior to an army made up entirely of one's own citizens. This example should suffice, because France would have been undefeatable had King Charles's decrees been followed and developed. But

55. See chapter 6.
56. Polybius, *Histories*, Book 1, chapter 9: "Finding the old mercenaries disaffected and seditious, he led an expedition against the barbarians who had occupied Messene. [...] But he held back his citizen cavalry and infantry at a distance and under his personal command, as if he meant to use them to attack another side, but sent the mercenaries on ahead, allowing them to be completely slaughtered by the barbarians."
57. King Charles VII of France (1403–61) was the father of Louis XI (1423–83). King Charles drove the English out of France (with the aid of Joan of Arc), and instituted sweeping reforms in his army by a series of ordinances, improving its recruitment and efficiency.

man's scant prudence will make him relish a dish that appears delicious while it conceals poison within.

A prince who does not perceive the ills in his principality as they arise is not truly astute. Such astuteness is afforded to few. If one considers the beginning of the decline of the Roman Empire, one will find that it began when Goth mercenaries were hired. It was then that the strength of the Roman army started to flag. All the skill and valor that was sapped from the Romans went to strengthen the Goths. Thus I conclude that no principality is safe without its own army. It is entirely at the mercy of Fortune, having failed to preserve the valor that will defend it in adversity. Wise men have always held to the maxim *quod nihil sit tam infirmum aut instabile quam fama potentiae non sua vi nixa.*[58] And "your own power" is an army composed either of your subjects, your citizens, or your dependents. Anything else constitutes a mercenary or auxiliary army. How one's army should be organized is easy to see if one weighs the four examples I have cited above[59] and if one takes into account the method by which Philip of Macedon, the father of Alexander the Great, and many republics and principalities armed themselves—a method I fully support.

58. An altered quotation from Tacitus's *Annales.* 13.19.1: *Nihil rerum mortalium tam instabile ac fluxum est quam fama potentiae non sua vi nixae.* (No human matter is as unstable and changeable as the reputation of power that has no support of its own.)
59. Cesare Borgia, Hiero of Syracuse, David, and Charles VII of France.

CHAPTER FOURTEEN

OF A PRINCE'S DUTIES
CONCERNING THE MILITARY

A prince must therefore have no other thought or objective, nor dedicate himself to any other art, but that of war with its rules and discipline, because this is the only art suitable for a man who commands. It is such a powerful art that it will maintain the position of one who is born a prince, but will also often raise mere private citizens to that rank. Princes who give more thought to luxury than to arms often lose their principality. In fact, the quickest way to lose a principality is to neglect the art of war, and the best way of acquiring one is to be a master in this art.[60]

Francesco Sforza, from being a private citizen, became Duke of Milan because he was armed, while his sons after him, shrinking from the hardships of military life, ended up as private citizens after having been dukes. Furthermore, being unarmed makes you, among other things, despised, which is one of the infamies from which a prince must shield himself, as I will discuss later.[61] There is no comparison between an armed man and an unarmed one. It is not reasonable to think that an armed man might be compelled to obey an unarmed one, or that an unarmed man might be safe among the armed mercenaries he has hired. The unarmed prince will always be wary of these merce-

60. See note 48 above.
61. See chapter 19.

naries, whereas they will harbor disdain for him. There is no way for them to work well together. Hence, beside the other misfortunes already mentioned, a prince who does not understand military matters will not be respected by his soldiers and cannot trust them.

The prince must therefore never shift his attention from the exercise of war, even in times of peace, and he must do this both in action and in mind. As for action, he must not only keep his troops well trained and organized, but must also himself continuously go out hunting, keeping his body accustomed to hardship, while learning the lay of the land: how the mountains rise and the valleys dip, how the plains lie, and the nature of the rivers and marshes. He must do this with the greatest application, for such knowledge is useful in two ways. First, he will familiarize himself intimately with his own country and understand how to defend it; second, with the knowledge and experience of his own terrain, he will more easily get to know any foreign terrain he might have to explore, because any hill, valley, river, plain, or marsh that exists in Tuscany will resemble those of other provinces. In short, familiarizing one with the terrain of one's own province helps to familiarize one with the terrain of other provinces as well. A prince who lacks this knowledge lacks the most essential quality in a general, because this will train him how to hunt the enemy, choose a campsite, lead troops, and direct them in the field and in besieging towns.

Among the things Prince Philopoemen of the Achaeans has been praised for by writers is that in times of peace he thought of nothing but ways of waging war.[62] When he was out riding in the country with his friends, he often stopped and reasoned with them: "If the enemy were up in those hills and we were here with our army, who would have the advantage? How could we attack without breaking formation? If we wanted to retreat, how would we do that? If they were to retreat, how would we pursue them?" And as Prince Philopoemen and his companions rode on, he would lay out all the circumstances that could befall an army. He would listen to the opinions of the others and share

62. Philopoemen (c. 252–182 BCE) was a renowned general of the Achaean League, known for his innovations in Greek military tactics. Machiavelli closely follows Livy's text (Book XXXV, chapter 28): "Philopoemen had a great talent for directing a campaign and choosing advantageous positions, which was the result of his experience acquired through much reflection in times of peace as well as war."

his opinions with them, which he would back up with detailed explanation, his aim being that through continuous deliberations, nothing unforeseen for which he might have no remedy would ever occur in battle.

As for the exercise of the mind, a prince must read histories and study the actions of great men so he can see how they conducted themselves in war and examine the reasons for their victories and defeats, in order to imitate the former and avoid the latter. Above all, the prince must follow the example of some great man of the past, who in turn followed the example of another great man who had been praised and honored before him, always keeping his predecessor's deeds and actions in mind. For it is said that Alexander the Great imitated Achilles, that Caesar imitated Alexander, and that Scipio imitated Cyrus. Anyone who reads Xenophon's life of Cyrus can see in Scipio's actions how much glory his imitation of Cyrus brought him, and to what extent Scipio conformed with what Xenophon wrote about Cyrus in matters of chastity, openness, humanity, and liberality.

A wise prince must observe such methods, and never remain idle in times of peace but vigorously take advantage of them so he can be ready for times of adversity, so that when Fortune changes, she will find him prepared to resist her.

CHAPTER FIFTEEN

OF THE THINGS FOR WHICH MEN,
AND PRINCES IN PARTICULAR,
ARE PRAISED OR BLAMED

It remains now to discuss what methods and measures a prince should employ with his subjects or friends. Many have written about this, and I fear I might be considered presumptuous, particularly as I intend to depart from the principles laid down by others. As my intention is to write something useful for discerning minds, I find it more fitting to seek the truth of the matter rather than imaginary conceptions. Many have imagined republics and principalities that have never been seen or heard of, because how one lives and how one ought to live are so far apart that he who spurns what is actually done for what ought to be done will achieve ruin rather than his own preservation. A man who strives to make a show of correct comportment in every circumstance can only come to ruin among so many who have other designs. Hence it is necessary for a prince who wishes to maintain his position to learn how to be able not to be good, and to use or not use this ability according to circumstances.

Casting aside imagined things about a prince, and considering only things that are true, I argue that all men, particularly princes, since they have a higher position, are judged by qualities that attract praise or blame. This is why some princes are considered generous and others miserly;[63] one is regarded as a giver, the other as a taker; one is seen

---

63. Machiavelli's note: "I am using the Tuscan term *misero* here, as *avaro* (miserly) in Italian still carries the implication of someone who wishes to acquire by robbery, while we use *misero* in Tuscan to mean someone who excessively abstains from using what is his own."

as cruel, the other as merciful, one faithless, the other faithful; one effeminate and pusillanimous, the other fierce and spirited; one humane, the other haughty; one lascivious, the other chaste; one frank, the other sly; one rigid, the other flexible; one grave, the other jovial; one religious, the other unbelieving; and so on. I know everyone will maintain that it would be commendable for a prince to have all the qualities I have just mentioned that are held to be good. But because a prince cannot wholly have or espouse all these qualities, as the human condition will not allow it, he must be wise enough to know how to evade the infamy of the qualities that are thought to be bad, which will cause him to lose his state. If possible he should also avoid the qualities which are considered bad but will not actually lose him his state, but if he must indulge in them, he need not concern himself about their consequences. He also should not concern himself about incurring the infamy of qualities that are considered bad if he needs them to save his state. For there are cases in which people might think a certain path is valorous, but following it would be the prince's ruin, while there are also cases in which a certain way might seem evil, but following it will result in the prince's safety and well-being.

CHAPTER SIXTEEN

OF GENEROSITY AND PARSIMONY

To begin with the first of these qualities: I propose that it is good to be thought generous. And yet generosity pursued in a way that makes people perceive you as generous will harm you, because if you exercise generosity in all modesty, as is appropriate, it will not be recognized, and you will not be able to avoid the reputation of miserliness. Hence, if one wishes to be perceived as generous among men, one will have to indulge in a great deal of sumptuous display. A prince who chooses this path will consume all his resources and eventually will have to overburden the populace with taxes, extort money from them, and do whatever else is necessary to raise money to maintain his reputation for being generous. This will make him hateful to his subjects, and, should he become poor, despised by all. With his generosity he will have hurt many and rewarded few. He will be vulnerable to the slightest unrest and fall prey to the first danger. When the prince who has chosen this path realizes this, his impulse is to draw back, which quickly brings him a reputation for miserliness.

Therefore a wise prince, seeing that he is unable to practice ostentatious generosity without harming himself, must not mind acquiring a reputation for miserliness. With time he will come to be considered generous once people see that his parsimony has produced sufficient funds and enabled him to defend himself from those who make war on him, and to launch campaigns without burdening the populace. In this way he will be considered generous by the great number of men from whom he takes nothing, and miserly by the few to whom he gives nothing. In our times we have seen great deeds accomplished only by those who were considered miserly; all the others came to ruin. Pope Julius II, though he made use of his reputation for generosity to gain the papacy, did not strive to maintain it afterward. This was so that he could wage wars. The present king of France[64] has launched many wars without imposing extra taxes on his people, which he has been able to do only because the additional expenditures have been provided for by his long parsimony. The present king of Spain,[65] had he been considered generous, could not have undertaken or won so many campaigns. Consequently, a prince must care little about gaining a reputation for parsimony if he does not want to rob his subjects and yet wishes to be able to defend himself without becoming poor and contemptible or being forced to become rapacious. Parsimony is one of the vices that permit him to reign.

Were someone to argue that Caesar acquired his empire through generosity, and that many others achieved the highest ranks because they were generous and were seen as such, my answer is: Either you are already a prince, or you are on your way to becoming one. In the first case, such generosity is damaging; in the second, it is quite necessary to be considered generous. Caesar was one of those who wanted to rule Rome. However, had he survived after he gained his principality and not tempered his spending, he would have destroyed Rome. But were someone to counter that there have been many princes who were considered most generous and who did great things with their armies, I would reply: A prince spends either his own wealth, or that of his subjects or of others. In the first case he must be frugal, while in the second, he must show every generosity. A prince who rides out with his army, sustaining himself by looting, sacking, and plundering, controlling the assets of others, such a prince needs to be generous. Otherwise his soldiers will not follow him. And it is easier to be a generous giver when the possessions you are giving away are not your own or those of your subjects. Cyrus, Caesar, and Alexander were of this class. Spending what belongs to others does not diminish your standing but

64. Louis XII.
65. Ferdinand II.

increases it. Only spending what is your own harms you. There is nothing that consumes itself like generosity: The more you use it, the more you lose the capacity of using it. You either become poor and disdained, or, to escape poverty, rapacious and hated. There is nothing a prince must avoid more than being at once disdained and hated, and generosity leads to both. It is therefore wiser to settle for a reputation of miserliness which incurs disdain without hatred, than to try to gain a reputation for generosity that brings with it a reputation for rapacity, incurring disdain with hatred.

OF CRUELTY AND MERCY, AND WHETHER IT IS BETTER TO BE LOVED THAN FEARED, OR THE CONTRARY

Proceeding to the other qualities I have already mentioned,[66] I maintain that every prince must wish to be considered merciful and not cruel. Nevertheless, he must avoid using mercy inappropriately. Cesare Borgia was considered cruel, yet his cruelty brought order to the Romagna, uniting it and making it peaceful and loyal. All things considered, Borgia proved far more merciful than the people of Florence, who allowed Pistoia to be destroyed simply in order to avoid a reputation for cruelty. A prince, therefore, must not fear being reproached for cruelty when it is a matter of keeping his subjects united and loyal, because with a few exemplary executions he will be more merciful than those who, through too much mercy, allow the kind of disorder to spread that gives rise to plunder and murder. This harms the whole community, while an execution ordered by a prince harms only a single individual.

Unlike an established prince, a new prince cannot escape a reputation for cruelty, since newly acquired states are filled with danger. As Virgil has Dido say: *Res dura, et regni novitas me talia cogunt / Moliri, et late fines custode tueri* (The harsh situation and the newness of my kingdom force me to act this way and post guards at my borders).

66. Chapter 15, paragraph 2.

Nevertheless, a prince must not be quick to believe the worst and act impulsively, becoming afraid of his own shadow. His actions must be tempered by prudence and humanity so that too much trust does not render him incautious, nor too much mistrust intolerable.

This raises the question whether it is better to be loved than feared, or the contrary. My reply is that one would like to be both, but as it is difficult to combine love and fear, if one has to choose between them it is far safer to be feared than loved. Because it can be said of men that they are ungrateful and inconstant, simulators and dissimulators,[67] and that they are hungry for profit and quick to evade danger. While you do them good they are devoted to you, offering you their lives, their possessions, their children, as I have said before—but only as long as danger is far off. The moment danger is at hand, they turn away. A prince who has based everything on their word without taking other precautions is ruined, because friendships acquired at a price and not through magnanimity and nobility of spirit can be bought but not owned, nor do they bring a return in difficult times. Men have less compunction about harming someone who has made himself loved than harming someone who has made himself feared, because love is held in place by chains of obligation, which, as men are evil, will quickly be broken if self-interest is at stake. But fear is held in place by a dread of punishment, which one can always rely on.

The prince, however, must make himself feared so that he avoids hatred, even if he does not acquire love. Being feared and not hated go well together, and the prince can always achieve this if he does not touch the property or the women of his citizens and subjects. If he finds he must execute someone, he should do so only if there is adequate justification and a manifest cause. But above all he must refrain from seizing the property of others, because a man is quicker to forget the death of his father than the loss of his patrimony. Furthermore, there are always ample reasons for seizing another's property, and he who begins to live by plunder will always find reasons to take what be-

---

67. Sallust, in his account of the Catiline conspiracy in *De conjuratione Catilinae,* described Catiline as *simulator ac dissimulator.*

longs to others, whereas the reasons for having to execute someone are rare, and frequently altogether lacking.[68]

Yet when a prince is with his army and has a multitude of soldiers under his command, he must not scruple about gaining a reputation for cruelty, because without it he can never keep his army united or willing to follow him into battle. One of Hannibal's many admirable achievements was that he marched his enormous army of myriad nationalities into battle in foreign lands. Whether Fortune smiled on him or not, there was never any dissension among them nor any rebellion against him. The only reason for this was his inhumane cruelty, which, combined with his infinite skill, made him venerated and feared in the eyes of his men. Without this quality, his other abilities would not have produced this effect. Some careless historians admire this quality while condemning the principal reason for it.

That his other abilities would not have sufficed to keep his army in check can be seen from the example of Scipio, an exceptional man not only in his time, but in all of history. His army rebelled in Spain for no other reason than his undue lenience, which allowed the soldiers more freedom than is suitable in military discipline. He was reproached for this in the Senate by Fabius Maximus, who called him the corrupter of the Roman army. The Locrians had been savaged and plundered by one of Scipio's officers, after which Scipio neither made reparations nor punished the officer, a consequence of Scipio's easygoing nature.[69] Subsequently, a Locrian spoke before the Senate and, in an attempt to excuse Scipio, said that there were many men who were better at not transgressing than they were at punishing the transgressions of others. With time, Scipio's nature would have thrown a shadow on his fame

---

68. See *Discourses,* Book III, chapter 6, in which Machiavelli develops these ideas in the paragraph beginning "The injury princes do to citizens is usually against their property, their honor, or their life. In the case of injury against life, threats are more dangerous than executions. In fact, threats are extremely dangerous, while executions are not at all: He who is dead cannot think about revenge, while he who remains alive will usually leave such thoughts to the dead."

69. Livy (Book XXIX, chapter 8) writes: "But Pleminius so surpassed General Hamilcar in crime and greed—the Roman soldiers so surpassing the Carthaginians—that they seemed to be rivaling one another not in battle but in vice. Nothing that renders the power of the strong hateful to the weak was left undone by the Roman general and his soldiers toward the towns-people."

and glory had he been a general in the times of the empire, but as he lived under the government of the Senate, this weakness was not only concealed, but brought him glory.

Returning to the question of being feared or loved, I conclude that since men love at their own will and fear at the will of the prince, a wise prince must build a foundation on what is his own, and not on what belongs to others. At the same time, he must do all in his power to escape being hated, as I have already said.

CHAPTER EIGHTEEN

OF THE NEED FOR PRINCES
TO KEEP THEIR WORD

Everyone knows how commendable it is for a prince to keep his word and live by integrity rather than by cunning. And yet our own era has shown that princes who have little regard for their word have achieved great things, being expert at beguiling men's minds. In the end, these princes overcame those who relied solely on loyalty.

There are two ways of fighting: either with laws or with force. The first is peculiar to men, the second to beasts. But because the first way often does not suffice, one has to resort to the second. Nevertheless, a prince must be expert in using both. This has been taught to princes allegorically by ancient writers, who tell us that Achilles and many other ancient princes were sent to Chiron the Centaur to be raised and tutored. What this means is that the ancient princes, whose tutor was half man and half beast, learned to use both natures, neither of which can prevail without the other.

Since a prince must know how to use the nature of the beast to his advantage, he must emulate both the fox and the lion, because a lion cannot defy a snare, while a fox cannot defy a pack of wolves. A prince must therefore be a fox to spot the snares, and a lion to overwhelm the wolves. The prince who models himself only on the lion does not grasp this, but a wise ruler cannot and should not keep his word when it would be to his disadvantage to do so, and when the reasons that made him give his word have disappeared. If all men were good, this rule would not stand. But as men are wicked and not prepared to keep their word to you, you have no need to keep your word to them. Nor does a prince ever lack legitimate pretexts for concealing the fact that he has broken his word. There are countless examples from our times of the many peace treaties and promises that have been rendered null and void through the fickleness of princes. The princes who have best used the nature of the fox to their advantage have been the most successful. But one must know how to conceal this quality and be a great simulator and dissimulator,[70] for men are so simple, and so prone to being won over by the necessity of the moment, that a deceiver will always find someone willing to be deceived.

There is an example from recent times that I do not want to pass over. Pope Alexander VI never thought or did anything except to deceive, and he always found someone to deceive. Never has a man made more grandiose promises or sworn greater oaths, and kept them less. And yet he always got away with his deceptions, because he was so well acquainted with this aspect of the world.

Consequently, although a prince need not have all the good qualities that I have mentioned, it is most necessary for him to appear to have them.[71] I will even be so bold as to say that it actually does a prince harm to have those good qualities and always observe them. But appearing to have them will benefit him. Of course, it is best to both seem and be merciful, loyal, humane, upright, and scrupulous. And yet one's spirit should be calculated in such a way that one can, if need be, turn one's back on these qualities and become the opposite. It is vital to understand that a prince, particularly a new prince, cannot afford to cultivate attributes for which men are considered good. In order to maintain the state, a prince will often be compelled to work against what is merciful, loyal, humane, upright, and scrupulous. He must have a spirit that can change depending on the winds and variations of Fortune, and, as I have said above, he must not, if he is able, distance himself from what is good, but must also, when necessary, know how to prefer what is bad.

Therefore a prince must be very careful that no word escape his

70. See text for note 67 above.

71. This idea is also echoed in *Discourses*, Book I, chapter 25: "Men cherish something that seems like the real thing as much as they do the real thing itself. In fact, they are often more affected by that which seems than by that which is."

mouth that is not filled with the five qualities I have mentioned. When one sees and hears him, he should be a paragon of mercy, loyalty, humaneness, integrity, and scrupulousness. Indeed, there is nothing more important than appearing to have this last quality. Men in general judge more with the eye than with the hand, because everyone can see, but few can feel. Everyone sees what you seem to be, but few feel what you are, and those few will not dare oppose the opinion of the many who have the majesty of the state behind them: In the actions of all men, and particularly the prince, where there is no higher justice to appeal to, one looks at the outcome.

The prince must acquire and keep his principality, and the means by which he does this will always be praised and judged honorable by all, because the common people will be convinced by appearances and by the end result. And the world is made up of common people, among whom the few dissenters who can see beyond appearances do not count when the majority can point to the prince's success. A certain prince of our times (whom I shall not name) preaches nothing but peace and loyalty, while he could not be more hostile to both.[72] Yet if he lived by what he preaches, he would by now have lost both his reputation and his state many times over.

---

72. Almost certainly an allusion to Ferdinand II.

CHAPTER NINETEEN

OF HOW TO AVOID CONTEMPT
AND HATRED

As I have already discussed the most important qualities[73] that attract praise or blame, I would like to touch on others in more general terms, so that the prince may note (as I have to some extent mentioned) how to avoid the things that would make him hated and scorned.[74] If he manages to do this he will have accomplished his duty, and will not face any risk should he perpetrate other infamies. What will make him hated above all, as I have said, is rapaciousness and seizing the property and women of his subjects, which he must refrain from. Men will generally live contentedly as long as their property and honor are not touched, and the prince need only counter the ambition of a few, which can be done easily and in many ways. What will make the prince contemptible is for him to be perceived as undependable, frivolous, effeminate, pusillanimous, and irresolute, against which a prince must guard himself as from the plague. He must do his utmost so that his actions will be perceived as imbued with greatness, courage, dignity, and power. And as for the private affairs of his subjects, he must be adamant that his decisions are irrevocable. He must maintain a standing such that no man would venture to cheat or deceive him.

---

73. See chapter 15, in which Machiavelli discusses "the qualities that attract praise or blame."
74. Throughout this chapter Machiavelli touches on ideas put forward in Aristotle's *Politics*, Book V. Aristotle writes (Book V, chapter 10, 1312b, 20): "There are two principal reasons that lead men to attack tyrannies: hatred and scorn."

A prince who creates this opinion of himself will be greatly esteemed, and it is difficult to attack or conspire against one who is greatly esteemed, so long as he is perceived as excellent and is revered by his people. But a prince must have two fears: one internal, based on his subjects; the other external, based on foreign powers. From the foreign enemy the prince can defend himself with good arms and good friends (and he who has good arms will always have good friends); and internal matters will always be stable when external matters are stable, so long as they have not been clouded by conspiracy. But even if external matters are volatile, the prince will always counter every violence if he has lived and ruled as I have mentioned and does not lose courage (as I have said Nabis of Sparta did).[75]

When external affairs are stable, the prince must still fear that his subjects might conspire secretly against him. But he will be quite safe from this as long as he avoids being hated or despised and keeps the populace on his side. It is important that he do this, as I have said at length above. One of the strongest remedies a prince has against conspiracy is not to be hated by the masses, because conspirators are invariably certain that they will satisfy the populace by killing the prince. But if on the other hand they think they will enrage the populace, they will not pluck up the courage for such an act, because the difficulties facing conspirators are infinite. Experience has taught that there have been many conspiracies, but few that have ended well, because whoever conspires cannot do so alone, nor can he attract cohorts other than those who he believes are malcontents. And the moment you take a malcontent into your confidence, you give him the opportunity to become quite content, pursuing his own advantage by betraying you.[76] So much so, that seeing the certain gain in that direction, and seeing doubt and peril in the other, it must be a rare friend or a most determined enemy of the prince who will keep his word to you.

In short, from the conspirator's point of view there is nothing but fear, rivalry, and the prospect of horrific punishment, whereas from the prince's perspective there are the majesty of the principality, the laws,

---

75. See chapter 9.
76. See *Discourses,* Book III, chapter 6: "If on the other hand you measure faithfulness by the discontent an ally has for the prince, you can be quite deceived, because the instant you take this malcontent into your confidence you provide him with the opportunity to become quite content at your expense."

and the protection afforded by friends and the state. If one also adds the goodwill of the people, it is unlikely that anyone would be so bold as to conspire against the prince, since under normal circumstances conspirators have much to fear before committing the evil deed, but in this case they have just as much to fear afterward, as they will have the whole populace against them. Once their deed is done, they cannot hope for refuge anywhere.

I could cite infinite examples of this, but shall limit myself to one incident that took place within the memory of our fathers. Annibale Bentivoglio, the Prince of Bologna and grandfather of the present Annibale Bentivoglio, was killed by the Canneschi, who conspired against him, leaving no one to succeed him except his son Giovanni, at that time still in swaddling clothes. Immediately after the murder, the people rose and killed all the Canneschi, a result of the people's goodwill toward the house of Bentivoglio. In all Bologna, after Annibale's death, there were no heirs who could rule the state, but the people's goodwill was so great that when they heard that there was a Bentivoglio living in Florence, who had been thought to be the son of a blacksmith, they went there to offer him the government of Bologna, which he accepted until young Giovanni Bentivoglio came of age.

I therefore conclude that a prince need not worry unduly about conspiracies when the people are well disposed toward him. But if they are his enemies and hate him, he must fear everything and everybody. Well-ordered states and wise princes have been careful not to anger the nobles and to keep the populace content, because this is one of the most important tasks that falls on a prince.

Among the well-ordered and well-governed states of our times is France. It has countless good institutions on which the king's liberty and security depend, of which the foremost is the *parlement* and its authority.[77] For he who set up this system was aware of the nobles' insolence and ambition and deemed that they needed a harness to keep them in check, but he was also aware of the people's hatred of the nobles, a hatred based on fear. The idea was to assuage both factions, but

---

77. The French *parlements* formed the supreme court under the Ancien Régime in France, divided into the Parisian *parlement*, which was the most powerful, and the regional *parlements*. The *parlements* saw to it that the king's edicts and measures conformed with the principles of law and justice. They provided a counterbalance to royal power. By Machiavelli's time, the *parlements* had adopted a course of systematic opposition to the king.

without the king's being seen to be involved. This removed any allegations the nobles might make that the king was favoring the populace, or any allegations the populace might make that he was favoring the nobles. This was the reason for establishing an independent institution that could keep the nobles in check, and favor the people without compromising the king. Such a decision could not have been better or more wise, nor could there be a better guarantee for the security of the king and the kingdom. From which one can draw another notable principle: Princes must delegate difficult tasks to others and keep popular ones for themselves. Once more I conclude that a prince has to respect the nobles, but must not make himself hated by the populace.

Many who have considered the way that certain Roman emperors lived and died might argue that they present examples that contradict my opinions, as some of these emperors did live excellently, showing much skill and spirit, but nevertheless lost their throne or were killed by their own men who conspired against them. I will respond to these objections by discussing the qualities of a few emperors, demonstrating that the reasons for their ruin are in accord with what I have cited. This should be of interest to anyone reading about the events of that era. I will limit myself to the emperors who came to the throne between the reigns of Marcus the Philosopher and Maximinus. These were Marcus, his son Commodus, Pertinax, Julianus, Severus, his son Antoninus Caracalla, Macrinus, Elagabalus, Alexander, and Maximinus.

First of all I would like to point out that while in most principalities one merely has to contend with the ambitions of the great and the hostility of the populace, the Roman emperors had to face a third problem: contending with the cruelty and plundering of their soldiers. This was so difficult that it proved the ruin of many, since it is hard to satisfy both army and populace. The populace wants peace and hence a modest prince, while the army wants a prince with a military spirit who is arrogant, cruel, and rapacious, and ready to unleash these qualities on the populace so that the soldiers can double their pay and give free rein to their greed and cruelty. The result was that those emperors who by nature or education did not have the standing that could keep the army or the populace in check invariably came to grief. Most of these emperors, particularly those who came to power as new princes, knew the difficulty of balancing these two opposing factions and chose to reward the soldiers with little thought of how this would harm the populace. This was a necessary decision. A prince cannot avoid being hated by one of the two factions. Hence he must first strive not to be hated by the people, and should that not be possible, he should do his utmost to avoid the hatred of the faction that is more powerful. Therefore emperors who were new princes and especially needed strong backing preferred to side with the army rather than the populace. This proved to be to the emperor's benefit or not, depending on whether he knew how to maintain his standing with the army.

It was for these reasons that Marcus, Pertinax, and Alexander—modest men who loved justice, spurned cruelty, and were kind and humane—met tragic ends. All, that is, except for Marcus, who lived and died with honor. He had come to the imperial throne by inheritance and did not need to show gratitude to the army or the populace, and he was a man of great skill, which made him venerated by all. Throughout his life he kept the soldiers in check and the people within bounds, and was never hated or disdained. But Pertinax was made emperor despite the opposition of the soldiers, who had been used to living licentiously under Commodus and could not bear the honest way of life that Pertinax wanted to force on them. Pertinax inspired hatred, and as he was an old man, contempt as well, so he came to ruin at the very start of his reign. And here one must note that hatred can be caused through good deeds as much as through bad. As I have said before, a prince who wants to maintain his state is often forced not to be good, because when the faction that you believe you need in order to rule is corrupt—whether it is the populace, the army, or the nobles—it is to your advantage to satisfy them, in which case good deeds are your enemy. But let us come to Emperor Alexander, who was so good that among the many things he was praised for was that not a single man was put to death without trial during his fourteen-year reign. Nevertheless, he was considered effeminate and a man who let himself be governed by his mother. This brought derision upon him, and the army conspired against him and killed him.

Let us now discuss, in contrast, the qualities of Commodus, Severus, Antoninus Caracalla, and Maximinus, all of whom you will find most cruel and rapacious. To satisfy their soldiers they did not spare any violence that could be inflicted on the populace. All these emperors, with the exception of Severus, came to a bad end. Severus was so skilled that he managed to keep the army on his side even though he oppressed the populace, and so had a successful reign. His skill made him so formidable in the eyes of the army and the populace that the former remained satisfied and reverent, and the latter awestruck and stupefied. For a new prince, Severus's actions were great and noteworthy, and so I would like briefly to demonstrate how well he used the traits of both the fox and the lion, which I have already referred to as necessary for a prince to emulate. When Severus was general of the Roman army in Slavonia he was aware of the indolence of Emperor Julianus, and he persuaded his men to follow him to Rome to avenge the death of Pertinax, who had died at the hands of the Praetorian Guard. Under this pretext Severus marched his army against Rome without revealing that he had any aspirations to the imperial throne, and was in Italy before anyone even realized that he had set out. When he arrived in Rome, the Senate elected him emperor out of fear, and sentenced Julianus to death. Severus now faced two difficulties in asserting his authority over the whole empire: One was Asia, where Niger, general of the Asiatic armies, had had himself proclaimed emperor, and the other was the West, where Albinus was aspiring to the throne.[78] Severus deemed it dangerous to declare himself an enemy to both men, and so decided to attack Niger and deceive Albinus. He wrote to Albinus that although the Senate had elected him, Severus, emperor, he wanted to share the throne with Albinus, and was sending him the title of Caesar. He informed him that through a pronouncement of the Senate he had made him his co-ruler. All of this Albinus believed. But no sooner had Severus defeated and killed Niger, bringing Asia under his control, than he returned to Rome and denounced Albinus in the Senate, charging that Albinus was plotting to kill him instead of showing gratitude for the favors he had been accorded. Severus announced that he was compelled to punish Albinus's ingratitude. He confronted him in France and took from him his state and his life.

Whoever considers Severus's actions will see that he was a ferocious lion and a cunning fox, feared and revered by all, and not hated

---

78. General Pescennius Niger was proclaimed emperor by his legions when Emperor Commodus's successor, Pertinax, was murdered in the spring of 193 CE, becoming ruler of the Greek-speaking East. General Albinus represented the aristocracy of the Latin-speaking West, and was an imperial candidate in the years 193-197 CE.

by the army. One should not be surprised that as a new prince he managed to secure so much authority, for his exceptional standing always shielded him from the hatred that his rapaciousness might have sparked among the people.

Severus's son Antoninus was also a man with qualities that made him formidable in the eyes of the people and popular with his soldiers.[79] He was a military man who could bear any hardship and who scorned delicate dishes and every other weakness. This raised him in the esteem of his soldiers. Nevertheless, Antoninus's ferocity and cruelty were so great and so unprecedented—after untold murders he had a large part of the population of Rome and the entire populace of Alexandria put to death—that all the world came to despise him. Antoninus was feared even by his own entourage, which resulted in his being killed by a centurion in the midst of his own army. From which it is to be noted that a prince cannot avoid assassination resulting from the deliberations of a determined mind, because he can be assaulted by anyone who does not care about dying himself. A prince need not fear this unduly, because such men are very rare.[80] He has only to refrain from inflicting grave injury on those who serve him and whom he keeps about himself in service of the state. Antoninus did inflict such injury, shamefully killing the brother of one of his own centurions and threatening the centurion every day, even though he retained him as his bodyguard.[81] Such rash conduct was bound to bring about his own ruin, and it did.

But let us come to Commodus, who, having inherited his throne from his father, Emperor Marcus, should have been able to hold on to it with ease. He had only to follow in his father's footsteps to satisfy both the army and the people, but he had a cruel and feral nature. In order to exercise his rapacity on the populace, he chose to favor the

---

79. Machiavelli follows Herodian's description in *History of the Empire*, Book IV, particularly chapters 4–9.

80. Aristotle (*Politics*, Book V, chapter 11, 1315a, 24) writes: "Among those who plot to assassinate the tyrant, those who are most worrisome, and should be most carefully watched, are those who do not strive to preserve their own lives while destroying his."

81. Aristotle (*Politics*, Book V, chapter 11, 1315a, 27) writes: "Therefore the ruler must be extremely wary of those who believe that he has harmed them or those under their care." King Agis IV (d. 241 BCE) attempted to introduce sweeping reforms that drew on Sparta's legendary lawgiver Lycurgus (c. seventh century BCE). Agis was, however, assassinated in the fourth year of his reign.

army, and allowed it every dissipation. Furthermore, he did not maintain his dignity, often descending into the arenas to fight with gladiators and doing other things that were contemptible and unworthy of imperial majesty, becoming a figure of scorn in the eyes of the soldiers. Being hated on one hand and scorned on the other, he was conspired against and killed.

It remains for us to consider the qualities of Maximinus. He was extremely pugnacious, but as the army had become weary of Alexander's weakness, which I discussed above, when he died, they elected Maximinus to the imperial throne. But Maximinus did not rule for long. Two things made him hated and disdained: First, he came from a very humble background, having herded sheep in Thrace (a fact that was widely known and looked down upon by all), and second, at the beginning of his reign he resisted going to Rome to take possession of the imperial throne. He also gave the impression of being unusually cruel, since through his prefects he had exercised great brutality in Rome and throughout the empire. As a result, everyone was filled with contempt for his lowly birth and with hatred that arose from fear of his ferocity. First Africa rebelled, then the Senate and the populace of Rome, and finally all of Italy conspired against him. His own soldiers rebelled during a difficult siege of Aquileia, and, tired of his cruelty and fearing him less because he had so many enemies, they killed him.

I will not discuss Elagabalus, Macrinus, or Julianus, who were so widely disdained that they were quickly eliminated, but shall come to the conclusion of this discourse. The princes of our era do not face the Roman emperors' problem of having to indulge their soldiers by unlawful means, though they do have to make some concessions to them. Issues are now resolved quickly, as none of our princes have the kind of established armies that evolved with the government and with the administration of the provinces, as was the case in imperial Rome. If in Roman times it was necessary to favor the army more than the people, that was because the soldiers carried more weight than the people. Now it is necessary for all princes, except the Ottoman sultan and the Sultan of Egypt, to favor the people above the army, because it is the people who carry more weight. But I make an exception of the Ottoman sultan: He always surrounds himself with an infantry of twelve thousand and a cavalry of fifteen thousand, on which the security and power of his rule depend. For him it is vital that he set aside all other considerations and keep his soldiers well disposed. Similarly, the Egyptian sultan's rule is also entirely in the hands of his soldiers, and so it behooves him to keep them on his side without consideration for the populace. It should be noted that the principality of the Egyptian sultan differs from other principalities in that it is similar to the Christian pontificate, which cannot be called a hereditary principality or a new principality because it is not the sons of the old prince who are the heirs and rulers. Princes are elected to that rank by those who have the authority to do so. As the Egyptian sultanate is an old institution, one cannot call it a new principality because it does not bring with it any of the difficulties of new principalities. Even if the prince is new, the institutions of that state are old and set up to receive him as if he were a hereditary ruler.

But let us return to our subject. If one weighs the above discourse, it is clear that it was hatred or contempt that brought about the ruin of the emperors I have mentioned. Though some followed one path and some the other, in each case some of the emperors ended well and some badly. It was futile and disastrous for Pertinax and Alexander, as new princes, to imitate Marcus, who was a hereditary ruler, and it was just as disastrous for Caracalla, Commodus, and Maximinus to imitate Severus, as they did not have the skill to follow in his footsteps. A new prince in a new principality cannot imitate the exploits of Marcus, but neither should he imitate those of Severus. He must take from Severus the necessary attributes to found a new state, and from Marcus the glorious attributes suitable for conserving a state that is already established and stable.

CHAPTER TWENTY

OF WHETHER FORTRESSES AND MANY OTHER THINGS PRINCES CREATE EVERY DAY ARE USEFUL

In order to hold their states securely, some princes disarm their subjects, others keep their conquered territories divided, while still others encourage hostility against themselves. Still others turn to winning over those whom they suspected at the beginning of their rule. Some princes build fortresses, others destroy them. Even though one cannot lay down a definite rule concerning these choices unless one examines the particulars of the states in question, I will nevertheless discuss this in as broad terms as the topic will allow.

No new prince has ever disarmed his subjects. In fact, whenever a prince found his new subjects disarmed, he has always armed them, because when he does so those arms become his. The men he did not trust become faithful, those who were faithful remain so, and his subjects become his partisans. And yet the prince cannot arm all his subjects, so when the ones he does arm receive benefits, he need not worry unduly about the rest: The armed subjects see that they are being preferred and are bound to the prince, while the others excuse the prince for showing preference, judging it necessary that those bearing arms should receive greater rewards since they have to shoulder more duties and face greater danger. But when you start to disarm them, they take offense. You show that you mistrust them, either out of cowardice or because you have little faith in them, both of which opinions will generate hatred toward you. Because you cannot remain unarmed, you will then have to turn to a mercenary army, which is of the quality that I have already described.[82] Even if the mercenary army is good, it can never be good enough to defend you from powerful enemies and subjects you cannot trust. But as I have already said, new princes in new principalities have always armed their subjects. History is filled with such examples. Only when a prince acquires a new state added like a limb to his old state[83] is it necessary for him to disarm the new state, unless his new subjects are his partisans, but even they, over time, must be made soft and effeminate, and things must be organized so that all the arms in the prince's state are in the hands of his actual soldiers who have been at his side in his old state.

Our forefathers, and those we thought wise, used to say that Pistoia was to be held by factions and Pisa by fortresses.[84] They therefore encouraged conflicts in some of their subject cities so they could hold them more easily. In those days, when there was a certain equilibrium in Italy, this might have been a good strategy, but I do not see how one can live by this principle today, because I do not believe that such divisions ever do anyone any good. In fact, it is inevitable that a divided city will fall the instant an enemy attacks: The weaker faction will ally itself with the external force, while the stronger faction will not be able to hold out.

I believe that the Venetians incited the Guelph and Ghibelline factions in the cities under their control for the reasons I have just mentioned.[85] The Venetians never actually let them shed each other's blood, but they did encourage their differences, so that the Guelphs and Ghibellines, occupied as they were with each other, did not unite against the Venetians. Yet as we have subsequently seen, this did not turn out to Venice's advantage, because when she was defeated at Vailà, one of the factions was quick to take courage and seize the whole state from her.[86] This strategy indicates weakness in a prince, because in a strong principality such divisions are never permitted. They bring advantages only in times of peace, enabling the prince to manage his sub-

---

82. See chapter 12.
83. See chapter 3.
84. See chapter 17.
85. The Guelphs supported the papacy and the Ghibellines the Holy Roman Emperors.
86. The Venetians were defeated in 1509 in the Battle of Agnadello by the forces of the League of Cambrai, after which the Ghibelline faction gained the upper hand in Venice.

jects with greater ease. But when war comes, this strategy reveals its flaws.

Without doubt, princes become great when they overcome difficulties and hurdles put in their path. When Fortune wants to advance a new prince, for whom it is more vital to acquire prestige than it is for a hereditary prince, she creates enemies for him, making them launch campaigns against him so that he is compelled to overcome them and climb higher on the ladder that they have brought him. Therefore, many judge that a wise prince must skillfully fan some enmity whenever the opportunity arises, so that in crushing it he will increase his standing.

Princes, particularly new ones, have found more loyalty and value in the men they distrusted at the beginning of their reign than in those who were considered sound. Pandolfo Petrucci, the Prince of Siena, ruled his state relying more on men he had initially distrusted than on his first supporters. But one cannot lay this matter out in broad terms, since it varies with every case. I will only say that men who are enemies of the prince at the beginning of his reign, but who are of quality and who need his support to maintain their position, can be won over with great ease. These men will be forced to serve him the more loyally, as they are aware that it is vital to rescind the negative opinion the prince initially had of them. Hence they are of greater use to him than are men who serve him with too much confidence in his goodwill and thus neglect his affairs.

Since our topic requires it, I do not wish to omit reminding princes who have recently acquired a state with the help of a faction within it that they should weigh the reasons that might have moved this faction to support them. If it is not natural affection toward the prince that made it favor him, but rather discontent with the former government, it will be only with much toil and difficulty that the prince will maintain these malcontents as his allies, because it will be impossible to satisfy them. If he looks closely at what can be deduced from ancient and modern examples, he will see that it is far easier to win over men who were content with the state before he conquered it, and therefore were his enemies, than to win over those who had not been satisfied, and so became his allies and supported his occupation of the state.

In order that princes might hold their states more securely, it has been their custom to build fortresses to act as a check on those who might have designs against them and to have a secure refuge against sudden rebellion. I praise this, as it has been a long-standing practice. And yet in our own times Niccolò Vitelli tore down two fortresses in Città di Castello in order to hold on to that state, while Guido Ubaldo, the Duke of Urbino, when he returned to his dominions from which Cesare Borgia had driven him, razed all the fortresses of that province to the ground, judging that he would be less likely to lose his state a second time without them. The Bentivogli, returning to Bologna, employed similar measures. Therefore, fortresses can be useful or not, depending on the times. If they are useful in one way, they can harm you in another. The question can be considered in this light: The prince who fears his people more than he does a foreign enemy must build fortresses, but the prince who fears a foreign enemy more than he does his people should not. The Castle of Milan built by Francesco Sforza has done and will do more harm to the House of Sforza than any turmoil in that state. The best fortress for the prince is to be loved by his people, because if he is hated by them, all the fortresses in the world will not save him. Once the populace has taken up arms, there will always be a foreign power eager to come to its aid.

In our time, we have not seen fortresses to be of any use to princes, except in the case of the Countess of Forlì when her husband, Count Girolamo, was killed. She managed to escape her people's uprising by retiring to her fortress and waiting there to recover her state with the help of Milan:[87] At that point in history, circumstances were such that a foreign power could not come to the aid of the people. But later the countess's fortresses were of little help to her when a foreign power—Cesare Borgia—attacked, and the populace, hostile to her, joined forces with him. Both then and before, it would have been safer for the countess to be loved by her people than to have fortresses. All things considered, I will praise both the prince who builds fortresses and the prince who does not, but I shall blame the prince who relies on his fortresses and thinks nothing of being hated by the people.

---

87. Caterina Sforza Riario (1463–1509) was the ruler of Imola and Forlì. When her husband, Girolamo Riario, was assassinated in 1488, she held out against the rebels in one of her fortresses until help arrived from her uncle, Ludovico Sforza of Milan. (Negotiations with Caterina Sforza Riario were the subject of Machiavelli's very first diplomatic assignment in July 1499.)

CHAPTER TWENTY-ONE

OF WHAT A PRINCE SHOULD DO
TO ACQUIRE PRESTIGE

Nothing can bring a prince more esteem than great feats and extraordinary actions. In our time we have Ferdinand of Aragon, the present king of Spain, who could almost be called a new prince because he started out as a weak monarch, but through fame and glory has become the foremost king of Christendom. If you consider his deeds, you will find that they are great, some of them even extraordinary. At the beginning of his reign he attacked Granada, an exploit that was to establish the cornerstone of his state. He did this quite casually, without the least concern that anyone might hinder him. He kept the attention of the barons of Castile trained on his enterprise, and, with their minds on this war, they did not think of introducing any changes. Before they realized what was happening, he had overshadowed them in prestige and power. He managed to build up his army with funds from the Church and the people, and during the long war in Granada he firmly established this army, which subsequently brought him much honor. To launch ever greater campaigns, he invariably made use of religion, resorting to a pious cruelty, robbing the Marranos[88] and routing them from his kingdom. No example of an extraordinary act is more pitiful and strange. Under the same mantle he attacked Africa. He campaigned in Italy, recently invaded France, and has always plotted and

88. Spanish Jews who converted to Christianity but continued practicing Judaism secretly.

carried out great feats that have captured the imagination of his people and kept their eyes on the outcome. He has launched these exploits in such quick succession that he has never given anyone an opportunity to conspire against him.

It also befits a prince to take extraordinary action in internal affairs, such as the exploits told of Bernabò of Milan.[89] When someone does something in civil life that is extraordinarily good or bad, the prince should find a way to reward or punish this person that will be much talked about. Above all, a prince must endeavor in all his actions to give the impression of being a superior man of extraordinary intelligence.

A prince is also revered when he is a true friend and a true enemy—in other words, when he declares himself without reservation in favor of one man against another. This kind of resolution is always more useful than if he remains neutral, because if two powerful neighbors come to blows, these neighbors will either be of the kind where you have to fear the winner, or not. In either case it will be more useful for you to take a position and wage an honest war. In the case where you have to fear the winner, if you do not commit yourself, you will fall prey to whoever wins, to the delight and satisfaction of whoever loses. Neither side will have reason or cause to come to your assistance, for the winner will not want the kind of ally who did not come to his aid in adversity, nor will the loser give you refuge, since you were not prepared to share his fate with your weapons drawn.

Antiochus was summoned to Greece by the Aetolians to expel the Romans. He sent orators to the Achaeans, who were allies of Rome, urging them to remain neutral, while Roman orators were urging them to take up arms for the Roman cause. The Achaeans weighed the matter in their council. When Antiochus's emissary argued that they should stay neutral, the Roman emissary replied: "Though they tell you not to intervene in our war, nothing would be further from your interests. Once you have lost esteem and character, you will end up as the victor's prize" (*Quod autem isti dicunt non interponendi vos bello, nihil*

---

89. Bernabò Visconti (1323–85), Lord of Milan, raised spectacular sums of money by unscrupulous taxation to fight constant wars, and gained great influence throughout Europe by providing enormous dowries for his many illegitimate daughters, whom he married off strategically to the European, particularly German, high nobility. (Among his sons-in-law were Leopold III of Austria, Stephan III of Bavaria, and Eberhard III of Württemberg.)

magis alienum rebus vestris est; sine gratia, sine dignitate, praemium victoris eritis).[90] He who is not your ally will always urge you to remain neutral, while your ally will urge you to come to his aid with your arms. The irresolute prince will most often follow the path of neutrality in order to avoid immediate danger, and will most often come to ruin. But when a prince boldly declares himself for one of the two sides, even if that side wins and is powerful and he remains in principle at its mercy, that side will be obliged to him and bound by contract of allegiance, and men are never so deceitful that they would subjugate someone in such a striking display of ingratitude after he had come to their aid. Furthermore, victories are never so decisive that the victor can wholly disregard justice. If the prince supported the losing side, that side will receive him and help him to the extent that it can, and he will become its companion in a destiny that may well resurge once more.

When they who fight one another are such that you need not fear whoever wins, it is all the more prudent for you to take sides. That way, you instigate the ruin of a ruler with the help of another ruler, who, were he wise, would be eager to save him. In this case, it is impossible for the side you are helping not to win, and in winning it remains in your debt. Here I would like to note that a prince should avoid forming an alliance with a power stronger than himself merely in order to attack another, unless, as I have said before, necessity compels him. Because if that power wins, he will end up its prisoner, and princes must do their utmost to avoid ending up in another's power. The Venetians allied themselves with France against the Duke of Milan even though they could have avoided this alliance, and it resulted in their ruin. If one cannot avoid such an alliance, as happened with the Florentines when the armies of the pope and Spain attacked Lombardy, then the prince must enter alliances for the reasons I have given. Nor should any state believe it can always make secure choices: In fact, all choices should be considered dubious, because it is in the nature of things that you can never escape one setback without running into another. Wisdom consists of knowing how to recognize the respective qualities of the setbacks and choosing the lesser evil.[91]

A prince must also prove himself someone who admires ability, fur-

90. A slightly altered quotation from Livy, Book XXXV, chapter 49.

91. See also *Discourses*, Book I, chapter 6: "If one looks carefully, this pattern can be observed in all human affairs: One can never remove one problem without another one's arising."

thering skillful men and honoring those who excel in what they do. He must also make certain that his citizens can go about their work unhampered—in trade, agriculture, and all the other professions—so that no one will be afraid of accumulating possessions out of fear that they might be taken away, or afraid of starting a business for fear of taxes. The prince must reward whoever wants to do these things and whoever wants to improve either the city or the state in some way. Furthermore, at certain times of the year, he has to keep the population busy with feasts and spectacles, and, as every city is divided into guilds and clans, he must also keep those groups in mind, meeting with them from time to time, and always showing himself as humane and munificent. He must always remain within the bounds of his majesty and dignity, which must never be absent.

CHAPTER TWENTY-TWO

OF THE ADVISERS OF PRINCES

The choice of advisers is very important for a prince: Advisers are able or not, depending on the prince's wisdom. One can assess a prince's intelligence by looking at the men with whom he surrounds himself. If they are capable and loyal, one can consider the prince prudent, because he was able to discern their ability and managed to keep them loyal. But when these men are lacking in quality, one can consider the prince as deficient, because it is in choosing his advisers that he can make his first mistake. Anyone who knew Antonio da Venafro, the minister of Pandolfo Petrucci, Prince of Siena, considered Pandolfo a most capable man for having chosen da Venafro.

There are three kinds of intelligence: One kind can understand on its own, the second can understand through others, and the third can understand neither on its own nor through others. The first kind is excellent, the second good enough, the third useless. Hence, if Pandolfo was not in the first category, he was at least in the second, because even if a prince does not possess great intelligence, if he can judge the good or bad that a man says or does, then he can distinguish between his adviser's good and bad deeds, and praise the good and punish the bad. The adviser cannot hope to deceive him, and so behaves well.

There is a dependable method by which a prince can know his adviser. When the prince sees that the adviser is more intent on furthering his own interest than that of the prince, and that his actions aim to further his own goals, this adviser will never be a good one, and the prince will never be able to trust him. A man who has the prince's affairs of state in hand must never think of himself but always of the prince, and must never involve the prince in matters that have nothing to do with him. And yet the prince, in order to keep the adviser loyal, must not forget to honor him and make him rich, obliging him by sharing with him honors and responsibilities, so that the adviser sees that he cannot exist without the prince. But the prince must also ensure that these many honors do not lead the adviser to desire even more honors, nor that great wealth lead him to desire even greater wealth, nor that his many responsibilities make him fear change. If advisers and princes are of this kind, they can have confidence in one another. If they are not, then things will end badly for one or the other.

CHAPTER TWENTY-THREE

OF THE WAY IN WHICH FLATTERERS
MUST BE AVOIDED

I do not wish to pass over an important point, a danger that a prince can escape only if he is extremely careful or has chosen his advisers well. This danger is the flatterers that fill all princely courts, because men are so self-congratulatory in the things they do, and so willing to deceive themselves, that they find it difficult to escape this plague, and in attempting to escape it they often run the risk of losing their standing. The only way for a prince to guard himself from flattering adulation is to make it understood that he will not be offended if he is told the truth. Then again, however, if every man is free to tell him the truth at will, the prince quickly becomes a figure of contempt. Therefore a prudent prince must approach the matter in an altogether different way: For his government, he must choose men who are wise and give them, and nobody else, free rein to speak their minds—but only on matters on which he consults them. Nevertheless, he must confer with them on every important issue, listen to their opinions, and then reach a decision on his own and in his own way. He must give his counselors to understand that the more freely they speak, the more he will rely on them. The prince must not listen to anyone other than these counselors, and he must carry out his decisions, unyielding in what he has decided. A prince who acts otherwise will either come to ruin because of his flatterers, or grow increasingly irresolute by following conflicting advice, which will result in his losing respect.

I would like to cite an example from our time. Father Luca, the counselor to the current emperor Maximilian, has said of His Majesty the Emperor that he never consults anybody, yet still has never managed to do what he wants. This resulted from his behavior, which is contrary to what I advised above. The emperor is a secretive man and does not inform anyone of his plans, nor does he take advice. But when his plans become clear as he starts putting them into effect, the men surrounding him begin to caution him. As the emperor is easily swayed, he yields, abandoning his plans. Consequently, what he does one day he undoes the next. One can never tell what he wants or intends to do, nor can one rely on his decisions.

Therefore a prince must be prepared to take counsel, but only when he seeks counsel. In fact, he should discourage anyone from offering counsel when he has not asked for it. But he must be an expert questioner and a patient listener to the truth in all matters on which he does seek counsel. If the prince realizes that someone is not telling him the truth, he must show his anger.

It is a common error to consider a prince prudent not because of his nature but on account of the good counselors with whom he surrounds himself. Yet it is an infallible rule that a prince who is not wise cannot be advised well, unless Fortune has placed him in the hands of one who is very wise and guides him in every matter. In this case the prince might fare well, but not for long, because soon enough that counselor will seize his state from him. Yet if a prince who is lacking in wisdom takes counsel from more than one man, he will invariably be given conflicting advice and find himself unable to reconcile it on his own. The counselors will have their own interests at heart, and the prince will not be able to keep them in check or see through their ruses. And all counselors are of this kind, because men never turn out to be faithful unless necessity makes them. Therefore it is to be concluded that good counsel, from whomever it comes, must be sparked by the wisdom of the prince, and not that the wisdom of the prince be sparked by good counsel.

CHAPTER TWENTY-FOUR

OF REASONS WHY ITALIAN PRINCES
HAVE LOST THEIR STATES

If the strategies I have mentioned above are carefully followed, a new prince will seem like an old, established prince. He will be more stable and secure in his state than if he had developed within it, because the actions of a new prince are more closely observed than those of a hereditary prince. If these actions are seen to be skillful, they will sooner attract and bind men to the new prince than an old bloodline would, because men are more inspired by things of the present than things of the past. If men see good in the present, they are content and do not yearn for anything else. In effect, they will stand by this prince in every way, as long as he is not otherwise lacking. He will have twice the glory, having established a new principality and having strengthened it with good laws, arms, allies, and good examples, just as a prince who is born a prince will have twice the shame if he loses his principality through lack of prudence.

If one considers the rulers of our time in Italy who have lost their states—such as the King of Naples, the Duke of Milan, and others—one can discern a common military weakness, as I have already discussed at length. One will also observe that some of these rulers had the populace against them, and that others had the populace on their side but did not know how to protect themselves against the nobles. States that are powerful enough to send an army into battle can be lost only through such defects.

Philip of Macedon (not Alexander the Great's father, but the king who was defeated by Titus Quintus)[92] did not have much power compared to the might of the Romans and Greeks who were attacking him. And yet, being a military man who knew how to inspire the populace and secure himself against his nobles, he managed to sustain a war against the Greeks and Romans for many years, and though he finally had to give up a few cities, he nevertheless kept his kingdom.

Therefore our Italian princes who were established in their principalities for many years and then lost them should blame their indolence and not Fortune. In times of peace they did not think that things might change (it is a common fault not to anticipate storms when the sea is calm), and with the advent of adversity our princes thought of escape, not defense. They hoped that the populace, angered by the victors' offensive ways, would call them back. Such a strategy might be good when others are lacking, but it is a mistake to prefer this remedy over others, because you should never let yourself fall in the hope that someone will be there to help you up. Either you will not be helped up, or, if you are, your continuing safety will be in question, because your defense was not sparked by you but by your cowardice, and defenses are secure and lasting only if they are sparked by your skill.

92. Philip V of Macedon (d. 179 BCE).

ON THE EXTENT TO WHICH FORTUNE WIELDS POWER IN THE AFFAIRS OF MEN, AND ON HOW THIS IS TO BE RESISTED

I am not unaware that many believe that the things of this world are governed to such an extent by Fortune and God that men, with all their foresight, cannot change them; that in fact there is no improving them. Those who believe this deem that they need not toil and sweat, but can let themselves be governed by Fortune. This opinion has been more prevalent in our time because of the great upheavals that we have witnessed and witness every day, and which are beyond anything we could have foreseen, and there have been times when even I have to some extent inclined to this opinion. Nevertheless, Fortune seems to be the arbiter of half our actions, but she does leave us the other half, or almost the other half, in order that our free will may prevail. I would compare Fortune to one of those violent torrents that flood the plains, destroying trees and buildings, hurling earth from one place to another. Everyone flees this torrent, everyone yields to its force without being able to stand up to it. As this is the torrent's nature, man should not neglect to prepare himself with dikes and dams in times of calm, so that when the torrent rises it will gush into a channel, its force neither so harmful nor so unbridled. The same is true with Fortune, who unleashes her force in places where man has not taken skillful precautions to resist her, and so channels her force to where she knows there are no dikes or dams to hold her back. If you consider Italy, which has been the scene of so many changes and has set so many changes in motion, you will find that it is a field without dikes or dams. Had Italy been protected with the appropriate skill, as Germany, Spain, and France were, this flood either would not have caused the great changes it did or would not have come at all.

So much for opposing Fortune in general terms. To limit myself more to particulars, I would like to remark that one can see a prince prospering one day and coming to ruin the next without having changed his nature or conduct in any way. I believe this is due, first and foremost, to the causes that I have already discussed at some length, namely, that the prince who relies entirely on Fortune will fall when Fortune changes. In my view, he who conforms his course of action to the quality of the times will fare well, and conversely he whose course of action clashes with the times will fare badly. One sees that men will proceed in different ways as they strive toward the common goal of wealth and glory: Some will proceed cautiously, others recklessly; some with force, others with guile; some with patience, others rashly. And in each of these ways one can prevail. If we take two cautious men, one might attain his goal and the other not; similarly, two men might succeed through entirely different courses of action, one through caution, the other through recklessness. The reason for this is the nature of the times that either conforms to or conflicts with their courses of action. Hence two men operating differently can obtain the same result, while when two men operate in the same way, one might achieve his goal, the other not. This also depends on the turning of Fortune's wheel from good to bad, because if a man acts with caution and patience and the wheel turns in a way that favors his course of action, he will flourish; but should the wheel turn again, he will be ruined if he does not change his manner of proceeding. One cannot find a man prudent enough to be capable of adapting to these changes, because man cannot deviate from that to which nature inclines him. Moreover, if he has always prospered by walking down a certain path, it will be difficult to persuade him to leave it. Consequently, when the time comes for a cautious man to act impetuously, he will not be able to do so, and will come to ruin. Even if he could adapt his nature to the times and circumstances, his Fortune would not change.

Pope Julius II acted impetuously in everything he undertook, and he found both the times and the circumstances in such agreement with this course of action that he always succeeded. Consider the first campaign that he launched against Bologna in the days when Giovanni Bentivoglio was still alive.[93] The Venetians were not pleased, nor was the King of Spain, and as for France, Julius was still in the midst of negotiations with them over this campaign. And yet Julius, wild and impetuous as he was, set out right away, heading the campaign himself. This move stopped the Venetians and Spaniards in their tracks: the former out of fear, the latter because of their desire to regain the entire Kingdom of Naples, while the King of France found himself drawn in despite himself. Seeing that Julius had already made his move, and wanting to ally himself with Julius in order to weaken the Venetians, the French king judged it impossible to refuse him troops without openly offending him. Hence, by his impetuous move, Julius achieved what no other pontiff could have achieved with all the prudence in the world. Had he waited for all the negotiations to be completed and everything arranged before setting out from Rome, as any other pontiff would have done, he would never have succeeded, because by then the King of France would have discovered a thousand excuses and the others a thousand doubts. I will not touch on Pope Julius's other actions, which have all been of the same kind and have all been successful. Moreover, the shortness of his life did not allow him to experience reverses, because if times had changed so as to compel him to act with caution, he would have come to ruin, for he could never have deviated from the way nature inclined him.

Therefore, I conclude that when Fortune changes and men rigidly continue in their ways, they will flourish so long as Fortune and their ways are in accord, but they will come to ruin the moment these are in discord. In my view, however, it is better to be impetuous than cautious, because Fortune is a woman, and if you wish to dominate her you must beat and batter her. It is clear that she will let herself be won by men who are impetuous rather than by those who step cautiously. Therefore, like a woman, she is more partial to young men, because they are less cautious, wilder, and command her with greater audacity.

93. Giovanni Bentivoglio (1443-1508) had been Gonfalonier of Bologna until Pope Paolo II made him chief senator for life in 1466. He was expelled from Bologna in 1506 by Pope Julius II.

CHAPTER TWENTY-SIX

AN EXHORTATION TO FREE ITALY
FROM THE BARBARIANS

I have given much thought to all the matters I have discussed until now, and have asked myself whether the time is ripe for Italy to greet a new prince, to offer to a prudent and skillful man the prospect of forging a government that would bring him honor and benefit all Italy. So many things have come together that are favorable to a new prince that I believe there has never been a more auspicious time. As I have already said, the people of Israel had to be slaves in Egypt so that the qualities of Moses would come to the fore, and for the Medes to oppress the Persians for the greatness of Cyrus to become apparent, and for the Athenians to be dispersed so that Theseus could demonstrate his skill. In the same way, that we may see the prowess of an Italian prince, it has been necessary for Italy to be reduced to the state it is in at present: more enslaved than the Jews, more in bondage than the Persians, more dispersed than the Athenians, without a leader, without order, beaten, plundered, flayed, overrun, exposed to all manner of adversity.

We have had occasional glimmers of hope that led us to believe that a certain man might have been ordained by God to bring redemption to Italy, but then we saw him rejected by Fortune at the pinnacle of his success.[94] And so Italy has lain prostrate, waiting for a savior who

94. Almost certainly a reference to Cesare Borgia.

would heal her wounds and put an end to the plundering of Lombardy and the taxation of Naples and Tuscany, a savior who would cure her sores that have been festering for so long. How she prays to God to send someone to save her from the barbaric cruelty and violence! How ardent and eager she is to follow a banner, if only there were someone who would raise it high. Italy has one hope, and that hope is Your illustrious House with its Fortune and prowess, a House of which You are now the prince favored by God and Church![95] Saving Italy would not be an insurmountable task if You kept before Your eyes the examples of Moses, Cyrus, and Theseus. Though they were extraordinary men, they were mere mortals, and they had less favorable prospects than those that Italy offers. Their campaigns were not more righteous, nor was their lot easier, nor did God look upon them with more benevolence than He looks upon You. There is great justice in our enterprise: "The only war that is just is one that is compulsory, and weapons righteous when there is no hope but in weapons."[96] [*Iustum enim est bellum quibus necessarium, et pia arma ubi nulla nisi in armis spes est.*] Circumstances are most favorable, and there cannot be great difficulty where circumstances are so favorable, as long as the House of Medici follows the models I have put forward. And we have seen extraordinary and unprecedented signs from God: the sea parting, a cloud showing the way, water pouring from a stone, manna raining from heaven. Everything has concurred for Your greatness. You must do the rest, for God does not want to do everything, lest he take from us our free will and that part of the glory that belongs to us.

One need not marvel that none of the Italians I have mentioned has been able to achieve what one hopes Your illustrious House will achieve. If it seems that our military prowess has been exhausted in so many upheavals and so many campaigns of war here in Italy, this is because Italy's old military institutions were not good and because there was nobody who was able to foster new ones. Nothing brings so much honor to a man who emerges as a new prince as the new laws and new institutions he creates, and when these have a sound foundation and

95. The House of Medici.
96. A slightly altered quotation from Livy, Book IX, chapter 1: *Iustum est bellum, Samnites, quibus necessarium, et pia arma, quibus nulla nisi in armis relinquitur spes.* [A war is just, Samnites, when it is compulsory, and weapons righteous when there is no hope except in weapons.]

greatness, they bring him esteem and admiration. Here in Italy there is ample matter that one can form: There is great spirit in the populace, even if it has been lacking in the leaders. Consider our duels and skirmishes, and you will see how the Italian is superior in strength, skill, and ingenuity. But when it comes to armies, the Italians have not shown themselves in the best light. All this goes back to the weakness of our commanders, because the finest among them are not followed, as every commander wants to go his own way. Until now there has been no one who has distinguished himself enough in skill or Fortune for the others to cede to him. The result has been that in the wars fought over the past twenty years, all the armies made up entirely of Italians have fared badly: the battles at Taro, Alexandria, Capua, Genoa, Vailà, Bologna, and Mestri all bear witness to this.

If Your illustrious House wishes to follow the excellent Moses, Cyrus, and Theseus who redeemed their lands, it will be vital above all else, as a true foundation of every campaign, to furnish yourself with an army of your own men. You will not find soldiers who are better, more faithful, or more true. Every man among them will be good, and all together they will become even better once they are commanded by their own prince and are honored and treated well by him. It is necessary, therefore, to create such an army, so one can defend oneself with Italian prowess from a foreign enemy. Even though the Swiss and the Spanish infantries are considered formidable, they both have shortcomings, which is why an army that is structured differently could not only match them on the field but be confident of defeating them. This is because the Spanish cannot stand up to a cavalry, and the Swiss to an infantry that is as fierce in battle as they are. Experience has shown and will show again that the Spaniards cannot stand up to the French cavalry, and the Swiss cannot stand up to a Spanish infantry, and though there is no actual proof of the latter, some evidence of it was seen in the Battle of Ravenna, when the Spanish infantry came face to face with the German battalions, which are set up along the same lines as the Swiss. In this battle, the Spaniards with their agility and their bucklers had cut through the German pikes and were primed to destroy the Germans, who were caught completely unawares. Had the cavalry not come to their rescue, the Germans would all have been killed. Hence, if one knows the weakness in the Spanish and Swiss infantries, one should create a new infantry that can resist the cavalry and not be intimidated by other infantries. This will be made possible by the type of arms furnished to the new infantry and a change in its disposition. It is these things which, newly organized, will bring prestige and greatness to a new prince.

This opportunity must be grasped. Italy, after so many years, must welcome its liberator. The love with which these lands that have suffered a flood of foreign armies will receive him will be boundless, as will be their thirst for vengeance, their iron loyalty, their devotion and tears. All doors will be flung open. What populace would not embrace such a leader? What envy would oppose him, what Italian withhold respect? For all here abhor the barbarian dominion. Your illustrious House must seize this matter with the kind of spirit and hope in which righteous tasks are seized, so that Italy shall be ennobled beneath its banners and under its auspices the words of Petrarch will come true:

> Prowess shall take up arms
> Against brutality, and the battle will be swift;
> For ancient Roman bravery
> Is not yet dead in Italian hearts.[97]

---

97. *Virtù contro a furore / Prenderà l'arme, e fia el combatter corto; / Ché l'antico valore / Nell'italici cor non è ancor morto.*

Selections from

THE DISCOURSES

Machiavelli wrote Discourses on the First Ten Books of Titus Livius *during his years of exile from Florentine politics, between 1512 and 1519. The work was published posthumously in 1531, one year before* The Prince. *If* The Prince *was a treatise on the ideal autocratic ruler,* The Discourses *are a vigorous championing of a republican form of government. Artists of the Renaissance looked to ancient Rome for inspiration in painting, sculpture, and literature, but* The Discourses, *despite taking Roman historian Livy as their point of departure, are extremely original. In them Machiavelli proposes for the first time a pragmatic study of Roman history, institutions, and politics, in search of guidance that would lead Renaissance Italy out of its dangerous and chaotic political conditions.*

The Discourses *are divided into three books, which are themselves divided into 142 chapters—mirroring the 142 books of Livy's* Histories.

NICCOLÒ MACHIAVELLI TO ZANOBI BUONDELMONTI AND COSIMO RUCELLAI, GREETINGS[1]

I am sending you a gift which, though it might not correspond to the obligations I owe to you, is without doubt the greatest gift that Niccolò Machiavelli can send you. In it I have gathered all that I know and have learned from my long experience and constant reading about the affairs of the world. No one can ask more of me, and no one can complain that I have not given more. You might be disappointed by the meagerness of my intelligence when what I narrate is weak, or when my judgment is erroneous, or when I may be mistaken in points of reasoning. And yet I am not sure whether you or I have more cause to be obliged to the other: I to you, who have compelled me to write what I would never have written of my own accord, or you to me, who in my writing have fallen short of your expectations. So I hope that you will accept this gift in the spirit in which all things are accepted by friends, where the intention of the giver is more important than the quality of the thing given. But the one satisfaction I have is that though my narration might be mistaken in many of its details, the one detail in which I have definitely not erred is in choosing you above all others to whom to address these *Discourses,* for in addressing them to you I feel that I am

1. Zanobi Buondelmonti (1491–1527) and Cosimo Rucellai (1495–1519) were young Florentine intellectuals with whom Machiavelli had frequent discussions in the Orti Oricellari, which were the gardens of the Palazzo Rucellai, the magnificent palace belonging to Cosimo's family.

showing gratitude for the benefits I have received. Furthermore, I believe I have managed to avoid the usual practice of writers, who, blinded by ambition or covetousness, dedicate their works to a prince, praising him as if he had every commendable quality when they ought to condemn him for having every shameful attribute. So as to avoid this error I have not chosen those who are princes, but those who have the kind of infinite good qualities that make them worthy to be princes; not those who could heap rank, honors, and wealth on me, but those who would do so if they had the means. Men who want to judge others properly must esteem those who are generous, not those who can be generous—those who know how to rule, not those who rule even though they do not know how. Historians praise Hiero of Syracuse more when he was a private citizen than they do Perseus of Macedon when he was king: because all Hiero was missing to be a prince was a principality, while the only kingly attribute that Perseus of Macedon had was a kingdom.[2] Therefore I hope you will enjoy this good or bad work that you yourselves have requested from me, and should you be misguided enough to find these ideas of mine pleasing, I will not refrain from sending you the rest, as I have promised. Farewell.

2. Hiero II of Syracuse (d. 216 BCE). See also *The Prince,* chapter 6, in which Machiavelli quotes a slightly altered line from Justin referring to Hiero as having "lacked nothing to make him a ruler except a kingdom." Also Polybius, in *Histories* (Book I, chapter 8), describes Hiero as always having had "a nature ideal for kingship and the administration of a state." Perseus of Macedon (d. c. 165 BCE) was the last king of Macedonia. Plutarch writes in *Parallel Lives* (Aemilius Paulus, 8) that Perseus, though a king, "was incapable of carrying out his designs, as he lacked courage and had a brutal nature that was beset by faults and diseases, among which greed was foremost."

BOOK I

PREFACE

Because of the envious nature of man, it has always been more perilous to establish new systems and institutions than to seek out new lands and seas, because men are more eager to blame than to praise the actions of others. Nevertheless, driven by the natural desire I have always had to work without fear on things that I believe bring a common benefit to everyone, I have decided to set out on an untrodden path. I am aware that this might bring me trouble and hardship, though it might also bring rewards from men who will view the result of these efforts with kindness. If my meager talent, my scant experience of present things, and my weak knowledge of ancient things make this attempt imperfect and of little use, they will at least open the way for someone with greater skill, eloquence, and judgment to carry out my intention, which, if it does not deserve praise, should at least not deserve blame.

Consider how much honor is attributed to antiquity. To cite just one example, think how often a man will buy a fragment of an ancient statue at a great price just to have it near him, to honor his house and have it imitated by those who delight in this art and are then compelled to replicate it in all their works. But when I consider the most skillful actions that the histories show us, actions accomplished in ancient republics and kingdoms by kings, generals, citizens, legislators, and others who strove to benefit their native land, I see that those actions are admired rather than imitated—or, I should say, they are avoided in every way. Indeed, no trace remains of that ancient process. I can only be amazed and saddened at the same time. So much more so when I see in the civil disputes that arise between citizens, or in the illnesses to which men succumb, that we always turn to the decrees and remedies that the ancients pronounced or prescribed: because civil laws are nothing more than the decrees pronounced by ancient jurisprudents, which, categorized, teach our present jurisprudents to judge. Nor is medicine anything more than experiments undertaken by ancient doctors on which present doctors base their diagnoses. And yet not a single prince or republic turns to the examples of the ancients for the organization of the state, the maintaining of states, the governing of kingdoms, the organization of an army, the conduct of war, the passing of judgment on their subjects, or the expansion of their dominion. This arises not so much from the weakness to which our present religion has brought the world,[3] or the ill that single-minded idleness has wreaked on many Christian provinces and cities, as from not having a true understanding of history. Reading the histories, we do not extract the meaning that is in them, nor do we relish the flavor they contain. The result is that countless people who read the histories take pleasure in the range of incidents they portray without thinking of imitating them, as they believe such imitation to be not only difficult, but impossible. As if the sky, the sun, the elements, and mankind had changed their motion, order, and power from what they had been in antiquity. Wishing to free men from this error, I have deemed it necessary to write these discourses on all the books of Livy that have survived the ravages of time, explaining, with my knowledge of ancient and modern things, whatever I deem necessary for better understanding these books, so that readers of my discourses can take

---

3. Machiavelli develops his argument of how Christianity brought weakness to the world in Book II, chapter 2: "Ancient religion only beatified men who were filled with worldly glory, such as generals and princes, while our religion glorifies men who are humble and contemplative rather than men of action. Our religion also places the highest value on humility, debasement, and disdain for worldly matters, while ancient religion placed the highest value on greatness of spirit, strength of body, and everything that makes men strong."

from them more easily what is necessary to understand history. Even though this undertaking is difficult, with the help of those who have encouraged me to bear this burden, I trust I will carry it far enough toward the destined place so that another might have to travel only a short distance.

CHAPTER ONE

On the origins of cities in general, and Rome in particular

Those who read about the origin of the city of Rome, its legislators, and how it was organized will not be surprised that so much excellence was sustained for so many centuries in that city, nor that Rome later managed to gain such an empire. As I would first like to discuss Rome's origins, I propose that all cities are built either by men born where the city was built, or by foreigners. The former case occurs when people live dispersed in many small communities and do not feel that they are living in safety, because, owing to the locations of these communities and the small number of people living in each, they cannot on their own resist the force of those who attack them. Nor can they unite in time to defend themselves once the enemy has arrived. (And even if they did manage to unite, they would be forced to abandon many of their refuges and so fall easy prey to their enemies.) To escape these dangers, the people living in these scattered communities unite either spontaneously or because they are stirred by one among them who is prominent in authority, and settle together in a single place more suitable to live in and easier to defend.

Athens and Venice are two examples among many of such cities. Athens was built under the authority of Theseus by inhabitants who had been living in dispersed communities.[4] In the case of Venice, many

4. According to Greek myth, the legendary king and hero Theseus, after fighting the Minotaur in the labyrinth in Crete, had united the scattered communities of Attica into a single Athenian state.

people gathered on the little islands at the head of the Adriatic Sea in order to escape the wars that after the decline of the Roman Empire raged every day in Italy with the arrival of new waves of barbarians. These first Venetians gathered without a prince to govern them, with the intention of living under laws that seemed most apt to sustain them. This succeeded only because of the long period of peace that their situation on the islands afforded them, as the sea had no harbor and the peoples attacking Italy did not have boats with which to overrun the islands. Thus the most modest beginning was enough to lead the Venetians to the greatness they have achieved.

The second case, when foreigners build a city, involves either free men or men who depend on others. Such are the colonies sent out by republics or princes either to relieve their lands of overpopulation or to defend a land that has been newly acquired, and they want to do this securely and without expense. The Romans built many such cities throughout their empire. Such cities were built by a prince, not for him to live in, but for his glory, as Alexandria was built by Alexander the Great. Since these cities do not have a free beginning, they rarely make much progress or grow to be counted among the capitals of an empire. This was the case with the building of Florence. It was founded by the soldiers of Sulla, or possibly by the inhabitants of the mountains of Fiesole, who, reassured by the long period of peace under Emperor Augustus, came down to live on the plain above the Arno River. But since Florence was built under the Roman Empire, it could not initially grow except at the pleasure of the emperor.

The builders of cities are free when a populace, either under a prince or of their own accord, are forced by disease, hunger, or war to abandon their native land and look for a new place to live. Such a populace will settle in cities that they find in the lands they acquire, as Moses did, or build new cities, as Aeneas did.[5] In such cases we know the skill of the builder and the fate of what he built, a fate more or less happy depending on the extent of its founder's skill. His skill can be distinguished first by the site he has chosen, and second by the organization of the laws. Man acts either by necessity or by choice, and it is recognized that he shows greater skill where there is less choice. Hence

5. In Machiavelli's interpretation, Moses, after leading the Israelites out of Egypt, sought towns to settle in, whereas the Trojan hero Aeneas had, according to legend, founded Rome after the destruction of Troy..

the question arises whether it is not better to choose a barren site to found a city, so that its inhabitants are forced to work hard and are less beset by idleness, and therefore live in harmony. This way, the barrenness of the site gives them less cause for discord. This was the case in Ragusa[6] and many other cities built in similar places. Such a choice would without doubt be wiser and more advantageous if men were content to live from their own resources and not seek to control those of others. But as men can secure themselves only with power, it is necessary to avoid barren terrain and settle in the most fertile regions, where the fercundity of the land allows them to multiply so that they can defend themselves from those who attack and subjugate those who challenge their prosperity. As for the idleness such a site might inspire in its inhabitants, one must organize things in such a way that any hardship not imposed by the site will be imposed by the laws. One must imitate those wise men who have lived in lands that were most pleasant and fertile, lands likely to produce indolent men unfit for any effective military activity. To remedy the shortcomings which the pleasantness of the land would have caused to make men indolent, rulers who are wise have made military training obligatory for men who are to become soldiers. As a result, they became better soldiers than the men of those states that were naturally rough and barren. Among the pleasant countries was the kingdom of the Egyptians,[7] which, despite its land being most abundant, had laws that imposed the kinds of hardship that produce excellent men. Had their names not been lost in the ravages of time, they would have merited more praise than Alexander the Great and many others whose memory is still fresh. And whoever considers the Egyptian sultanate and the institutions of the Mamluks and of their army before the Grand Turk, Sultan Selim, destroyed them[8] would have seen the prodigious training that was imposed on soldiers, and would have seen how they shunned the indolence that the mildness of the land might have induced had they not avoided it by means of the strictest laws.

I propose, therefore, that it is more prudent to settle a fertile place when this fertility can be subjugated to the laws. The architect Dinoc-

6. Today the Croatian port town of Dubrovnik.
7. The Mamluk sultanate, 1250–1516.
8. The Ottoman sultan Selim I defeated the Mamluk armies at the battles of Marj Dabiq in 1516 and Raydaniyah in 1517, bringing Egypt under Ottoman rule.

ιαιɛъ had gone to Alexander, who wanted to build a city to his glory, and shown him how he could build it on top of Mount Athos, a place that was secure and that could also be constructed to represent a human form. This would have been a most wonderful and rare thing, worthy of Alexander's greatness; but when Alexander asked Dinocrates how the inhabitants would live, he replied that he had not thought of that. Alexander laughed, and casting aside Mount Athos had Alexandria built on a site where men would gladly want to live because of the abundance of the land and the convenience of the Nile and the sea.[9]

So whoever examines the building of Rome, if he takes Aeneas as its founding father, will regard it as one of the cities built by foreigners, and if he takes the founder to be Romulus,[10] a city built by men born in that place. In either case, he will regard it as having had a free beginning without being dependent on anyone. He will also see, as I will discuss further on in my discourses, how much hardship was imposed on the city by the laws made by Romulus, Numa,[11] and the other early rulers, so that the fertility of the place, the convenience of the sea, the frequent victories, and the greatness of the empire did not manage to corrupt it for many centuries, maintaining it in more glory than any other city or state was ever adorned with.

And because the things accomplished by Rome and which are celebrated by Livy came about either through private or public decisions, either inside or outside the city, I will begin my discussion with the matters that occurred within the city and by public decision. I believe these merit more comment, and will add to them everything dependent on them. With these discourses I will end this first book, or rather this first part.

9. Vitruvius (first century BCE), in his preface to Book II of *De architectura*, reports that Dinocrates said: "I have created a design for shaping Mount Athos into the statue of a man. In his left hand there will be a great city with strong fortifications, and in his right hand a bowl to capture all the rivers from the mountain, which will pour from the bowl into the sea." To which Alexander replies: "I am delighted, but anybody who would found a city in such a place would be censured for bad judgment."
10. Romulus was the legendary founder and first king of Rome, who was said to have ruled from Rome's founding in 753 until 715 BCE.
11. Numa Pompilius was the legendary second king of Rome, said to have ruled from 715 to 673 BCE.

CHAPTER TWO

ON HOW MANY KINDS OF REPUBLIC THERE ARE, AND WHAT KIND THE ROMAN REPUBLIC WAS

I would like to set aside the discussion of cities that had their origin through an outside power, and discuss those that had their origin without any external servitude but were governed from the start by their own free will, either as republics or as principalities. With their varied beginnings, these cities had different laws and institutions. Some were given their laws by a single ruler and all at once, either at the time of their founding or soon thereafter, like the laws given by Lycurgus to the Spartans. Other cities received their laws by chance on different occasions and depending on circumstances, as was the case with Rome. A state can be considered most fortunate if it can bring forth a man who is so wise that he establishes laws organized in such a way that the state can exist securely under them without these laws needing to be revised. It can be seen that Sparta respected her laws for more than eight hundred years without corrupting them, or without dangerous turmoil.

On the other hand, a state can be considered to some degree unfortunate if it does not chance to have a wise organizer and has been obliged to reorganize itself on its own. Of these states, the most unfortunate is the one furthest from order, and the state furthest from order is the one whose institutions stray from the path that could lead the way to a perfect and proper existence. States in this position find it almost impossible to be put in order by some unforeseen event. The other cities, which might not have perfect institutions but have at least made a good start and have acted to become better, can become perfect by a concurrence of events. But it is true that the states will never introduce this order without risk, because most men will never agree to a new law connected with a new order in the state unless necessity makes clear to them that it has to be done, and as such a necessity cannot come without risk, it is easy enough for this state to be destroyed before it can bring its institutions to perfection. The Republic of Florence can bear witness to this: It was reformed by the Arezzo incident in 1502, and destroyed by the Prato incident in 1512.[12]

As I would like to discuss the institutions of the city of Rome and the incidents that led to its perfection, I say, as have some who have written about republics, that they have one of three forms of government: principality, aristocracy, or democracy. These writers also point out that those who organize a city must turn to one of these three forms, depending on which seems to them most apt. Others who many consider wiser say that there are six different kinds of government, of which three are very bad, while the other three are good in themselves, but so easily corruptible that they, too, become pernicious. The kinds that are good are the three mentioned above, while the ones that are bad are the other three that depend on them, for each of these kinds of government is similar to the one it is linked to, which means that it can easily enough turn into its counterpart: A principality can easily become a tyranny, an aristocratic state a government of the few, and a democracy can easily turn into chaos.[13] Thus if the founder of a republic institutes one of these three kinds of government, he cannot hope for it to last long, for no precaution can keep it from lapsing into its opposite because of the similarity in this case between virtue and vice.

12. The crisis provoked by the revolt of Arezzo drove the Florentine Republic to sweeping constitutional reform. See also "On How to Treat the Populace of Valdichiana After Their Rebellion." In the Prato incident of 1512, the Pope demanded that Florence dismiss its current leaders and allow the exiled Medici to return. Florence was forced to submit by a Spanish army that sacked Prato, one of its cities.
13. In this paragraph Machiavelli closely follows Polybius in *Histories* (Book VI, chapter 3): "Most of those who profess to give us authoritative instruction on this subject distinguish three kinds of constitutions, the first of which they call kingship, the second aristocracy, and the third democracy. [...] Therefore we must mention six types of government—the three that everyone talks about that I have just mentioned, and three others that are related to them, by which I mean despotism, oligarchy, and rule of the crowd."

These varieties of government arise by chance, since at the beginning of the world, when its inhabitants were few, they lived for a time dispersed like wild beasts. As the generations multiplied, these early inhabitants came together, and in order to defend themselves better began looking among themselves for a man who was stronger and had more courage, making him their leader and obeying him. From this arose man's understanding that what is good and honest differs from what is destructive and evil: When a man harmed his benefactor, that man inspired hatred and compassion among people, who blamed the ungrateful and honored the grateful, as they realized that the same harm could be done to them. To avoid such evils they felt constrained to make laws, and to set up punishments for those who contravened them. This gave rise to the awareness of the concept of justice. Later, when they had to elect a prince, they did not elect the boldest man, but the one who was most prudent and just. But then as princes began coming to power by succession and not by election, the successors were quick to depart from their forefathers and discard virtuous works, convinced that princes had nothing else to do but surpass others in sumptuousness and dissipation and every other form of licentiousness. The result was that the people began to hate the prince, who grew frightened at this hatred and was quick to proceed from fear to attack, which promptly gave rise to tyranny. This then initiated the conspiracies against the prince and the beginning of his downfall. These conspiracies were not instigated by those who were timid or weak, but by those who surpassed others in generosity, magnanimity, wealth, and nobility, men who could not bear the reprehensible ways of the prince. The populace followed the authority of these powerful men and took up arms against the prince, and when he was eliminated, the populace obeyed these men as their liberators. The new rulers, abominating the very idea of a single leader, formed a government among themselves, and in the beginning, mindful of the past tyranny, kept to the laws they had instituted, putting the common good before their own interests, governing and conserving private and public affairs with the utmost diligence. But then their government passed down to their sons, who did not know how changeable Fortune can be, never having experienced adversity. This new generation of rulers was not content with civil equality and soon turned to covetousness, ruthless ambition, the abducting of women, and turning the government of aristocrats into a government of the few without the slightest regard for civil law. As a result, they soon suffered the fate of the tyrants, because the populace grew weary of their government and became the instrument of whoever designed to attack these rulers. Soon someone would rise who with the help of the populace would destroy this government of the few. As the memory of the former prince and his offences was still fresh, the populace, having destroyed the government of the few and not wanting to recreate that of a principality, turned to democracy, setting it up in such a way that neither a few powerful men nor a single prince would hold power. And because all states at the beginning are to some extent respected, this democracy is maintained for a while, but not for long, at most until the demise of the generation that founded it, because it would invariably fall into disorder, when neither private nor public men were feared. Everyone lived as he pleased and the citizens did each other a thousand injustices every day until necessity, or a single capable man, constrained them to return once more to principality in order to escape such disorder. And from this principality, stage by stage, they returned to disorder in the way and for the reasons I have discussed.

This is the cycle of all states, regardless of how they are governed. And yet they rarely return to the same form of government because almost no state can exist long enough to go through these changes many times and still remain standing. Turmoil, however, can lead a state lacking resolution and strength into becoming the vassal of a neighboring state that is better governed. Were this not to happen, however, a state might go infinitely through this cycle of governments.

Hence, I propose that all the modes of government I have mentioned are pernicious because of the brief life of the three good forms of government and the malignity of the three bad ones. Prudent rulers setting up laws were aware of this shortcoming, and steered clear of each of these forms in itself, choosing a government that combined them all, judging it steadier and more stable, because one form can keep the other in check when there are a principality, an aristocracy, and a democracy in the same city. Among the men who have deserved the most praise for such a government is Lycurgus, who constituted his laws in Sparta in such a way that the kings, the aristocracy, and the populace all had their function. In doing this, he created a state that lasted for more than eight hundred years, with the utmost glory to him and peace for Sparta. The opposite happened to Solon, who organized the laws of Athens. He only set up a democracy, which had such a short life that he saw the tyranny of Pisistratus arise before he died.[14] After forty years the heirs of Pisistratus were chased out and Athens returned to liberty, but because the democracy that was reinstated followed Solon's laws, it did not last more than a hundred years, even though to conserve the democracy, many laws not envisioned by Solon were drawn up to keep the arrogance of the aristocracy and the unruliness of the populace in check. Nonetheless, since in his laws Solon had not combined the power of a principality with that of an aristocracy, Athens prevailed for only a brief time compared to Sparta.

But let us consider Rome, which, despite not having a Lycurgus to give it laws in the beginning in such a way that it could prevail in freedom over a long period, there were nevertheless so many incidents arising from the discord between the plebeians and the Senate that what a founder did not do was subsequently done by chance. If Rome did not have Fortune on her side the first time, she did later, because Rome's initial laws, though imperfect, nevertheless did follow a straight path that led it to perfection. For Romulus and all the other kings made many good laws that were suitable for living in freedom, but because their aim was to found a kingdom and not a republic, when Rome became free she lacked many things necessary to secure liberty that had not been set up by those kings. These rulers lost their power for the reasons I have already discussed, and yet those who chased them out immediately established two consuls[15] who took their place, so that what was driven from Rome was only the name of king and not kingly power. As the republic had only the consuls and the Senate, it was a combination of only two of three forms of governments described above, in other words, that of the principality and that of the aristocracy. It remained to the city only to give a place to democracy. But the Roman nobility became arrogant, for reasons I will discuss later, and the populace rose against them. So as not to lose

14. Solon (c. 630–c. 560 BCE) was an Athenian statesman who introduced sweeping economic, political, and legal reforms that ended the aristocrats' control of the Athenian government. Pisistratus (d. 527 BCE) was tyrant of Athens three times. After his death, his sons Hippias and Hipparchus succeeded him. See also Book II, chapter 2 below.

15. After the expulsion of the Tarquin kings (509 BCE), the Romans replaced the kingship with two annually elected chief magistrates called consuls.

everything, the nobility was constrained to concede to the populace their share, and, on the other hand, the Senate and the consuls kept enough power over the republic that they managed to maintain their positions. This is how the tribunes of the plebeians came to be, after which the republic became more stable since each of the three forms of government had its part. Fortune was so favorable to Rome that although the city passed from a government of kings and aristocrats to one of the populace, through the same stages and for the same reasons discussed above, the kingly qualities were never entirely relinquished to the aristocrats, nor was the authority of the aristocrats ceded to the populace. Rather, the authority remained mixed, creating a perfect republic. Rome reached this perfection through the discord between the plebeians and the Senate, as will be seen in the following two chapters.

On the incidents that led to the creation of the plebeian tribunes in Rome, which made the republic more perfect

Those who reason about civic life argue—and the history books are filled with examples—that it is necessary for a ruler who is setting up a republic and organizing its laws to presuppose that all men are evil, and that whenever they have the opportunity they will act according to the malignity of their nature. When such malignity is concealed for a while, it is linked to a hidden cause which, not being visible, is not recognized. But time, which people call the father of all truth, will in the end expose this malignity.

In Rome after the Tarquins[16] were expelled there seemed to exist a wonderful accord between the plebeians and the Senate. The nobles seemed to have laid down their pride and taken up the popular cause and were supported by everyone, even the lowliest. But this was a ruse, and the motivation of the nobles remained hidden, nor was the reason for it apparent as long as the Tarquins, whom the nobles feared, were alive. The nobles felt that mistreating the plebeians would draw the plebeians closer to the Tarquins, and so the nobles conducted themselves toward the plebeians outward with respect. But no sooner were the Tarquins dead than the nobles' fear vanished and they began spewing at the plebeians all the venom concealed in their hearts, attacking

---

16. Tarquin the Proud, who according to tradition reigned from 534 to 510 BCE, was the last of the seven legendary kings of Rome.

them in every way they could.[17] This bears testimony to what I said before, that men never do good except out of necessity.

But where choice is overabundant and one has recourse to every freedom, everything is soon beset by confusion and disorder. It is said that hunger and poverty make man industrious, and that laws make him good, but that laws are not necessary when things work well on their own accord without them. When these good customs are missing, however, then laws become vital. With the Tarquins gone—the fear of whom had kept the nobility in check—it was necessary to find a new order that would have the same effect that the Tarquins had had while they were alive. Thus, after many uproars, and clashes between the plebeians and the nobility, the tribunes were created for the security of the plebeians. These tribunes were of such standing and reputation that they were always able to act as mediators between the plebeians and the Senate, and to curb the arrogance of the nobles.

17. Livy (Book II, chapter 21) writes: "This year is notable for the news of Tarquin's death. [. . .] The news delighted the patricians and delighted the plebeians. But the patricians' happiness went out of control. Up to that time they had treated the plebeians with great deference, but now their leaders began to inflict injustice upon them."

ON HOW DISCORD BETWEEN THE PLEBEIANS AND THE ROMAN SENATE MADE THE ROMAN REPUBLIC FREE AND POWERFUL

I do not want to pass over the tumults that occasionally arose in Rome between the time the last Tarquin king died and the time the tribunes were created. I would also like to say a few things against the opinion of those who hold that Rome was an unruly republic beset by so much confusion that if good fortune and military skill had not made up for its defects, it would have been inferior to all other republics. I cannot deny that Fortune and the army were reasons for the power of Rome, but it seems clear to me that those who are of the opinion that Rome was unruly do not realize that where there is a good army there must also be good institutions, and this only rarely occurs where there is no good fortune. But let us proceed to the other aspects of Rome. I say that those who censure the discord between the nobles and the plebeians are blaming things that played a foremost part in keeping Rome free, and that they consider only the tumult and shouts engendered by such disorder rather than the good results they generate. Nor do they consider how in the body of every republic there are two different humors—that of the people and that of the nobles—and that all the laws that are passed in favor of liberty arise from their discord, as can easily be seen to have happened in Rome. From the era of the Tarquins to that of the Gracchi, a period of more than three hundred years, the clashes in Rome rarely resulted in exiles and even more rarely in bloodshed.[18] Nor can one judge these clashes as detrimental, or the republic divided. In all that time, in its periods of strife, it did not send more than nine or ten citizens into exile, executed very few, and did not force many to pay fines. Nor can one reasonably claim that Rome was a republic in disarray when there are so many examples of excellence: because good examples arise from good education, good education from good laws, and good laws from those clashes which so many rashly condemn. If one examines the outcome of these clashes, one will find that they did not result in exile or violence against the common good, but in laws and institutions that benefited civic liberty. Some might say that the means were extreme and almost savage, seeing the populace gathered to shout against the Senate, the Senate against the people, everyone running riot through the streets, closing the shops, the plebeian masses leaving Rome—things that frighten even those who only read about them. I would like to propose that every city has to have methods that allow the populace to give vent to their ambitions, above all those cities that want to engage their populace in important matters. Rome had such a method. When the populace wanted to obtain a law, they either caused unrest as mentioned above, or refused to enlist to go to war, so that to placate them Rome had to satisfy them in some way. The desires of a free populace are rarely dangerous to liberty, because the danger arises either from a populace being oppressed or from the suspicion that they might be oppressed. Where these fears were false, there was the remedy of the public assemblies at which some good man could rise and make a speech demonstrating that they were mistaken. And as Cicero says, the populace, though ignorant, are capable of understanding the truth, and readily acquiesce when they are told the truth, by a man worthy of trust.[19]

One should therefore criticize the Roman government more moderately, and realize that the many good results that came out of that

18. Tarquin the Proud, the last king of Rome, was deposed in 510 BCE. The Gracchi brothers were influential statesmen and reformers. The elder, Tiberius Sempronius Gracchus, was killed in 133 BCE, his brother, Caius Sempronius Gracchus, in 121 BCE.
19. In *De amicitia* (*On Friendship*) XXV, Cicero writes: "A public assembly, though composed of inexperienced men, nevertheless will be able to judge the difference between a mere flatterer and untrustworthy citizen seeking popularity, and a man of principle, standing, and solidity."

republic could only have been brought about by the best causes. And if the discord was the reason for the creation of the tribunes, it deserves the highest praise, because, besides affording the populace a role in the government, the tribunes were formed to guard Roman liberty, as will be shown in the following chapter.

CHAPTER FIVE

ON WHETHER THE PROTECTION OF LIBERTY IS MORE SECURE IN THE HANDS OF THE POPULACE OR OF THE NOBLES, AND WHETHER THOSE SEEKING TO ACQUIRE OR THOSE SEEKING TO MAINTAIN HAVE GREATER CAUSE TO SOW DISCORD

Among the most important institutions set up by the wise founder of a state is legislation to protect liberty. Living in freedom will last for a greater or lesser time depending on how well founded that freedom is. In every state there are nobles and populace, and so the question arises in whose hands it would be best to place the protection of liberty. In ancient Sparta, as in modern Venice, it was placed in the hands of the nobles, while in Rome it was placed in the hands of the plebeians. Therefore it will be useful to examine which of these states made the better choice. If we look at the reasons for these choices, there is something to be said for both sides. But if we examine the results, one would choose the side of the nobles, as Sparta's and Venice's liberty lasted longer than that of Rome.

As for the reasons for these choices, let me first argue the case of the Romans, and say that the protection of liberty ought to be given to those who have less desire to usurp it. For without doubt, if one considers the respective aims of the nobles and the populace, one sees in the former a strong desire to dominate, and in the latter merely a desire not to be dominated.[20] Consequently, the populace have a stronger

20. This idea is echoed in *The Prince*, chapter 9: "One acquires this principality through the favor of either the people or the nobles, because in every city there are two opposing humors. This arises from the fact that the nobles want to command and oppress the people, but the people do not want to be commanded or oppressed by the nobles."

will to live free, having less hope to usurp freedom than the nobles. Thus if the populace are set up as the protector of liberty, it is reasonable to conclude that they will take better care of it. Not being able to seize power themselves, they will not permit others to seize it.

On the other hand, the defenders of the Spartan and Venetian model will counter that he who places the protection of liberty in the hands of the nobles does two good things. First, it satisfies the nobles' aspiration to rule, and with that power in their hands they consequently play a larger part in the state and have more reason to be satisfied. Second, it removes authority from the plebeians with their restless spirits, which are the cause of infinite discord and upheaval in a state and certain to reduce the nobility to despair, which over time brings bad results. The defenders of the Spartan and Venetian model cite Rome itself as an example: The tribunes of the plebeians acquired so much authority that they were no longer content with one consul being a plebeian, but wanted both to be. Achieving that, the tribunes then demanded the office of censor, the office of praetor, and all the other positions of power in the city, and it was this same passion that before long drove them to venerate any man capable of assaulting the nobility. This gave rise to the power of Marius and the ruin of Rome.[21]

But in fact, whoever weighs both sides might be in doubt as to which side he would choose to be the protector of such liberty, not knowing which humor would be more injurious in a state: the humor that seeks to preserve the rank and offices it already holds, or the humor that seeks to gain that which it does not have. Yet examining everything carefully, one will come to the following conclusion: One is considering either a state that is striving toward an empire, like Rome, or a state content to maintain itself as it is. In the first case, the state has to do exactly as Rome did, and in the second it can follow the example of Venice and Sparta, for reasons I shall explain in the following chapter.

But let us discuss which men are most injurious to a state: those who desire to acquire, or those afraid of losing what they have acquired. I propose that once Marcus Menenius was made dictator, and Marcus Fulvius his Master of the Horse (both were plebeians), in order to in-

21. Gaius Marius was a Roman general of plebeian background who was first elected consul in 107 BCE. Many of his reforms led to the fall of the republic.

vootigate conspiracies against Rome that had arisen in Capua, they were also given authority by the people to seek out those men in Rome who, through ambition and illegal means, strove to gain the consulship or other high positions in the city.[22] In the nobility's eyes such authority had been given to the dictator against them, and they began spreading the rumor throughout Rome that it was not the nobles who were seeking these high positions out of ambition and illegal means, but men from the plebeian ranks, who, unable to rely upon their birth and skill, were seeking to acquire the highest ranks through illegal means.[23] They particularly accused the dictator. Their accusation was brought with such force that the dictator, Menenius, gave an oration in which he complained about the calumnies which the nobles had launched against him and laid down his office, submitting himself to the judgment of the populace. His case was deliberated and he was absolved: at which point the question arose, who was more ambitious, he who wants to maintain what he has or he who wants to acquire what he does not have, as it is easy enough for either aspiration to be the reason for the greatest discord. Nevertheless, in most cases the discord is caused by those who possess, because the fear of losing generates in them the same desires as those who wish to acquire. Men do not feel their possessions secure if they do not also acquire the possessions of others. And the more they possess, the more power and capacity they have to cause turmoil. Furthermore, their improper and covetous behavior ignites in the hearts of those who do not possess the urge to avenge themselves and rob those who do, gaining the wealth and honors that they see so badly misused by others.

22. The dictator was a chief magistrate with absolute authority, elected for six months during great emergencies. The Master of the Horse assisted the dictator in managing the state. Gaius Maenius (not Marcus Menenius) became dictator, with Marcus Folius (not Fulvius) as his Master of the Horse. Livy describes these incidents in Book IX, chapter 26.
23. Livy (Book IX, chapter 26) writes: "The nobility, not only those who were being accused, but all the nobles, protested that the charge should not be brought against the patricians to whom the path to honors was always open, unless it was obstructed by intrigue, but against plebeian upstarts."

CHAPTER SIX

ON WHETHER A FORM OF GOVERNMENT COULD HAVE BEEN SET UP IN ROME THAT COULD HAVE REMOVED THE ENMITY BETWEEN THE POPULACE AND THE SENATE

We have discussed the effects of the clashes and conflicts between the populace and the Senate. Since these continued until the time of the Gracchi,[24] leading to the end of liberty in Rome, one might have wished that Rome had attained its greatness without such enmities. But it seems relevant to consider whether a government that was able to remove such clashes could have been instituted in Rome. To examine this, one must look at the states that managed to remain free for a long time without enmities and clashes, and see what form of government they had, and whether one could have set up such a government in Rome. There are ancient Sparta and modern Venice, both of which I have already touched on. Sparta set up a king and a small senate to govern it,[25] while Venice did not organize its government by ranks, but rather under a single appellation: All those with the right to enter the administration were called gentlemen. This system was given to the Venetians more by chance than by the wisdom of their legislator. They were confined to those little islands on which the city now stands, for the reasons I have already mentioned, and as the Venetians had grown to such a number, they needed laws if they wanted to live together,

24. The reforms of Tiberius and Gaius Gracchus acted as a catalyst to end the Roman Republic, opening the way to imperial Rome.
25. In fact, Sparta had *two* kings, who were elected as lifetime co-rulers. The Spartan senate, or *gerousia*, was made up of twenty-eight elders.

and so they set up a form of government. They often convened in councils to deliberate on matters concerning the city, and when it seemed that they had enough members in their councils to form a vital civic system, they closed the doors to all further newcomers to Venice, preventing them from participating in their government.[26] Then, once enough inhabitants were excluded from government, the men of the government acquired a standing and were called gentlemen, while the others were called commoners. This system could arise and maintain itself without discord because when it originally came into being, everyone living in Venice was made part of the government, and so nobody could complain. Those who arrived later found the government established and closed, and so did not have cause or opportunity to spark turmoil. There was no cause because nothing had been taken from them, and there was no opportunity because whoever was ruling held them in check and did not call upon them in matters in which they could end up gaining power. Furthermore, those who later came to settle in Venice were not many, not enough in number to cause an imbalance between those who governed and those who were governed. The proportion of gentlemen to commoners was either equal or greater, so Venice could set up this kind of state and keep it united.

Sparta, as I have already mentioned, was governed by a king and a small senate. It managed to maintain itself for such a long time because it had few citizens, and did not accept immigrants. Sparta had also adopted and observed the laws of Lycurgus, which took away all cause for discord, and the Spartans managed to live united for a long time. The laws of Lycurgus brought more equality in wealth and less equality in rank. Hence there was equality in poverty, and the populace were not as politically ambitious, since the positions of power in the city were open to so few citizens and were kept from the populace, nor did the nobles ever give them reason to desire these positions by treating them badly. This stability arose from the kings of the Spartans, who, being called into office and placed in the midst of that nobility, had no better way to hold on to their office than by keeping the populace secure from harm. The result was that the populace neither feared nor desired power; and since they neither had power nor feared that of the nobles, the struggle they would have had with the nobility and the causes for clashes did not arise, and they could live in harmony for a long time. But two principal matters brought about this harmony: first, Sparta had few inhabitants and so could be governed by a few, and second, by not accepting foreigners into their state, they did not have occasion either to adulterate themselves or to grow to such an extent that the state would become unrulable by the few who governed it.

Considering all these matters, it is clear that the Roman legislators, if they wanted Rome to remain as peaceful as the states I have mentioned, had to do one of two things: either not use the plebeians in war, like the Venetians, or not open their doors to foreigners, like the Spartans. The Romans, however, did both, which gave the plebeians power, helped them grow in number, and gave them infinite occasion to cause turmoil. But had the state of Rome become more peaceful it would have become weaker, as this would have blocked the path to the greatness it achieved. In other words, had Rome removed the causes of turmoil, it would have also removed the causes for its growth. If one looks carefully, this pattern can be observed in all human affairs: One can never remove one problem without another one's arising.[27] If you strive to make a populace numerous and armed in order to build a large empire, you end up unable to control it as you wish; if you keep it small or disarmed you can control it, but if you acquire new dominions you will be unable to keep them, or they will become so weak that you will fall prey to whoever attacks you. So in all our deliberations we should consider where the fewest drawbacks lie and choose the best solution, because there is no choice that is entirely clear and certain. Rome, therefore, like Sparta, could have created a prince for life and a small senate; but unlike Sparta, Rome could not have avoided expanding the number of its citizens, as it wanted to create a large empire. This would have meant that the king for life and the small senate would have been of little benefit to Rome as far as its harmony was concerned.

Therefore, anyone wishing to set up a republic from the start should first consider whether his aim is to expand his dominion and power, like Rome, or to remain within strict limits. In the first case, he has to follow the model of Rome and allow the tumult and popular dis-

---

27. See also *The Prince*, chapter 21: "It is in the nature of things that you can never escape one setback without running into another. Wisdom consists of knowing how to recognize the respective qualities of the setbacks and choosing the lesser evil."

cord to the extent that he can; because without a great number of men, and well-armed ones, a state can never grow, or if it does, it will be unable to maintain itself. In the second case, the founder of a republic can set it up following the model of Sparta or Venice; but because expansion is poison to such states, he who sets them up has to do his utmost to hinder them from acquiring territory. Such territorial acquisitions, when a state is weak, will be its utter ruin. This is what happened in Sparta and Venice. The former, having subjugated almost all of Greece, showed its weak foundation in a minor incident: When Pelopidas[28] sparked a rebellion in Thebes, other cities followed suit, and the Spartan state was destroyed. Similarly, Venice had occupied a large part of Italy—most of it not through war but through money and ingenuity—and yet the moment it had to prove its strength, it lost all its territories in a single day.[29]

Therefore I propose that the way to create a republic that will last a long time is to set it up like Sparta or Venice, and to found it in a strong location and with such power that nobody would consider it easily subjugated, but on the other hand not allow it to become so large that it would instill fear in its neighbors. This way, a state can prevail for a long time, since one makes war on a state for two reasons: in order to subjugate it, or out of fear that one might be subjugated by it. The model I have proposed above will almost entirely remove these reasons, because if it is difficult to conquer a state (since I presuppose its defense would be skillfully devised), it would be rare or out of the question for someone to set his sights on acquiring it. If the state remains within its own borders, and experience demonstrates that it does not harbor ambitions of expansion, nobody will declare war on it out of fear, and even less so if it has a constitution or laws that prohibit expansion. I have no doubt that if such a balance could be kept it would lead to a proper living according to law and the true tranquillity of a city. But as all affairs of this world are in motion and will not remain fixed, they must either rise or fall, and many endeavors to which reason will not induce you, necessity will. If one has set up a republic that is able to maintain itself without expanding, but necessity

28. Pelopidas freed Thebes from Spartan occupation in 379 BCE, which Plutarch describes in *Parallel Lives* in his chapter on Pelopidas.
29. In the Battle of Agnadello in 1509, Venice suffered a total defeat by the French king Louis XII and lost all its cities on the Italian mainland.

leads it to expand, one will see its foundations crumble under it, and it will quickly come to ruin. And yet, if the heavens smile upon it and it never has to wage war, idleness might make this republic effeminate or divided. These two problems together, or each by itself, can be enough reason for the republic's ruin. Therefore, since it is not possible, in my opinion, to find a balance or to maintain a middle way, in setting up a republic one must think of the most honorable choices, and set it up in such a way that even if necessity induces it to expand, it will be able to conserve what it has acquired.

But to return to my first argument: I believe that it is necessary to follow the institutions of Rome and not those of other states, because I do not believe it is possible to find a middle way. One must tolerate the kinds of clashes that arose in Rome between the populace and the Senate, regarding them as a necessary ill on Rome's road to greatness. Beyond the other reasons I have submitted, which demonstrate that the authority of the tribunes was necessary for the protection of liberty, one can easily see the benefit that states derive from the power of public indictment, which was granted, among other things, to the tribunes, as will be discussed in the following chapter.

CHAPTER SEVEN

ON THE EXTENT TO WHICH
PUBLIC INDICTMENTS ARE NECESSARY
IN A REPUBLIC TO KEEP IT FREE

The most useful and necessary authority that can be granted to institutions entrusted with the protection of the republic's liberty is the ability of indicting publicly, or before some magistrate or council, citizens who in some way have offended the public. Such institutions have two very useful results. First, citizens, out of fear of being indicted, will not attempt anything against the state; if they do, they are immediately persecuted regardless of who they are. Second, it is a way to provide an outlet for the humors that arise in different ways within cities against particular citizens. When these humors do not have a lawful outlet they seek one that is unlawful, which can bring the whole state to ruin. Therefore, nothing makes a republic more stable and firm than to be set up so that the change in such humors that agitate it have an outlet that is regulated by the laws.

This can be demonstrated by many examples, but best of all by what Livy writes of Coriolanus.[30] The Roman nobility had been angered because in their view the plebeians had too much power through the creation of the tribunes, who protected them. At that time there was a great scarcity of provisions in Rome, and while the Senate had sent to Sicily for grain, Coriolanus, who was hostile to the popular

---

30. Gaius Marcius Coriolanus is a legendary figure believed to have lived in the fifth century BCE. Livy describes this episode in Book II, chapters 33–35.

faction, advised that the time had come to punish the plebeians and take back the authority that they had seized from the nobility. The plebeians, Coriolanus advised, should be kept hungry, and the grain should not be distributed among them. When this reached the ears of the populace, such anger flared up against Coriolanus that the crowd would have lynched him as he came out of the Senate had the tribunes not summoned him to argue his case. This incident reinforces what I have said above: How useful and necessary it is for the laws of a republic to provide an outlet for the anger that the masses feel toward a single citizen. When these legal means do not exist, the masses will resort to illegal means, which without doubt have far worse results than the former.

When a citizen is punished by legal means, even if he is wronged, little or no unrest follows, because the law is enforced without private or foreign forces that ruin the state's freedom. Order is upheld with public forces and laws that have precise boundaries, which they do not transgress and so ruin the state. I feel that the example of Coriolanus from ancient times should suffice, as anyone can judge what harm would have befallen the Roman Republic had he been lynched in a riot. Once private citizens harm other private citizens, the harm generates fear, and fear seeks defense, for which partisans are secured, who then cause factions in states, and factions lead to the destruction of these states. But as the matter has been mediated by those who have public authority, all the harm that might have come from controlling it with private authority falls away.

We have seen in our own times the disorder that ensued in the Florentine Republic when the multitude could not vent its anger against one of its citizens within the boundaries of the law, as happened in the era when Francesco Valori ruled the city like a prince.[31] Many in Florence saw him as a man of unbridled ambition who strove to transcend the law through audacity and violence, but there was no way to resist him except by starting a faction that would oppose his. As he had nothing to fear unless illegal steps were taken against him, he began surrounding himself with supporters. In the meantime, those who opposed

31. Francesco Valori was one of the main political figures involved in the ousting of the Medici from Florence and the restoration of a republican government influenced by the ideas of the radical Dominican prior Girolamo Savonarola. Valori was murdered shortly before Savonarola's execution in 1498.

him had no legal means of countering him, and so they turned to illegal means, finally resorting to arms. Had they been able to oppose him with legal means, his authority would have been destroyed with harm done to him alone, but having to destroy his authority by illegal means, his opponents did harm not only to him, but also to many outstanding citizens. In support of this conclusion I could also add another incident that occurred in Florence, involving Piero Soderini.[32] This, too, came about solely because there were no institutions in the republic through which one could indict the ruthless ambition of powerful citizens, as it is not sufficient to indict a powerful citizen before eight judges in a republic:[33] There have to be many judges, because the few always look out for the interests of the few. Had such institutions existed, the citizens could have indicted Soderini if he had comported himself badly, and so have given vent to their anger without calling in the Spanish army; and had Soderini not comported himself badly, the citizens would not have dared indict him, out of fear of ending up indicted themselves. This way, the forces that were the occasion for the scandal would have been removed.

It can therefore be concluded that whenever we see a faction in a city calling in foreign forces, we can be certain that this arises from the city's bad system, which has no institutions within its walls providing a legal outlet for the malignant humors that arise in man. This problem can be fully anticipated by establishing a system of bringing indictments before a large number of judges and giving these indictments weight. In Rome this system was so well set up that in the many conflicts between the plebeians and the Senate, neither the Senate nor the plebeians nor any private citizen ever considered using foreign forces. They had the remedy at home, and so were not compelled to seek it abroad.

Though the examples I have cited furnish ample proof of this, I would like to add another that Livy relates in his *Histories*. In Chiusi, the foremost city of Etruria in those days, a chief magistrate raped one of the sisters of a certain Arunte, who, unable to avenge himself because of the rank and position of the rapist, turned to the Gauls, who

32. In 1502 Piero Soderini had been elected Gonfalonier for life in Florence, but in 1512 he was deposed by the Medici with the help of a Spanish army. Soderini had been Machiavelli's patron.
33. *Otto di guardia*, eight Florentine magistrates who administered justice.

were ruling present-day Lombardy, and encouraged them to come to Chiusi with their army, arguing that they could avenge him to their advantage.[34] Had Arunte been able to avenge himself through the institutions of the city, he would not have sought the help of the barbarian forces. But as useful as such indictments are in a republic, false accusations are harmful, as I shall discuss in the following chapter.

34. In fact Livy (Book V, chapter 33) writes: "Arruns's wife had been seduced by an Etruscan prince whose tutor Arruns was. But since the prince was an influential young man, Arruns could not get justice without seeking help from abroad. In revenge, he led the Gauls across the Alps and encouraged them to attack Clusium."

CHAPTER EIGHT

As useful as public indictments are to states, false accusations are harmful

Furius Camillus's brilliance in liberating Rome from the oppression of the Gauls[35] made the Roman citizens cede to him without feeling that they were losing standing or rank. Manlius Capitolinus, however, could not bear to see such honor and glory awarded to Furius Camillus. He himself had saved the Capitol, and felt that he had done as much for the protection of Rome as Camillus had, and that he was in no way inferior to him in feats of military glory. He was filled with envy and rankled by Camillus's glory. As Manlius Capitolinus could not sow discord among the senators, he turned to the plebeians, spreading dark rumors, including one that the treasure that had been gathered for the Gauls, but then had not been given to them, had been seized by private citizens: If this treasure could be regained, it could be used for the public good, relieving the plebeians of taxes or private debts.[36] These words had a great effect on the plebeians, and they

35. Marcus Furius Camillus (d. 365 BCE) was a Roman general, statesman, and five-time dictator of Rome. His greatest triumph was the conquest of the Etruscan city of Veii (also discussed in chapter 55 below). Later Romans celebrated him as the second founder of Rome after the Gauls sacked the city in 396 BCE. Machiavelli is discussing the events described by Livy in Book VI.

36. Livy (Book VI, chapter 14) writes: "[Manlius] delivered speeches in his house as if he were haranguing the Senate. Unconcerned about truth or falsehood, he insinuated that the treasure that had been collected for the Gauls had been sequestered by the senators, who were not content with seizing public lands, but also wanted to embezzle public funds. With

began causing turmoil in the city. The Senate saw the gravity of the situation and elected a dictator to look into the matter and put a stop to the violence that Manlius was unleashing. The dictator immediately summoned him to be confronted before the public, the dictator standing among the nobles, Manlius among the plebeians. He ordered Manlius to reveal who, according to him, had seized that treasure, since the Senate was as eager to know as the plebeians. Manlius evaded the question, saying that there was no need for him to inform the Senate of what it already knew. As a result, the dictator had him imprisoned.

It is to be noted from this incident from Livy how detestable false accusations are in free states or in any other form of society, and that no legislation to repress such false accusations should be neglected. In fact, there is no better system for eliminating false accusations than providing ample opportunity for public indictments, because just as indictments are beneficial to a state, false accusations are harmful. The difference between the two types is that false accusations need neither witnesses nor proof to substantiate them: Anybody can falsely accuse anybody else, but not everyone can be lawfully indicted, as public indictments need proof and circumstances that demonstrate the truth of the charge. Men are publicly indicted before magistrates, the people, and the councils, while they are falsely accused in town squares and market stalls. Calumny is more common where there are fewer opportunities for public indictments and where the states are not as well set up to receive them in their judicature. Therefore, a founder of a state must plan the legislature in such a way that any citizen can indict any other citizen without fear or deference to rank, and once the charges have been made and have been carefully looked into, false accusers must be severely punished. And the false accuser cannot complain if he is punished, as he could have made his accusations by lawful means rather than in spreading calumnies in market squares. Whenever this system is not well set up, clashes and disorder always follow, because calumnies provoke but do not punish citizens, and the provoked have their minds set on retaliation, as they hate rather than fear the things being said against them.

---

this treasure the populace could be freed of its debts." See also chapter 24, in which Machiavelli further discusses Manlius Capitolinus's sedition.

As I have already mentioned, the system of public indictment was set up well in Rome, but badly here in Florence. And just as in Rome this institution did much good, in Florence its absence did much harm. Whoever reads the history of Florence will see how much calumny in every era was perpetrated on those of its citizens who were employed in the important affairs of the city. Of one man they said that he had stolen money from the state, of another that he had been unsuccessful in a military campaign because he had been bribed, and that another had done this or that misdeed out of ruthless ambition. Hatred surged from all sides, leading to division; division led to factions, and factions led to ruin. Had there been institutions in Florence for bringing indictments against citizens and punishing false accusers, the infinite scandals would not have continued. Those citizens who were either condemned or acquitted would not have been able to harm the city, and there would have been fewer men indicted than falsely accused, for it is easier, as I have said, to accuse a man falsely than to indict him officially. Among the devices used by a citizen to achieve greatness have been calumnies, for leveling false accusations against powerful citizens who have opposed a man's appetite for power can be very effective. When the false accuser takes the part of the populace, and confirms their bad opinion of the powerful citizen, he wins them to his side. I could cite many examples, but will limit myself to one. The Florentine army was on a campaign against the city of Lucca under the command of Giovanni Guicciardini, who was its commissary.[37] Lucca did not fall, either because of Guicciardini's bad leadership or his bad fortune, and yet, whichever the case might have been, he was held culpable, as it was said that he had been bribed by the Luccans. This calumny was promoted by his enemies and almost drove Guicciardini to the brink of desperation.[38] He put himself in the hands of the Captain of the People in order to clear his name,[39] but even so, he never managed to clear himself entirely, as there was no system in Florence

37. Giovanni Guicciardini (c. 1385–1435) was the commissary of the Florentine army that attacked Lucca in 1430, which at the time was under the rule of Pagolo Guinigi, who is mentioned in passing in *The Life of Castruccio Castracani:* "Lucca, which remained under his family's rule [the Guinigi] until the reign of his great-great-grandson Pagolo."
38. Giovanni Guicciardini was an opponent of the faction of Cosimo de' Medici, who was exiled in 1433 but managed to seize power again the following year.
39. The Capitano del Popolo was the magistracy in charge of leading the military forces of the populace and ensuring that justice was done to wronged members.

for him to do this. Much indignation resulted among Guicciardini's friends, who were for the most part men of great influence and wanted to bring about a change in Florence. This incident, along with others like it, grew to such an extent that the ruin of the republic ensued.

Hence Manlius Capitolinus was a false accuser, and not a legitimate one, and in his case the Romans demonstrated precisely how false accusers must be punished. Calumniators have to be turned into public accusers, and where the accusation proves to be true, either they must not be punished or they must be recompensed, but in cases where the accusation proves false, they must be punished in the way Manlius was.

CHAPTER NINE

ON THE NECESSITY TO ACT ALONE IF ONE WISHES TO FOUND A STATE OR ENTIRELY REFORM ITS OLD INSTITUTIONS

Some might argue that I have gone too deeply into Roman history without having yet discussed its founders or military and religious institutions. As I do not want to keep in suspense any readers who wish to hear something about this, I will first say that many might judge it a bad example that a founder of a state, such as Romulus, would first have killed his brother, and then consented to the death of Titus Tatius, the Sabine, whom he had chosen as co-ruler of the Kingdom of Rome.[40] The reader will judge from this that the citizens of such a state might follow the example of their prince and harm those who oppose their own ambition and desire for power. This opinion would be correct, if one did not consider the aim that led Romulus to these murders.

It is a general rule that rarely, if ever, has a republic or kingdom been set up well from the beginning, or had its old institutions entirely reformed, unless this was done by a single man. In fact, it is necessary that one man alone give it form. Its organization must depend entirely on his ideas. But the prudent organizer of a republic who does not seek to benefit himself but rather the people, not his own heirs but his whole state, must do his utmost to keep all the power to himself. Nor

40. Livy (Book I, chapter 14) writes: "Romulus is said to have been less distressed at [Tatius's murder] than he should have been, either because of the suspicion inherent in joint sovereignty, or because he thought that Tatius had deserved his fate."

will a wise man ever reproach him for acting outside the law in order to set up a kingdom or establish a republic. While his actions might accuse him, the result excuses him, and when the result is good, as it was in the case of Romulus, the result will always justify his actions. Only the man who is violent in order to ruin things should be reproached, not the man who is violent in seeking to repair things. The founder of a state must be prudent and skillful enough not to leave his power for another to inherit, because as men are more prone to evil than to good, his successor might use with greed what the founder used with skill. A single man might be capable of establishing a state, but the state established tends not to last long if it remains on the shoulders of one man, while it does last when it remains under the control of many and relies on many to maintain it. For just as many men are not able to establish something from the start, as they are unable to recognize the good in it since they all hold conflicting opinions, once they do recognize the good they will not let go of it. It is clear that Romulus was one ruler who deserves to be pardoned for the death of his brother and his co-ruler. What he did was for the common good and not for his own ambition, as he immediately set up a senate which he always consulted, making decisions with the senate's views in mind. If one weighs the authority that Romulus reserved for himself, one sees that he only kept for himself the power to command the armies when war had been declared, and to convene the senate. This was apparent when Rome became free after the Tarquins[41] were driven out and the Romans did not reform any of the old institutions, except that in place of a king for life there were two annual consuls. This proves that all the original institutions of Rome were more fitting for a free state than an absolute and tyrannical one.

One could give countless examples to support the matters I have written about above, such as Moses, Lycurgus, Solon, and other founders of kingdoms and republics, who could make laws for the common good because they had seized absolute power. But I would like to pass over them, as they are well known, and put forward only one, not so renowned, but worthy of consideration by those who might wish to be the legislators of good laws. Agis, King of Sparta, wanted to

---

41. Tarquin the Proud, who according to tradition reigned from 534 to 510 BCE, was the last of the seven legendary kings of Rome.

return the Spartans to the boundaries that the laws of Lycurgus had set for them, for it seemed to him that they had deviated from these laws, and that Sparta had consequently lost much of its ancient prowess, and also strength and power. But the Spartan ephors[42] killed Agis during his initial endeavors, since they perceived him to be a man who wanted to establish a tyranny. But Cleomenes became king after him, and he was resolved to follow Agis's example, after he found Agis's memoirs and writings in which his thoughts and intentions were clearly described. Cleomenes, too, realized that he could not help Sparta if he did not become the sole authority. He recognized that men being ambitious, he would not be able to do good for the many against the will of the few. Waiting for an opportune moment, he had all the ephors killed, and anyone else who might oppose him. Then he reformed all the laws of Lycurgus. This decision would have resuscitated Sparta and afforded Cleomenes a reputation comparable to that of Lycurgus had there not been the power of the Macedonians and the weakness of the other Greek states. After Cleomenes's reforms, the Macedonians attacked, and as he was inferior in strength and finding himself without allies, he was defeated. And so his design, though just and praiseworthy, remained incomplete.[43]

Having considered all these things, I conclude that in setting up a republic it is necessary to act alone, and that Romulus deserves pardon, not blame, for the deaths of Remus and Titus Tatius.

---

42. The ephors were a group of five magistrates who, with the kings, formed the executive branch of the Spartan state.
43. Plutarch describes these incidents in a section on Agis and Cleomenes in *Parallel Lives.*

On how the founders of a republic or kingdom are as much to be lauded as founders of a tyranny are to be rebuked

Among all the men who are praised, those praised most highly are the founders and heads of religions. Following closely are men who have founded republics or kingdoms, who in turn are followed in status by military men who have enlarged their own dominions or those of their state, and men of letters who are of so many kinds that they are each celebrated according to their quality. All other men, their number infinite, merit some praise according to their craft and the skill with which they practice it. In contrast, infamous and detestable are the men who are destroyers of religion, who dissipate kingdoms and republics, and enemies of accomplishment, letters, and all the crafts that bring value and honor to mankind. Such men are impious, violent, ignorant, worthless, idlers, and cowards. No one will be so foolish or so wise, so bad or so good that, when faced with the choice of two qualities in man, he will not praise what is praiseworthy and blame what is blamable. Nevertheless, in the end, almost all rulers, beguiled by a false good and a false glory, allow themselves to slip either voluntarily or unaware into the ranks of those who merit more blame than praise. Though to their everlasting honor they are able to found a republic or kingdom, they turn to a tyranny, not seeing how much fame, glory, honor, security, tranquillity, and peace of mind they are rejecting, and how much infamy, vituperation, blame, danger, and insecurity they are bringing upon themselves.

It is unthinkable that men living as private citizens in a republic, even if they become princes by fortune or skill, would prefer to be a Scipio rather than a Caesar after they have read the histories and have benefited from the records of ancient things.[44] It is unthinkable that if they are already princes they would prefer to live as Agesilaus, Timoleon, or Dion, rather than as Nabis, Phalaris, or Dionysius, because they would see that the former have been accorded the highest praise, and the latter the strongest opprobrium.[45] They would also see how Timoleon and the others had more authority in their states than Dionysius or Phalaris in theirs, and more security over a long period.

And let no one be deceived by Caesar's glory just because historians showered him with the highest praise. Those who praised him were beguiled by his good fortune and intimidated by the duration of the empire which, ruled as it was under his name,[46] did not permit historians to write freely about him. If one wishes to gauge what free historians would have said of Caesar, one need only look at what has been written about Catiline.[47] Caesar is all the more detestable, since a man who does a deed is more blameworthy than a man who intends to do one. One will also see with how much praise the historians showered Brutus: Unable to blame Caesar because of his power, they celebrated his enemy.

Anyone who has become the prince of a state should consider how much more praise is merited by emperors who lived as good rulers according to the law after Rome became an empire than by emperors who did not. Titus, Nerva, Trajan, Hadrian, Antoninus, and Marcus did not need the Praetorian Guard or whole legions to defend them. They were defended by their conduct, the goodwill of the populace, and the love of the senate. On the other hand, Caligula, Nero, Vitellius, and so many other wicked emperors found that their eastern and western armies were not enough to save them from the enemies their

44. Machiavelli compares Scipio Africanus (who defeated Hannibal), as a champion of the Roman Republic, to Caesar, as founder of imperial Rome.
45. Plutarch in *Parallel Lives* praises Agesilaus of Sparta, Timoleon of Corinth, and Dion of Syracuse as heroic rulers. Nabis was the last ruler of independent Sparta; Phalaris, tyrant of Acragas, was alleged to have roasted his victims alive in a bronze bull; Dionysius the Elder was tyrant of Syracuse.
46. Machiavelli is referring to the Roman emperors who adopted Caesar as a title.
47. Catiline was a Roman politician of the first century BCE who is best known for the Catilinian conspiracy, an attempt to overthrow the Roman Republic.

evil ways had generated. A new prince who considers their history carefully will find it excellent training, showing him the path to glory or to blame, the path to security or fear. Of the twenty-six emperors between Caesar and Maximinus, sixteen were murdered and ten died of natural causes. If among the murdered emperors there was a good one—like Galba or Pertinax—he was murdered on account of the corruption that his predecessors had instilled in the soldiers. And if among the emperors who died of natural causes there was one who was evil—as Severus was—this arose from his exceptional good fortune and skill, two things that are rarely found together in one man. A new prince reading this history will also see how a good kingdom can be set up, because all the emperors who came to power through a hereditary line, except for Titus, were evil, while all those who came to power through adoption were good, as were the five emperors from Nerva to Marcus. When the empire fell back into a hereditary line, it was destined once more for ruin.

Let a prince, therefore, first consider the times from Nerva to Marcus and compare them to those before and after, and let him choose in which era he would have liked to have been born, or in which he would have wanted to rule. Because in the era of a good emperor he will see a ruler secure among steadfast citizens, and the world steeped in peace and justice. He will see the Senate with its authority, the magistrates with their honors, wealthy citizens enjoying their wealth and seeing their nobility and skill exalted. He will see tranquillity and well-being and the eradication of all rancor, licentiousness, corruption, and ruthless ambition. He will see a golden age in which everyone can have and defend any opinions. He will see the triumph of a world filled with reverence and glory for the prince, and love and security for the populace. The prince should then carefully weigh the times of the other emperors, and will see in them terrible strife, discord, and sedition, and cruelty both in war and peace. So many princes dead by the sword, so many civil wars and wars with outside powers, Italy afflicted and filled with novel disasters, her cities sacked.[48] He will see Rome torched, the Capitol torn down by its citizens, the ancient temples devastated,

48. In this paragraph Machiavelli is paraphrasing a passage from Tacitus's *Histories* (Book I, chapter 2) that begins: "I am entering a period of history replete with brutal war, discord, and sedition, torn by civil strife, savage even in peace. [. . .] Italy was brought to her knees by disasters that were entirely novel."

the rites corrupted, the cities rife with adulteries, the sea teeming with exiles, the shores covered in blood. He will see untold cruelty in Rome, and noble rank, riches, past honors, and above all excellence, charged as capital sin. He will see slanderers rewarded, corrupted servants turning against their masters, freedmen against their patrons, and those without enemies will be overpowered by their friends. He will see clearly then what debt Rome, Italy, and the world owe to Caesar.

And without doubt, if the prince is of human birth he will be troubled by the idea of imitating evil times, and will be inspired by an immense desire to follow those who were good. In fact, if a prince seeks the glory of the world, he should desire to possess a corrupt city: not in order to ruin it entirely, as Caesar did Rome, but to reorganize it, as Romulus did. Truly, the heavens cannot give man greater prospect for glory, nor can man wish for a greater glory. Should a prince have to jeopardize his position in order to set up his state properly, it would be better for him to refrain. But there is no excuse if he can keep his principality and organize the state well, but does not do so. In conclusion, he to whom the heavens give such an opportunity should consider that there are two paths: one that will make him secure during his lifetime and glorious after his death, and the other that will make him live in constant anguish and after his death leave behind a legacy of everlasting infamy.

CHAPTER ELEVEN

ON THE RELIGION OF THE ROMANS

Rome's founding father was Romulus, and Rome, like a good daughter, recognized that she owed to him her birth and upbringing. And yet the heavens determined that Romulus's institutions were not adequate for a state like Rome, and so they inspired the Roman senate to elect Numa Pompilius as Romulus's successor, so that what Romulus had neglected was instituted by Numa.[49] He found the populace of Rome most ferocious[50] and, wanting to bring them to civil order through the arts of peace, turned to religion as vital if he wanted to maintain civil order, and so he constituted it in such a way that for many centuries there was never so much fear of God as there was in that state.[51] This also helped all the undertakings of the Senate and the great men of Rome. Whoever considers the countless ventures of Roman individuals or the populace as a whole will see how Roman citizens were more afraid of breaking an oath than they were of breaking the law, just as are men who esteem the power of God more than the power of man. This is clearly evident in the examples of Scipio and Manlius Torqua-

49. Numa Pompilius was the second of the seven legendary kings of Rome, who was said to have ruled from 715 to 673 BCE.
50. Machiavelli is directly translating Livy's words (Book I, chapter 19): *ferocem populum.*
51. King Numa Pompilius was believed to have founded many of Rome's religious institutions. Livy describes Numa's reforms in Book I, chapters 19–21.

tus. After Hannibal had defeated the Romans at Cannae,[52] many Roman citizens had given up their city as lost and decided to abandon Italy for Sicily. When Scipio heard this, he faced them sword in hand, and forced them to swear that they would not abandon their city.[53] In the case of Lucius Manlius, the father of Titus Manlius (who was later called Torquatus), he had been indicted by Marcus Pomponius, the plebeian tribune, but before the day of the trial Titus went to Marcus Pomponius and threatened to kill him if he did not swear to lift the indictment against his father, and forced Marcus Pomponius to take an oath. Marcus, having taken the oath in terror, saw himself compelled to withdraw the accusation.[54] Likewise, the Romans whose love of their city and its laws had not been enough to keep them in Italy were kept there by an oath they had been forced to take. And the tribune put aside the hatred he had for the father, the offense of the son, and his personal honor, in order to keep the oath he had taken. This arose from the religion that Numa had introduced into Rome.

Anyone who looks closely at Roman history can see how religion served to govern the armies, encourage the plebeians, keep good men good, and shame the evil. If one were to debate to which of its kings Rome was more indebted—Romulus or Numa—I believe Numa would have to be ranked first, for where there is religion, an army can be introduced with ease, though where there is an army but no religion, religion can be introduced only with difficulty. It is evident that Romulus did not need divine authority in order to set up a senate and other civil and military institutions, but Numa did need it, and feigned familiarity with a nymph who advised him how to counsel the populace:[55] all this, because Numa wanted to establish new and drastic laws in Rome, and doubted that his own authority would suffice.

In fact, there has never been a legislator of drastic laws who did not turn to God, for otherwise his laws would not be accepted. A wise legislator can see many good things that are perhaps not evident enough

52. A major battle (216 BCE) between the forces of Rome and Carthage during the Second Punic War. The Roman army was utterly crushed by Hannibal. Of 80,000 Roman troops, only 14,000 managed to escape.
53. Livy describes this incident in Book XXII, chapter 53.
54. Livy describes this incident in Book VII, chapter 4.
55. Livy (Book I, chapter 19) writes: "But he needed some miraculous contrivance in order to convince them, and so pretended that he held nocturnal meetings with the goddess Egeria."

in themselves to persuade others. Therefore, wise legislators who want to avoid this difficulty have recourse to God. Lycurgus and Solon did this, as did many others who had the same goals. The Roman populace admired Numa's goodness and wisdom and embraced all his ideas. It is true that in that era, filled as it was with religion, the men with whom he had to work being rough and simple, Numa achieved his designs with ease, as he was able to imprint on these men whatever new form he pleased. Without doubt, whoever wants to create a republic in our day will find it easier to do so among the people of the mountains, who are uncivilized, than among people who are used to living in cities, where civilization is corrupt, since it is far easier for a sculptor to shape a beautiful statue from a rough piece of marble than from one that has already been badly chiseled by another.

Weighing these matters, I conclude that the religion introduced by Numa was among the foremost reasons for the happiness of the city, because it brought with it good institutions; good institutions brought good fortune, and good fortune brought successful enterprises. As the observance of religious worship is the reason for the greatness of a republic, so the contempt for religious worship is the reason for its ruin. A state in which a fear of God is missing will either come to ruin or be sustained by the people's fear of a prince who can make up for the lack of religion. But because princes are transient, it stands to reason that that kingdom will fail as soon as his skill is absent. Therefore, states that depend only on the skill of a single prince do not last, because that skill will cease to exist with the life of the prince, and it is rare for this skill to resurge in a successor, as Dante wisely says:

> Rarely does human worth descend from branch
> to branch: so it is demanded by Him who grants
> this gift, as He wants us to pray to Him for it.[56]

Therefore the security of a republic or kingdom is not in having a prince who merely reigns wisely during his lifetime, but in having one who can establish institutions in such a way that the state will be maintained after his death. And though it is easier to persuade unrefined

---

56. Machiavelli quotes Dante's *Purgatory*, Canto VII, line 120, with a slight alteration. Where Machiavelli has human worth "descending" from one branch to another, Dante says *risurge*, "rises."

men to embrace a new institution or idea, it is nonetheless possible to persuade civilized men who do not like to think of themselves as being unrefined. The people of Florence did not consider themselves rough or ignorant and yet Brother Girolamo Savonarola persuaded them that he was talking to God. I do not wish to judge whether he was being truthful about this or not, because one must speak of such a man with reverence, but I will say that countless people believed him without ever having witnessed any extraordinary event that might compel them to do so. But his life and doctrine, and the subjects of his sermons, were enough to make them believe him. Thus nobody should despair of attaining what has been attained in the past by others, because men, as we have said in our preface, have always been born, and have lived and died, within the same order of things.

ON THE IMPORTANCE OF TAKING RELIGION INTO ACCOUNT, AND HOW, DUE TO THE CHURCH OF ROME, ITALY HAS BEEN RUINED THROUGH LACK OF RELIGION

Princes or republics that wish to maintain themselves intact must above all else keep the ceremonies of their religion uncorrupted and in veneration. There is in fact no greater harbinger of a state's ruin than signs of religious worship being held in contempt. This is easy to assess if one knows the foundation on which the religion is based in a state, because every religion has its beginnings in one of a state's principal institutions. The religion of the pagans was founded on the responses of oracles and the sects of diviners and haruspices.[57] All the subsequent ceremonies, sacrifices, and rites of the pagan religion depended on these, because the pagans were prepared to believe that the god who could foretell what would be good or bad in their future could also bring it about. There followed temples, sacrifices, supplications, all the ceremonies for venerating the gods, the oracle of Delos, the temple of Jupiter Ammon, and other famous oracles that filled the world with devotion and admiration. But when the oracles began to make pronouncements in favor of the powerful and the oracles' falseness was discovered, men became skeptical and ready to destroy all institutions.

The rulers of a republic or kingdom must preserve the foundation

57. Soothsayers who practiced divination by the inspection of the entrails of animals.

of their religion. If they do so, they will find it easy to keep their state religious, and in consequence keep the state benevolent and harmonious. They must also keep and cultivate everything that contributes to favor their religion, even things they consider false. The wiser and more knowledgeable in natural phenomena a ruler is, the more he will do so. This method was followed by wise rulers, and so belief in miracles arose, which has been celebrated even in false religions: Because wise men amplify the importance of miracles, regardless of what might have caused them, they rely on the awe of the people at these miracles to gain their trust. In Rome there were many such miracles, among them the one that occurred when the Romans were sacking the city of Veii.[58] Soldiers entered the Temple of Juno, and approaching her image, asked, *Vis venire Romam?* ("Do you want to come to Rome?") Some of the soldiers were convinced that she nodded her head, others that she said yes. As these men were in the grip of religion (for as Livy tells us, the soldiers entered the temple devoutly and with reverence), they thought that they were quite unexpectedly hearing the answer that they in fact expected.[59] Their faith and credulity were encouraged by Camillus and the other rulers of the city.[60] If religiosity had been supported by the rulers of the Christian republic as it had been set up by its founder, the Christian states and republics would be more united and much happier than they are. Nor can there be a better surmise about the decline of religion when one sees how the men closest to the Church of Rome, the head of our religion, are not very religious. Anyone considering the origins of our religion will see to what extent our current practices have strayed, and would doubtless judge our religion near ruin.

Many are of the opinion that Italian cities owe their well-being to the Church of Rome, but I would like to offer some arguments against this that occur to me. I will cite two cases which, in my view, cannot be

58. Veii was a wealthy Etruscan city-state that lay ten miles northwest of Rome (modern Veio), and was conquered by the Romans in 396 BCE.
59. Livy describes this incident in Book V, chapter 22, but quotes the Roman soldier as asking the statue: *Visne Romam ire, Iuno?* ("Would you like to go to Rome, Juno?")
60. Marcus Furius Camillus conquered Veii in 396 BCE. He had been appointed Dictator of Rome to direct Rome's second major war of expansion into Etruscan territory. See also chapter 8 above and chapter 1 of Book III below.

contested. First, the papal court and the bad example it sets has led to an utter loss of piety and religion in Italy. This has brought about endless disadvantages and turmoil, because as one might presume that where there is religion there is every good, where religion is lacking one might presume the opposite. We Italians have the Church and the priests to thank for the fact that we have become irreligious and evil. But we also owe the Church another, greater debt, the second cause of our ruin: This is that the Church has kept, and is still keeping, Italy divided. In fact, no land has ever been united or happy unless it is completely under the rule of a republic or prince, as has happened in France and Spain. It is because of the Church that Italy is not in such a position and does not have a single republic or prince ruling it. Although the Church has resided in Italy and held temporal power here, it has not been powerful or skillful enough to occupy the rest of Italy and become its ruler. Nor has it been so weak that, for fear of losing control of its temporal possessions, it refused to call in foreign powers to defend it against anyone in Italy who had become too powerful. There are many examples from our distant past, such as when the pope called upon Charlemagne to drive out the Lombards who practically ruled all of Italy,[61] and there are also examples from our own times, as when with the help of France the Church seized power from the Venetians and then proceeded to drive out the French with the help of the Swiss.[62] The Church has not been powerful enough to occupy Italy, but has not allowed anyone else to occupy it either. Hence the Church has been the reason why Italy remains under many princes and lords, unable to unite under a single ruler. From this has sprung so much discord and weakness that Italy has become easy prey to powerful barbarians and whoever else might attack it. For this, we Italians

61. The Lombard king Alboin had conquered much of northern Italy in 569 CE, as well as territories in central and southern Italy. In the winter of 753–54, Pope Stephen II traveled to Gaul and consecrated Pepin and his sons, Charlemagne and Carloman, kings of the Romans when they promised him help against the Lombards. Charlemagne marched on Rome in 774 when he was called upon by Pope Adrian I, ending the rule of the Lombard dynasty.
62. In 1509, Pope Julius II formed an allegiance with the Holy Roman Emperor Maximilian I, Louis XII of France, and Ferdinand II of Aragon against the Republic of Venice. This allegiance came to an end in 1510, when the pope switched sides and re-allied himself with Venice. Julius II set his sights on expelling the French from Italy, and managed to do so in 1512 with the aid of Swiss troops.

owe thanks to the Church, and to the Church alone. If one could send the papal court with all its authority to settle in the lands of the Swiss—who today are the only people living as the ancients did, both in their religiosity and military institutions—the evil ways of the papal court would soon cause more discord in that country than any other calamity in all its history.

CHAPTER THIRTEEN

ON HOW THE ROMANS MADE USE
OF RELIGION TO REFORM THEIR STATE,
CONDUCT THEIR CAMPAIGNS, AND PUT
A STOP TO TURMOIL

I do not think it inappropriate for me to cite several instances of how
the Romans used religion to reform their state and conduct their campaigns. Livy provides many examples, but I believe that the few I shall
mention here will suffice. The Roman populace had created tribunes
with consular powers who, with one exception, were all plebeians.[63]
There had been a plague and a famine that year, and miracles had occurred which the nobles seized on in electing new tribunes. They
claimed that the gods were angry because Rome had misused the dignity of its government, and that the only way to please them was to restore the election of tribunes to the way it had been done before. The
plebeians were awestruck when religion was made an issue, and they
elected tribunes who were all nobles.[64] The conquest of the city of Veii
shows how the Roman generals used religion to induce their soldiers
to continue the campaign. The soldiers were weary of the long siege
and wanted to return to Rome. But Lake Albanus had miraculously

63. Livy (Book IV, chapter 13) describes the growing tension between the plebeians and the
patricians as the plebeians tried to expand their political power. A tribune was an official appointed to protect the rights of the plebians. The institution of the tribunes had existed since
the fifth century BCE, and became increasingly powerful in the later years of the republic.
64. Livy (Book V, chapter 14) writes: "[The voters] were impressed not only by the dignity
and pomp of the candidates, but by the religious argument. As a result they elected all the
consular tribunes from among the patricians."

risen that year, and the Romans discovered that Apollo and certain haruspices had said that Veii would be defeated the year that Lake Albanus rose and overflowed its shores. This made the soldiers willing to endure the hardship of the siege, since they now had hope of conquering the city, and they agreed to continue the campaign. Camillus was then made dictator of Rome, and Veii was captured after it had been under siege for ten years.[65] So religion, used well, aided in the taking of the city and the restitution of the tribunes to the nobility. Without religion, neither the one nor the other would have been possible.

I would like to offer another example. Much turmoil erupted in Rome when the tribune Terentillus proposed a certain law for reasons I will discuss later.[66] Religion was among the first means the nobility used to counter him. They did this in two ways. First they had the Sibylline Books consulted,[67] and had them respond that Rome, because of sedition, was in danger of losing its liberty that year. Though the tribunes exposed this ruse, it still put so much fear in the hearts of the plebeians that they were no longer as eager as they had been to follow the tribunes. The second way the nobility used religion was when a certain Appius Herdonius occupied the Capitol one night with a crowd of exiles and slaves numbering four thousand men. This created such turmoil in Rome that there was concern that if the Aequi and the Volsci, age-old enemies of Rome, were to attack the city, they would conquer it with ease.[68] Despite this, the tribunes maintained that the possibility of an attack was a mere fabrication and so did not cease demanding that Terentillus's law be enacted. Consul Publius Valerius, a solemn and authoritative man, came out of the Senate, and in words that were at times amicable, at times menacing, laid out for the plebeians the untimeliness of their demands and the dangers that these demands brought upon the city. He compelled them to swear that they would stand by their consul, upon which the obedient plebeians retook the Capitol by force. But as Publius Valerius was killed during the

---

65. Livy describes this incident in Book V, chapter 15. See also notes 35 and 60 and chapter 55 on Marcus Furius Camillus.
66. Terentillus, tribune of the plebeians, proposed (c. 460 BCE) the creation of military tribunes with consular power. Livy discusses this incident in Book III, chapter 9.
67. The Sibylline Books contained the prophecies of the Cumaean Sibyl and were kept in the Temple of Jupiter on the Capitoline Hill. They were consulted only when Rome was in a state of emergency.
68. Livy describes this incident in Book III, chapter 15.

attack, Titus Quinctius was immediately made consul again.[69] He did not want the plebeians to have time to catch their breath or turn their minds to Terentillus's law, so he commanded them to march from Rome on a campaign against the Volsci, declaring that the plebeians, by the oath they had sworn to stand by the consul, were now obliged to obey him. The tribunes opposed this, arguing that the oath they had sworn had been to the dead consul and not to him, but Livy shows how the plebeians, through fear of religion, preferred to obey the consul rather than follow the tribunes, and writes the following words in favor of the ancient religion: "The negligence toward the gods that prevails in our time did not yet exist, nor did people put an interpretation on oaths and laws that suited their own practice."[70] The tribunes feared they would lose power, and so formed an allegiance with Consul Titus Quinctius, agreeing that they would obey him and not bring up the Terentillus's law for a year, while both consuls agreed that they would not send the plebeians to war for a year. This was how religion helped the Senate overcome difficulties it could never have overcome on its own.

---

69. Livy mentions Lucius Quinctius, not Titus.
70. Machiavelli quotes Livy (Book III, chapter 20) in Latin: *Nondum haec quae nunc tenet saeculum neglegentia deum uenerat, nec interpretando sibi quisque ius iurandum et leges aptas faciebat.*

IF SOME INCIDENT SHOULD FREE A POPULACE ACCUSTOMED TO LIVING UNDER A PRINCE, THEY WILL BE ABLE TO MAINTAIN THIS FREEDOM ONLY WITH DIFFICULTY

In the annals of ancient history there are countless examples that demonstrate the difficulty a populace that is accustomed to living under a prince have in conserving their freedom should they by some chance obtain it, as the Romans did after the Tarquins were expelled. This difficulty is to be expected, because such a populace is not unlike a wild animal, which might be fierce and feral by nature but has been raised in captivity and servitude. If this animal is released into the open, not used to feeding itself or knowing where to take shelter, it will fall prey to the first man who seeks to chain it up again.

The same thing happens to a populace who are accustomed to living under the government of others without knowing how to reach decisions in matters of public defense or offense. Not understanding the new rulers or being understood by them, this populace quickly end up under a yoke that is often heavier than the one they had managed to shake off. Although their nature is not corrupted, the populace find themselves in this difficulty because a people that is corrupted through and through cannot live in liberty for even a short period, as I shall discuss in the following two chapters. Therefore our discourse will concern peoples in whom corruption has not spread too widely, and in whom there remains more of the good than the corrupted.

Added to this difficulty is that a state which becomes free creates hostile factions, as opposed to factions that are on its side. All those who took advantage of the previous tyrannical state and fed off the wealth of the prince become hostile factions. Having lost the opportunity of partaking of the tyrant's wealth, they cannot live contentedly in the new state, and will try to restore the tyranny so they can regain their power. Nor will this new state acquire friendly supporters, as I have already said, because a free state can offer honors and prizes on only a few honest occasions, beyond which it will offer neither prizes nor honors to anyone. For once a man has secured the honors and benefits he thinks he deserves, he no longer feels obligated to those who rewarded him. Furthermore, the common benefit that results from living in freedom is not recognized by people while they possess it: In other words, being able to enjoy one's possessions freely and without fear, not having to worry about the honor of one's women or sons, or to fear for oneself. In fact, no one will ever admit to owing an obligation to someone who does not harm him.

But, as I have said above, a state that is free and newly created inevitably has hostile factions and not friendly ones. To resolve this problem, and the turmoil created by the difficulties I mentioned above, there is no stronger remedy or one more valid, secure, and vital, than killing the sons of Brutus.[71] These, as history shows, were driven to conspire with other Roman youths against their city for no other reason than that they did not enjoy the same status under the consuls as they had under the kings.[72] In their eyes, the liberty of the people had brought about their own slavery.

Whoever undertakes to govern a multitude, either by means of liberty or by means of a principality, and does not secure himself from those who are hostile to the new order, is creating a state that will be short-lived. In fact, I consider those princes unfortunate who are compelled to secure their state by exceptional means because the populace is their enemy, for he who has as his enemy the few can secure himself easily and without much turmoil, but he who has the whole populace as his enemy can never secure himself. And the more cruelty he em-

71. According to Roman tradition, Lucius Junius Brutus, a legendary figure of the sixth century BCE, ousted the last Tarquin king of Rome in 509, founding the Roman Republic. He condemned his own sons to death when they joined in a conspiracy to restore the Tarquins. See also Book III, chapter 3 above.
72. Livy (Book II, chapter 3) writes: "[The youths] missed their former freedom to do as they pleased, and complained that the liberty others enjoyed had turned into slavery for them."

ploys, the weaker his principality becomes. Hence the best remedy is to seek to make the populace his friend.[73]

My discussion here might deviate from what I have written above, as I am speaking here of princes and there of republics, but I would nevertheless like to mention this matter briefly so that I will not have to return to it again. Should a prince wish to win over a populace hostile to him—I am speaking of princes who have become tyrants of their own cities—he has to weigh what the people desire. He will find that they always want two things: first, to avenge themselves against those who are the cause of their becoming enslaved, and second, to regain their liberty. The first desire the prince can fulfill entirely, the second partially. I can offer a perfect example of how a ruler can fulfill the first desire: Clearchus, the tyrant of Heraclea, was in exile when there was a clash between the people and the nobles of Heraclea.[74] Realizing that they were at a disadvantage, the nobles turned to Clearchus for support and, conspiring with him, put him in power against the will of the people, taking away their liberty. Clearchus, finding himself caught between the arrogance of the nobles, whom he could neither curb nor satisfy, and the anger of the populace, who could not endure having lost their freedom, he decided to free himself from the ballast of the nobles and win over the people in a single stroke. A good opportunity arose and he seized it, massacring all the nobles, to the great satisfaction of the populace. By this means he fulfilled one of the populace's desires, that of vengeance. But as for their second desire—to regain their liberty—the prince, unable to fulfill it, would have to examine the reasons that made them want liberty. Here the prince will find that a small part of the populace desire liberty so they can rule, but that all the rest, who are innumerable, desire liberty only so that they can live securely. In all states, regardless of how they are organized, the ranks of command are never attained by more than forty or fifty citizens. As this is a small number, the prince can easily protect himself, either by

---

73. See *The Prince,* chapter 9: "A prince who obtains a state with the help of the people maintains his position with less difficulty than a prince who acquires it with the help of the nobility, because in the latter case he is surrounded by men who consider themselves his equals and whom he therefore cannot command or govern as he pleases."

74. Clearchus (d. 353 BCE) was tyrant of Heraclea, a Greek city on the Black Sea. Machiavelli closely follows the incidents described by Justin in *Epitome of the Philippic History of Pompeius Trogus* (Book XVI, chapters 4 and 5).

getting rid of these few citizens or by heaping them with so many honors that, depending on their status, they will for the most part be happy. The rest of the citizenry, desiring merely to live securely, can easily be satisfied with institutions and laws that protect both the prince's power and public safety. When a prince does this, and the populace see that he will not break those laws under any circumstances, they will soon enough begin living securely and happily. We have the example of the kingdom of France, which exists securely for no other reason than that its kings are bound by innumerable laws that also ensure the security of all their subjects. The founder of the French state intended these kings to act as they pleased in military and financial matters, but in all other things under their jurisdiction they had to do as the laws specified. The princes or republics that do not secure themselves at the beginning must do so as soon as they can, as the Romans did. The ruler who lets the opportunity slip by will later regret that he did not do what he should have done.

As the Roman populace was not yet corrupted when they regained their liberty after the death of Brutus's sons and the elimination of the Tarquin kings, they managed to maintain it through the means and institutions I have already discussed. Had the Roman populace been corrupted, there would have been no effective way for them to keep their liberty, as I will show in the following chapter.

On how, when corrupt populaces gain their freedom, they will be able to maintain it only with the greatest difficulty

I believe that had the kings of Rome not been eliminated, Rome would very quickly have become worthless and weak. If we consider how corrupt these kings had become, if two or three more generations of their kind had followed, and the corruption within them had begun to spread throughout their branches, once the branches were corrupted, it would have been impossible ever to reform Rome again. But because the head was lost while the body was still whole, the Romans could easily adjust to living in freedom and good order. We must accept as an absolute truth that a corrupt state under a prince will not be able to adjust to liberty, even if the prince and all his offspring are eliminated. In fact, it would be better if one prince ousted another. Without the creation of a new ruler, the state will never be sound if the goodness and skill of a single ruler does not keep it free. But this liberty will last only for the duration of that ruler's life, as was the case in Syracuse with Dion and Timoleon. Their skill kept the state free while they were alive, but after their deaths it reverted to its former tyranny. However, there is no better example than that of Rome, which managed immediately to seize and maintain that liberty once the Tarquins were expelled. But with the deaths of Caesar, Gaius Caligula, and Nero, and the whole of Caesar's line extinguished,[75] Rome could not

---

75. Nero (d. 68 CE) was the fifth Roman emperor and, by adoption, the last descendant of Caesar.

maintain its liberty, let alone lay a foundation for it. Such diverse results came about only because in the era of the Tarquin kings the Roman populace were not yet corrupted, while by the later imperial times they had become quite corrupt. In the early years it was sufficient to make the populace swear that they would never consent to anyone becoming king of Rome. In later years, Brutus's authority and severity, with all his eastern legions, were not enough to make the Romans want to maintain the liberty that he, like the first Brutus,[76] had restored to them. This was the result of the corruption that the factions of Caius Marius had triggered among the people. Caesar, as the leader of these factions, could blind the masses so that they did not see the yoke into which they were slipping their own heads.

This Roman example is the best, but I would nonetheless like to mention examples from our times. I suggest, for instance, that no incident, however momentous or violent, could ever render Milan or Naples free, their natures being so corrupt.[77] This can be seen after Filippo Visconti's death, when Milan strove to regain its liberty but did not know how to maintain it.[78] Hence it was Rome's great fortune that its kings became corrupt quickly, so that they were driven out before their corruption could spread into the bowels of the city. This absence of corruption in the Roman populace was the reason that Rome's infinite clashes and tumults, sparked by men of good intentions, did no harm but were in fact beneficial to the republic.

One can come to the following conclusion: When a city's nature is not corrupted, the clashes and tumults are not harmful, but when it is corrupted, even the soundest laws are of no use unless they are enacted by someone who can ensure with great force that they are observed, so that the state's nature becomes good. I do not know whether this has ever occurred or if it even can occur, because it is clear that a state which has gone into decline through the corruption of its nature can rise again only through the skill of a single ruler who happens to

---

76. Machiavelli is contrasting Lucius Junius Brutus, who led the revolt that overthrew the last king of Rome, with Marcus Junius Brutus, who was one of Caesar's assassins.

77. See chapter 55 below, in which Machiavelli further discusses the corruption of the Kingdom of Naples, the Papal States, the Romagna, and Lombardy.

78. When Filippo Maria Visconti died in 1447, the short-lived Ambrosian Republic of Milan (1447–50) followed. After internal dissension, Francesco Sforza, who had married Visconti's daughter Bianca, took over the city and had himself declared duke.

be alive at the time, and not by the skill of the whole populace supporting the good institutions. But the moment that ruler dies, the state will regress to its original ways, as happened in Thebes, which through the skill of Epaminondas was able, while he was alive, to have the form of a republic and an empire. When Epaminondas died, Thebes returned to its previous disarray.[79] The reason is that no man can live long enough to tame a state that has had bad habits for a long time. One ruler with an exceptionally long life, or two skillful rulers in a row, can restore a state, but the lack of such rulers, as I said above, will ruin it, unless with great danger and much blood they have brought about its rebirth. Hence, such corruption and lack of capacity for maintaining a life of liberty arise from an inequality that exists in such a state. Should one wish to restore equality, it will be necessary to use the most exceptional measures, which few want or know how to use, as I will discuss in greater detail elsewhere.[80]

79. Epaminondas (c. 410–362 BCE) was a Theban statesman and general who ended Spartan dominance over Thebes and the other Greek city-states when he defeated the Spartans at the Battle of Leucra in 371. His Theban empire, or predominance over the other Greek states, lasted only from 371 to 362 BCE, when he was killed in the Battle of Mantineia.

80. See chapter 26 below, in which Machiavelli outlines some of the "exceptional measures" a ruler must take to restore equality: "He must create a new government with new offices that have new names and new powers and are occupied by new men. He must make the rich poor and the poor rich."

ON HOW A FREE GOVERNMENT CAN BE MAINTAINED IN A CORRUPTED STATE IF A FREE GOVERNMENT ALREADY EXISTS, OR, IF IT DOES NOT, HOW IT CAN BE ESTABLISHED

I do not believe it is out of place or at odds with what I have been discussing to consider whether one can maintain a free government in a corrupted state if a free government already exists, or, if it does not, how to establish it. I would like to point out right away that it is extremely difficult to do one or the other. It is almost impossible to lay down a rule on how to proceed, because in such a situation it would be necessary to act according to the extent of the corruption. However, I do not want to pass over this, as it is good to discuss all cases. As an example, I would like to consider a state that is extremely corrupted, though this will make the subject more difficult, because such a state will not have any laws or institutions formidable enough to halt a corruption that is widespread. For just as good customs require good laws so that they can be maintained, laws require good customs in order to be observed. Furthermore, the institutions and laws created in a state at its birth, when men were good, are no longer relevant once men have become evil. Even if laws in a state vary according to circumstances, its institutions rarely, if ever, do. This means that new laws are not enough, because the institutions that remain unchanged will corrupt them.

To clarify this further, I suggest that in Rome there was originally a system of government, or rather of the state, and later, laws, that, in conjunction with magistrates, kept the citizens in check. The system of the state included the power of the populace, the Senate, the tribunes, and the consuls, as well as the method of proposing and appointing magistrates and the method of making laws. During all that occurred in Rome, these institutions changed little, if at all. What did change as citizens became increasingly corrupted were the laws that put a check on them: the adultery law, the sumptuary law, the law against ruthless ambition, and many others.[81] But the institutions of the state remained fixed, unable to counter the corruption, while the laws that were being redrawn did not suffice to keep men good. And yet such laws would have been quite useful if the institutions of the state had been changed along with them.

That it is true that such institutions in a corrupted state would not be good can be clearly seen in two principal matters: the creating of magistrates and the making of laws. The Roman populace accorded the consulship and the other foremost positions of the city only to men who sought these positions. This system was good in the beginning, because those who wanted these positions were citizens who judged themselves worthy, and to be rejected would have been a disgrace. Hence, in order to be judged worthy, they comported themselves well. Later, in the corrupted city, this system became extremely destructive, for it was no longer the men with the greatest skill who stood as candidates for the magistrature, but those with the most power, while men without power, though skillful, declined to stand out of fear.

Rome did not reach this dire condition all at once, but by degrees, as all dire conditions are reached. Once the Romans had subjugated Africa and Asia and had reduced almost all of Greece to their rule, they became complacent about their liberty and did not feel that they had any enemies left whom they needed to fear. This sense of security, and the weakness of their enemies, made the Roman populace value popularity over ability when selecting their consuls, electing those who were best at amusing the populace and not those best at conquering the enemy. Then the Romans slipped even further, not giving the office to men who were popular but to men with the most power. The

---

81. The *Lex Iulia de adulteriis coercendis* (18 BCE) made conjugal unfaithfulness a public and private offense; various sumptuary laws were passed to prevent general extravagance in the private expenses of citizens, such as inordinate expenditure for banquets and clothes; the *Lex Cornelia de ambitu* proscribed the purchasing of votes or public offices.

faultiness of this system resulted in worthy men being entirely excluded from office. A tribune or any other citizen could propose a law, and every citizen could debate either in favor or against it before the law was put in effect. This system worked when the citizens were good, because it has always been proper for anyone who thinks something is for the common benefit to propose it. And it is right that everyone can speak his mind so that the populace, having heard all sides, can then choose what is best. But once the citizens had become corrupt, this system became very bad indeed, because only those with power proposed laws, and the laws they proposed were not for the common good but for their own power. Out of fear of the powerful, nobody could speak up against this, so that the populace ended up being either deceived or forced into choosing their own ruin.

If Rome was to remain free amid the corruption, it was therefore necessary for it to create new institutions, just as it had created new laws throughout its history, because when a populace is corrupt, institutions and ways of living must be organized differently than when a populace is good. There cannot be the same form in matter that is completely different. These institutions must be reformed either in a single stroke the moment it is clear that they are no longer good, or little by little before everyone realizes they are no longer good. But I maintain that both these options are practically impossible to execute. If one wants to reform the institutions little by little, then the reformer must be someone extremely prudent, who can see the nascent problems from a distance as they begin to emerge. Such a man might never appear during the entire existence of a state, and even if he does, he might not be able to persuade the other citizens of what he himself can discern. Men used to living in a certain way do not wish to change, especially if they cannot actually see the evil for themselves, but need to have it explained to them with theories and conjectures. As for changing the state's institutions all at once, when everyone can clearly see that they are not good, I propose that a problem, once it is clearly visible, is difficult to set right again. It will not be enough to use ordinary means, as ordinary means will have become corrupt. Exceptional means such as violence and arms will be necessary, and the legislator will have to strive to become the prince of that state so that he will be able to set it up as he wishes. Rearranging a state in order to make it a vital civic system presupposes a good man, while becoming a prince through violent means presupposes a bad man. Therefore it is quite rare that a good man will want to become a prince through evil means even if his aims are good, or that an evil man, once he has become a prince, would want to do good or would ever consider using beneficially the authority he has acquired in such an evil way.

The difficulty or the impossibility of a corrupt state's creating or maintaining a republic arises from all the things I have mentioned above. Such a state would have to be shaped more as a monarchy than a democracy, so that arrogant men who cannot be controlled by the laws would in one way or another be held in check by an authority that is almost regal. Attempting to make them good by other means would be either an extremely cruel undertaking or entirely impossible. I have already cited the example of Cleomenes. He murdered the ephors in order to rule alone, just as Romulus killed his brother and Titus Tatius for the same reason.[82] After these deeds, Cleomenes and Romulus made good use of the power they gained, but we must nevertheless remember that neither of them had subjects tainted by the corruption we have been discussing in this chapter. Therefore they could set their goal and achieve it.

---

82. See chapter 9 above, in which Machiavelli describes Cleomenes's tactics in detail, and discusses Romulus's murder of his brother and the death of his co-ruler, Titus Tatius. In that chapter, however, Machiavelli does not state that Romulus murdered Titus Tatius, but only that he "consented to the death of Titus Tatius."

CHAPTER TWENTY-FOUR

STATES THAT ARE WELL ORGANIZED INTRODUCE REWARDS AND PUNISHMENTS FOR THEIR CITIZENS, BUT NEVER LET THE GOOD DEEDS EXCUSE THE BAD

Horatius's merit was great, as evidenced by his skill in defeating the Curiatii. But as he killed his sister, his sin was atrocious, and the murder so infuriated the Romans that they wanted to condemn him to death despite his merit having been so great and so recently demonstrated.[83] Whoever considers this matter cursorily might regard it as an example of the ingratitude of the populace. But if one examines the matter more closely and gives some thought to the institutions that a state must have, one will sooner blame the populace for ultimately absolving Horatius than for having wanted to condemn him for his deed. The reason is that no state that is properly set up will ever allow a citizen's merits to cancel out his demerits. A state ensures rewards for a good deed and punishment for a bad one. In other words, having rewarded a man for having done something good, the state must also punish him if he acts badly, and this without regard for any past good deeds. If this system is observed, a city will live in freedom for a long time; otherwise, it will rapidly come to ruin. Citizens who have committed a notable deed for the state are given the status that this deed brings them, but if they then become overweening and confident that

---

83. In Roman legend, there were two sets of warring triplet brothers, the Roman Horatii and the Alban Curiatii. After two of the Horatii triplets were killed, the third—the Horatius whom Machiavelli mentions—killed the Curiatii triplets single-handedly. His sister, who was betrothed to one of the Curiatii, could not conceal her grief and was killed by Horatius.

they can commit bad deeds without fear of punishment, they will soon become so insolent that every form of civil life will disappear.

If one wishes to punish evil deeds it is also necessary to offer rewards for good deeds, as we have seen was the case in Rome. Even if a state is poor and can give only a little, it must not abstain from doing so, because any small gift given to reward a good deed, regardless of how great the deed might be, will be esteemed by him who receives it as an honorable and great reward. The story of Horatius Cocles is well known, as is that of Mucius Scaevola: The first held off the enemy at a bridge until the bridge was destroyed, the other burned his hand for failing to kill Porsenna, the King of the Etruscans. The public gave each of these men a plot of land for their deeds.[84] The story of Manlius Capitolinus is also noteworthy:[85] He saved the Capitol from the Gauls who were besieging it, and was given as a reward a small measure of flour by his fellow citizens, who were besieged alongside him. This was a great reward if one considers the ill fortune that had befallen Rome.[86] And yet when Manlius, moved either by envy or his evil nature to stir up sedition in Rome, tried to rouse the populace in dissension, he was cast down from the same Capitol that he had saved with so much glory, without regard for his past merits.

---

84. Machiavelli writes *due staiora*, two bushels, meaning the amount of land that can be sown with two bushels of grain.

85. See chapter 8 above, in which Machiavelli discusses Manlius Capitolinus's envy of Marcus Furius Camillus and Manlius's subsequent sedition.

86. Livy writes in Book V, chapter 47: "Each brought half a pound of grain and a dram of wine to his quarters, which had been set up in the fortress. It does not sound like much, but the scarcity made it a prodigious evidence of their affection."

CHAPTER TWENTY-FIVE

ON HOW A RULER WHO WANTS TO REFORM AN OLD SYSTEM OF GOVERNMENT IN A FREE STATE MUST KEEP AT LEAST A VENEER OF THE OLDER INSTITUTIONS

A ruler who desires to reform the government of a state and wants the government to be accepted and maintained to the satisfaction of everyone will have to keep at least a veneer of the old ways, so that it will not seem to the populace that the institutions have changed, even if the new institutions are completely different from the old ones. Men cherish something that seems like the real thing as much as they do the real thing itself. In fact, they are often more affected by that which seems than by that which is.[87] When they achieved liberty at the beginning of the republic, the Romans knew that in creating two consuls instead of one king, they would not want them to have more than twelve lictors,[88] so that they would not surpass the number that had ministered to the king. There was also an annual sacrifice in Rome that had been offered only by the king, and since the state did not want the people, for want of a king, to lack any of the old practices, they created a "king" of the sacrifice, and made him subordinate to the high priest.[89]

87. See also *The Prince*, chapter 18: "Though a prince need not have all the good qualities that I have mentioned, it is most necessary for him to appear to have them."
88. Functionaries who walked before the consuls when they appeared in public, carrying the fasces, a bundle of rods bound together around an ax as an emblem of authority.
89. Livy writes in Book II, chapter 2: "Certain public rites had always been performed by the kings in person, and so that the lack of a king be nowhere regretted, a 'King of Sacrifices' was created. This office was made subordinate to the high priest, lest the combination of office and name threaten the people's liberty, which at that time was a leading fear."

In this way the populace was satisfied by the sacrifice, and never had a reason, through its absence, to desire the return of the kings. This path must be followed by all who wish to eliminate an old way of life in a state and introduce a new and free way of life: because as new things change men's minds, one must do one's utmost to keep as much of the old as possible. If new magistrates differ in number, authority, and duration of office from the old ones, they should at least retain the titles that they had. This, as I have said, must be done by a legislator who wishes to set up a vital civic system, either by way of a republic or kingdom. But he who wishes to create a despotism, which the ancient authors called "tyranny," will have to make everything new, as I will discuss in the following chapter.

ON HOW A NEW PRINCE MUST MAKE EVERYTHING NEW IN A CITY OR STATE HE HAS TAKEN

A man who becomes the ruler of a city or state and does not follow the path of a monarchy or republic in establishing a civic life will find that, as a new ruler, the best way to keep this city or state is to make everything in it new. This is even more advisable when his footing is weak. In other words, he must create a new government with new offices that have new names and new powers and are occupied by new men. He must make the rich poor and the poor rich, as David did when he became king: "He has filled the hungry with good things and sent the rich away empty."[90] Furthermore, he must build new cities and demolish those already built, move inhabitants from one place to another, and not leave a single thing intact in all the land. There must be no rank, institution, government, or wealth of which the owner does not acknowledge that it comes from the prince. The prince must take as his model Philip of Macedon, the father of Alexander the Great, who by these methods turned himself from a small king into the King of Greece. Justinius, writing about Philip, says that he moved men from province to province the way shepherds move their flocks.[91] These

90. Machiavelli quotes the Bible, Luke 1:53, in Latin: *Esurientes implevit bonis et divites dimisit inanes.*
91. In *Epitome of the Philippic History of Pompeius Trogus*, Justin writes (Book VIII, chapter 5): "Just as shepherds drive their flocks at times into winter pastures, at times into summer pastures, so he transplanted people and cities from one place to another."

methods are very cruel and hostile to every way of life, not only the Christian, and a ruler should avoid them and prefer to live as a private citizen rather than as a king who unleashes so much ruin on people. Nevertheless, if he wishes to remain in power, a prince who does not want to choose the good course must choose the course of evil. Men, however, usually take a middle course that is most destructive, because they do not know how to be entirely good or entirely bad, as I will discuss in the following chapter.

CHAPTER TWENTY-SEVEN

ON THE RARITY OF MAN BEING ENTIRELY

GOOD OR ENTIRELY BAD

When Pope Julius II went to Bologna in 1505 in order to drive out the Bentivogli,[92] who had been princes in that city for a hundred years, he also wanted to remove Giampaolo Baglioni from Perugia, of which he was tyrant, as the pope conspired against all the tyrants who were occupying the lands of the Church. Arriving before Perugia with that spirit and intent known to all, he did not wait to enter the city with his army that would have protected him, but entered unarmed, even though Giampaolo was inside with the many men he had gathered to defend him. Thus the pope, escorted only by his personal entourage, and driven by the rage with which he conducted all his affairs, put himself in the hands of his enemy Giampaolo, who then meekly followed him out of the city, leaving behind a governor who would do justice in the name of the Church. The prudent men who attended the pope commented on the pope's recklessness and Giampaolo's cowardice,[93] nor could they understand why Giampaolo had not, to his everlasting fame, crushed his enemy the pope and enriched himself with plunder, since all the cardinals in the pope's entourage carried much wealth with them. Nor could they believe that he had refrained

---

92. Giovanni Bentivoglio (1443–1508) had been Gonfalonier of Bologna until Pope Paul II made him chief senator for life in 1466. Pope Julius II, however, excommunicated and ousted him from Bologna in 1506.

93. Machiavelli was in Pope Julius II's retinue at Perugia.

out of goodness or conscience: There could hardly have been any pious respect in the heart of a ruthless man who kept his sister as mistress and who had killed his cousins and nephews in order to rule.[94] So the consensus was that men often do not know how to be perfectly good or honorably evil, and when an evil deed has grandeur or is in some part generous, a man will often not know how to carry it off.

Thus Giampaolo, who was unconcerned about committing incest and ostentatiously murdering his family, did not know how, or to put it better, did not dare, when the perfect opportunity presented itself, to pull off a feat for which everyone would have admired him, making a name for himself to all eternity for being the first to show the prelates how little those who live and rule as they do should be esteemed. The greatness of this feat would have surpassed any infamy or danger that could have sprung from it.

94. Giampaolo Baglioni (c. 1470–1520). In 1500, when his uncle Guido Baglioni was ruler of Perugia, Giampaolo's cousins Carlo and Grifonetto attempted to seize power by assassinating all the other members of the family. Giampaolo violently suppressed their attempt and seized power himself.

CHAPTER TWENTY-NINE

ON WHO IS MORE UNGRATEFUL,
A POPULACE OR A PRINCE

It seems to me relevant to our subject to examine who has shown greater instances of ingratitude, a populace or a prince. So that we can weigh this question more effectively, I would like to suggest that the vice of ingratitude is sparked by either avarice or suspicion. If a populace or a prince has sent a general on an important campaign through which he will attain much glory if he is victorious, the prince or populace must reward the general when he returns. But if instead, when the general returns, he is dishonored or harmed and not given the reward he deserves out of parsimony or greed, then this is an unforgivable error that carries with it everlasting infamy. Yet many princes have committed this error, and Tacitus gives us the reason in the line: "Man is much more inclined to requite wrongs than reward any benefit done to him, because gratitude is burdensome, while revenge seems to offer gain."[95] But when the reason that a prince or populace does not reward the victorious general but harms him is not parsimony, but suspicion, the prince or the populace can be excused. One reads much about this kind of ingratitude. It happens because the general, who with exceptional skill and prowess has acquired an empire for his prince—conquering his enemies, and covering himself with glory and his sol-

95. Machiavelli quotes Tacitus, *Histories,* Book IV, chapter 3, in Latin: *Tanto proclivius est iniuriae quam beneficio vicem exolvere, quia gratia oneri, ultio in quaestu habetur.*

178 · *The Essential Writings of Machiavelli*

diers with riches—will unavoidably gain so much standing with his soldiers, his enemies, and even the prince's citizens that the general's victory cannot augur well for the prince who sent him. Because man's nature is ruthless and suspicious, and will not set limits to its aspirations, it is inevitable that the suspicion immediately sparked in a prince after his general's victory will be triggered by some arrogant action or remark of the general. Consequently, the prince cannot think of anything but how to secure himself against the general, and to do this will consider killing him or taking away the standing and reputation he has gained with the army or populace, demonstrating that this victory was the result not of the general's skill and courage but of Fortune, the cowardice of the enemy, or the judicious tactics of the other commanders involved in the battle.

When Vespasian was in Judea his troops declared him emperor.[96] Antonius Primus, who was leading another army in Illyria,[97] formed an allegiance with him and marched on Italy against the Emperor Vitellus, who was reigning in Rome. With great skill Antonius Primus destroyed two of Vitellus's armies and occupied Rome, so that when Mucianus, who had been sent by Vespasian, arrived in Rome, he found that Antonius had skillfully seen to everything and that every difficulty had been overcome. Yet Antonius's reward was that Mucianus immediately stripped him of command of the army, and little by little took away any authority he had in Rome. Antonius turned to Vespasian, who was still in Asia, but he stripped Antonius of all military rank, and Antonius later died in quite desperate circumstances. The histories are filled with such examples. In our own times we all know with what skill and application Gonsalvo Ferrante fought in the Kingdom of Naples for King Ferdinand of Aragon against the French. Gonsalvo Ferrante was victorious over the French and conquered Naples, but the reward for his victory was that King Ferdinand immediately came to Naples, stripped him of his command, took from him his fortresses, and then brought him back to Spain, where he soon died in obscurity.

This suspicion in princes is so natural that they cannot avoid it, which makes it impossible for them to show gratitude to a general who

96. Vespasian was Roman emperor from 69 to 79 CE. Tacitus, in *Histories*, Book II, describes his rise from humble origins to the throne.

97. According to Tacitus (Book II, chapter 86), Antonius was not in Illyria, but in Pannonia.

has been victorious and has made great acquisitions under their flags. If a prince cannot avoid this, it is no miracle that a populace cannot either, because if a state living in freedom has two goals—one to acquire territory, the other to remain free—it stands to reason that it will err from excessive zeal in achieving either of these goals. Regarding the errors that a state makes in its attempts to acquire territory, I shall discuss those at an appropriate point.[98] As for the errors it makes to secure its freedom, there are, among others, harming the citizens it ought to reward, and suspecting those it should trust. In a republic that has become corrupted, these methods are a cause of great evil, and many times such a republic is quick to turn into a tyranny, as happened in Rome with Caesar, who seized by force what ingratitude had denied him. Nevertheless, in a republic that is not corrupted, these methods are the cause of much good: They ensure that the republic stays free, since men, out of fear of punishment, tend to remain good and less ambitious for power. It is true that, for the reasons I have discussed above, Rome proved the least ungrateful among all the peoples who ever had an empire. It can be said that the only example of Rome's ingratitude was that to Scipio, because Coriolanus and Camillus were exiled on account of their offenses against the plebeians.[99] Coriolanus was never forgiven, because he had always been hostile toward the populace, while Camillus was not only called back from exile, but subsequently venerated for the rest of his life as if he were a prince. The ingratitude shown Scipio, however, arose from suspicion that the citizens began to have of him such as they had never had of others. This was because of the greatness of the enemy whom Scipio had defeated,[100] the standing that a victory after such a long and perilous war had secured him, the speed of this victory, and the favors that his youth, prudence, and other memorable qualities had acquired for him. These were so many factors that even the Roman magistrates were afraid of his power, which displeased wise men as a thing unheard of in Rome. Scipio's position seemed so extraordinary that Cato the Elder, who was known for his saintly temperament, was the first to attack him, maintaining that a state could not call itself free if one of its citizens was feared by the magistrates. Had the people of Rome followed

---

98. In the following chapter.
99. For Coriolanus, see chapter 7 above; for Camillus, chapter 8 above.
100. The enemy was Hannibal.

Cato's opinion in this case, they would have deserved the excuse that I offered above for those princes and populaces that are ungrateful out of suspicion. Concluding this discourse, I would like to emphasize once more that the vice of ingratitude occurs either from parsimony or suspicion. But we will find that a populace never shows ingratitude out of parsimony, and they are less inclined than are princes to show ingratitude out of suspicion, since a populace has less reason to be suspicious, as I will discuss below.

CHAPTER THIRTY

ON THE MEANS A PRINCE OR REPUBLIC MUST EMPLOY TO AVOID THE VICE OF INGRATITUDE, AND ON WHAT A GENERAL OR CITIZEN MUST DO NOT TO FALL VICTIM TO IT

To escape the need of living in constant suspicion or being ungrateful, a prince must himself go out on military expeditions, as the Roman emperors initially did and as the Turk does in our times.[101] This is what skillful princes have done and still do, because when the prince is victorious, the glory and the conquest is entirely his. But if he is not there the glory belongs to another, and the prince feels he cannot profit from the conquest if he does not extinguish the general's glory, a glory which the prince did not know how to gain for himself. Such princes become ungrateful and unjust, and without doubt they lose more than they gain. If through negligence or lack of prudence the prince remains idly at home and sends a general to war, the only course of action I could suggest to the prince is the one he would be following anyway. But as the general will not be able to escape the sting of the prince's ingratitude, I would advise the general to do one of two things: Either leave the army immediately after his victory and put himself in the hands of his prince, being careful not to commit any insolent or ambitious act, so that the prince has no reason to suspect

101. Machiavelli is referring to the Ottoman sultans, who in the sixteenth century still led their armies into battle. See *The Prince*, chapter 14, in which Machiavelli argues in the opening line that a prince must "have no other thought or objective, nor dedicate himself to any other art, but that of war with its rules and discipline, because this is the only art suitable for a man who commands."

him and every reason to reward him, or at least not harm him; or, if this does not seem the prudent thing to do, energetically take the opposite course, and consider all the means by which he can make what he acquired in battle his own, and not his prince's. He must secure the goodwill of soldier and subject, forge new alliances with neighbors, occupy the fortresses with his men, bribe the commanders of his army, and take measures against those he cannot bribe. By these means he must punish his prince for the ingratitude the prince would otherwise show him. There are no other alternatives, but, as I have mentioned previously, men do not know how to be entirely evil or entirely good.[102] And it is always the case that immediately after a victory, generals do not want to leave their armies, cannot show modesty, and do not know how to adopt means that are violent and create respect. Indecisive at this crucial moment, trapped by their own indecision and uncertainty, they are crushed.

A republic that wants to avoid the vice of ingratitude cannot use the same remedy as the prince—go to battle itself and not send someone else—as it is obliged to send one of its citizens. It is fitting, however, for me to suggest that the republic adopt the same solution the Roman Republic did, in other words, that of being less ungrateful than other republics. Rome's solution arose from its system of government. As the entire city was involved in war—nobles and commoners alike—there existed in Rome throughout its history so many exceptional men crowned by numerous victories that the populace had no reason to doubt any of them; since there were many exceptional men, they checked one another. Moreover, these men remained loyal and careful not to show even a shadow of ruthless ambition or other reason for the populace to harm them, so that when these men were elected dictator, they gained the more glory the sooner they accomplished their duties and stepped down.[103] As this conduct could not cause suspicion, it did not generate ingratitude either. Hence, a republic that does not wish to have reason to be ungrateful must act as Rome did, and a citizen who wishes to escape the sting of ingratitude must observe the limits observed by the Roman citizens.

102. See chapter 27 above, "On the Rarity of Man Being Entirely Good or Entirely Bad."
103. The Roman dictator was a chief magistrate with absolute power, elected in periods of emergency for up to six months. Livy gives examples throughout his *Histories* of dictators who within a few days resolved emergency situations and ended their dictatorship.

CHAPTER THIRTY-TWO

ON HOW A REPUBLIC OR PRINCIPALITY MUST NOT WAIT FOR DIFFICULT TIMES TO OFFER BENEFITS TO ITS POPULACE

Rome was successful in its generosity to its populace, and overcame the danger when Porsena invaded Rome to restore the Tarquin kings to power.[104] And yet the Senate, uncertain whether the populace might not prefer living under the kings to living through a war, lifted the tax on salt and all other duties, declaring that the poor were doing enough for the public good by feeding their children. It was for these benefits that the Roman populace was prepared to bear a siege, hunger, and war. But no ruler should rely on this example and wait for dangerous times in order to win over the populace, because he will never manage to do what the Romans did. In the eyes of the populace, it will not be that ruler who grants them their new benefits, but his enemy, and they will have every reason to fear that once the adversity has passed, their ruler will take back what he was forced to give. Consequently, the populace will not feel bound to him in any way. The reason the Senate's action turned out well was that the Roman Republic was new and not yet stable, and the populace had seen laws being made that benefited them in times of peace, such as the right of appeal. They could be per-

---

104. Livy (Book II, chapters 8 and 9) describes how the Etruscan king Porsena unsuccessfully attempted to regain the throne for the last king of Rome, also an Etruscan. "The Tarquin king had now fled for refuge to Lars Porsena, king of Clusium, [who] considered that Rome should have a king, and one of an Etruscan line, and so marched upon Rome with his army." Throughout this chapter, Machiavelli closely paraphrases Livy's text.

suaded, therefore, that the assistance granted them during Rome's adversity had been granted more because of the Senate's disposition to benefit them than because of the advent of the enemy. Furthermore, the memory of the kings who had oppressed them in many ways was still fresh. But such circumstances are rare, and it is also rare for such policies to work. A state, whether it is a republic or a principality, must try to foresee what adversity might befall it and which men it might need in such times, and then treat these men in a fitting way. A state which acts otherwise, whether a principality or a republic—but particularly a principality—and then believes that during perilous times it can win back the populace with benefits is deceiving itself. Not only will such a state not win over the populace, but it will bring about its own ruin.

CHAPTER THIRTY-THREE

WHEN A PROBLEM WITHIN A STATE OR AGAINST A STATE HAS GROWN, IT IS BETTER TO BIDE ONE'S TIME THAN TO TACKLE IT WITH FULL FORCE

As the Roman Republic grew in reputation, strength, and dominion, its neighbors, who at first had not foreseen how much harm the new republic might do them, recognized their error too late. They wanted to remedy what they had not remedied from the start, and so forged an alliance of some forty peoples against Rome.[105] As a result, the Romans created the institution of dictator, along with the other measures they usually resorted to in times of grave danger, giving full power to a single man who could reach decisions without consulting anyone, and implement these decisions without anyone's having the right of appeal. This solution, which was useful at the time, and the reason the Romans prevailed over the dangers I have just mentioned, invariably proved most useful in the problems which the Roman Republic encountered as it expanded its domains.

But first we must discuss how, when a problem arises within a state or against it, whether triggered by internal or external causes, and becomes so grave that it begins to alarm everyone, it is a far more secure course of action to bide one's time than to try to eliminate it. Those who try to eliminate the problem in fact increase it, and so amplify the evil that was expected. Such problems in a state are more often

---

105. Livy (Book II, chapter 18) writes that "some thirty Latin peoples were conspiring against Rome."

brought about by internal causes than external ones, such as when a citizen is allowed to gain more power than is reasonable, or a law that is at the root of the free state begins to be corrupted, and these errors have been allowed to grow to an extent that makes it more harmful to attempt a remedy than to let them continue. In fact, it is more difficult to recognize these problems when they arise, since man tends to favor the introduction of new enterprises, and will usually prefer enterprises that have mettle and are advanced by young men. If, for instance, a young nobleman of unusual skill emerges in a state, the eyes of all citizens turn toward him as they rush blindly to honor him. And if he has even a grain of ruthless ambition, the combination of these circumstances and the favors nature has granted him quickly enables him to attain such a position that by the time the citizens recognize their error, they have recourse to only a few remedies and, in attempting to use them, they in fact increase his power.

One could cite many examples, but I would like to limit myself to one from Florence. Cosimo de' Medici,[106] to whom the House of Medici owed its rise to power in our city, achieved such standing through his prudence and the ignorance of the Florentines that the government began to fear him. The Florentines judged it dangerous to attack him, but even more dangerous to leave him as he was. Niccolò da Uzzano, a contemporary who was considered an expert in civic affairs, made the first error in not perceiving the dangers that could arise from Cosimo de' Medici's growing power. But throughout his life Niccolò da Uzzano was resolved not to permit the Florentines to commit the second error, in other words to attempt to eliminate Cosimo, as he deemed that this would lead to the destruction of the state. After his death, da Uzzano was in fact proved right, because the Florentines did not follow his advice and joined forces against Cosimo, chasing him from Florence. As a result, Cosimo de' Medici's faction, resenting this action, managed to bring him back soon after and made him the prince of the state, a rank he could never have attained without this manifest opposition.[107] The same thing happened in Rome with Caesar, whose skill and prowess assured him the favor of Pompey and others. But this favor soon turned to fear, as Cicero testified when he said that Pompey

106. Cosimo de' Medici (1389–1464) was the founder of the Medici dynasty.
107. Cosimo de' Medici had been exiled from Florence in 1433, and returned as its ruler exactly one year later.

had begun to fear Caesar too late.[108] This fear made Pompey's faction seek solutions, but these solutions hastened the fall of the Roman Republic.

Consequently, I would like to suggest that since it is difficult to recognize these evils when they arise, a difficulty caused by their deceptiveness in their early stages, it is a far wiser course once they are recognized to bide one's time than to fight them. If one bides his time, they will either fade on their own, or at least be postponed to some time in the future. Princes who plan on eliminating these difficulties, or forcefully countering them, must keep their eyes open so as not to exacerbate the evil instead of diminishing it, under the impression that they are pushing it away by dragging it behind them, as one might drown a plant by overwatering it. The power of the disease must be carefully gauged, and if you see yourself capable of curing it, you must apply yourself with determination. Otherwise, you must let the disease run its course and not try in any way to intervene, because you will suffer the fate of Rome's neighbors I mentioned above: Once Rome had become very powerful, it would have been a better tactic to attempt to placate it by peaceful means, and so keep it in check, than forcing it through war to invent new institutions and new defenses. The only thing that the scheme of Rome's neighbors accomplished was to make the Romans more united and more courageous, and to invent new means by which the Romans could increase their power in the shortest possible time. Among these new means was the creation of the institution of dictator, through which Rome overcame the immediate danger and averted the infinite evils that the Roman Republic would have incurred without this remedy.

108. Machiavelli is quoting from Cicero's letter to Tiro (Cicero, *Letters*, XVI, 11).

CHAPTER THIRTY-FOUR

ON HOW THE POWER OF THE DICTATORS DID NOT HARM THE ROMAN REPUBLIC BUT BENEFITED IT, AND ON HOW THE POWER A CITIZEN SEIZES FOR HIMSELF, UNLIKE THAT ACCORDED TO HIM BY FREE ELECTION, IS DESTRUCTIVE TO CIVIC LIFE

Some historians condemn those Romans who created the institution of dictator, maintaining that it was this that eventually brought about tyranny in Rome. They allege that the first tyrant ruled the city under the title of dictator, and that had this title not existed, Caesar would not have been able to disguise his tyranny beneath an official designation. Those holding this opinion, however, have not examined it carefully. It has been believed without good reason, because it was not the title or rank of dictator that enslaved Rome, but the power that the dictator seized from the citizens for the duration of his office. If the title of dictator had not existed in Rome, another would have been chosen, because power easily acquires a title, while titles do not easily acquire power. It is clear that the office of dictator, when it was bestowed in keeping with the public institutions and not seized by one man's authority, always benefited the city. Republics are harmed when magistrates are created and granted power by exceptional and not ordinary means as was the case in Rome, when over such a long period of time no dictator did anything but good for the republic.

There are very clear reasons for this. First, for a citizen to do harm and seize illegal power for himself, he must have many faculties which he could not have developed in an uncorrupted state. He would have to be extremely rich and have many adherents and followers, which he could not have in a state where the laws are observed, and even if he did have followers and adherents, such a man would have been so dreaded that free votes would not have been given to him. Moreover, a dictator was elected for a brief period of time, not forever, and only to handle the emergency for which he was elected.[109] He had the authority to decide on his own what measures needed to be taken to counter urgent danger, and he could do this without consultation, punishing any individual without right of appeal. But the dictator could not take any action that would diminish the power of the state, such as removing authority from the Senate and the people, or eliminating old institutions and establishing new ones. Hence, if one takes into account a dictator's brief term of office and the limits on his power, and that the populace of Rome was not corrupted, it was impossible for the dictator to transcend the limits of his office and harm the city. And history has shown that the dictatorship was always useful.

In fact, among all Roman institutions, that of dictator deserves to be esteemed and numbered among those that led to the greatness and power of Rome. Without such an institution, a state has difficulty emerging from extraordinary circumstances. The usual institutions of a state move slowly, since no council or magistrate can run everything but will need to confer with others. This takes time, which makes this course of action perilous when it is a matter that cannot wait. Therefore states need to create an institution similar to that of the Venetian Republic, which is an excellent republic of our times. It has given authority to a few chosen citizens to deliberate on urgent matters without the need to consult others if they are all in agreement.[110] If such a system is lacking in a state, it will either come to ruin as it clings to its laws or, in order to escape ruin, breaks them. And in a state it is bad for anything to take place that forces it to be governed by exceptional means, because even if the exceptional means are beneficial for a time, the example nevertheless causes harm. It sets a precedent for contravening the state's laws for a good purpose, and later, under the same pretext, the laws might be contravened for bad. Thus there never was a perfect state that did not make provisions for everything in its laws, and set up remedies for every circumstance. In conclusion, I sug-

109. Roman dictators were elected for a maximum period of six months.
110. The Council of Ten, established in 1310, watched over the security of the Venetian state.

gest that those states that have no recourse to a dictator or a similar authority when in urgent danger inevitably come to ruin.

It is to be noted with what foresight the Romans set up the method of electing a dictator. The creation of a dictator brought some shame on the consuls: They were the heads of state but, after the election of a dictator, would have to obey him like everyone else. The founders of the dictatorship, foreseeing that this would cause the citizens to disdain the consuls, decided that the power to elect a dictator should remain with the consuls, the idea being that when a dire circumstance beset Rome and a monarchical authority was necessary, the consuls would willingly appoint a dictator. If they made the appointment, their own loss of authority would pain them less, because any harm that man does to himself voluntarily and by his own choice ultimately hurts less than harm done to him by others. In later years, however, the Romans gave dictatorial authority to the consul and not to a dictator with the words: "Let the consul see to it that no harm befalls the Republic."[111]

But to return to our subject, I conclude that Rome's neighbors, by trying to suppress Rome, forced the city to create institutions that would not only be suited to its defense, but also give it the ability to counterattack with greater cohesion, force, and power.

---

111. Machiavelli quotes from Livy (Book III, chapter 4) in Latin: *Videat consul, ne respublica quid detrimenti capiat.*

• • •

CHAPTER THIRTY-EIGHT

ON HOW WEAK STATES ARE INDECISIVE AND CANNOT REACH DECISIONS, AND HOW WHEN THEY DO IT IS USUALLY BECAUSE THEY HAVE BEEN FORCED TO, NOT BECAUSE THEY HAVE CHOSEN TO DO SO

There was a severe outbreak of pestilence in Rome, and the Volsci and the Aequi took the opportunity to mount an attack.[112] They assembled a large army and assailed Rome's Latin and Hernici provinces, ravaging their lands and forcing them to call the Romans to their defense. Rome was afflicted by the plague, and so replied that it would allow these provinces to defend themselves with their own forces, as it was unable to defend them.

This is an example of the wisdom and generosity of the Roman Senate, how it always strove in good and bad times to be the arbiter of decisions concerning its subject provinces. Nor was it ashamed, when necessity demanded, of ruling in a way contrary to custom. I say this because on other occasions the same Senate had forbidden the Latins and the Hernici to arm and defend themselves.[113] A less prudent senate might have considered that it was jeopardizing its standing by allowing its provinces to provide their own defense, but the Roman Senate always judged things as they ought to be judged, invariably choosing the least bad alternative as the best. For reasons I have already mentioned, and for many others that are obvious, the Senate was

112. Livy describes the plague and Rome's inability to help her allies in Book III, chapters 6–8.
113. Livy in Book II, chapter 30, mentions that when the Aequi attacked Latium, the Roman Senate felt it was "safer to have unarmed Latins defended by Romans than to allow them to rearm."

aware how bad it was for Rome not to be able to defend its subjects, and allowing them to arm themselves on their own. But the Senate was also aware that the provinces had no choice, since the enemy was at their gates. So the Senate took the honorable course in deciding that the provinces should do what they had to do with Rome's consent. If they now had to disobey out of necessity, they would not later disobey out of choice. Though this might appear to be a resolution any state would take, states that are weak and badly advised are not able to, nor do they know how to manage similar extraordinary circumstances. Cesare Borgia, for instance, had taken Faenza and forced Bologna to accept his terms. He then wanted to return to Rome by way of Tuscany, and sent word to Florence to request that he and his army be granted passage. The Florentines consulted on how to handle the matter, but nobody proposed that his request be granted: The Florentines did not follow the Roman practice. As Cesare Borgia was heavily armed, and the Florentines were not well armed enough to forbid him passage, it would have been a more honorable course of action for them to be perceived as allowing him passage of their own free will rather than being forced to do so. What ensued was Florence's utter disgrace, though it would have been only a minor matter had they acted differently. The worst attribute of weak states is their irresolution, so that all the decisions they ultimately make are made by force. If they come to any good decisions it is because they are forced to, not because they do so out of their own wisdom.

I would like to give two more examples of this, concerning the government of our city of Florence, that have taken place in our times. In 1500, after King Louis XII of France had retaken Milan, he wanted to give Pisa back to Florence for the fifty thousand ducats that the Florentines had promised him for such a restitution. He sent his army to Pisa under the command of Monsignor de Beaumont, who, though a Frenchman, was a man the Florentines trusted. Commander and army marched to the area between Cascina and Pisa in order to attack the city walls, but during the few days in which they were preparing the siege, Pisan emissaries came to Beaumont and offered to hand Pisa over to the French army on condition that King Louis would pledge not to deliver the city to the Florentines before a period of four months had passed. The Florentines spurned this proposal, with the result that they marched against Pisa only to march away again in disgrace. The proposal had been rejected for no other reason than the Florentines' distrust of the king's word, even though they had in the first place put themselves in his hands through bad counsel. They did not trust him, but they could not see how it made more sense for the king to restore Pisa to them once he had occupied it—and that if at that point he did not restore it, he would be revealing his true nature. But as Louis XII had not yet occupied Pisa, he could only promise it to them and force them to pay for that promise. Thus it would have been far more advantageous for the Florentines to have agreed to Beaumont's taking the city under any condition. There was a similar occurrence in 1502, when the city of Arezzo rebelled and the French king sent Monsignor Imbalt with French troops to aid the Florentines. As Monsignor Imbalt marched toward Arezzo he was approached by the Arezzans, who were prepared to give up their city for certain pledges, much as the Pisans had been. This proposal was rejected in Florence, and Monsignor Imbalt, convinced that the Florentines had little understanding of the matter, began to conduct negotiations on his own without involving the Florentine representatives. As a result, he drew up the agreement in his own manner, and under this agreement entered Arezzo with his men, giving the Florentines to understand that he considered them simpletons. If they really wanted Arezzo, they should address themselves to King Louis, who could hand them the city much more easily now that the French had occupied it than when they had been camped outside. There was much cursing and blaming of Imbalt in Florence until the Florentines finally realized that if Beaumont had acted the way Imbalt had, the Florentines would have had not only Arezzo, but Pisa too.

Hence, to return to our topic, irresolute states never make good choices except by force, because their weakness never lets them reach decisions where any doubt exists. And if this doubt is not eliminated by a violent act that presses them forward, they remain forever suspended in indecision.

CHAPTER FORTY-ONE

On the imprudence and ineffectiveness of sudden change from humility to haughtiness and from mercy to cruelty without appropriate measures

Changing too quickly from one quality to another was among Appius's principal injudicious measures for maintaining his tyranny.[114] His cunning, on the other hand, in feigning to be a man of the people in order to deceive the plebeians, was effective.[115] Also effective were his methods for reappointing the Decemvirs,[116] as was the audacity of appointing himself against the wishes of the nobility and then putting his entourage into power. But having done all this it was injudicious, as I said above, for Appius suddenly to change his nature, turning himself from a friend of the plebeians into their enemy, from benevolent to arrogant, from generous to difficult, and all this so suddenly and without excuse that anyone could see his falsity. If a man has been perceived as good at a certain time but wants to become evil for his advantage, he must do so on an appropriate occasion and in a way that gives the

114. Appius Claudius was the most tyrannical of the Decemvirs, a legislative commission appointed in 451 and 450 BCE, given the task of resolving the power struggle between the patricians and the plebeians.

115. Livy (Book III, chapter 33) writes: "By means of the plebeians' favor, the leadership of the magistracy was granted to Appius. He feigned such a new personality that instead of being seen as a savage persecutor of the plebeians, he suddenly became their champion, ready to capture every breath of popularity."

116. Livy (Book III, chapter 33) writes: "The Decemvirs were elected without right of appeal."

impression that his actions are being forced by circumstances, so that before his changed nature deprives him of old favors, it will have secured so many new ones that his power will not be diminished. Otherwise he will find himself exposed and without friends, and so will come to ruin.

CHAPTER FORTY-TWO

ON THE EASE
WITH WHICH MEN CAN BE
CORRUPTED

It is also worth noting, concerning the Decemvirate, how easily men can be corrupted and made to assume an altogether different nature, no matter how good or educated they might be.[117] Consider how the young men with whom Appius surrounded himself became supporters of his tyranny for the scant benefits it brought them, or how Quintus Fabius, one of the second group of Decemvirs and an excellent man, was blinded by ambition and persuaded by Appius's evil ways, turning from good to bad and becoming like him.[118] Were lawgivers in republics or kingdoms to examine this matter carefully, they would be more ready to put a check on men's appetites and deprive them of the hope of transgressing without punishment.

---

117. In 449 BCE, the Decemvirs were forced to abdicate, as they had become tyrannical.
118. Livy (Book III, chapter 41) writes: "The foremost among the Decemvirs were Quintus Fabius and Appius Claudius. [. . .] Fabius's character was deficient in soundness and integrity rather than actively evil. In fact this man, formerly distinguished at home and on the battlefield, was so changed by the Decemvirate and his colleagues that he chose to be like Appius rather than be himself."

CHAPTER FORTY-THREE

On how men who fight for their own glory are good and faithful soldiers

Another issue to be considered concerning the matter discussed above is the difference between an army that is content and fights for its own glory and an army that is discontented and fights for the ambition of others. While the Roman armies tended to be victorious under the consuls, they were invariably defeated under the tyranny of the Decemvirs.[119] This example also indicates to some extent why mercenary soldiers are of no use, since the meager salary they are paid is the only motive they have to keep fighting.[120] This is not enough of a reason, nor can it be, to make them loyal to you, nor so much your friend that they will want to die for you. In an army whose soldiers do not have the kind of love for the man they are fighting for to make them his devoted supporters, there can never be enough skill and valor to resist an enemy who is even moderately skillful. And because such love and fervor cannot be inspired in anyone but one's subjects, it is necessary, in order to sustain a government or to maintain a republic or kingdom, to arm oneself with one's own subjects. All those who had their own armies had great success. The Roman armies under the Decemvir

---

119. Livy (Book III, chapter 42) writes: "The soldiers, determined that nothing anywhere should prosper under the leadership and auspices of the Decemvirs, allowed themselves to be defeated."
120. See *The Prince*, chapter 12, titled "Of the Different Types of Armies, and of Mercenaries."

tyranny had the same skill as previous Roman armies, but because they did not have the same disposition, they did not achieve the same results. The moment the Decemvirs were abolished and the Roman soldiers once again fought as free men, their former valor returned. The result was that their campaigns became as successful as they had been before.

• • •

CHAPTER FORTY-SIX

ON HOW MEN PROGRESS FROM ONE AMBITION TO ANOTHER, AND HOW THEY SEEK TO AVOID BEING HARMED BUT READILY HARM OTHERS

Once the Roman populace had regained its liberty[121] and become as it had been before—except that now the populace was in an even better position, as it had created many new laws guaranteeing its own power—it seemed reasonable to expect that within a short period calm would be restored. But quite the opposite happened, with new turmoil and discord breaking out every day. Livy cogently points out the reason for this, so it seems fitting to use his exact words when he says that either the populace or the nobility always became insolent when the other was humiliated: When the plebeians were happy enough to remain quietly within their station, young noblemen took to attacking them. Nor could the tribunes take any measures as they too were under attack. The nobility, on the other hand, even though they thought their young men too violent, still felt that if the line was to be crossed it should be by their faction and not by the plebeians.[122] And so in its desire to defend its own liberty each faction strove to oppress the other, because men in their quest to live without fear will attempt to instill fear in others. The harm they dispel they impose on others, as if the only way to prevail is either to harm or be harmed. Here can be seen one of the ways in which republics disintegrate, and how men

---

121. In 449 BCE, when the Decemvirs were forced to abdicate.
122. Machiavelli is quoting Livy, Book III, chapter 65.

progress from one ambition to another. The words that Sallust puts in Caesar's mouth are very true: "For all bad examples arise from good beginnings."[123] As I have already mentioned, the first thing a ruthlessly ambitious citizen of a republic will seek to do is guard himself from being harmed, not only by private citizens, but by magistrates as well. To do this he will seek allies, which he acquires by means that appear honest enough, either by offering money or by offering to defend the allies from those in power. This seems honest, so it easily fools everyone and is not remedied. Soon enough the ambitious citizen, continuing along his course without encountering any obstacles, reaches a position where private citizens are afraid of him and magistrates respect him. And once he has attained this position, he is at a point where it is extremely dangerous to counter him. I have already discussed the danger of trying to deal with a problem within a state when the problem has grown too great:[124] In a nutshell, one must seek either to eliminate it and run the danger of immediate ruin, or let it run its course and feign servitude until a death or some other incident frees you. Once citizens and magistrates are frightened of offending the powerful man and his allies, he does not have to do much more to have the magistrates pass rulings or attack others as he dictates. Consequently, a state must have institutions and laws that will hinder a citizen from doing evil under the guise of doing good, thus ensuring that he can develop only the kind of standing that will benefit and not harm liberty, as will be discussed in its proper place.

---

123. Machiavelli quotes *Bellum Catilinae,* 51, 27, in Latin: *Quod omnia mala exempla bonis initiis orta sunt.* Regarding *Bellum Catilinae,* see note 250 to Book III, chapter 6, below.

124. In chapter 33 above, titled "When a Problem Within a State or Against a State Has Grown, It Is Better to Bide One's Time Than to Tackle It with Full Force."

CHAPTER FIFTY

ON HOW A SINGLE COUNCIL OR MAGISTRATE SHOULD NOT BE ABLE TO BLOCK THE PROCEEDINGS OF A STATE

When Titus Quinctius Cincinnatus and Gnaeus Julius Mento were consuls in Rome they were always at odds, and this brought all the proceedings of the republic to a halt.[125] As a result, the Senate decided to create a dictator to do what the consuls were unable to do because of their constant wrangling. The consuls, however, though they disagreed about everything else, did agree on one thing: They did not want a dictator. So the Senate had no other recourse than to turn to the tribunes for help. The tribunes, with the backing of the Senate, forced the consuls to obey. This demonstrates the usefulness of the office of tribune, which was valuable not only in keeping the ruthless ambition of the powerful against the plebeians in check, but also the conflict of the plebeians among themselves. It demonstrates too that one should never establish an institution in a state that will enable the few to block a decision that might be vital in keeping the state from harm. For example, if you give a council power to distribute honors and rewards, or give a magistrate the power to direct an affair, it makes sense either to impose a stipulation that will compel these authorities to act in all circumstances, or to set things up in such a way that if they do not want to act, someone else can and will. Otherwise such an institution is defective

---

125. In 431, during the wars with the Volsci and Aequi, Titus Quinctius Cincinnatus and Gnaeus Julius Mento were elected consuls. Livy (Book IV, chapter 26) writes: "The consuls' perverse discord and constant wrangling in the Senate greatly alarmed the Romans."

and dangerous, as it would have been in Rome had the power of the tribunes not been able to oppose the obstinacy of the consuls. In the Republic of Venice, it is the Greater Council that distributes the honors and rewards. There were times, however, when members of this council, out of contempt or false conviction, did not appoint successors to magistrates and those who administered Venice's empire. This led to great turmoil, because suddenly Venice and its foreign dominions lacked legitimate judges. Nor could anything be done unless all the members of the Greater Council were satisfied or dissuaded from their false conviction. This problem would have brought Venice to a bad end if prudent citizens had not made provision for it. When the opportunity presented itself, they passed a law that no Venetian magistrate inside or outside Venice could vacate his post unless a successor had been appointed. This removed the possibility of the council impeding public actions and so endangering the republic.

CHAPTER FIFTY-ONE

ON HOW A REPUBLIC OR PRINCE MUST MAKE A SHOW OF DOING OUT OF GENEROSITY WHAT HE MUST DO FROM NECESSITY

Prudent men know how to make a merit of each of their actions even when necessity forces them to take these actions. The Roman Senate was prudent in this way when it chose to pay men in military service out of public funds even though the men had always been accustomed to supporting themselves. The Senate realized that otherwise it would be impossible to wage war over long periods and that the Roman armies would be unable to lay siege to cities or dispatch the soldiers far from Rome. The Senate saw that it was necessary to be able to do both, and so decided that salaries would be paid to the soldiers, but in such a way that made a merit of what in fact necessity was forcing it to do. The plebeians so welcomed this gift that all Rome went wild with happiness, and regarded the Senate's decision as a great benefit that they could never have hoped for or sought on their own.[126] The tribunes did their best to abolish this resolution, arguing that as the plebeians would have to pay taxes in order to cover the military salaries, it would burden them, not provide relief, but the tribunes did not manage to convince the plebeians. The Senate even managed to increase the plebeians' enthusiasm in the way it distributed taxes, by imposing the heaviest and largest taxes on the nobility, taxes which would have to be paid first.

126. Livy (Book IV, chapter 60) writes: "It is told that nothing was ever welcomed by the plebeians with such rejoicing. They flocked to the Senate, grasped the senators' hands as they emerged, saying that they were rightly called 'Fathers,' and proclaiming that now no man, while he had any strength left, would spare his body or blood for such a generous state."

CHAPTER FIFTY-THREE

ON HOW, DECEIVED BY A FALSE KIND OF GOOD, THE POPULACE OFTEN DESIRES ITS OWN RUIN, AND HOW EASILY IT IS MOVED BY GREAT HOPES AND BOLD PROMISES

After the city of Veii was defeated, the populace of Rome came upon the idea that it might be good if half the Romans went to live in Veii.[127] They reasoned that as Veii was rich in territory and buildings and was also close to Rome, half the population of Rome could be made richer without great upheaval. The Senate and the wiser Romans, however, considered this so futile and dangerous that they openly declared they would rather face death than consent to such an idea. Consequently, when the matter came up for debate, the plebeians were so incensed against the Senate that arms and bloodshed would have ensued had not the Senate used some elderly and esteemed citizens as a shield, the reverence the plebeians had for them putting a halt to the clamor.[128] Two things are of note here. First, the populace will often be misled by a deceptive appearance of good, and consequently end up desiring its own ruin; for if the populace is not made to understand what is good and what is bad by someone it trusts, endless danger and harm can come to a state.[129] And when fate has it that the populace does not have faith in anyone, as sometimes happens, having been duped in the past

127. Rome defeated Veii, a wealthy and important Etruscan city-state that lay ten miles northwest of Rome (modern Veio), after a decade-long siege in 395 BCE. Machiavelli is closely following the text of Livy (Book V, chapter 24).
128. Machiavelli closely follows Livy's text (Book V, chapter 25).
129. The second thing of note is discussed at the beginning of the following chapter.

by men or events, this inevitably leads to ruin. In his discourse *De monarchia,* Dante says that the populace at times shouts: "Long live their death! Death to their life!"[130] Because of this lack of faith, states sometimes do not reach good decisions, as I have said above about the Venetians: When all their enemies came together and assaulted them, the Venetians did not manage to decide, before they were ruined, to give back territories they had occupied (which had given rise to the conspiracy of princes[131] and the war that was waged against them), even though giving back these territories would have won over some of their enemies.

Therefore, in considering what it is easy to persuade a populace of, or what is difficult, the following distinction can be made: What you must persuade it of appears at first glance a gain or a loss, or appears courageous or cowardly. And when the populace sees a gain in the matters placed before it, even if there is a loss hiding behind these matters, it will always be easy to persuade it to follow that path as long as it seems courageous, even if it leads to the ruin of the republic. Likewise, it will always be difficult to convince the populace about those decisions where there is seeming cowardice or loss, even if behind them there is hidden security and gain. My point is confirmed by countless examples, Roman and foreign, ancient and modern. From this arose the bad opinion in Rome concerning Fabius Maximus,[132] who could not persuade the Roman populace that it would be good for the republic to proceed slowly in the Punic War, and to endure Hannibal's attacks without confronting them. The populace considered this option cowardly, and did not see the value hidden behind it, nor did Fabius Maximus present enough reasons to convince them. The Roman populace was so blinded by its opinion that even though it had committed the error of authorizing Fabius's Master of the Horse[133] to

130. In fact, Dante's *Il Convivio* (*The Banquet*), I, 2.

131. Machiavelli is referring to the League of Cambrai, formed in 1508 by Pope Julius II with the Holy Roman Emperor Maximilian I, Louis XII of France, and Ferdinand II of Aragon against Venice, with the aim of dividing its territorial possessions among them.

132. Fabius Maximus Quintus (d. 203 BCE) was a Roman commander and statesman whose cautious delaying tactics during the war against Hannibal gave Rome time to recover its strength and take the offensive. Machiavelli is discussing the events described by Livy in Book XXII, chapters 25–27.

133. Fabius's effective delay tactics sparked controversy in Rome and a quarrel with Minucius Rufus, his Master of the Horse and second in command. In an unprecedented action, the people of Rome then divided the command between Minucius and Fabius.

fight Hannibal, though Fabius was against it, the Roman army would have been destroyed if Fabius had not with his prudence saved the day. But the Roman populace did not learn from this, and went ahead and made Varro consul for no other merit than his promises in Rome's public places and squares to defeat Hannibal if he were given the authority to do so.[134] The result was the utter disaster at Cannae and the near destruction of Rome.

I would also like to put forward another Roman example: Hannibal had been in Italy for nine or ten years, killing Romans throughout the land, when Marcus Centennius Paenula, a man of very humble origins (though he did hold a position of rank in the army), came to the Senate and declared that if he were given the authority to gather an army of volunteers anywhere in Italy he pleased, he would in short order deliver Hannibal dead or alive.[135] The Senate saw his demand as extremely rash, but felt that if it were to turn him down and the populace were to find out, much turmoil and resentment against senatorial order would have ensued. So Paenula's request was granted, as the Senate preferred to put all those who followed him in danger than to spark new anger in the people, knowing that such a decision would be popular and how difficult it would be to dissuade the people from it. So Paenula marched out with a disorderly and unruly rabble to find Hannibal, and at the very first encounter was routed and killed along with all the men who followed him.

In Greece, in the city of Athens, a most grave and prudent man by the name of Niceas could not persuade the populace that it was a bad idea to invade Sicily, so when this idea was adopted against the wishes of the wise, the result was the complete destruction of Athens. When Scipio was made consul and wanted to conquer Africa, promising the destruction of Carthage, the Senate was unresolved, as Fabius Maximus was against it. So Scipio threatened to put the matter before the people, knowing very well how they liked such enterprises.

One could also give examples from our own city of Florence: Er-

---

134. The Roman consuls of 216 BCE, Lucius Aemilius Paulus and Gaius Terentius Varro, set out to meet Hannibal in the disastrous Battle of Cannae with eighty thousand men, of whom only fourteen thousand escaped. (Livy, Book XXII, chapter 35.)
135. Livy (Book XXV, chapter 19) comments: "The promise was foolish, but just as foolish was the credence it received. As though the skills of an ordinary soldier could be the same as those of a commander."

cole Bentivoglio, along with Antonio Giacomini, commander of the Florentine troops, after having routed Bartolommeo d'Alviano at San Vincenti, besieged the city of Pisa. This campaign had been agreed to by the populace following the bold promises of Ercole Bentivoglio, even though many wise citizens condemned it. But the wise could do nothing, forced as they were by the will of the people, which was based on the rash promises of the commander. Hence I suggest that there is no easier way to ruin a republic where the populace has power than to engage it in bold campaigns, because where the populace carries weight in the deliberations, bold campaigns will be always accepted: Whoever might be of a different opinion will not be able to do anything about it. But if this causes the ruin of the state, it also causes—and this even more often—the ruin of the citizens in charge of such enterprises, because when the populace has taken victory for granted, when the defeat comes it does not accuse Fortune or the circumstances of war but the commander's wickedness and ignorance. In most cases he is then killed, imprisoned, or banished, as happened to countless Carthaginian generals and many Athenians. Previous victories are of no use to them because their present defeat cancels everything. This was the case with our Florentine general Antonio Giacomini, who, failing to conquer Pisa as he had promised and as the populace had been certain he would, fell into such disgrace with the people that, despite his countless successes in the past, he remained alive more because of the indulgence of those in power than that of the people.

CHAPTER FIFTY-FOUR

ON THE EXTENT TO WHICH A MAN

OF GRAVITY AND RESPECT CAN HALT

AN AROUSED MULTITUDE

The second thing of note concerning my discussion in the previous chapter is that nothing is as effective at halting an aroused multitude as its reverence for a man of gravity and authority who confronts them. Virgil does not say without reason:

> Yet if they see a man who is revered through goodness and merit,
> they will fall mute and crowd around him to listen to his words.[136]

Therefore a man who is given command of an army, or who finds himself in a city where there is turmoil, must step before the crowd with as much dignity as he can, surrounded by all the insignia of his rank, in order to make himself more revered. A few years ago Florence was divided into two factions, the Frateschi and the Arrabbiati, as they called themselves.[137] These factions came to blows and the Frateschi were crushed. Among them was Pagolantonio Soderini, a citizen of repute in those days, and during the turmoil the armed mob headed to his house to sack it. His brother Francesco, then the Bishop of Volterra and today a cardinal, happened to be there, and the instant he heard the clamor and saw the crowd, put on his most venerable garment and

---

136. Machiavelli quotes Virgil's *Aeneid*, I.151–52, in Latin: *Tum pietate gravem ac meritis si forte virum quem / Conspexere, silent, arrectisque auribus adstant.*
137. The Frateschi were the followers of Savonarola, the Arrabbiati opposed him.

over it the episcopal vestment. He confronted the armed crowd, and by his august presence and words managed to stop them. This incident was admired and celebrated throughout the city for many days.

Hence I conclude that the best and most certain way of halting an aroused multitude is the presence of a man who appears venerable and is revered. Thus, to return to the incident discussed in the previous chapter, it can be seen with what obstinacy the Roman plebeians entertained the idea of moving to Veii because they judged it sensible and did not perceive the dangers it concealed, and how there would have been endless turmoil and upheaval had the Senate not used grave and revered men to halt the plebeians' frenzy.

CHAPTER FIFTY-FIVE

On how easily things can be accomplished in a state where the populace is not corrupted, and on how one cannot create a principality where there is equality, or a republic where there is no equality

I have already discussed at length what is to be feared or hoped for from a corrupted state,[138] but it nevertheless strikes me as fitting to consider a decision of the Roman Senate concerning Camillus's vow to give Apollo one-tenth of the spoils gathered from the people of Veii.[139] These spoils had come into the hands of the Roman plebeians, and as the Senate was unable to check their value, it passed an edict that everyone should deliver to the treasury a tenth of what they had plundered. To the plebeians' relief, however, the Senate ultimately decided on a different course of action, having settled on another way of pleasing Apollo, and this decision was not carried out.[140] Nevertheless, it is evident to what extent the Senate had confidence in the plebeians' honesty, and how it thought that no one would refrain from delivering exactly what the edict commanded. It is also evident that the plebeians did not think of cheating by giving less than they owed, since they

---

138. In chapters 16–18 above.
139. Livy writes (Book V, chapter 21) that before setting out to conquer Veii, Camillus had sworn to give Apollo one-tenth of the plunder, should he be successful.
140. Livy writes (Book V, chapter 25) that it was decided that as Rome had gained the territories of Veii, one-tenth of their worth would be estimated and the money taken from the treasury. "But when it turned out that the money was not enough [...] the matrons brought jewelry to the treasury."

strove instead to free themselves of the edict by voicing their outright indignation at it. This example, along with many others already cited, shows how much honesty and pious integrity this populace possessed, and how much good one could expect of it. In fact, nothing good is to be expected where such honesty is lacking, as we see from the states of our era which are so corrupted—Italy above all others. Even France and Spain have some of that corruption, though one does not see as much tumult in those countries as Italy faces every day. In those other countries this does not come so much from the populace's honesty, which is to a large extent absent, as it does from their having a king who keeps them united, not only through his expertise and skill, but with the help of institutions that are not yet corrupted. This honesty and pious integrity are very apparent in Germany, with the result that many of its states are free, and observe their laws, so that no one dares occupy them, from within or without.[141] In order to demonstrate how true it is that there is a good measure of this ancient honesty in the German states, I would like to give an example similar to the one cited above concerning the Roman Senate and plebeians. When the German states need to spend an amount of money for the benefit of the public, the empowered magistrates or councils solicit from all citizens one or two percent of what each has in revenue. When this decision has been made according to the institutions of the state, each citizen presents himself before the tax collectors and, taking an oath to pay the proper sum, drops whatever his conscience compels him to donate into a box set up for that purpose. The man who pays is the sole witness of the amount he pays. From this we can conjecture how much honesty and pious integrity is still present in these men, and it must be assumed that everyone pays the correct sum, otherwise the tax revenue anticipated based on previous collections would not have tallied with the amount received. Should the amounts not tally, the deception would be discovered and another method of collection would have been instituted. Such honesty is all the more admirable in our times, when it has become rarer. In fact, it now seems to exist only in Germany.

There are two reasons for this. The first is that the Germans have

141. On the freedom of German cities see also *The Prince*, chapter 10, titled "Of How the Strength of Principalities Is to Be Measured."

not had extensive contact with their neighbors, because neither they nor their neighbors travel to each other's lands; each is content with his goods and produce, and happy enough to clothe himself in the wool his land provides. This has removed the reason for any contact and the source of any corruption, because the Germans have not been able to pick up French, Spanish, or Italian customs, these nations taken together being the corruption of the world. The second reason is that the states that have an uncorrupted and vital civic order do not allow for any of their citizens to act or live in the manner of a "gentleman": In fact the citizens maintain equality among themselves and are great enemies of the gentlemen and men of substance of that land. If by chance they get their hands on any of these worthies, they are killed as the source of corruption and the reason for turmoil.

I shall clarify what the title "gentleman" signifies. A gentleman lives in idleness and luxury off the profits of his possessions; he does not concern himself with the cultivation of the land, or submit himself to any of the toil necessary to live. In every state and land such men are pernicious, but even more pernicious are those men who have even greater fortunes, with castles and subjects who obey them. The Kingdom of Naples, the Papal States, the Romagna, and Lombardy are filled with both these kinds of gentleman. This is the reason that no republic or vital civic order has ever come about in those lands, because men of this kind are entirely hostile to any form of civil life. To introduce a republic into such states would be impossible, but if someone wanted to reorganize them entirely—that is, if someone were to serve as arbitrator—his only recourse would be to establish a kingdom. This is because where there is so much corruption that laws are not sufficient to halt it, one must combine laws with a larger force. This larger force must be a royal hand that with extreme and absolute authority restrains the excessive ambition and corruption of the powerful. This idea is supported by the example of Tuscany, where for a long time three republics—Florence, Siena, and Lucca—existed over a relatively small territory. Although the other states of Tuscany are in a sense subservient to them, it is evident from their spirit and their institutions that they maintain, or at least would like to maintain, their liberty. This has come about because in Tuscany there is no lord of the castle and very few if any gentlemen, but rather the kind of equality that would enable a ruler with foresight and some knowledge of ancient civilizations to introduce civic life. Yet the ill fortune of Tuscany itself has been so great that up to our times this task has fallen to no man who has known how to do this, or has been able to accomplish it.

It is therefore possible to draw the following conclusions from this discourse: He who wishes to set up a republic in a state that has many gentlemen cannot do so unless he first eliminates them all, and he who wishes to set up a kingdom or principality where there is great equality cannot do so unless he raises many of the restless and ambitious spirits out of that equality and makes them gentlemen in fact and not just in name, giving them castles and possessions and favoring them with property and men. Placed in their midst, the new ruler will then maintain his power, while they, through him, will satisfy their ambitions. The rest of the citizenry can be compelled to bear the yoke that force and force alone will make them bear. With this method there will be a balance between the citizenry who oppress and the citizenry who are oppressed, and so all men will remain within their rank. Turning a state suited to be a kingdom into a republic, or one suited to be a republic into a kingdom, is a task for a man of rare intellect and power: Many have tried but few have succeeded. The magnitude of the task partly bewilders and partly hinders them, so that they inevitably fail in the very first stages of their attempt.

My argument that one cannot set up a republic where there are gentlemen might appear to be challenged by the example of the Venetian Republic, in which only gentlemen have any standing. My only reply to this is that the Venetian example does not conflict with what I have said, because the gentlemen of Venice are gentlemen in name more than in actuality, as they do not draw great revenues from their possessions. Their great wealth is founded on commerce and trade. What is more, none of these gentlemen owns a castle or has any jurisdiction over others. In Venice, the appellation of "gentleman" is one of dignity and rank and without any of the characteristics associated with gentlemen in other states. Just as the citizenry of all republics are divided into various appellations, so is Venice divided between gentlemen and commoners. Venetian gentlemen hold or can hold any office, while commoners are entirely excluded. This, however, does not create unrest in Venice, for reasons that I have already discussed.[142] Thus you can found a republic where great equality exists or has existed, or set up a principality where there is great inequality. Otherwise you will create a system that lacks balance and will not endure.[143]

142. See chapters 5 and 6 above.
143. Machiavelli means a system that will lack proportion between those who rule and those who are ruled.

CHAPTER FIFTY-EIGHT

ON HOW THE POPULACE IS WISER AND
MORE CONSTANT THAN THE PRINCE

Nothing is more erratic and unstable than the populace, Livy and all the historians maintain, because often in the historians' narrations one sees the multitude condemning a man to death and afterward fervently wishing him back. This was the case with the Roman populace, which condemned Manlius Capitolinus to death and then lamented him. In Livy's words: "Soon enough, after he no longer presented a threat, the populace began to long for him."[144] And elsewhere, when Livy describes the incidents in Syracuse after the death of Hieronymus, Hiero's grandson, he says: "That is the nature of the multitude: It will either serve humbly or dominate arrogantly."[145]

I do not know if in upholding an idea which, as I have said, is contrary to the opinion of so many historians, I will be entering a terrain that is so difficult that I shall either have to abandon it with shame or follow it and draw censure upon myself. And yet I do not judge it wrong, nor have I ever done so, to defend an opinion with reasoning, and not with power or force.

I propose that all men—and princes more than anyone else—can be accused of the defect of which historians accuse the populace. In

144. Machiavelli is quoting Livy (Book VI, chapter 20) in Latin: *Populum brevi, posteaquam ab eo periculum nullum erat, desiderium eius tenuit.*
145. Machiavelli is quoting Livy (Book XXIV, chapter 25) in Latin: *Haec natura multitudinis est: aut humiliter servit, aut superbe dominatur.*

fact, any ruler who is not held in check by laws is apt to make the same errors as an unruly multitude. This is quite evident, because there are and have been many princes, and yet only a few of them good and wise. I am referring here to princes who have managed to break the constraints that might have held them in check. The kings of Egypt, when that land was governed by law in ancient times, were an exception, as were the kings of Sparta and also today's kings of France, a kingdom better controlled by its laws than any other that we know of in our era. The kings who exist under such constitutions need not be grouped together with those whose natures must be considered separately to see if each is unchecked like the populace. To do so one would have to compare these kings to a populace that is equally kept in check by the laws. And one will find in these kings too the same goodness one sees in the populace, as the populace neither arrogantly dominate nor humbly serve. This was the case with the Roman populace, which, while the republic remained uncorrupted, never served humbly nor dominated arrogantly. In fact, the Roman populace, with their own institutions and magistrates, bore their ranks with honor, and when it became necessary to rise up against a powerful man, the populace did so, as in the cases of Manlius, the Decemvirs, and others who strove to oppress them. And when, for the safety of the public, it was necessary to obey a dictator or the consuls, the Roman populace did so. It is not surprising if the populace lamented Manlius Capitolinus after they had condemned him to death, because they longed for his valor, which was such that the memory of it evoked sympathy in all. Manlius's valor would have had the same effect on a prince, because it is the verdict of all historians that valor is praised and admired even in one's enemies. And yet if Manlius could have been resurrected by all that fervent longing, the Roman populace would have passed the same sentence on him as they did when they dragged him from prison and condemned him to death. Nevertheless, we also see princes who were considered wise and still put a man to death and then lamented him, as Alexander the Great had done with Cleitus and other friends, or as Herod had done with Mariamne.[146]

But Livy, in talking about the nature of the populace, is not talking

---

146. In a drunken fit, Alexander the Great killed Cleitus, one of his foremost commanders, after which he was inconsolable. King Herod had his wife Mariamne put to death in a fit of jealousy.

about a populace restrained by laws, as in Rome, but about a populace not held in check, as was that of Syracuse, where the populace made all the errors usually made by infuriated men not restrained by laws, as was the case with Alexander the Great and Herod. Yet the nature of the populace should not be blamed more than the nature of princes, because both tend to err equally when they can err without fear. There are enough examples of this besides the ones I have just cited, both among the Roman emperors and among other tyrants and princes, who behaved more inconsistently and erratically than any populace ever has.

I therefore disagree with the common opinion that a populace in power is unstable, changeable, and ungrateful, and maintain that a populace can be as guilty of this as an individual prince. If one were to accuse both populace and prince of these shortcomings, one would probably be right. But it would be deceiving oneself to accuse the populace and not the prince: because a well-regulated populace that is in power will be stable, prudent, and grateful, just like a prince, or even better than a prince, even if that prince is considered particularly wise. The prince, on the other hand, unchecked by laws, will be more ungrateful, unstable, and imprudent than a populace. The instability of his conduct does not arise from his having a different nature, because all men have the same nature. If there is a greater amount of good, it lies with the populace, because the populace will more or less keep to the laws by which it lives. If we consider the Roman populace, we will see that for four hundred years the people were hostile to the very name of king and championed the glory of the city's common good, and there are a great number of examples that testify to this. If someone were to point out the ingratitude of the Roman populace toward Scipio, I would respond with the same argument I have already made at length concerning this matter, where the people showed themselves less ungrateful than the princes.[147]

But in matters of prudence and stability, I propose that a populace is more prudent, more stable, and has better judgment than a prince. It is not without reason that the voice of the people has been compared to the voice of God. One sees public opinion making surprising prog-

147. See chapter 29 above, titled "On Who Is More Ungrateful, a Populace or a Prince," and also chapter 30.

nostications, so that it seems that the populace, as if by some hidden skill, can foresee their good and bad fortune. As for judging things, it is rare that a populace hearing two orators of equal skill arguing for opposing sides will not understand the truth it is hearing and choose the better side. And if the people err in matters of action that are bold or appear to be useful, as I have already discussed, a prince will often be misled by his own passions, which are more numerous than those of the populace.

We also see that in the appointment of magistrates the populace will make far better choices than a prince, nor can one ever persuade a populace that it is good to elect a wicked man with corrupt ways to public office. This is something a prince can easily be persuaded to do in a thousand ways. We also see that when a populace begin to detest something, they can do so for many centuries. This does not happen with princes. In both these matters I would like the Roman populace to suffice as example: In so many elections of consuls and tribunes over the centuries, they did not make four choices that they had cause to repent. And the populace had, as I have said, so much hatred for the name of king that no citizen, however meritorious, who aspired to that name could avoid the deserved punishment. We also see that states ruled by the populace are able to expand their territories quite remarkably in the shortest period, much more so than states that have always been under a prince. Rome proved to be such a state after the expulsion of its king, as was Athens after it freed itself from Pisistratus. This can mean only that a government of the populace is better than that of a prince. Nor do I want all that Livy says in the passage I have cited, or in any other, to be set against my argument, because if we compare all the disorder caused by the populace with all the disorder caused by princes, and all the glories of the populace with all those of princes, we will see that the populace is far superior in goodness and glory. And if princes are superior to the populace in establishing laws, creating civic orders, and organizing statutes and new institutions, the populace has been so much superior in maintaining institutions in an orderly way, that without doubt they add to the glory of those who established them.

Finally, in conclusion, I propose that the states of princes have endured for a long time, as have republics, and that both the one and the other have had to be regulated by laws: A prince who can do as he pleases will prove himself mad, just as a populace who can do as they please will prove themselves unwise. Therefore, if one looks at a prince and a populace who are bound by laws, one will see that there is more skill in the populace than in the prince. If one looks at a prince and a populace who are not bound by laws, one will see fewer mistakes in the populace than in the prince, and these will be less serious and easier to resolve. A good man can speak to an unruly and riotous multitude and easily set it on the right path, but there is no one who can speak to an evil prince, nor is there any other remedy than the blade of a knife. From which one can assess the gravity of the populace's or the prince's disorder: To cure that of the populace one needs only words, while to cure that of the prince requires a blade—and here one can only conclude that where one needs a more incisive cure, there are greater ills.

When the people are completely unchecked by laws, their foolish acts are not feared, nor is one afraid of any present evil, but rather of the evil that might arise, since so much confusion can bring forth a tyrant. But with evil princes the opposite happens: One fears the present evil and has hope for the future, since men persuade themselves that the prince's evil life can give rise to liberty. Hence you can see the difference between the one and the other as a difference between the things that are and the things that will be. The cruelty of the populace is directed against those who the populace fears will seize public property, while the cruelty of the prince is directed against those he fears will take his property. But the bad opinion one has of the populace arises because, even while it is in power, everyone will speak badly about it quite openly, without fear of reprisal, while of princes one always speaks with a thousand fears and a thousand cautions.

· · ·

BOOK II

Preface

Men praise the old times and find fault with the present, though not always with justification. They so admire things of the past that they esteem not only what they have come to know through accounts that historians have left us, but also the times that they as old men remember from their youth. When their opinion is flawed—as it is more often than not—I feel certain that this happens for a number of reasons. The first reason, in my view, is that no one knows the whole truth about the past, since in most cases incidents that would have brought disgrace upon earlier times have been concealed, while glorious incidents are rendered fully and are described as having been quite magnificent. This is because most historians bow to the fortunes of conquerors, and in order to make their victories glorious they aggrandize not only what the conquerors have skillfully achieved but also the exploits of the enemy, so that anyone born later, either in the land that was victorious or the land that was defeated, has reason to marvel at those men and those times and is compelled to admire and praise them.

Furthermore, men hate either from fear or from envy. Consequently, two most compelling reasons for hating things of the past are eliminated: Things of the past cannot harm you, nor is there any cause to envy them. Yet the opposite is true of things you can see, or in which you are involved. As these things are not in any way hidden from you, you can understand them fully and can discern precisely what you like as well as many things you dislike. As a result, you judge these things inferior to those of the past, even if in fact the things of the present deserve far more fame and glory. I do not mean matters concerning the arts, which are so brilliantly clear that time cannot diminish their glory or give them more glory than they deserve, but matters connected to life and customs, in which one cannot see such clear testimony.

I would like to point out, however, that though men tend to praise the past and find fault with the present, they are not always wrong to do so. Sometimes it is necessary for us to arrive at such a judgment, as human affairs are always in motion and will consequently either rise or fall. We see a city or country founded with a vital political order by an excellent man, and see it continue to develop toward the better, for a time, through the skill of its founder. Anyone who is born in such a land and praises ancient more than modern times is deceiving himself, which is caused by the issues that I pointed out above. But men born later in that city or country, during the period of its decline, do not deceive themselves.

As I contemplate how these things develop, I judge the world as having always been in the same condition: that there has always been as much good as evil, with the good and evil varying from country to country. We can see this from what we know of ancient kingdoms that differed from one another because of the variety of their customs, while the world remained the same. The only thing different in those times was that the world initially channeled all its resourcefulness first into Assyria, then into the land of the Medes, and then Persia, until it reached Italy and Rome. After imperial Rome, no empire has lasted, nor has there been a single place where the world has channeled all its resourcefulness, and yet this resourcefulness can be seen scattered among many nations where men lived worthily. This was true of the kingdom of the Franks, the Turks, the Mamluk sultans of Egypt, and today the peoples of Germany, and before them in the Saracen sect that accomplished such great feats and occupied so much of the world that it destroyed the Eastern Roman Empire.[148] Thus, after the Romans came to ruin, this resourcefulness continued in all these countries and

148. Saracen sect: the Muslim Ottoman Turks who invaded and ultimately destroyed the Eastern Roman (Byzantine) Empire.

sects, and still exists in some of them, where it is cherished and much prized. Whoever is born in these lands and praises the past more than the present may be deceiving himself. But whoever is born in Italy or Greece and has not joined the foreign invaders (if he is Italian) or turned Turk (if he is Greek) has reason to blame his own times and praise the past. The past could boast of much that was admirable, while the present has nothing that can raise it out of the greatest misery, infamy, and shame, with no observance of religion, laws, or military traditions, and stained by every kind of filth. These vices are all the more detestable when they are found in men who sit as judges, command others, and strive to be honored.

But to return to our argument: If the judgment of men is distorted in assessing whether the present or the past is superior, it is because men cannot know the past as well as they know the present, owing to the passage of time. Old men, too, should not let their judgment be distorted when they compare the days of their youth with those of their old age, even though they have in fact seen and experienced both. Such a comparison would be sound if a man's judgment and desires were the same throughout his life, but as these vary, even if the times do not, the times cannot appear the same to a man when in old age he has different desires, pleasures, and considerations than he did in his youth. As men grow old, they lose strength but gain in judgment and prudence, so it is unavoidable that what appeared bearable and good when they were young later becomes unbearable and bad. In this they ought to blame their judgment, but instead they blame the times. Furthermore, human appetites are insatiable because nature gives us the ability and the will to desire everything, while Fortune gives us the ability to acquire only little. The result is continuous discontent in the minds of men, and dissatisfaction with the things that they possess. This leads them to blame the present, praise the past, and long for the future, even though they have no reasonable grounds for doing so.

Consequently, if in these *Discourses* I praise the times of ancient Rome too highly and find fault with our times, I do not know whether I deserve to be numbered among those who deceive themselves. Without doubt, if the worthiness that held sway then and the vice that holds sway now were not clearer than the sun, I would speak more cautiously for fear of being duped in the same way as those I have just blamed. But as the matter is so clear to whoever considers it, I shall be bold and say openly what I understand of past and present times, so that the minds of the young who will read my work can avoid the mistakes of our times and be prepared to imitate ancient times whenever Fortune gives them the opportunity. For it is the duty of a good man to teach others the goodness that, because of Fortune and the malignity of the times, he himself has not been able to achieve; among the many who are capable of good actions, those more favored by heaven might be able to accomplish them. In the previous book I spoke of the Romans' decisions concerning the internal affairs of their city; in this book I shall speak of the decisions that the people of Rome made concerning the expansion of their empire.

CHAPTER ONE

ON WHETHER THE
EMPIRE THE ROMANS ACQUIRED WAS
A RESULT OF SKILL OR OF FORTUNE

Many have been of the opinion—among them Plutarch, a writer of great importance—that in acquiring its empire the Roman populace was favored more by Fortune than by skill.[149] One of Plutarch's arguments is that the Romans plainly attributed all their victories to Fortune, since they built more temples to Fortune than to any other deity. It seems that Livy was of the same opinion, because he rarely has a Roman speak of skill without adding to it the role that Fortune played. I, however, reject this view entirely, as I do not believe it can be sustained. If no republic was as successful in expanding its territories as Rome, this is because there has never been a republic better organized than Rome to accomplish such expansion. It is the skill of Rome's armies that enabled it to acquire its empire, while the organization and procedures established by Rome's founder enabled it to maintain what it acquired, as I shall discuss later in greater detail.

The historians claim that if Rome never fought two major wars at the same time, it was due to Fortune, not to the skill of its populace. The Romans did not fight a war against the Latins before the Romans

---

149. Plutarch writes in *De fortuna Romanorum*, chapter 11: "The smooth course of events, and Rome's swift expansion and progress to supreme power, proves to all who weigh this matter that Rome's rule did not arise from the toils and tactics of man but was sped on by divine escort and the winds of Fortune."

crushed the Samnites so totally that they then had to wage a war to defend them.[150] The Romans did not have to fight the Etruscans until they had subjugated the Latins and almost entirely crushed the Samnites. If two of these powers had joined forces when they were whole and strong, one could easily imagine them destroying Rome. Be that as it may, it never came about that the Romans had to fight two major wars at the same time: In fact, it always seemed that when one war began, another ended, and when one war ended, another began. This is clear from the sequence of the wars they fought, because if we set aside the wars before Rome was taken by the Gauls,[151] we see that while the Romans battled the Aequi and the Volsci, no other state waged a war against the Romans while the Aequi and the Volsci were still powerful. It was only after Rome was victorious that the war against the Samnites began,[152] and though the Latins rebelled against the new Roman dominion before the Samnite War was over, by the time the rebellion took place the Samnites had already allied themselves with Rome, which then used Samnite soldiers to curb the Latins' insolence.[153] Once the Latins were crushed, the Samnite War resurged,[154] and after the Samnites were beaten by constant routs, the war against the Etruscans began. When this war was over, the Samnites rose again when King Pyrrhus arrived in Italy.[155] After King Pyrrhus was repulsed and sent back to Greece, the Romans initiated their first war against the Carthaginians, a war that had barely ended when all the Gauls, from both sides of the Alps, conspired against the Romans until they were finally defeated after a great massacre between Popolonia and Pisa, where today the tower of San Vincenti stands.

Once this war was over, for the next twenty years there were wars of

150. The Samnites were a group of tribes of the southern Apennines who united to repel Roman expansion.
151. The Gauls sacked Rome in 390 BCE. The Aequi, an Italic people hostile to Rome, were repulsed by the Romans in 431, but not entirely subdued until the end of the Second Samnite War (304 BCE).
152. The First Samnite War was fought from 343 to 341 BCE.
153. The Romans and the Samnites fought the Latins between 340 and 338 BCE.
154. The Second Samnite War (326–304 BCE).
155. In 281 BCE the Samnites asked Pyrrhus, King of Epirus, for assistance against Rome. He crossed to Italy with some twenty-five thousand men, and won a series of costly victories against the Romans. In 275, however, he suffered heavy losses in the Battle of Beneventum and returned to Epirus.

minor importance, because the Romans fought only the Ligurians and whatever Gauls were left in Lombardy. This period continued until the beginning of the Second Punic War, which kept Italy engaged for sixteen years. When the Punic War ended with supreme glory for Rome, the Macedonian War began, and when that war ended there was another with Antiochus and Asia.[156] After this victory there was no prince or republic in all the world who could oppose the Roman forces, alone or in joint effort.

Yet even before this last victory, anyone who considers the sequence of these wars and how they were conducted will see great skill and wisdom linked with Fortune. The reason for this good fortune is quite clear, because it is most certain that when a prince or populace reaches such powerful standing that all neighboring princes or populaces are afraid of attacking them individually and of being attacked by them, it is inevitable that no one will assault them unless they are forced to do so. The powerful prince or republic can choose what neighbor to engage in battle while attentively calming the others, who can be assuaged easily enough because of their deference to power and the deceptiveness of the methods used to assuage them. Other states that are more distant and do not have much contact with the powerful prince or republic will regard the matter as far off and of little concern. These distant states will continue in their mistaken view until the blaze of war reaches them. By that time their only means of extinguishing it will be with their own forces, which will no longer be sufficient, as the enemy will have become too powerful.

I would like to pass over how the Samnites stood by and watched the Romans conquer the Volsci and the Aequi, and, in order not to be too long-winded, will begin with the Carthaginians, who, in the days when the Romans were battling the Samnites and the Etruscans, were very powerful and greatly revered, as Carthage already held all of Africa, Sardinia, and Sicily and parts of Spain. Carthage, because of its power and its distance from the provinces of Rome, never sought to attack the Romans or come to the aid of the Samnites or the Etruscans. The Carthaginians, in fact, acted as one does when everything is progressing in one's favor, even forming alliances with the Romans. Nor

---

156. The Second Macedonian War, 200–196 BCE, and the war against Antiochus the Great of the Hellenistic Syrian Empire.

did they realize their mistake until the Romans had subjugated all the territories between the Roman provinces and those of Carthage and began fighting Carthage for its possessions in Sicily and Spain. The Carthaginians fell into the same trap as had the Gauls, Philip of Macedon, and Antiochus, who had all been convinced that the Romans would be vanquished by one of the others, and that they themselves would have ample time to defend themselves from the Romans through either peace or war. Hence I believe that the Romans' good fortune in this matter is of the kind that any prince would have who proceeds as they did and is as skillful as they were.

Here I would have liked to discuss the ways the Romans had of entering the territories of others, had I not discussed this at great length in my treatise on principalities.[157] So I will say only that in new territories, the Romans always did their best to have allies who could serve as a door or ladder enabling them to enter and retain these territories. We see that the Romans entered Samnium with the help of the Campanians, and Etruria with the help of the Camertines; the Mamertines helped them enter Sicily, the Saguntines Spain, the Massinissa Africa, the Aetolians Greece; Eumenes and other princes helped Rome enter Asia, and the Massilienses and the Aedui helped them enter Gaul. The Romans never lacked this kind of support, which facilitated their campaigns and helped them acquire and keep new provinces. States that follow the Roman example will find they need Fortune less than states that do not. To clarify how skill more than Fortune can lead a state to such an empire, we will discuss in the following chapter the character of the peoples whom the Romans engaged in battle, and how determined these peoples were in defending their liberty.

---

157. Machiavelli is referring to *The Prince*, chapters 3 and 5.

On the peoples the Romans had to fight, and how those peoples resolutely defended their liberty

For the Romans, nothing presented a greater obstacle in their drive to conquer the peoples surrounding them, as well as those in more distant lands, than these peoples' love for liberty. In fact, they defended their liberty so resolutely that they would never have been subjugated had not the Romans been exceptionally skillful. There are many examples of the dangers to which these peoples exposed themselves in order to keep their liberty or regain it, and of their acts of vengeance against those who had occupied them. We also know from reading the histories how these people and cities suffered on account of their servitude to Rome. In our times there is only one land where there are states one can call free,[158] while in ancient times all lands had peoples living in freedom. It is clear that in Italy, in those ancient times we are now discussing, from the mountains that divide present-day Tuscany and Lombardy to the southern tip of Italy, all the peoples were free: the Etruscans, Romans, Samnites, and many others that populated the rest of Italy. Nor is it ever argued that there were any kings, other than those of Rome or the Etruscan king Porsena, of whom history does not tell us how their lineage was extinguished. But we can see that during the era when Rome besieged Veii, the Etruscan lands were free and passionate about their freedom, hating the word "king" so much that

158. Machiavelli is referring to Germany.

when the people of Veii appointed a king for their defense against the Romans, and then called upon the Etruscans for help, the Etruscans, after much deliberation, decided against helping a people that lived under a king. The Etruscans decided that they would not come to the defense of a people that had already allowed itself to be subjugated by a ruler.[159]

It is easy enough to understand how a people's love of freedom arises, because we have seen from experience that states have grown in land and wealth only if they are free: The greatness that Athens achieved within a century of liberating itself from the tyranny of Pisistratus[160] is astonishing, and even more astonishing the greatness that Rome achieved after it freed itself from its kings. The reason these cities flourished is easy to understand, because it is the pursuit of the public interest, not private interest, that will make a city great. Without doubt, the pursuit of the public interest is seen as crucial only in a republic, because everything vital to the republic is carried out. During this process harm is done to this or that private individual, but there are so many who benefit from the common good that the majority sees to it that it is carried out despite the resistance of the few who are harmed. The opposite occurs when there is a prince, because more often than not what he does in his own interest will harm the city, and what he does for the city will harm his interests. Consequently, the moment a tyranny replaces freedom, the least harm that can be expected for that state is that it no longer progresses, and stops growing in power and wealth. But in most cases—in fact, always—these states begin to regress. Even if by chance the tyrant proves capable, expanding his dominions through courage and military skill, it will not result in any benefit to the state but only to him. He will not be able to honor any of the good and valorous citizens under his yoke, as he does not want to have to be suspicious of them. Nor can he subjugate the states he conquers into offering tribute to the state of which he is tyrant, be-

159. Livy (Book V, chapter 1), however, writes: "The Etruscans were offended, as they hated kingship as much as they did the new king himself. They found him odious for his wealth and pride. He had once sacrilegiously broken up the games of a solemn religious festival in fury that another man had been preferred to himself as priest."

160. Pisistratus and his sons ruled Athens from 546 to 510 BCE, after which Athens entered its Golden Age, which lasted until it was defeated by Sparta in the Peloponnesian War in 404 BCE.

cause it is not to his advantage to make his own state powerful. It is in fact to his advantage to keep the territories under his control divided, each recognizing him alone. As a result it is the tyrant who benefits from his new dominions, not his state. Anyone who wishes to confirm this opinion can find many examples in Xenophon's treatise *On Tyranny*.[161]

Hence it is not surprising that the ancients, in their desire to live in freedom, persecuted tyrants with such vigor, and held the word "liberty" in such high esteem. An example is when Hieronymus, Hiero's grandson, was assassinated in Syracuse.[162] As soon as the news of his death reached his army, which was not far from Syracuse, the soldiers took up arms against his assassins, but when they heard all Syracuse shouting the word "liberty," they relented, enthralled by that word. Hieronymus's army put aside their anger against the tyrannicides and began to consider how a free government might be set up in that city.

Nor is it surprising that populaces have been known to undertake extraordinary feats of revenge against those who deprived them of their liberty. I could cite many examples, but will limit myself to one that occurred during the Peloponnesian War in Corcyra, a Greek city. Greece was divided, some of the states supporting the Athenians, others the Spartans. One result was that opposing classes within many Greek cities sought support from Sparta or Athens to further their cause. In Corcyra the noble faction prevailed, and deprived the populace of its freedom. But the populace, with the help of the Athenians, regained power, rounded up the nobles, and locked them in a prison large enough to hold them all. From there they brought out nine or ten men at a time under the guise of sending them into exile to different places, but instead slaughtered them in many cruel ways.[163] When the remaining nobles realized what was awaiting them, they decided to avoid an ignominious death and armed themselves as best they could. They repulsed all who tried to enter the prison. They defended the gate

---

161. In Xenophon's treatise *On Tyranny*, also known in English as *Hieron*, the tyrant Hiero of Syracuse and the poet Simonides argue over the benefits and disadvantages of exercising tyranny.

162. Hieronymus was assassinated in 215 BCE, "stabbed many times before help could be called" (Livy, Book XXIV, chapter 7).

163. Machiavelli follows Thucydides's dexcription in *The Peloponnesian War*, Book IV, chapters 46–48.

until the populace, roused by the clamor, came running and knocked down the roof of the prison, crushing the nobles beneath the ruins. There were many other such terrible and notable cases in Greece, which shows that man will seek greater vengeance for liberty that is taken from him than for liberty that someone intends to take from him.

If one reflects on why in those ancient times men were greater lovers of liberty than in our times, one will conclude that it is for the same reason that men today are less strong. The reason is, I believe, the difference between our upbringing and that of ancient times, which is caused by the difference between our religion and that of the ancients. Though our religion has revealed the truth to us and the true path, it has made us value worldly honor less, while the pagans valued it greatly, considering it to be the highest good, and consequently were fiercer in action. This is evident in many of their customs, beginning with the magnificence of their sacrifices in comparison to the humbleness of ours, whose ceremonies are subdued rather than magnificent and have no action that is fierce or bold. The ceremonies of the ancients, on the other hand, had great pomp and magnificence, and also had sacrifices filled with blood and ferocity, countless animals slaughtered, a terrible sight that made men ferocious. Furthermore, ancient religion beatified only men who were filled with worldly glory, such as generals and princes, while our religion glorifies men who are humble and contemplative rather than men of action. Our religion also places the highest value on humility, debasement, and disdain for worldly matters, while ancient religion placed the highest value on greatness of spirit, strength of body, and on everything that makes men strong. If our religion does demand that you be strong, it is so that you will be able to bear suffering rather than carry out feats of strength. It is this way of life that seems to have rendered the world weak, delivering it to wicked men to be ransacked. And these men have no trouble in doing so, since mankind, its eyes set on paradise, strives to endure pain rather than avenge it. If the world seems to have become effeminate, and heaven disarmed, this doubtless arises more from the cowardice of men who have interpreted our religion through the prism of indolence, and not through that of skill and valor. Were they to consider how our religion permits the exaltation and defense of one's native land, they would see how it also wants us to love and honor it, and to prepare ourselves to be the kind of men who can defend it. Our up-bringing and the false interpretation of our religion has resulted in there no longer being as many republics in the world today as there were in ancient times, nor do we consequently see as great a love for liberty. Another compelling reason for this, however, is that with its arms and grandeur the Roman Empire destroyed all the republics and free states it occupied. Even though the Roman Empire later col-lapsed, very few of its provinces have been able to regroup or reorga-nize themselves into free states. Be this as it may, in every corner of the earth the Romans had encountered alliances between states which were heavily armed and fought doggedly to defend their liberty. This demonstrates that the Romans would never have been able to over-come them without their own exceptional skill.

As an example of a state within such an alliance I would like to limit myself to the Samnites. It is amazing, and Livy himself admits this, that they were so powerful, and their army so effective, that they were able to resist the Romans until the days when Papirius Cursor, the son of Papirius the Elder, was consul—a period of forty-six years—despite the routs and the devastation of their lands and all the carnage in their territories.[164] It seems all the more amazing that today the former Samnite lands, where there were so many cities and such great popu-lations, are almost uninhabited, whereas in ancient times there was so much order and power that Samnium would have been unconquerable had it not been assaulted by Roman skill. It is easy to understand where such order came from and where such disorder: It all came from their having first lived freely and then in slavery. All lands and coun-tries that live freely, as I said above, prosper. In them one finds thriving populations, with marriage easier and more desirable because any man will gladly procreate sons when he believes he can feed them, without worrying that their patrimony will be seized, and knowing that they will not only be born free and not slaves, but that they can, through their own skill, become rulers. Riches are seen to multiply more swiftly, both from agriculture and from crafts. Everyone gladly works to increase these things, seeking to obtain the goods he believes he can

---

164. Livy (Book X, chapter 31) writes: "I will not now recount the destruction of all those years that overtook both peoples, and the troubles they endured, and yet all this was power-less to break the resolution or the spirit of the Samnites."

enjoy once he has acquired them. As a result, men will vie to think about private and public benefit, with the result that both grow quite miraculously.

The opposite happens in the states that live in slavery. The more they recede from the good to which they were accustomed, the harsher their slavery becomes. And of all harsh servitude, the harshest is to be subjugated by a republic: first, because it is more lasting and one cannot hope to escape; second, the aim of a republic is to enervate and weaken all the bodies around it so that its own body will grow. A prince who subjugates you, on the other hand, will not enervate and weaken you, unless he is a barbarian prince and a destroyer of lands and civilizations, as oriental princes are. But if the prince has an ordinary and humane disposition, more often than not he will love his subject states as his own and leave their crafts and almost all their old institutions intact, so that even if these states cannot grow as they would if they were free, they will not come to ruin as if they were slaves: By this I mean the slavery the states fall into when they are subjected to a foreign prince, as I have already discussed those which had one of their own citizens as prince.

Anyone who weighs all the things I have said will not be surprised at the power the Samnites had when they were free, and the weakness into which they declined once they were enslaved. Livy testifies to this on many occasions, most of all when he discusses Hannibal's war, when the Samnites, oppressed by a Roman legion stationed in Nola, sent emissaries to Hannibal pleading with him to rescue them.[165] These emissaries proclaimed in their speeches that the Samnites had fought the Romans for a hundred years with their own soldiers and generals, often withstanding two consular armies and two consuls, but that they had now fallen so low that they could barely defend themselves against a small Roman legion stationed in Nola.

---

165. Livy in Book XXIII, chapters 41 and 42, describes these incidents and their speech to Hannibal, which begins: "We fought the Romans for a century without aid from a foreign general or army."

On how Rome became a great state, destroying the states that surrounded it, and how it took foreigners into its ranks

"All the while Rome grows on the ruins of Alba."[166] Those who intend their city to become a great empire must endeavor to fill it with inhabitants, because without an abundance of men it will never become a great city. This can be done in two ways: through love or through force. If it is through love, one must keep the roads open for foreigners who aspire to come live in one's city, everyone living there willingly. If it is through force, one will destroy the neighboring cities and send their inhabitants to live in one's own city. Rome followed this practice so diligently that by the time of their sixth king, Rome had eighty thousand men capable of bearing arms. The Romans wanted to adopt the ways of the good farmer who will prune the first branches that a tree sprouts so that it will grow well and produce ripe fruit, and so that the power remaining in the roots can with time make it grow more lushly and bear more fruit. The examples of Sparta and Athens demonstrate that this way of enlarging a state and creating an empire is effective: These two states had powerful armies and the best laws, and yet they did not reach the greatness of the Roman Empire, even if by comparison Rome seemed unruly and disorganized. No other reason for Rome's greatness can be put forward than the one I have already suggested: Rome had enlarged the body of its state in both these ways and

---

166. Machiavelli quotes Livy (Book I, chapter 30) in Latin: *Crescit interea Roma Albae ruinis.*

was able to arm eighty thousand men, while Sparta and Athens never surpassed twenty thousand each. This was not the result of Rome's having a more advantageous location, only that it had a different way of proceeding. Lycurgus, the founder of the Spartan state, believed that nothing would corrupt his laws more than introducing new inhabitants into Sparta, and consequently did his utmost to prevent foreigners mixing with Spartans. Not only did he forbid intermarriage, citizenship, and other interaction that brings people together, but he decreed that only money made of leather could be used in his state. He did this in order to discourage merchants from coming to Sparta with goods or crafts. The result was that the city could never grow in inhabitants. And as all of our actions imitate nature, it is neither possible nor natural that a delicate trunk will be able to sustain heavy branches. Therefore a small republic cannot occupy cities and kingdoms that are more effective or bigger than it is, and if it does, it will meet the same fate as a tree whose branches are larger than its trunk: holding them up with difficulty, the trunk will break in the slightest breeze. This was the case of Sparta, which successfully occupied all the city-states in Greece. And yet the moment Thebes rebelled, all the other cities followed suit and the trunk remained alone and without branches. This could not happen to Rome, as its trunk was so thick that it could support branches of any size. This and other ways of proceeding that I shall describe are what made Rome powerful and great. Livy demonstrated this in his well-chosen phrase: "All the while Rome grows on the ruins of Alba."

• • •

CHAPTER THIRTEEN

ON HOW ONE RISES FROM LOW TO HIGH ESTATE THROUGH DECEPTION MORE THAN THROUGH FORCE

I consider it true that men of low fortune rarely if ever reach high rank without using either force or deception, though such rank can also be reached by gift or heredity. I also believe that force alone is never enough, though deception alone can be. Anyone who reads about the lives of Philip of Macedon, Agathocles of Sicily,[167] and many other such men will see that those of the lowest or at least limited fortune have gained kingdoms or great empires through deception. Xenophon in his life of Cyrus also demonstrates the necessity of deception.[168] If one considers Cyrus's first expedition against the king of Armenia, one will see that it is marked by deception, and that Cyrus occupied that kingdom through trickery, not force.[169] One can only conclude that a

167. Machiavelli also refers to Philip of Macedon (360–336 BCE) and Agathocles (361–289 BCE) in *The Prince*. In chapter 12: "The Thebans had made Philip of Macedon their general after the death of Epaminondas, but once Philip was victorious in battle he took away the Thebans' liberty." And in chapter 8: "One morning Agathocles called together the people and the senate of Syracuse as if to discuss important issues concerning the republic, and then at a signal to his soldiers had them kill all the senators and the richest men of the city." (See also note 30 in *The Prince*.)

168. Machiavelli is referring to Xenophon's *Cyropaedia*: In Book I, chapter 6, young Cyrus asks his father how one overcomes the enemy in battle, to which the father answers: "My son, this is not a simple question you are asking. He who intends to do this must be a plotter, cunning, deceitful, a cheat, a thief, and rapacious, and outdo his enemy in everything."

169. Xenophon in *Cyropaedia*, Book II, chapter 4, has Cyrus explain his tactics of organizing hunting expeditions with his men near the borders of Armenia. When the day comes for him

prince who aspires to great deeds must learn to deceive. Cyrus also deceived his maternal uncle Cyaxares, the king of the Medes, in many ways, and Xenophon demonstrates how Cyrus would not have been able to achieve the greatness that he did without this deception.

Nor do I believe that any man of low fortune who attained great power managed to do so through sincerity and open force, but only through deception. Giovanni Galeazzo's seizing power and control of Lombardy from his uncle, Messer Bernabò, is another example.[170] And what a prince is compelled to do as he begins to expand his state, a republic must also do until it has become powerful enough to use force alone. Rome prevailed because by choice or chance it always used any means necessary to achieve greatness. As Rome began to expand, it could not have resorted to greater deception than it used in acquiring allies, which I have described above, because through these alliances it made these allies its slaves, which was the fate of the Latins and the other peoples surrounding Rome. First Rome used these peoples' armies to subjugate the peoples living adjacent to their territories and strengthen Rome's standing and prestige, and then, having subjugated them, Rome grew to such an extent that it could vanquish anyone. And all the while, the Latins did not realize they had become slaves until they saw the Samnites twice defeated and forced into a treaty.[171] Through this victory, the Romans increased their standing with distant princes, who now encountered Rome's prestige though not Rome's armies. But this victory also generated envy and suspicion among those who did encounter and experience Rome's armies, among them the Latins. This envy and fear were so great that not only the Latins, but also their colonies in Latium, along with the Campanians, who had only recently been defended by the Romans, all conspired against Rome. The Latins started the war, as I have already mentioned, in the way most wars are started: They did not attack the Romans, but defended the Sidicini against the Samnites, who were fighting with the sanction of the Romans. Livy shows us that the Latins attacked once they became aware of the Roman deception. He has Annius Setinus

---

to invade, his presence with a large force of men will not arouse the suspicions of the Armenians.
170. Gian Galeazzo Visconti (1351–1402), ruler of Pavia, seized Milan and other territories of Lombardy from his uncle after imprisoning and executing him.
171. Livy describes these incidents in Book VII, chapters 33, 36, and 37.

say: "For under the semblance of a treaty between equals we have already been enslaved."[172] So it is clear that in their initial expansions the Romans were ready enough to resort to deception, which has always been necessary for those wanting to reach sublime heights from small beginnings. This deception is less deserving of vituperation the more it is concealed, as was the deception of the Romans.

---

172. Machiavelli is quoting Livy, Book VIII, chapter 4, in Latin: *Nam si etiam nunc sub umbra foederis aequi servitutem pati possumus.*

CHAPTER FIFTEEN

WEAK STATES HAVE ALWAYS WAVERED IN THEIR DELIBERATIONS, AND SLOW DELIBERATIONS ARE ALWAYS HARMFUL

If one considers the beginning of the war between the Latins and the Romans, one can see how important it is in an assembly to keep to the matter at hand and not waver or be uncertain about the issue. This became apparent in the assembly the Latins called together when they considered breaking their alliance with Rome.[173] The Romans sensed the ill humor that had arisen among the Latin people, and to evaluate the matter and see if they could be won back without Rome's having to resort to arms, requested that they send eight citizens to Rome to consult with them.[174] The Latins, aware that they had done many things against the will of the Romans, called together an assembly to decide who should go to Rome and what they should say. During the debate, Annius, their praetor, spoke these words: "I think it would be more vital to our interests if you were to give greater consideration to what we should do rather than what we should say. Once a decision has been reached it will be easy enough to accommodate our words to the situa-

173. Rome had entered into an uneasy alliance with the Latin League, a confederation of Latin tribes living in the vicinity of Rome, in 493 BCE. Tensions rose over the next century as Rome's power grew and the power of the Latin League diminished.
174. Livy writes in Book VIII, chapter 3: "Though the collapse of the Latin alliance was no longer in any doubt, the Romans, as if they cared for the Samnites and not for themselves, summoned ten Latin chiefs to Rome to inform them of their wishes."

tion."[175] This statement must be heeded by every prince and republic, because words cannot be accommodated to the ambiguity and uncertainty of what one might wish to do. But once a decision has been reached and what is to be done determined, it is easy enough to find words. I have noted Annius's statement all the more willingly as I have often seen the harmful effect of such ambiguity on public actions, with damage and shame to our republic of Florence as the outcome. And it will always be the case that in doubtful decisions calling for courage, when it is weak men who gather to deliberate, there will be wavering.

Slow and ponderous deliberations are no less harmful than ambiguous ones, particularly those that need to be made to help an ally, because slowness helps no one and only hurts you. Such deliberations are the result of weakness of spirit and lack of strength, or the result of a malignity among those who are deliberating and who hamper and impede decisions out of their desire to ruin the state or fulfill some other aspiration. Good citizens, even when they see the public's enthusiasm turning to a bad choice, will never impede deliberations, particularly not when time is pressing. Hieronymus, the tyrant of Syracuse, died while war was raging between the Carthaginians and the Romans, and the Syracusans debated whether they should form an alliance with Rome or with Carthage.[176] The vehemence of the opposing factions was so great that the matter remained unsettled, and no resolution was reached until Apollonides, one of Syracuse's foremost citizens, in a speech filled with prudence, pointed out that neither those who argued for holding to Rome nor those who argued for Carthage should be spurned. It was vital, he argued, to overcome the wavering and slowness at reaching a decision, because such ambiguity would lead to the ruin of the state. Once a decision was reached, regardless of what it might be, one could hope for some good. Livy could not have demonstrated more effectively in this passage the damage indecision brings with it.

He shows this again in the case of the Latins: After they had asked the Lavinians for help against the Romans, the Lavinians dragged out

---

175. Machiavelli quotes a slightly altered passage from Livy, Book VIII, chapter 4, in Latin: *Ad summam rerum nostrarum pertinere arbitror ut cogitetis magis quid agendum nobis quam quid loquendum sit. Facile erit, explicatis consiliis, accommodare rebus verba.* (Machiavelli has added to Livy's text the words *ut cogitetis magis* ("if you were to give greater consideration").

176. Machiavelli closely follows Livy's text from Book XXIV, chapter 28.

the deliberations for such a long time that when they were finally marching out the city gates to come to the Latins' aid, they were greeted by the news that the Latins had been defeated. Milionius, their praetor, said: "These few steps we have marched will cost us much with the Roman people."[177] The Lavinians should have decided swiftly either to help or not to help the Latins. By not helping them, the Lavinians would not have angered the Romans, and by helping the Latins—had their help been in time—they might with their combined forces have defeated the Romans. Since the Lavinians wavered, they were bound to lose either way, as proved to be the case.

Had the Florentines heeded Livy's text, they would not have had to face so much trouble from the French when King Louis XII marched on Italy against Duke Ludovico of Milan. As he prepared his campaign, Louis sought an alliance with the Florentines. The Florentine emissaries at his court agreed that Florence would remain neutral, and that should he march on Italy he would leave their government intact and take them under his protection. With everything agreed upon, he gave Florence a month to ratify this agreement. But the ratification was delayed by those who, through lack of prudence, favored Duke Ludovico's cause, until Louis was on the brink of victory, at which point Louis turned down the ratification that the Florentines hastily offered him. He was aware that they were not pledging their friendship voluntarily but out of necessity. Florence now had to pay him a very large sum of money and its government almost fell, as on another occasion it did in fact fall for a similar reason.[178] This wavering deliberation was all the more blameworthy because it was of no use to Duke Ludovico either, who, had he been victorious, would have shown a good deal more hostility toward the Florentines than did Louis XII. I have discussed the harm that comes to republics that have this weakness in a previous chapter,[179] but I took the opportunity to do so again here with a new example, as it seems to me a most vital matter for all republics such as Florence to take note of.

177. Machiavelli translates Milionius's statement directly from Livy (Book VIII, chapter 11).
178. Machiavelli is referring to the Battle of Ravenna in 1512.
179. See Book I, chapter 38 above, titled "On How Weak States Are Indecisive and Cannot Reach Decisions, and How When They Do It Is Usually Because They Have Been Forced to, Not Because They Have Chosen to Do So."

CHAPTER TWENTY

ON THE DANGERS TO A PRINCE OR REPUBLIC IN MAKING USE OF AN AUXILIARY OR MERCENARY ARMY

Had I not discussed at length in another of my works the uselessness of a mercenary and auxiliary army as opposed to the usefulness of one's own, I would have extended my discussion further in this chapter.[180] But as I have already discussed this matter extensively, I shall be brief. However, I did not think it appropriate to pass over it entirely, as I found in Livy so many examples of the use of auxiliary troops. Auxiliary troops are those which another prince or republic sends to help you, and which they pay and command. Turning to Livy's text,[181] the Romans had in two instances routed Samnite armies with troops that they had sent to help the Campanians who were warring with the Samnites. Having freed the Campanians from the Samnites, the Romans returned to Rome, leaving two legions in their city of Capua as a defense force so that the Campanians would not fall prey to the Samnites again. These legions succumbed to idleness, which they came to enjoy so much that they forgot Rome and their duty to the Senate, and decided to take up arms and become masters of the territory they had so skillfully defended. In their view, the Campanians were not worthy

---

180. See *The Prince*, chapter 12, titled "Of the Different Types of Armies, and of Mercenaries," and chapter 13, titled "The Auxiliary Army, the Citizen Army, and the Army That Combines the Two."
181. Livy, Book VII, chapter 33 and following.

of owning the land they could not defend.[182] When Rome realized what was happening, it intervened, as I shall discuss in greater detail when I talk about conspiracies.[183] Therefore I repeat: Of all the kinds of soldiers, auxiliary troops are the most harmful, because the prince or republic that resorts to them has no authority over them; only he who has sent the auxiliary troops does. As I have pointed out, auxiliary troops are sent by a ruler under the command of his own generals and banners, and are paid by him, as was the army that the Romans had sent to Capua. After a victory, such troops will in most cases prey on those who called upon them for defense as well as those whom they were there to fight. These auxiliaries will do this either through the malignity of the ruler who sent them, or because of their own ambitions. Though Rome had intended to uphold its treaties and agreements with the Campanians, those two legions had overcome the Campanians with such ease that Rome did not long hesitate to seize their government and territories. One could cite many examples, but I would like this one to suffice, along with that of the people of Rhegium, whose lives and lands were taken by a legion that the Romans had sent to defend them.[184]

Therefore, princes or republics must choose any means other than auxiliary troops to defend them if they have to depend on them entirely, because any pact or agreement with the enemy, no matter how harsh, will be easier to bear than this alternative. If one reads carefully about past events and examines present events, one will find that for every ruler who benefited from auxiliary troops there have been countless rulers who were deceived. An ambitious prince or republic cannot hope for a better opportunity to occupy a city or country than

---

182. Livy (Book VII, chapter 38) writes: "The soldiers, beguiled by all the pleasures and delights around them, soon relinquished all memory of Rome. In the winter they gathered together to conspire on how they might seize Capua by illicit means. [...] 'Why should these lands, the most fertile in all of Italy, and this worthy city, belong to the Campanians, who cannot even defend their lives or their possessions? Why should Capua not belong to our victorious army, the army that drove away the Samnites with our sweat and blood?' "
183. See Book III, chapter 6, p. 285.
184. Polybius in *Histories* (Book I, chapter 7) writes: "The people of Rhegium, when Pyrrhus was crossing to Italy [...] requested protection and help from the Romans. A Roman garrison of four thousand, under the command of a Campanian named Decius, entered the city and for a time preserved it and the people's faith [...] but attracted to the pleasant land and the private wealth of the citizens, they seized the city."

to be asked to send in his army to defend it. Consequently, anyone so ambitious as to call in an auxiliary army, not only in his own defense but in order to attack others, is seeking to acquire territory he cannot hold and which can easily be taken from him. But man's ambition is so great that in order to satisfy a wish of the moment, he will not think of the evil that will soon enough descend upon him as a result. Nor do examples from ancient times move him in this or any other matter we have discussed, because if man took notice of them, he would understand that the more generosity he shows toward his neighbors and the more disinclination to occupy them, the more eager they will be to throw themselves into his arms.

Insults and affronts give rise to hatred against those who use them, without conferring any benefit

I believe that one of man's most prudent courses of action is to abstain from threatening or abusing with words, because neither the one nor the other reduces the enemy's strength: threats make the enemy more cautious, while verbal abuse will fan their hatred of you and make them think more actively of ways to harm you. One can see this in the example of the people of Veii, who, to the injury of war against the Romans, added the insult of dishonoring them with words.[185] Any prudent commander will prevent his soldiers from doing this, as it only stirs up the enemy and inspires them to vengeance without in any way impeding their attack, so that dishonoring with words is in fact a weapon that turns against you.

A noteworthy example of this occurred in Asia: Cobades, commander of the Persian army, had been besieging the city of Amida for a

---

185. Livy (Book II, chapter 45) writes: "[The soldiers of Veii] rode right up to the Roman camp and challenged the Romans. When this had no effect, they shouted insults at army and consuls alike, declaring that the consuls were using internal discord as an excuse to cover up the cowardice of their men [. . .] Right beside the ramparts and gates of the camp the Etruscans shouted comments, true as well as false, on the upstart nature and descent of the Roman race. The consuls remained calm, but the ignorant soldiers were filled with rage and shame [. . .] So contemptuous and arrogant were the enemy's taunts that all the soldiers crowded around the general's tent, demanding battle."

long time and decided to retreat, worn out by the tedium of the siege. He was already decamping when the men of Amida came out onto the walls and, arrogant in their victory, unleashed every kind of abuse, insulting Cobades and his men and rebuking them for their cowardice and indolence. Cobades was so angered by the insults that he resumed the siege, and in his fury took and sacked the city within a few days. The same happened to the people of Veii, who, as I have said, were not content with waging war on the Romans, but also attacked them with words. The men of Veii climbed onto their stockades and shouted insults at the Romans, hurting them more with their words than with their weapons: and the Roman soldiers, who had initially been pressed into this war against their will, now compelled the consuls to take up the fight. Consequently the people of Veii, like the people of Amida, paid the penalty for their arrogance.

Hence good generals and statesmen must take every measure so that insults and invective are not used by the state or the army, neither among themselves nor against the enemy. If they insult the enemy, they run the risk of the trouble I have just mentioned, and if they insult each other it is even worse, unless they are careful, as wise men have always been. The Roman legions left stationed in Campania conspired against the Campanians, and the conspiracy gave rise to a mutiny, as I shall narrate in the proper place.[186] The mutiny was then suppressed by Valerius Corvinus, and among the provisions in the agreement was that the severest penalties would be used against anyone who rebuked any of the soldiers for that mutiny.[187] During the Punic War, Tiberius Gracchus was given command of a number of slaves whom the Romans had armed because they were short of men. One of the first things he did was to introduce capital punishment for anyone who would hold the former slavery of any of these men against them. The Romans considered insulting a man or reproaching

186. See Book III, chapter 6 below. See also Machiavelli's other discussions of the Campanians (pp. 243 and 285)
187. Livy (Book VII, chapter 41) writes: "[The dictator] with the permission of the Senate had the populace, which was assembled in the Petilian Grove, swear that no proceedings would be brought against soldiers who had defected. He also asked the people to grant him the favor that they would never, either in jest or in earnest, reproach any of them."

greater anger, whether the words were true or spoken in jest. "For him for a shameful matter extremely harmful, as has been mentioned above, because nothing would inflame his spirit so much nor generate when they draw excessively from the truth, sharp jests leave a bitter memory."[188]

188. Machiavelli presents in Latin an altered quote of Tacitus: *Nam facetiae asperae, quando nimium ex vero traxere, acrem sui memoriam relinquunt.* Tacitus in fact writes (Annals XV, 68): *[Nero] ferociam amici metuit, saepe asperis facetiis inlusus, quae ubi multum ex vero traxere, acrem sui memoriam relinquunt.* ("[Nero] feared the ferocity of his friend, who often mocked him with the kind of cruel humor that, when it draws too much on the truth, leaves a bitter memory").

PRUDENT PRINCES AND REPUBLICS SHOULD BE CONTENT WITH VICTORY, BECAUSE WHEN THEY ARE NOT, THEY USUALLY LOSE

Insulting the enemy usually arises from arrogance brought on by victory, or a false hope of victory. This false hope makes men err not only in what they say, but also in what they do. Once hope enters the heart, it causes man to go too far and risk losing a benefit that is certain in the hope of gaining an even better one that is, however, uncertain. This is a point that merits consideration, because men often let such hope lead them astray to the detriment of their city or state. As I cannot demonstrate my point as clearly with pure reasoning, I would like to demonstrate it with ancient and modern examples.

After Hannibal had routed the Romans at Cannae, he sent emissaries back to Carthage to inform them of his victory and request help.[189] The Carthaginian senate deliberated, and Hanno, an old and prudent citizen, advised that Carthage use its victory wisely and make peace with the Romans. As victors, Hanno argued, the Carthaginians could negotiate a peace with optimal stipulations: It would be a mistake to wait for a defeat to negotiate peace. The Carthaginians' intention should be to prove to the Romans that the Carthaginians were capable of defeating them, and having achieved victory, Hanno declared, they should not risk losing this opportunity in the hope of an

---

189. A major battle (216 BCE) of the Second Punic War in southeastern Italy in which Hannibal utterly defeated a Roman army of eighty thousand men, of whom only fourteen thousand escaped.

even greater one. Hanno's suggestion was not adopted, though later the Carthaginian senate, after the opportunity had been lost, saw only too clearly how wise his suggestion had been.

After Alexander the Great had conquered all the East, the Republic of Tyre became aware of Alexander's importance. Tyre was illustrious and powerful in those days, as its city, like Venice, was on the sea. They sent emissaries to him, avowing that though they were prepared to honor him in every way, they were not prepared to accept him or his men on their land. Alexander was angered that a city would, unlike the rest of the world, close its gates to him. He rebuffed their offer, refused their conditions, and began a siege. Situated on the water, the city was well supplied with the provisions and ammunition necessary for its defense. Within four months Alexander realized that, to Tyre's glory, this single city had taken up more of his time than many of his other conquests, and so he proposed a treaty, agreeing to all the conditions Tyre had initially stipulated. But the people of Tyre, swollen with pride, did not want to accept his offer, and even killed the emissaries he had sent. Alexander was outraged, and attacked Tyre with such fury that he conquered and destroyed it, killing and enslaving all its people.[190]

In 1512 a Spanish army marched into Florentine territory to return the Medici to power and levy tribute on the city. They had been summoned by citizens who had given them hope that the moment they set foot on Florentine land the inhabitants would take up arms in their support. When they marched in, however, they found no one there, and as they were short of supplies they attempted to reach an agreement with Florence. But swollen with pride, the people of Florence rejected this offer, which led to the loss of Prato and the fall of the Florentine government.

Therefore rulers who are attacked cannot make a greater mistake, when they are attacked by men far more powerful, than to refuse a treaty, particularly when it is offered to them. This treaty will never be so unfavorable that it will not in some way benefit the ruler who accepts it, and will be part of his victory. The people of Tyre should have been satisfied that Alexander accepted the conditions he had at first

190. In 332 BCE, Alexander the Great, during his campaigns in Phoenicia, had laid siege to Tyre for eight months, finally capturing the city.

refused. It would have been a sufficient victory for them to have been able, weapons in hand, to make such a man bow to their will. The Florentines also should have been satisfied with the lesser victory of the Spanish army, ceding to some of their wishes without satisfying them all, because the intention of the Spanish army was to overthrow the government of Florence, sever its connection with France, and extract a tribute from the city. If of these three intentions the Spanish army had achieved the last two and allowed the Florentine people to keep their government intact, both sides would have had some honor and some satisfaction. Nor, if they could have kept their liberty, would the Florentine people have needed to care about their old alliance with France or having to pay a tribute to the Spanish army. The Florentines, even if they saw a bigger and almost certain victory within their grasp, put their fate at the discretion of Fortune, staking everything on one card, something a prudent man will do only as a last resort.

After sixteen years of glory, Hannibal left Italy, called back to Carthage to save his fatherland, where he found Hasdrubal and Syphax defeated, the Kingdom of Numidia lost,[191] and Carthage reduced to the limits of its city walls, with himself and his army as its last hope. Aware of this, he did not wish to risk the city until he had tried all other measures, and was not ashamed to beg for peace, judging that if his city were to have any hope, it was in peace and not in war. When the enemy turned this down, Hannibal decided to fight with all his might, judging that he might still be able to win, or if he lost, he would lose with glory.[192] If Hannibal, who was so valiant and skilled and had his army intact, sought peace before battle when he saw that in losing, Carthage would be enslaved, then what should another man with less valor, skill, and experience do? But men make the mistake of not being able to set limits to their hopes. They base themselves on these hopes without assessing their feasibility, and so come to ruin.

191. Hasdrubal, Hannibal's brother, had formed an allegiance with King Syphax of Numidia to fight the Roman forces in North Africa.
192. Machiavelli is discussing the events described by Livy in Book XXX, chapters 16–31.

BOOK III

CHAPTER ONE

ON THE NEED TO KEEP BRINGING A SECT[193]
OR A STATE BACK TO ITS ORIGINS
IF IT IS TO ENDURE

It is too true that all the things of this world have an end, but those things that manage to pass through the entire cycle that Heaven has ordained for them do so only because they do not let themselves fall into disarray, but maintain themselves in an ordered fashion. They do not let their system change, or if they do, it is a change that benefits rather than harms them. Here I am talking about mixed bodies, such as states or sects, and I propose that changes that restore them to their origins are to their benefit. Accordingly, the sects and states that are best organized and have the longest life are those which can keep renewing themselves through their institutions, or by some event from outside. It is quite clear that if they do not renew themselves they will not endure.

The way to renew these bodies is, as I have said, to take them back toward their origins, because the origins of all sects, republics, and kingdoms inevitably have some good through which they can reclaim their initial worth and growth. As time passes, this original goodness becomes corrupted, and if something does not intervene to restore the body to its roots, the corruption will inevitably kill it. As the doctors of medicine say: "Every day the body absorbs something that will sooner or later require a cure."[194]

193. *Setta* (sect): here in the sense of a political or religious body.
194. Machiavelli quotes in Latin the aphorism (probably inspired by the teachings of the Greek physician Galen) *Quod quotidie aggregatur aliquid, quod quandoque indiget curatione.*

This restoration to origins, when speaking of states, is done either by extrinsic events or intrinsic foresight. As for extrinsic events, it was clearly necessary for Rome to be taken by the Gauls[195] in order for it to be reborn, and once reborn it gathered new life and strength and again embraced religion and justice, which had begun to be corrupted. This is quite clear in Livy's *Histories*, in which he shows how, in sending the army out against the Gauls and in creating tribunes with consular power, the Romans no longer observed religious ceremony.[196] Similarly, the Romans not only did not punish the three Fabii who had fought against the Gauls in a way that was *contra ius gentium*, but in fact made them tribunes.[197] It is easy to assume that the Romans had begun to turn away from the sound laws created by Romulus and other judicious rulers after him, laws that were reasonable and necessary to preserve a free way of life. Then came the shock from outside when the Gauls occupied Rome, with the result that all the institutions of the state were subsequently renewed. The people of Rome realized that it was not only necessary to maintain religion and justice, but also to hold its good legislators in esteem. The people saw that it was important to place more value on the skill of these legislators than on any conveniences they might be deprived of because of the policies of these legislators. This is precisely what happened. The instant the Romans reclaimed Rome from the Gauls, they renewed all the institutions of their old religion, punished the Fabii who had fought *contra ius gentium*, and valued the skill and goodness of Camillus so highly that the Senate and everyone else set aside their jealousies and placed the heavy burden of government entirely in his hands.[198]

195. In 390 BCE, the Gauls laid siege to Rome, occupying and destroying much of the city before they were finally bought off.
196. Livy writes (Book V, chapter 38) that the Roman military tribunes had the army march into battle "without giving thought to man or gods, without auspices or sacrificial offerings."
197. Latin: "against the law of nations." In 391 BCE, Quintus Fabius Ambustus and his two brothers were sent as Roman emissaries to Clusium, which was being besieged by the Gauls. According to Livy, the three brothers violated "the law of nations" by intervening in the battle and fighting on the side of Clusium. Livy writes (Book V, chapter 36): "Contrary to the law of nations, the emissaries took up arms, and the Fates began to drive Rome toward its ruin." Livy writes that the Gauls demanded that the Fabii be delivered to them, but Rome refused, and instead elected the brothers consular tribunes, upon which the Gauls invaded and sacked Rome.
198. Marcus Furius Camillus was the legendary Roman general and dictator who had captured Veii. See note 35 to Book I, chapter 8 above. He is also discussed in Book I, chapter 55

Hence it is necessary, as I have already said, for members of any kind of body to examine themselves frequently, whether instigated by eternal or internal events. If by internal events, it is best when these arise either institutionally, which will often make members of the body reexamine matters, or by a good man who, through his example and good works, produces the same effect.

Consequently, this benefit comes about in a state through the skill either of a man or of an institution. As for the latter, the institutions that drew the Roman Republic back toward its origins were the tribunes of the plebeians and the censors, together with all the laws instituted against men's ruthless ambition and insolence. These institutions must be given life through the skill of a single citizen who bravely sets out to enforce them against the power of those who will not comply. In the era before Rome was seized by the Gauls, there were notable incidents of such enforcement, such as the killing of Brutus's sons, the deaths of the Decemvirs, and the murder of Maelius the Grain-dealer.[199] In the era after Rome was occupied by the Gauls, there were the deaths of Manlius Capitolanus and of Manlius Torquatus's son, the attempt of Papirius Cursor to condemn to death Fabius, his master of cavalry, and the charges against the Scipios.[200] Because these incidents were extreme and noteworthy, they recalled men to order. But when these incidents became more rare, they gave men more space in which to become corrupt and behave in ways that were dangerous and resulted in turmoil.

---

above. According to Roman historians, he was again made dictator when the Gauls were sacking Rome, at which point he defeated the Gallic army and recovered Rome's treasury from the Gauls.

199. For the killing of the sons of Brutus, see Book I, chapter 16 above, and note 71; also chapter 3 below. The Decemvirs were a legislative commission that was forced to abdicate in 449 BCE, when it became too tyrannical. The Decemvirs, however, were exiled, not killed (though according to Livy, two subsequently committed suicide). Spurius Maelius (d. 439 BCE) was a Roman plebeian who bought up a large amount of grain during the famine of 439 and sold it cheaply to the populace. He was then accused of trying to gain popularity to make himself king, and was murdered.

200. For Manlius Capitolinus, see Book I, chapter 8 above. During the Roman war against the Latins, Consul Titus Manlius Torquatus (thereafter a symbol of Roman sternness) decreed the execution of his son for having disobeyed the order of not engaging in single battle with the enemy. Quintus Fabius Maximus Rullianus had been consul five times, and was dictator in 315. During Lucius Papirius Cursor's term as dictator, Fabius had been victorious in battle against the Samnites, but his disobeying orders led Papirius Cursor to condemn him to death. On the charges against the Scipios, see Book I, chapter 29 above.

These extreme incidents should not occur more than ten years apart, because with the passing of time men begin to be careless with their customs and to break the law; if nothing occurs to remind them of the punishment and to rekindle fear in their hearts, there will be so many offenders that they can no longer be punished without danger.

The Medici, who ruled Florence between 1434 and 1494, always said that they had to retake power every five years, otherwise it was difficult to maintain. What they meant by "retaking power" was instilling in their subjects the kind of fear and terror that the populace had experienced when the Medici first seized power, crushing those who, in their view, had opposed them. When the memory of such terror fades, men speak out, becoming bold and striving for change.

So it is necessary to make provision to take the state back toward its origins. This can also be achieved by the skill of a single man who is not vulnerable to any law that involves punishment. But this man must be of such standing, and so exemplary, that good men will want to imitate him and bad men will be ashamed of leading a contrary way of life. Horatius Cocles, Scaevola, Fabricius, the two Dexii, Regulus Atilius,[201] and a few others were Romans of exceptional quality, who by their rare and valiant example had an effect on the state that was almost as powerful as that of the laws and institutions. Had these punishments and these exemplary individuals arisen at least every ten years, the inevitable result would have been that Rome would never have become corrupted. But as those punishments and individuals were increasingly few and far between, corruption grew. After Marcus Regulus there were no exemplary individuals, and though Rome had the two Catos, there was such an interval between them and Marcus Regulus, and then between the two Catos themselves, that their example remained isolated and did not have much effect,[202] especially that of the

---

201. Machiavelli is listing some of the foremost legendary heroes of Rome: In the sixth century BCE, Horatius Cocles and one other soldier held back the entire Etruscan army at the Sublician bridge by Rome, and Gaius Mucius Scaevola had demonstrated his courage before the Etruscan king by placing his hand in an altar fire until it burned, after which the king withdrew his forces from Rome. In the third century BCE, the statesman Gaius Fabricius Luscinus was regarded as a model of incorruptible Roman virtue, and Marcus Atilius Regulus as a model of heroic endurance.

202. Cato the Censor (234–149 BCE). Marcus Porcius Cato (95–46 BCE), Cato the Younger, was the great-grandson of Cato the Censor. He was one of the foremost statesmen fighting to preserve the Roman Republic.

second Cato, who found Rome so corrupted that he could not set the citizens a good example. These instances should suffice as far as republics are concerned.

As for sects, we can see from the example of our religion that such renewal is necessary. Had our religion not been drawn back toward its origins by Saint Francis and Saint Dominic,[203] it would have died out. These saintly men, with their poverty and their adherence to the example of Christ's life, brought our religion back into the minds of men after it had already died out. Their orders were so powerful that they kept the dishonesty of the prelates and religious leaders from destroying our religion. The friars lived in poverty, but were so trusted by the people in the confessional and in their preaching that they managed to convince the people that it was wrong to speak ill of evil men, and right to live in obedience to the Church: If the men of the church committed sins, it was up to God to punish them. As a result of this, the men of the Church can be as evil as they wish, because they do not fear a punishment they cannot see and do not believe in. Thus this renewal, begun by Saint Dominic and Saint Francis, has maintained and continues to maintain our religion in the state it is now in.

Kingdoms also need to renew themselves and take their laws back to their origins. It can be seen what a good effect this had in the Kingdom of France, which lives under laws and institutions more than any other kingdom. Its *parlements,* particularly the *Parlement* of Paris,[204] are the custodians of these laws and institutions, which are renewed by them every time they bring a legal action against a prince of that kingdom or condemn the king in their judgments. Until now these *parlements* have maintained themselves by being determined enforcers of the law against the nobles, but should they ever have allowed a nobleman's crimes to go unpunished, or such crimes to multiply, they would have ended up having to restore order through great upheaval, and the Kingdom of France would have run the risk of collapsing.

In conclusion, therefore, nothing is more vital in a community—whether it be a sect, a kingdom, or a republic—than to give it the status it had in its origins, and to endeavor that this be achieved by good institutions or good men, so that the return to origins does not have to

---

203. In the early thirteenth century, Saint Francis of Assisi founded the Franciscan Order, and Saint Dominic the Dominican Order.
204. See note 77 on page 73.

be effected by an external force. Even though an external force might sometimes be a perfect remedy, as the invasion of the Gauls was for Rome, it is so dangerous that it should at all costs be avoided. To demonstrate how the actions of particular men made Rome great and brought about many good results in that city, I shall proceed to a discussion of them, and with this I shall bring this third book and last part of the *Discourses* on Livy to its conclusion. And though the actions of the kings of Rome were great and significant, I shall refrain from discussing them at any length, as history has already done so, and I will mention them only when the kings did something pertaining to their private interests. I shall begin with Brutus, the father of Roman liberty.

CHAPTER TWO

On how wise it is at times
to feign foolishness

No man was ever so prudent or thought so wise for an exceptional action as Junius Brutus deserves to be for pretending to be a fool. Livy mentions only one reason that induced Junius Brutus to feign idiocy: to live more securely and maintain his patrimony.[205] Yet if one considers the progression of his actions, one might conclude that Junius Brutus did this in order to be less conspicuous and have a better prospect of toppling the king and freeing Rome when the opportunity arose. That this was on his mind becomes apparent from Junius Brutus's interpretation of the oracle of Apollo, when he pretended to fall down so that he could kiss the earth, believing that by doing this the gods would favor his designs.[206] Later Junius stood over the dead Lucretia in the presence of her father, her husband, and other of her relatives, and

205. Livy writes (Book I, chapter 56): "Lucius Junius Brutus, the son of Tarquinia, the king's sister, was a young man very different in intelligence from the dullard he pretended to be. For since his uncle had killed the leading men of the state, including his own brother, he decided to leave nothing in his person for the king to fear or in his possessions for him to covet. Safety lay in being an object of scorn."

206. According to Livy, King Tarquin had sent his sons Titus and Aruns to consult the oracle at Delphi to interpret a dire omen. Junius Brutus had accompanied them "as a figure of fun." The king's sons also asked the oracle who would be the next king of Rome, to which the oracle replied that he who kissed his mother first would be king. Livy writes (Book I, chapter 56): "But Brutus thought the Pythia's words meant something quite different. Pretending to slip, he fell to the ground and pressed his lips to the earth, the mother of us all."

was the first to pull the knife from her wound, making those present swear that they would never consent to any king's reigning over Rome again.[207]

Those who are dissatisfied with a prince can learn from Junius's example. But they must first measure and weigh their own strength, and if they are powerful enough to reveal themselves to their enemy and wage open war, they must follow his course as the least dangerous and most honorable. But if they do not have sufficient power to wage open war they must do their utmost to make their enemy their friend, doing whatever they judge necessary, finding pleasure in everything in which the prince finds pleasure, and taking delight in all the things that they see delight him. Such intimacy will, first of all, enable one to live in security. Without running any danger you can enjoy the prince's good fortune at his side, and furthermore you will have every opportunity to achieve your ends. It is true some will say that you should not stand so close to a prince that his ruin will drag you down with him, nor at such a distance that you will be unable to capitalize on his ruin. Of course the middle course would be best—that is, if a middle course were possible—but as I believe it to be impossible, I suggest following one of the two methods I have just mentioned, either distancing oneself from the prince or drawing closer to him. He who does otherwise, even if he is a man of notable qualities, will live in constant danger. Nor is it enough for him to proclaim: "I want no honors, no gains, I want to live quietly and without care!" Such excuses are heard, but not believed. Nor can a man of standing choose to step back in such a manner. Even if he is sincere in wishing to live without ambition, nobody would believe him. Consequently, even if he does wish to live in that manner, others will not allow it. It is therefore advisable to play the fool as Junius Brutus did, and one can look quite the fool when one praises, discusses, and does things contrary to one's nature and way of thinking just to please a prince. As I have spoken of Junius's wisdom in how he recovered liberty for Rome, I shall now speak of his severity in maintaining it.

---

207. Sextus Tarquinius, the king's son, raped Lucretia, who subsequently called together the men of her family, and, informing them of what had happened, killed herself. Livy describes the scene in Book I, chapter 59.

On how, if one wants to maintain a newly gained liberty, one must kill the sons of Brutus

Junius Brutus's severity was as necessary as it was expedient in maintaining the liberty he had just gained for Rome. His example is most rare in recorded history: a father sitting in judgment over his sons, and not only condemning them to death but also being present at their execution.[208] Those who read about ancient matters will always see that after a state has changed from a republic to a tyranny or from a tyranny to a republic, a memorable action is needed against the enemies of the new state. The ruler who chooses a tyranny and does not kill Brutus, or who chooses a republic and does not kill the sons of Brutus, will not hold power for long. As I have already discussed this at length I will say no more on the subject, except to offer one memorable example from our times and our city of Florence. Piero Soderini believed wrongly that with goodness and patience he could overcome the appetite of the sons of Brutus for returning to power under a new government.[209] Soderini was wise enough to be aware of the need to

---

208. See Book I, chapter 16 above. Livy (Book II, chapter 5): "The traitors were condemned to death, and what was extraordinary was that the consuls imposed on a father the duty of punishing his own children. The father who should not even have been present at the execution, was made by Fortuna to carry it out."

209. In 1502 Piero Soderini had been elected Gonfalonier for life in Florence. Soderini was Machiavelli's patron. By "the sons of Brutus" Machiavelli means the Medici, who were the former and subsequent rulers of Florence, as Soderini was deposed by them in 1512.

act, and furthermore Fortune and the ambition of his enemies gave him every opportunity to eliminate them. Yet he never took action, because he believed he could extinguish such evil humors with goodness and patience and by bestowing gifts and rewards on some of his enemies, thus eliminating a part of their enmity. Furthermore, Soderini felt—as he often confided to his friends—that if he had chosen to counter his opponents with open force and had crushed them, he would have had to assume illegal power and sweep aside the laws of equal rights among citizens. Even if Soderini had subsequently not made use of his power tyrannically, his actions would have dismayed the people of Florence to such an extent that after he died they would never again have wanted to elect a Gonfalonier for life, an office that Soderini wanted to build up and perpetuate. In this sense, Soderini's aspirations were wise and good. And yet one must never let evil progress for the sake of something good when that good can easily be usurped by the evil. While Fortune and life were his, Soderini should have believed that his works would be judged by their result, and it would have been an easy thing for him to persuade everyone that what he had done was for the good of Florence and not for his own advancement. He could have arranged things in such a way that his successor would not have been able to do for the sake of evil what Soderini had done for the sake of good. But he was deceived in his idea of being able to rely on goodness and patience to extinguish the evil humors in his state, not realizing that evil cannot be tamed by time, nor placated by any gift. Consequently, unable to be like Junius Brutus, he lost his state, his rule, and his standing. That it is as difficult to save a free state as to save a kingdom I shall demonstrate in the following chapter.

ON HOW A PRINCE CANNOT LIVE SECURELY IN HIS PRINCIPALITY WHILE THOSE WHO WERE DEPRIVED OF IT ARE STILL ALIVE

The death of Tarquinius Priscus, which was brought about by the sons of King Ancus, and the death of Servius Tullius, brought about by Tarquinius Superbus, show how dangerous it is to strip a man of his kingdom and then leave him alive, even if you try to win him over with favors.[210] It is clear that Tarquinius Priscus was deceived in believing that, as the kingdom had been given him by the people and confirmed by the Senate, he had gained possession of it lawfully, nor did he believe that the sons of King Ancus would be so resentful that they would not be pleased with what pleased all of Rome. Servius Tullius too was deceived in believing that he could win over the sons of King Tarquinius with favors.[211] Consequently, in the first case, every prince should be warned that he will never live secure in his principality while those who were stripped of it are still alive. As for the second case, any man of power should be reminded that old injuries cannot be

210. According to Roman lore, Tarquinius Priscus, the legendary fifth king of Rome, had been the guardian of the sons of King Ancus, the fourth king of Rome, but had assumed the throne after the king died. King Ancus's sons subsequently had him murdered. The legendary sixth king of Rome, Servius Tullius, was said to have been born a slave in the household of King Tarquinius Priscus. He usurped the throne, but was subsequently murdered by Tarquinius Superbus, the seventh and last king of Rome.
211. According to Livy (Book I, chapter 46), King Servius Tullius had given his daughters in marriage to Tarquinius Superbus and his brother.

redressed by new benefits,[212] even less so when the new benefits are not as great as the injury had been. Without doubt, Servius Tullius showed little foresight in thinking that the son of King Tarquinius would be content to remain the son-in-law of Servius Tullius, whose king he believed he should have been.

The hunger to rule is so great that it enters the hearts not only of those who might have a claim to rule but also of those who do not, as in the case of Tarquinius Superbus's wife, who was the daughter of King Servius Tullius. Driven by the passion to rule she forgot all filial piety and drove her husband to take from her father his life and his kingdom: So much more did she value being queen than being the daughter of a king. If, therefore, Tarquinius Priscus and Servius Tullius lost their kingdom by not thinking to secure themselves against those from whom they had usurped it, Tarquinius Superbus lost it by not observing the practices of the former kings.

---

212. The idea is also echoed in *The Prince,* chapter 7: "For whoever believes that great advancement and new benefits make men forget old injuries is mistaken."

CHAPTER SIX

On conspiracies

I do not think it appropriate to pass over discussing conspiracies, since they are as dangerous to princes as they are to private citizens who conspire against princes. We see many more princes losing their lives and principalities through conspiracy than through open warfare, because few citizens have the means of waging open war against a prince, while everyone has the means of conspiring. And yet a private citizen can embark on no more rash and dangerous a venture than a conspiracy, because there are difficulties and perils at every stage. As a result, many attempt to conspire, but few attain their desired goal. I shall speak on this matter at some length, not omitting any notable documented conspiracy, so that princes will learn to guard themselves, while private citizens who are resolved to conspire will do so with more caution and perhaps even learn to live content under the princely authority that fate has allotted them. Tacitus's axiom is golden, that men must honor things of the past and abide by those of the present, and though they might desire good princes they must tolerate those they have regardless of their qualities.[213] Without doubt, whoever does not follow this axiom will risk bringing himself and his state to ruin.

213. Tacitus (*Histories,* Book IV, chapter 8) has Marcellus Epirus say in the Senate after Emperor Vespasian's election: "I admire the past, but comply with the present, and, though I pray for good emperors, I tolerate whoever we have."

In embarking on this subject we must first consider against whom conspiracies are directed. We will find that they are directed against either one's state or one's prince. It is these two I wish to discuss, because in a previous chapter I have already discussed at length conspiracies that seek to hand a state over to an enemy who is besieging it.[214] Consequently, in the first part of this chapter I would like to consider conspiracies against a prince, and would like first to examine the many reasons for such conspiracies, of which one, the populace's hatred of the prince, is far more important than the rest.[215] When a prince has inspired widespread dislike in the masses, it is reasonable to assume that there will be some individuals who are more harmed by him than others and who want to avenge themselves. Their desire for vengeance is fanned by the populace's anger, which the conspirators see all around them. A prince, therefore, must avoid the hatred of the populace, though I will not talk about how he ought to go about doing this, as I have done so elsewhere.[216] I will, however, say that if a prince resorts to simple, individual offenses instead of angering the public as a whole, he will encounter less hostility: first, because one rarely finds men who consider the harm done them so grave that they will put themselves in great danger in order to seek vengeance, and second, even if they have the courage and power to do so, they are held back if the prince has inspired the affection of the people.

The injury princes do to citizens is usually against their property, their honor, or their life.[217] In the case of injury against life, threats are more dangerous than executions. In fact, threats are extremely dangerous, while executions are not at all: He who is dead cannot think about revenge, while he who remains alive will usually leave such thoughts to the dead. But a man who is threatened by a prince and sees himself compelled either to act or suffer becomes very dangerous for the prince, as I shall discuss in its proper place. After an attack on a man's life, an attack on his property and honor are the two things that will of-

214. See Book II, chapter 32 above.
215. In *The Prince*, chapter 19, Machiavelli writes: "One of the strongest remedies a prince has against conspiracy is not to be hated by the masses, because conspirators are invariably certain that they will satisfy the populace by killing the prince."
216. See *The Prince*, chapter 19.
217. In *The Prince*, chapter 17, Machiavelli writes: "Being feared and not hated go well together, and the prince can always achieve this if he does not touch the property or the women of his citizens and subjects."

fend him most. A prince should refrain from these kinds of attack, because he can never strip a man of so much that he will have no knife left for revenge, nor can he dishonor a man to such an extent that he will not have enough spirit left to seek vengeance. When it comes to a man's assaulted honor, that regarding his womenfolk is foremost in importance, after which public insult takes second place. This was what drove Pausanias to conspire against Philip of Macedon,[218] and many others against many princes. In our times, Giulio Bellanti was driven to conspire against Pandolfo, the tyrant of Siena, only after Pandolfo[219] had given him one of his daughters as a wife and then taken her away again, as I shall discuss later in this chapter. The main reason the Pazzi conspired against the Medici was the inheritance of Giovanni Borromei, which they had ordered seized.[220]

Another major motive that will lead a citizen to conspire against a prince is the desire to free his state that has been seized by the prince. This motive moved Brutus and Cassius to conspire against Caesar,[221] and has moved many others to conspire against princes such as Phalaris, Dionysius, and others who occupied states.[222] Nor, unless he abandons the tyranny, can any tyrant protect himself against such hatred. But as one never finds a tyrant who is prepared to give up his tyranny, one rarely finds a tyrant who comes to a good end. As Juvenal says:

> How few of all the boastful men that reign
> Descend in peace to Pluto's dark domain![223]

---

218. In *Politics,* Aristotle used Pausanias, a young nobleman and one of Philip of Macedon's bodyguards, assassinating Philip as an example of a king being murdered because of a personal offense.
219. Giulio Bellanti, the son-in-law of Pandolfo Petrucci (1452–1512), the tyrant of Siena, tried to assassinate him in 1508.
220. See *Florentine Histories,* Book VIII, chapter 2.
221. Gaius Cassius Longinus and Marcus Junius Brutus were the two foremost conspirators in Julius Caesar's assassination in 44 BCE.
222. Phalaris (sixth century BCE), the tyrant of Acragas (modern Agrigento in Sicily), was legendary for his cruelty. Dionysius the Elder (fourth century BCE) was the tyrant of the neighboring state of Syracuse.
223. Machiavelli quotes Juvenal's *Satirae,* Book X, verses 112–13, in Latin: *Ad generum Cereris sine cæde et vulnere pauci / Descendunt reges, et sicca morte tyranni.* (Literally: "To the land of Pluto few kings descend without fatal wounds, and few tyrants without a dry death.")

As I have already mentioned, the dangers that conspirators face are great and must be borne at every stage of the conspiracy. A conspirator faces risks while preparing the conspiracy, while carrying it out, and after it has been carried out. A conspirator can be either a single person or many. If it is a single person, one cannot really call it a conspiracy, but rather one man's firm resolve to kill the prince. Of the three dangers one runs in a conspiracy, the single conspirator avoids the first—the danger during its planning—because prior to carrying out his conspiracy he does not run any risks since other men are not privy to his secret, nor is there a danger of the prince hearing of his plan. The will to conspire can manifest itself in a man of whatever station: great, small, noble, common, a man known to the prince or one completely unknown to him. Everyone has the opportunity to come before the prince, and whoever does so also has the opportunity to give vent to his feelings. Pausanias, whom I have mentioned, killed Philip of Macedon when Philip was going to the temple accompanied by a thousand armed men and walking between his son and his son-in-law. Pausanias was a nobleman and also well known to the king. A poor and wretched Spaniard stabbed King Ferdinand of Spain in the neck: the wound was not fatal, but it proved that the man had the courage and the opportunity to attempt it. A dervish—a Turkish priest—struck at Bayezid, the father of the present sultan, with a scimitar.[224] He did not wound him, but he too had the courage and the opportunity to do so. I believe there are many valorous men who have the desire to commit such an act, because the desire itself carries neither danger nor punishment. But there are few who would actually carry it out, and of those who do, none can avoid being killed on the spot—and there is no one who wants to go to certain death.

But let us pass over those who act alone and proceed to conspiracies that involve more men. I propose that all conspiracies in recorded history have been undertaken by powerful men or those closest to a prince, because others, unless they are completely mad, cannot conspire. Weak men and those not close to the prince lack any of the prospects or opportunities needed to carry out a conspiracy. First, a weak man has no recourse to individuals who will put their trust in him: No one would do his bidding in the absence of the kind of

224. Sultan Bayezid II (1447–1512) was the father of Sultan Selim I, who was the ruler of the Ottoman Empire (from 1512 to 1520) while Machiavelli was writing *The Discourses*.

prospects that make men face great dangers. In consequence, as their conspiracy expands to two or three individuals, they encounter a traitor and come to ruin. And even if they are lucky enough to avoid traitors, they face such difficulty in carrying out their conspiracy (as they do not have easy access to the prince) that they inevitably come to ruin: If powerful conspirators who have access to the prince are overwhelmed by the formidable difficulties I shall discuss, then it is to be expected that those difficulties will be endlessly multiplied for men who are weak. Accordingly, when conspirators are aware that they are weak—since men are not complete fools when it comes to their life and property—they tread carefully, and when they have had enough of a prince, they resort to cursing him and wait for others with more strength than they have to avenge them. Even if one comes across a weak conspirator who does attempt to carry out his intention, one is forced to praise his intent, not his prudence.

One therefore sees that conspirators were generally powerful men or men close to the prince, and that many were moved to conspire either by having been subjected to too much harm or accorded too much preference, as was the case in Perennius's conspiracy against Commodus, Plautianus's against Severus, and Sejanus's against Tiberius.[225] These men had all been given so much wealth, honor, and rank by their emperors that the only thing that seemed lacking to their power was the empire itself. Wanting that, too, they conspired against their emperors, and their conspiracies had the end that their ingratitude deserved. And yet in more recent times such conspiracies have had a better end, as that of Iacopo di Appiano against Piero Gambacorta, the prince of Pisa.[226] Iacopo, after being been raised, nurtured, and given great standing by the prince, usurped his state. A similar conspiracy of our times was that of Coppola against King Ferdinand of Aragon. Coppola had risen to such power that he felt the only thing lacking was the

---

225. Roman Emperor Commodus (161–192 CE) had his prefect Perennius assassinated in 185 CE after receiving proof that he was conspiring against him. Emperor Severus (146–211 CE), who ruled after Commodus, had advanced his Praetorian Prefect Plautianus until the latter had almost complete control over the administration of Rome. Severus's son, the future Emperor Caracalla, assassinated Plautianus in 205 CE. Emperor Tiberius (14–37 CE) advanced Sejanus until he was the single most powerful man in Rome. Tiberius had Sejanus executed in 31 CE after his conspiracies were uncovered.

226. Iacopo di Appiano (d. 1398) was the chancellor of Piero Gambacorta, the prince of Pisa, whom he assassinated in 1392 when he seized power.

kingdom itself, and through this desire lost his life.[227] In fact, if any conspiracy of powerful men against princes seemed destined to succeed it should have been Coppola's conspiracy, as it was a conspiracy that was led, one could say, by one prince against another with every opportunity of fulfilling his desire. But the lust for power that blinds men also blinds them in carrying out their venture, because if they knew how to execute their evil endeavor with prudence they would be bound to succeed. A prince who wishes to protect himself against conspiracies must therefore be more wary of those to whom he has granted too many benefits than of those whom he has excessively harmed, because the latter lack the means to conspire successfully, while the former possess them in abundance. And yet the desire is the same, because the desire for power is as great as or even greater than the desire for revenge. Consequently, a prince must give only so much power to his friends as will leave some space between that power and his principality, always allowing for something more to be desired in between; otherwise it will be quite out of the ordinary if this prince does do not suffer the fate of the princes I have just discussed.

But to return to our subject, I suggest that as conspirators are powerful men who can easily approach the prince, the outcome of their conspiracies and the reasons for their success or failure must be discussed. As I have already stated, there are three points of danger in a conspiracy: before, during, and after. Few conspiracies end well, because it is almost impossible to pass successfully through all three points. To begin with a discussion of the initial dangers, which are the most important, I suggest that one must be quite prudent and have great luck in conducting the conspiracy in order not to be discovered. Conspirators are discovered either when one of the conspirators talks, or if he acts suspiciously. Someone talking comes about when there is a lack of loyalty or prudence in the men with whom you are interacting. A lack of loyalty is not at all unusual, as you can discuss a conspiracy only with the most trusted friends who will face death out of friendship to you, or with men who are extremely dissatisfied with the prince. As for your most trusted friends, you can find one or two, but as the conspiracy grows you cannot find more. Furthermore, their good-

227. Francesco Coppola, the extremely wealthy and influential Count of Sarno, took part in the "Conspiracy of Barons" in 1485 against Ferdinand the Catholic. See *Florentine Histories,* Book VIII, chapter 32.

will toward you must be so great that the danger and fear they will encounter will not seem greater. But men are often deceived in their assessment of the friendship someone bears for them. They can never assure themselves of it until it has been put to the test, and in this case testing it is extremely perilous. Even if you have tried that friendship in some other dangerous affair in which your friends proved true, you cannot rely on it, for a conspiracy surpasses by far any other type of danger. If on the other hand you measure faithfulness by the discontent an ally has for the prince, you can be quite deceived, because the instant you take this malcontent into your confidence you provide him with the opportunity to become quite content at your expense.[228] His hatred will have to be quite great, or your authority even greater, for you to be able to keep him loyal to you.

As a consequence, many conspiracies are discovered and crushed in their very first stages. In fact, it can be considered a miracle when a conspiracy has remained a secret among many men for a long time, as was the conspiracy of Piso against Nero,[229] and in our times that of the Pazzi against Lorenzo and Giuliano de' Medici, in which more than fifty men were involved and were discovered only when they were on the point of carrying out their plot.[230] As for being discovered because of a lack of prudence, this comes about when a conspirator is incautious in what he says and a servant or some third person overhears him, as happened with the sons of Brutus, who, while arranging their conspiracy with the envoys of Tarquinius, were overheard by a servant who denounced them. One can also be discovered when one is careless and irresponsible enough to confide in a woman or boy one loves, as was the case with Dymnus, Philotus's co-conspirator against Alexander the Great, who revealed the conspiracy to Nicomachos, a boy he loved, who immediately told his brother, Cebalinas, who told Alexander. As for being discovered through suspicious behavior, there is the example of Piso's conspiracy against Nero, in which Scaevinus, one of the conspirators, the day before he was to assassinate Nero, made a

---

228. Also in *The Prince,* chapter 19: "And the moment you take a malcontent into your confidence, you give him the opportunity to become quite content, pursuing his own advantage by betraying you."

229. As Tacitus writes in *Annals,* Book XV, chapter 54: "It is astonishing that with so many people of different rank, age, sex, and wealth that the conspiracy remained a secret."

230. See *Florentine Histories,* Book VIII, chapter 3.

272 · The Essential Writings of Machiavelli

will, ordered his freedman Milichius to sharpen one of his rusty daggers, freed all his slaves and gave them money, and ordered bandages to be made for binding up wounds.[231] When Milichius became aware of the plot through this unusual behavior, he denounced Scaevinus to Nero. Scaevinus was then arrested along with Natalis, another conspirator who had been observed in a long and secretive conversation with him the previous day. When their accounts of this conversation did not agree, a confession was forced out of them, with the result that the conspiracy was uncovered and all the conspirators came to ruin.

It is impossible to guard oneself from the reasons conspiracies are uncovered—malice, imprudence, or thoughtlessness—whenever those in the know exceed three or four in number. If more than one conspirator is caught, it is impossible not to uncover the plot, because two men will never manage to make their explanations tally. When only one conspirator is caught he can, if he is a strong and courageous man, remain silent about the other conspirators, but the other conspirators must not have any less courage than he and stand firm, not revealing themselves by taking flight. If courage is missing on either side—either on that of the arrested conspirator or that of the conspirator who is free—the conspiracy will be uncovered. The example Livy provides concerning the conspiracy against Hieronymus, the King of Syracuse, is remarkable. When Theodorus, one of the conspirators, was seized, he valiantly concealed the names of all the other conspirators and instead accused the friends of the king. The other conspirators, for their part, had so much faith in Theodorus's valor that none of them fled Syracuse or showed any sign of fear. [232]

In setting up a conspiracy one must overcome all these dangers. To avoid them, these are the remedies: The first and most certain, or I should say the only remedy, is not to give your fellow conspirators enough time to denounce you. You should inform them of your plan only at the time you want to carry it out. Conspirators who have followed this path escaped the dangers of preparing the conspiracy, and often other dangers too. In fact, their conspiracies all had successful outcomes, and any prudent man would prefer to conduct himself in this manner. I would like to cite only two examples:

231. Tacitus, *Annals*, Book XV, chapters 54–56.
232. Machiavelli closely follows Livy's text in Book XXIV, chapter 5, though Livy names the conspirator as Theodotus, not Theodorus.

Nelematus was unable to bear the rule of Aristotimus, the tyrant of Epirus, and gathered in his home many friends and relatives, exhorting them to free their state. Some asked for time to think the matter over and make arrangements, upon which Nelematus had his servants lock the doors, and said: "Either you swear to carry out our plan now or I will deliver you all as prisoners to Aristotimus." Roused by these words, they swore, and immediately carried out Nelematus's plan.

A magus had taken over the kingdom of Persia through deceit, and Ortanes, one of the great men of the kingdom, understood and uncovered his trickery. He conferred with six other princes, announcing that he wanted to rid Persia of the magus's tyranny. When one of the princes asked for more time, Darius, another of the princes, said: "Either we carry out this plan right away, or I shall denounce you all." And so without time for second thoughts they rose in agreement, and immediately carried out their plan.

Similar to these two examples is the way in which the Aetolians set about to kill the Spartan tyrant Nabis. Under the guise of sending aid to Nabis, they sent Alexamenes, an Aetolian citizen, with thirty horsemen and two hundred foot soldiers. They informed only Alexamenes of the secret, while they forced the horsemen and foot soldiers to obey Alexamenes blindly under penalty of exile. He went to Sparta and did not reveal his commission to the other men until it was time to carry it out, and so managed to kill Nabis.[233] By such methods these men managed to escape the dangers that arranging conspiracies bring, and anyone who imitates them will always manage to avoid these perils.

To show how any man can follow their example, I would like to offer that of Piso, which I have already touched on. Piso was powerful, a man of great standing, and a close friend and confidant of Nero, who often came to his garden to dine with him. In other words, Piso was in a position to befriend men who had the courage, heart, and disposition to carry out the conspiracy (which is quite easy for a great man to do).[234] When Nero was in Piso's garden he could have communicated

233. Machiavelli closely follows Livy's text from Book XXXV, chapter 35.
234. The Piso Conspiracy of 65 CE against the emperor Nero (37–68 CE) involved forty-one conspirators ranging from soldiers to senators to literary figures, including Lucan and Seneca. Machiavelli bases himself on Tacitus's description of the conspiracy in *Annals*, Book XV, chapters 48 and following.

to these friends with apt words and spurred them to do what they would not have time to refuse to do, and which would not have failed to succeed. If we examine all other conspiracies, few will be found that could not have been carried out in this way. But as a rule, men have so little understanding of the affairs of the world that they often commit the gravest errors, even more so in illicit matters such as these. Hence a conspirator must never communicate his plan unless it is necessary, and then only at the moment it is to be carried out. And if he must communicate his plan, then to one person alone of whom he has long experience, or who is moved by the same motives. Finding a person like this is far simpler than finding many, and hence less dangerous. Furthermore, even if this one person deceives you, you can find a way to defend yourself, which is not the case when there are many conspirators. I have heard from the mouth of a prudent man that you can speak with one individual about anything, because the "yes" of one man is worth as much as the "no" of another—that is, if you avoid writing anything down in your own hand. You must avoid this as you would the plague, because nothing is more incriminating than something written in your own hand. When Plautianus wanted to have Emperor Severus and his son Antoninus killed, he took the tribune Saturninus into his confidence. The tribune wanted to denounce him, but doubting that his word would be believed against that of Plautianus, asked him for a note in his hand to confirm the commission. Plautianus, blinded by ambition, wrote the note, with the result that Saturninus successfully denounced him. Without this note and other evidence, Plautianus would have had the upper hand, as he was so vehement and convincing in his denials. It is, in other words, possible to find a remedy against such a denunciation as long as you cannot be convicted by a note in your hand or by some other evidence, in which matter you should be extremely careful.

In the Piso conspiracy there was a woman called Epicharis, who had once been Nero's mistress. She felt it would be useful to have among the conspirators a captain of the triremes that Nero kept as a bodyguard, and so told him of the conspiracy, but not who the other conspirators were. Consequently, when the captain denounced her to Nero, Epicharis was so vehement in her denial that Nero became confused, and she was not condemned.[235] Hence there are only two dangers in informing a single person of a conspiracy: first, that this person might denounce you with proof, and second, that if he is arrested on account of suspicious behavior or some sign of guilt, he might denounce you once he is convicted and tortured. But there is a remedy for both these dangers: It is possible to deny the first by accusing the denouncer of bearing some resentment against you, and the second by the allegation that torture compelled your denouncer to lie. Consequently, it is wise not to inform anyone of the conspiracy and to follow the examples I have cited, or, if you should inform anyone, then not more than one person. For even if a conspiracy involves great danger, that danger is still less than that of informing many people about the conspiracy.

A related situation occurs when necessity forces you to do to the prince what the prince would do to you, particularly when the necessity is so urgent that you have no time to weigh your actions. Such urgency, however, almost always leads to the desired end, and to prove this I would like to offer two examples. Emperor Commodus counted Laetus and Eclectus, captains of the Praetorian Guard, among his best and closest friends, while Marcia was his preferred concubine. They all sometimes reproached the emperor for the way in which he was bringing disgrace on his person and position, as a result of which he decided to have them put to death.[236] He wrote their names—Marcia, Laetus, and Eclectus—on a piece of paper along with the names of a few others he intended to have executed the following night, and placed the paper under his pillow. He had gone to bathe when a boy, a favorite of his who was playing around the room and on his bed, came upon the piece of paper and, leaving the room with it in his hand, encountered Marcia, who took it from him. When she read it and realized what it meant, she immediately sent for Laetus and Eclectus. All three understood the danger they were in, conferred on how to counter it, and promptly killed the emperor the following night.[237]

235. Tacitus writes in *Annals,* Book XV, chapter 51: "Epicharis was summoned and, confronted with the informer, easily rebuffed him as he had no witnesses. But Nero kept her in custody, for he suspected that though it [the informer's accusation] had not been proven true, it could not be entirely false, either."

236. The rule of Emperor Commodus (161–192 CE) became increasingly brutal and chaotic as he declined into insanity.

237. Machiavelli follows Herodian's description in *History of the Empire,* Book I, chapters 16 and 17.

Emperor Antoninus Caracalla was in Mesopotamia with his army and left Macrinus back in Rome as his prefect, a man more apt in civil matters than in military ones. Weak rulers always fear that others might be plotting against them in a manner they feel they deserve, and so the emperor wrote to Maternianus, a friend in Rome, that he should ask the astrologers if anyone was aspiring to the imperial throne. Maternianus wrote back that Macrinus had such aspirations. But the letter happened to fall into Macrinus's hands, and he immediately realized the necessity of either killing the emperor before Maternianus sent the emperor a new letter, or to die himself. So he commissioned a trusted centurion by the name of Martial, whose brother the emperor had put to death a few days earlier, to kill the emperor, a commission that Martial successfully carried out. Hence it is evident that urgent necessity which does not allow conspirators any time has almost the same effect as the method I have described above with Nelematus of Epirus. This again underlines what I said toward the beginning of this chapter, that the threats that a prince makes will put him in greater danger and are the reason for more successful conspiracies than are any actual attacks he might launch. A prince must keep himself from making threats because he must either treat men kindly or secure himself against them. He must not lead them into a situation where they feel their only choice is to kill or die.

As for the dangers incurred in carrying out a conspiracy, these come about when plans are suddenly changed, when the courage of those carrying it out falters, when the conspirators make errors through a lack of prudence, or when they do not carry out their purpose to the end, leaving alive some of those they intended to kill. First, I suggest that nothing will cause so much disorder or present such an obstacle to any planned action as suddenly changing a plan, moving away from what was initially decided upon. Such changes cause disorder in matters of war and conspiracy, because nothing is as vital as mustering one's courage to execute the affair at hand. If men have set their thoughts for many days on a certain method or way and then this is suddenly changed, it is impossible for them not to be disconcerted and for everything not to be ruined. In fact, it is far better to carry out something according to a set plan, even if there is a sudden drawback, than to create a thousand irregularities by trying to circumvent it. This happens when there is no time to reorganize the plan, because when there is time, a man can adapt.

The conspiracy of the Pazzi against Lorenzo and Giuliano de' Medici is well known. The plan had been that the Cardinal of San Giorgio would be invited to a banquet at the palace of the Medici, where the Medici would then be killed.[238] Everything had been determined: who would kill them, who would seize the palace, and who would run through the city rousing the populace to liberty. On the agreed-upon day the Pazzi, the Medici, and the cardinal were at a solemn ceremony in the Cathedral of Florence when it suddenly became clear that Giuliano de' Medici would not be joining them at the banquet. As a result, the conspirators quickly decided that they would do in the cathedral what they had intended to do in the Medici palace. This threw their entire plan into disarray, because Giovan Battista da Montesecco did not want any part in a murder committed in a church. Every action had to be reassigned to a different conspirator, who did not have time to steady his mind. In the end, the conspirators made so many mistakes that their plot was crushed.[239]

A man's courage to carry out such a conspiracy fails either out of respect for the victim or out of cowardice. The majesty and reverence that the presence of a prince brings with it can be so great that it is not unusual for a conspirator to lose his nerve or be gripped by fear. When Marius[240] was captured by the people of Minturnae, a slave was sent to kill him—but the slave, intimidated in the presence of such a great man and of his former glory, became cowardly and lost the resolve to kill him. And if this powerful presence can emanate from a man who is imprisoned, in chains, and crushed by ill fortune, one can imagine how much more powerful is the presence of a prince who appears with all the majesty of his insignia, pomp, and entourage! Such pomp might intimidate you or also soften you when accompanied by a pleasant

238. Girolamo Riario, the Cardinal of San Giorgio, was the nephew of Pope Sixtus IV. Both the pope and his nephew were also part of the Pazzi conspiracy, along with the Archbishop of Pisa and other important figures.

239. Giuliano de' Medici was killed by Francesco Pazzi, but Lorenzo de' Medici managed to escape. The people of Florence rallied around Lorenzo, and many of the conspirators were killed.

240. Plutarch in *Parallel Lives,* "Caius Marius" (39, 2), describes how a "Cimbric or Gallic" soldier was sent to assassinate the imprisoned Marius: "But the soldier thought that he saw flames shooting from Marius's eyes, and that he heard a loud voice rising from the shadows: 'Are you the man who would dare kill Caius Marius?' The barbarian immediately fled, dropping his sword."

greeting. A group of men conspired against King Sitalces of Thrace, and chose the day on which they would kill him. They gathered at the designated place, but none of them moved to attack the king, so that they left, blaming each other and unable to understand what it was that had hindered them. They tried to carry out their conspiracy several times to no avail, until their plan was uncovered and they suffered the penalty for the crime which they wanted to commit but could not bring themselves to.

Two brothers of Duke Alfonso of Ferrara plotted against him using Giannes, the duke's priest and cantor, as an intermediary. At their request, Giannes had brought the duke into their presence several times so that they would have the opportunity to kill him. Nevertheless, neither of them dared do it, so that when their plot was uncovered they suffered the penalty of their evil intentions because of their lack of prudence. This negligence could have been caused only by the duke's presence intimidating them, or by some kindness on the duke's part humbling them. In such enterprises there is the problem of a mistake due to a lack of prudence or a lack of courage: Both these problems can disturb and confuse you, leading you to do or say things you should not.

Livy clearly shows how men can become bewildered and confused at the point at which they are about to execute a conspiracy when he describes the state of mind of Alexamenes the Aetolian as he was about to kill Nabis of Sparta in the conspiracy I have already mentioned. When the moment arrived to carry out the deed and Alexamenes disclosed to his men what was to be done, Livy says, "Even he had to summon up his courage, perplexed as he was by the contemplation of such a great task."[241] It is in fact impossible for a man not to be perplexed—even a man of courage who is used to carrying a sword and seeing men die. Therefore, in a conspiracy one must choose a man experienced in such matters and not put one's trust in anyone else, no matter how courageous he is thought to be, because where courage for a great deed is needed, one cannot not take a definite outcome for granted if that courage has not been tested in that specific kind of deed. Bewilderment at the crucial moment either can make a man's weapons fall

---

241. Machiavelli quotes Livy (Book XXXV, chapter 35) in Latin: *Collegit et ipse animum, confusum tantae cogitatione rei.*

from his hands or might make him say words that will lead to the same result. Lucilla, Emperor Commodus's sister, ordered Quintianus to kill the emperor. Quintianus waited for Commodus at the entrance of the amphitheater and threw himself on him with his dagger unsheathed, shouting: "The Senate sends you this!"[242] These words resulted in Quintianus being restrained before he could bring his arm down to inflict the wound. Antonio da Volterra, as I have already mentioned, had been appointed to kill Lorenzo de' Medici, and when he threw himself at Lorenzo, shouted: "You traitor!" That shout proved to be Lorenzo's salvation and the ruin of the conspiracy.[243]

A conspiracy might fail for the reasons I have given when it is aimed at a single prince, but it is even more likely to fail when it is aimed at two. In fact, it becomes so difficult that it is almost impossible to succeed, because to mount such an action in two different places simultaneously is almost impossible, since it cannot be done at different times, when one assassination would ruin the other. Consequently, if conspiring against a prince is an uncertain, dangerous, and most imprudent enterprise, then conspiring against two is futile and reckless. If I did not hold the historian Herodian in such high esteem I would never believe possible what he says of Plautianus, that he commissioned the centurion Saturninus to kill both Severus and Antoninus though they lived in different places, because that is so unreasonable that I would refuse to believe it if it came from any other source.[244]

Some young Athenians conspired against Diocles and Hippias, tyrants of Athens. They killed Diocles, but Hippias remained alive and avenged him. Chion and Leonidas, citizens of Heraclea and disciples of Plato, conspired against the tyrants Clearchus and Satyrus. They killed Clearchus, but Satyrus, who remained alive, avenged him. The Pazzi, whom we have already mentioned a number of times, managed to kill only Giuliano de' Medici. Consequently, such conspiracies against more than one prince should be avoided, because one does

242. Herodian describes these events in *History of the Empire,* Book I, chapter 8, 5–6.
243. See *Florentine Histories,* Book VIII, chapter 5.
244. Herodian describes this incident in *History of the Empire,* Book III, chapters 4–12. He writes (Book III, chapter 12): "As usual, [Saturninus] made his rounds through the entire palace unhindered, but realized that it was impossible to kill the two emperors as they lived in different sections of the palace."

good neither to oneself, one's state, or anyone else: In fact, the princes who survive become even more insufferable and brutal, as Florence, Athens, and Heraclea can attest.

It is true that Pelopidas's conspiracy to free Thebes, his native city, evinced all possible difficulties, because Pelopidas conspired not against two tyrants, but ten. And yet his conspiracy was successful. Not only was he not close to the tyrants in any way, he did not even move in their circles. Pelopidas was in fact a rebel. Yet he managed to enter Thebes, kill the tyrants, and liberate his city. However, he accomplished this with the help of a certain Charon, a counselor to the tyrants, who gave him the opportunity to approach the tyrants and carry out his plan. But nobody should follow his example, because it was an impossible undertaking and it was a miracle that it succeeded, and historians have considered it a rare incident that is practically without parallel.[245]

The completion of a conspiracy can be interrupted by a false conjecture or an unforeseen event at the crucial moment. The morning on which Brutus and the other conspirators intended to kill Caesar, it happened that Caesar stopped and spoke for a long time with Gnaeus Popilius Laenas, one of the conspirators, and when the others saw the long discussion they were suddenly convinced that Popilius Laenas might have revealed the conspiracy to Caesar. They were about to attempt to assassinate Caesar immediately, without waiting for him to go to the Senate, and would have done so had the conversation not ended without Caesar acting strangely in any way.[246] Such false conjectures must be considered and weighed, particularly in situations when false conjectures are so readily at hand, because he who has a guilty conscience will easily conclude that he is being talked about. A word said about an entirely different matter might perturb him and lead him to believe that it involves his conspiracy. This might prompt him to reveal it by his taking flight, or lead him to bring forward an action in-

---

245. Machiavelli's following Plutarch's *Parallel Lives*, "Pelopidas," chapters 5–12.
246. Machiavelli is closely following the text of Plutarch's *Parallel Lives*, "Brutus," chapter 16, 3: "The conspirators (for so they must be called) could not hear his words but judging from their suspicion that what he was telling Caesar was about their plot, their minds fell into confusion. They looked at one another, mutually agreeing by their expressions that they must not wait for their arrest but face death right away."

tended for later, hence throwing the whole conspiracy into disarray. This happens much more readily when there are many conspirators.

As for unforeseen events, since they are unforeseen one can only present them as warning examples to conspirators. Giulio Bellanti of Siena, whom I mentioned at the beginning of this chapter, decided to kill Pandolfo out of hatred, since Pandolfo had taken back his daughter after having given her to Giulio as his wife. Pandolfo was in the habit of going almost every day to visit a sick relative, and on his way would pass Giulio's house. Giulio was aware of this, and arranged to have his co-conspirators waiting at his house so that they could kill Pandolfo as he passed. He had them wait, armed, inside the entrance and had one man keep watch at a window, who was to give a sign as Pandolfo walked past. It happened, however, that after Pandolfo had appeared and the man at the window alerted the others, Pandolfo ran into a friend who stopped him, while some of Pandolfo's men went on ahead. They saw and heard the weapons and uncovered the trap, with the result that Pandolfo was saved while Giulio and his fellow conspirators had to flee Siena. The unforeseen event of Pandolfo's encountering a friend impeded the action and ruined Giulio's plot. As unforeseen events are rare, they cannot be provided for. It is vital, however, to consider any event that might arise, and to take every precaution.

All that now remains for us to discuss are the dangers incurred after carrying out a conspiracy, these dangers being in fact only one: if someone who will avenge the dead prince is left alive. It could be his brothers, his sons, or other followers who expect to inherit the principality. They might have been left alive either through the conspirators' negligence or for the reasons I have already mentioned. This happened in the case of Giovanni Andrea da Lampognano, who along with his fellow conspirators murdered the Duke of Milan.[247] But as one of the duke's sons and two of his brothers remained alive, they ultimately avenged the dead man.[248] In truth, the conspirators can be ex-

247. Andrea da Lampugnano, Carlo Visconti, and Girolamo Olgiati set out to restore a republic in Milan by assassinating Duke Galeazzo Maria Sforza in the Cathedral of Santo Stefano during the Christmas festivities (December 1476).
248. The conspirators were caught and put to death. After the assassination, the duke's wife, Bona of Savoy, initially ruled as a regent for her son Gian Galeazzo (1469–94). His power was then usurped by the murdered duke's brother, Ludovico the Moor.

cused in such cases, as they could not have acted differently; but when someone is left alive through imprudence or carelessness, the conspirators do not merit excuse. Some conspirators from Forlì killed their lord, Count Girolamo, and captured his wife and small sons.[249] The conspirators felt that they would not be safe unless they occupied the castle, and as the castellan refused to hand it over, Madonna Caterina (that was the countess's name) promised the conspirators that if they let her enter the castle, she would see to it that it was delivered to them: They could keep her sons as hostages. With this promise, the conspirators allowed her to enter the castle. But the instant she was inside she began shouting at them from the walls, abusing them for killing her husband and threatening every kind of revenge. To show them that she did not care about her sons, she revealed her genitals, saying that she still had the means to produce more. Thus the conspirators, not knowing what to do and realizing their mistake too late, paid for their lack of prudence with perpetual exile.[250]

But of all the dangers that can come to pass after a conspiracy has been carried out, none is more certain or more to be feared than if the populace loves the prince you have killed. Here the conspirators have no remedy, since they will never be able to secure themselves. Caesar is an example: The Roman populace was on his side, and they avenged his death. The conspirators were chased from Rome, and were all killed at different times and places.

Conspiracies against one's own state are less dangerous for the conspirator than conspiracies against princes, because there are fewer dangers in preparing them, the same amount of danger in carrying them out, and no danger at all afterward. The reason there is not much danger in setting up a conspiracy is that a citizen can prepare to seize power without revealing his purpose or designs to anyone. If his plans are not interrupted, he can successfully carry out his endeavor, and should they be halted by some law, he can bide his time and carry them

---

249. Count Girolamo Riario, who had been involved in the Pazzi conspiracy, was himself killed in a conspiracy mounted by Francesco d'Orso in 1488. His wife was Caterina Sforza, the Duke of Milan's illegitimate daughter, who subsequently, as ruler of Imola and Forlì, was one of the foremost women of the Renaissance. See also *The Prince*, chapter 20, and *Florentine Histories*, Book VIII, chapter 34.

250. Caterina Sforza barricaded herself in the fortress until her uncle, the new Duke of Milan, Ludovico the Moor, came to her rescue. See *Florentine Histories*, Book VIII, chapter 34.

out by different means. This would be the case in a republic where there is some corruption, because in an uncorrupted republic, where no evil has sprouted, such thoughts cannot arise in any of its citizens. Hence, since he does not run the risk of being crushed, a citizen in a republic can aspire to become a prince by many means and in many ways, because republics are slower to act than a prince, are less suspicious and in consequence less cautious, and also because they have more respect for their powerful citizens, who as a result are more audacious and spirited in their actions against the republic. Everyone has read Sallust's description of the Catiline conspiracy,[251] and knows how, once the conspiracy was discovered, Catiline not only remained in Rome but came to the Senate and made insulting speeches against the senators and the consul;[252] so much respect did that city have for its citizens. And after Catiline had left Rome and was already with his army,[253] Lentulus and the others would not have been arrested had they not been carrying letters they had written that incriminated them quite clearly.[254] Hanno, a great citizen of Carthage, aspiring to become tyrant, intended during the wedding of one of his daughters to poison the entire senate and then assume power. When his conspiracy was revealed, the senate's only countermeasure was to put limits on expenditure at banquets and weddings—so highly did they esteem his qualities.[255]

On the other hand, carrying out a conspiracy against one's own

251. Sallust's *Bellum Catilinae* (*Catiline's War*) deals with the corruption in Roman politics involving the conspiracy of Catiline, who attempted to overthrow the Roman Republic in 63 BCE.

252. Sallust in *Bellum Catilinae* (31) writes: "[Catiline] was about to utter more slander when they all clamored, calling him a traitor to Rome, at which he furiously exclaimed, 'As I am surrounded by dire enemies and driven to desperation, I shall quench the fire around me with destruction.'"

253. Sallust writes in *Bellum Catilinae* (32): "[Catiline] and a few other men set out in the dead of night to Manlius's encampment, leaving behind Lentulus [and] Cethegus, of whose bravery he was certain [. . .] to further the plots against the consul, start a massacre, set fire to the city, and plot other destructive actions of war. He promised that he would soon march on the city with a large army."

254. Sallust writes in *Bellum Catilinae* (41): [The Allobroges] demanded an oath in writing from Lentulus, Cethegus, Statilius, and Cassius, which they could carry back with them under seal, otherwise, they said, it would not be possible to secure support for such a great endeavor."

255. Machiavelli follows Justin's description in *Epitome of the Philippic History of Pompeius Trogus,* Book XXI, chapter 4.

284 · The Essential Writings of Machiavelli

state can also involve difficulties and dangers, because rarely will your forces be sufficient to conspire against so many. And not everyone is commander of an army, as were Caesar, Agathocles, Cleomenes, or others like them, who with their forces swiftly occupied their own state. For such men the road is easy and safe; but others who do not have recourse to armies such as theirs must do things either through deception and guile or with the help of foreign forces. As for deception and guile, when the Athenian Pisistratus defeated the city of Megara and so gained the support of the people, he came out one morning wounded, saying that the nobility, jealous of his standing, had attacked him, and he demanded that he be granted an armed guard. With the power of this guard he easily rose to such greatness that he became tyrant of Athens.[256] Pandolfo Petrucci returned with other exiles to Siena[257] and was given an armed force and guardianship of the public square, a position everyone else had turned down as insignificant. Nevertheless, with time Petrucci's armed men gave him enough power and standing to become prince. Many other men used different ways and means of achieving their purpose without danger over time. Men who conspired to take over their own state using their personal army or a foreign one had various results, depending on whether Fortune favored them or not. Catiline, whom I have already mentioned, came to ruin, and Hanno, when his plot to poison the senators failed, armed his thousands of followers, which led to his and their deaths.[258] Some of the foremost citizens of Thebes brought in a Spartan army, and with its help set up a tyranny. Consequently, when one examines all the conspiracies that men made against their own state, one finds that few if any were crushed during the period of organization, but

256. Pisistratus had gained influence in Athens after his victories in the Battle of Megara (635 BCE), and established his own political faction. Plutarch in *Parallel Lives*, "Solon," describes how Pisistratus inflicted wounds on himself and made a dramatic entrance into the Athenian agora in his chariot, claiming that his enemies had attacked him. The Athenians accorded him an armed bodyguard with which he subsequently seized power.

257. Pandolfo Petrucci, 1452–1512, had been exiled from Siena for his involvement with the Noveschi (Council of Nine), the former ruling party of Siena. Petrucci returned to Siena in 1487.

258. Justin writes in *Epitome of the Philippic History of Pompeius Trogus*, Book XXI, chapter 4: "Frightened of being sentenced he rounded up twenty thousand armed slaves and captured a fortress.... There he was captured, and after being whipped, and having his eyes gouged out and his arms and legs broken, as if penance as to be drawn from every single limb, he was slaughtered before the eyes of the people."

that all either succeeded or came to ruin while being carried out. Once they were carried out, the conspirators faced no further dangers except those facing any prince. Once a man has become a tyrant, he encounters the natural and usual dangers a tyranny brings with it, against which he can only turn to the solutions I discussed at the beginning of this chapter.

This is what it occurred to me to write about conspiracies. And if I have explored those carried out with dagger and sword instead of poison, it is because they follow the same pattern. Conspiracies which make use of poison are also more dangerous because less certain: not everyone has an opportunity to administer the poison, so one has to confer with someone who does, and this necessity places one in danger. Furthermore, there are many reasons why a poisonous potion might not be fatal, as happened to the conspirators who killed Emperor Commodus.[259] The emperor vomited up the poison they had administered, and they were forced to strangle him.

In short, a prince has no greater enemy than conspiracy, because when he is conspired against he will be either killed or shamed. If the conspiracy succeeds he will die, while if it is uncovered and he kills the conspirators, people will always believe that he fabricated the conspiracy in order to satisfy some covetous motive and exercise his cruelty on the life and possessions of those he has killed. Nonetheless, I want to warn the prince or republic that has been conspired against to exercise caution before taking action to punish a conspiracy when they become aware of it. They must strive to comprehend its quality and measure their power against that of the conspirators. If the prince or republic finds that the conspiracy is extensive and strong, they should not expose it until they have mustered enough forces to crush it. If they do otherwise, they will only bring about their own ruin. For this reason, they must endeavor to act as if they know nothing, because if the conspirators are suddenly exposed, necessity will force them to act immediately. We have the Romans as an example, who, after they had left two legions of soldiers to guard the Campanians from the Samnites, as I have said elsewhere,[260] the captains of the legions conspired to subjugate the Campanians. When word of this reached Rome, Ru-

259. See discussion of Laetus and Eclectus's conspiracy earlier in this chapter.
260. Book II, chapter 26, above.

tilus, the new consul, was commissioned to see to the matter. To lull
the conspirators into a false sense of security he made it known that
the Senate was going to keep the Campanian legions stationed in
Capua indefinitely. The conspiring soldiers believed the news and felt
that they would have ample time to carry out their design, and so did
not hurry their plot. They did nothing until they realized that the consul was separating them from one another. This made them suspicious,
and they quickly carried out their plot.[261] This is the best example for
both sides of the coin, because it demonstrates how slowly men will act
when they believe that they have time, and how fast they will act when
necessity is at their heels. A prince or republic wishing to defer the uncovering of a conspiracy to its advantage can use no better device than
artfully offering the conspirators an opportunity to carry out their
plan in the foreseeable future. This way, the conspirators wait for that
moment to come, under the impression that they have ample time,
while the prince or the republic has every opportunity to punish them.
Whoever has acted differently has only hastened his own ruin, as was
the case with the Duke of Athens and also with Guglielmo de' Pazzi.
The Duke of Athens had become the tyrant of Florence.[262] When he
realized that there was a conspiracy against him, he immediately had
one of the conspirators seized without first weighing the matter, and
the result was that the other conspirators immediately took up arms
and seized the state from him. Guglielmo de' Pazzi was the Florentine
commissioner in Valdichiana in 1501, when he heard that there was a
conspiracy in Arezzo in favor of the Vitelli to seize Arezzo from the
Florentines. He immediately marched on Arezzo without weighing
the strength of the conspirators against his own and without first gathering a military force. There, on the advice of his son the bishop, he
arrested one of the conspirators, as a result of which the other conspirators immediately took up arms and seized the city from the Florentines, and Guglielmo went from being commissioner to being a
prisoner.

But when conspiracies are weak they must be crushed without
much reflection. However, one should definitely not imitate two
schemes that are almost diametrically opposed: The first scheme was

261. Livy describes the incident in Book VII, chapters 38–41.
262. In 1342, Walter de Brienne, titular Duke of Athens, became Signore of Florence. He
was, however, deposed the following year.

used by the Duke of Athens. To demonstrate that he believed he had the goodwill of the Florentine citizens, he put the man who told him of the conspiracy to death.[263] The second scheme was used by Dion of Syracuse. To test the intentions of a certain man he suspected, he allowed Callippus, whom he trusted, to pretend that he was setting up a conspiracy against Dion.[264] Both these rulers ended badly: The Duke of Athens discouraged informers and encouraged conspirators, while Dion of Syracuse paved the way for his own death and was even the leader of his own conspiracy, because, as it turned out, once Callippus was free to conspire against him he did so with such zeal that he took from Dion his state and his life.

263. As Machiavelli writes in *Florentine Histories,* Book II, chapter 36: "[The Duke of Athens] wanted to show everyone that he believed himself beloved by all. Thus, when Matteo di Morozzo, either to acquire his favor or free himself from danger, revealed to the duke that the Medici were conspiring against him, not only did not inquire into the matter, but had the informer put to a cruel death."
264. Plutarch describes the incident in *Parallel Lives,* "Dion," chapters 54 and following.

Selections from

THE ART OF WAR

The Art of War *is a richly woven work on military tactics, poli-*
tics, and the philosophy of war. Machiavelli wrote it in 1519 or
1520, and it is his only political work published in his lifetime.
Though since its first publication in English L'Arte della Guerra
has been known as "The Art of War," a more correct rendering of
the title might be "The Craft of War."

 Machiavelli wrote this work at a time when Italy—and Flor-
ence in particular—was beset by wars and international intrigue.
He regarded these ills as caused by political and military blunders.
As in The Prince *and* The Discourses, *the message of* The Art
of War *is that ancient history—particularly the Roman model—*
could be relied upon as a paradigm to bring Renaissance Italy out of
its dire straits. Though in his preface Machiavelli professes that "it
is an audacious act for a man like myself to take up matters of
which he has no professional experience," one must be careful not to
take him at his word; as Secretary of the Second Chancery in the
Republican government of Florence he was responsible for military
strategy.

 Machiavelli divided The Art of War *into a preface and seven*
books, presenting the narrative in a series of dialogues between the
great mercenary general Fabrizio Colonna and a company of young
Florentine noblemen. Machiavelli gives Colonna lengthy mono-

logues in which Machiavelli's ideas and philosophy are systematically presented. Modern scholars have argued that Machiavelli was weak as a practical military strategist and that he underestimated the degree to which firearms and artillery would shape the future of warfare. But for centuries after its first publication, The Art of War *was extremely influential, military leaders relying upon it for strategy. In Voltaire's words: "Machiavelli taught Europe the art of war."*

PREFACE

By Niccolò Machiavelli, Citizen and Secretary of Florence,
on the Books of the Art of War,
to Lorenzo di Filippo di Strozzi,[1]
Florentine Patrician

Many, Lorenzo, have held the opinion, and still do, that nothing in the world is more unlike civilian life than military life. Therefore one often sees an immediate change in a man who chooses life in the army: not only in his clothes, but also in his manner, habits, and voice as he distances himself from every civilian convention. This man will not believe that, striving to be unencumbered and ready for any violence, he can assume a civilian manner. Nor can a man keep civilian customs and habits when he sees the customs as effeminate and the habits as unfavorable to his task, nor does it seem right to him to maintain his ordinary appearance and words when, with his beard and blasphemies, he wants to instill fear in other men. This is the way of thinking in our times. But if one considers ancient institutions, one will not find anything more united, more harmonious, and of necessity with greater affinity for each other than civilian and military institutions. All the professions pursued in a society for the common good of man, and all the institutions created to make him live in fear of the laws and of God, would be in vain if provision were not made for their defense. If this defense is well organized it will also maintain those institutions that are weaker, while good institutions without military backing become

1. Lorenzo di Filippo Strozzi (1482–1549) was a member of the group of gentlemen and intellectuals who met in the Orti Oricellari, the gardens of Cosimo Rucellai's family, and was a patron and friend of Machiavelli.

as disordered as the bejeweled chambers of a proud and regal palace without a roof: If the chambers are not covered, they will have nothing to protect them from the rain. If in the civil institutions of a city or a kingdom every diligence is employed to keep men loyal, peaceful, and filled with the fear of God, such diligence should be redoubled in the military. Where can a state find greater loyalty than in a man who must promise to die for her? Who would have a greater love of peace than a man who can only be harmed by war? Who would have a greater fear of God than a man who every day faces infinite perils and has more need for God's help? This necessity, considered carefully by legislators and men in the military profession, had the effect in ancient times that the life of the soldier was praised, imitated, and carefully followed by other men. But military institutions are now completely corrupted and much changed from the ancient ways, which has led to mistaken ideas that make men hate the military and avoid any interaction with those who have soldiery as their profession.

I have come to the opinion, from what I have seen and read, that it is not impossible to restore the army to the ancient ways and bring back some form of past skill and prowess. In order not to let my leisure pass without doing something constructive, I have decided to write what I know of the art of war for the satisfaction of those who are admirers of ancient deeds. Although it is an audacious act for a man like myself to take up matters of which he has no professional experience, I do not believe it amiss to assume with words a position that many, with far greater conceit, have assumed with deeds. The errors I might commit in writing about these things can be rectified without anyone's coming to harm, while the errors others have committed with actual deeds come to light only with the downfall of their government.

Consider therefore, Lorenzo, the quality of my efforts, and evaluate them with the kind of blame or praise you believe they merit. But I send them to you to show myself grateful for all the benefits I have received from you—though my efforts in no way equal my debt to you—and also because it is the custom to dedicate works such as this to those who are resplendent in their nobility, wealth, intellect, and generosity. And I know that you have few equals in wealth and nobility, fewer in intellect, and none in generosity.

BOOK I

• • •

Fabrizio Colonna passed through Florence on his return from Lombardy, where he had fought long and gloriously for the Catholic king,[2] and decided to stay several days to visit His Excellency the Duke[3] and several gentlemen of his acquaintance. Cosimo[4] took the opportunity to invite him to his gardens, not so much to show his generosity as to have an opportunity to converse with him at length and learn all the things one can expect from such a man. Cosimo looked forward to spending a day discussing matters that would satisfy his curiosity.

As Cosimo hoped, Fabrizio Colonna came, and was received by him and several of his closest friends, among whom were Zanobi Buondelmonti, Battista della Palla, and Luigi Alamanni.[5] Cosimo was close to these young men, who shared his passion for the same studies, and whose qualities I need not touch on, as they shine forth every day and every hour.

---

2. Fabrizio Colonna (d. 1520) was a nobleman of the powerful Colonna family and a mercenary general for King Ferdinand the Catholic (1452–1516), King of Aragon, Sicily, Castile, and Naples.

3. Lorenzo de' Medici, to whom Machiavelli dedicated *The Prince*, was the ruler of Florence. His uncle, Pope Leo X (Giuliano de' Medici), made him Duke of Urbino.

4. Cosimo Rucellai (1494–1519), the host at the gardens of the Orti Oricellari.

5. The three young men were frequent guests at the meetings in the Orti Oricellari (the gardens of Cosimo Rucellai) and were close friends and admirers of Machiavelli. Zanobi Buondelmonti (1491–1527) was a wealthy Florentine merchant, banker, and patron of the arts.

Colonna was received with great honor. The banquet was soon over, the tables cleared and the festivities concluded, which happens quickly with great men whose minds are turned to lofty thoughts. As the day was long and the heat intense, Cosimo decided to take the opportunity to escape the sun by leading his friends to the more secluded and shaded part of his garden. When they sat down there—some on the grass, which in that spot is very fresh, some on chairs in the shadow of the tallest trees—Colonna praised the place as delightful. But he gazed bemused at the trees, not recognizing some of them. Cosimo noticed this and said, "It might be that you have no knowledge of a number of these trees, but this should not surprise you, as some of them were more highly prized in ancient times than they are today." Cosimo told him their names, and how his grandfather Bernardo had worked hard to cultivate them.

"I thought that might be the case," Fabrizio replied. "This place and this pursuit bring to mind several princes of the Kingdom of Naples, who delighted in what the ancients cultivated and the shadows it cast." He fell silent, and then, as if hesitating, added, "I would give you my opinion, were I not concerned that I might offend you. And yet I do not believe I would be offending you, because when one converses with friends one simply discusses, one is not finding fault. How much better would your grandfather and the princes have done—may they rest in peace—to seek resemblance with the ancients in rough and solid matters, not in what is delicate and soft; in matters accomplished under the sun, not within the shadows, to choose the ways of a true and perfect antiquity, not ways that are false and corrupt. Because once such pursuits began to please the Romans, our country came to ruin." To which Cosimo replied . . . —But so that I may avoid repeating "he said" and "the other added," I shall note only the name of whoever is speaking, without repeating anything else.[6]

COSIMO: You have opened the way to a discussion that I hoped for, and I beg you to speak freely, for I shall not hesitate to ask you questions just as freely. And if in a question or answer I should defend or

---

The *Discourses* are dedicated to him and Cosimo Rucellai, and *The Life of Castruccio Castracani* is dedicated to him and Luigi Alamanni.

6. Machiavelli borrowed this formula from Cicero's *On Friendship* (I, 3): "So that I may avoid always repeating 'I say' and 'he says,' I shall use the form of a dialogue."

accuse anyone, I will do so not in order to defend or accuse that person, but only as a matter of argument in order to hear the truth from you.

FABRIZIO: I will be happy to tell you what I know about anything you ask, and will leave you to judge whether it is true or not. I will be grateful for your questions, because I wish to learn as much from you in what you ask as you will from me in what I answer. For often a wise questioner leads one to consider many things and to realize many others, things that would never have been realized had the question not been asked.

COSIMO: I want to return to what you said first, that my grandfather and the princes of Naples would have done better to resemble the ancients in rough things rather than in delicate ones, and I wish to defend my side because I hope you will defend yours. I do not believe that any man of my grandfather's era disliked living in ease more than he did, and he was very much a lover of the rough life that you praise. Nevertheless, he recognized that he himself could not live by these norms or compel his sons to do so, as he had been born into such a corrupted era that anyone wanting to depart from the common way would be defamed and vilified by all. If a man were to roll naked in the sand under the hottest sun, or roll in the snow during the coldest months of winter, as Diogenes did, he would be thought mad.[7] If a man were to raise his children outside the city the way the Spartans did, making them sleep in the open, go about with bare head and feet, and bathe in cold water to harden them, so that they might endure every ill and have less love of life and less fear of death, he would be derided by everyone and considered a beast rather than a man. Or if one sees someone living off vegetables and scorning gold, as Gaius Fabricius Luscinus[8] did, he would be praised by few and followed by none. Hence, constrained by our present way of living, my grandfather

7. Machiavelli is quoting Diogenes Laertius's *Lives of Eminent Philosophers,* "Diogenes" (Book 6:2:23): "In summer he rolled in the hot sand and in winter embraced statues covered with snow, always practicing to endure anything."

8. A Roman commander and statesman (c. third century BCE), praised by Roman historians as a model of incorruptible Roman virtue. After King Pyrrhus of Epirus invaded Italy and defeated the Romans at Heraclea, he was so impressed by Gaius Fabricius Luscinus's refusal to accept a bribe that he released all Roman prisoners without ransom.

turned from the ways of the ancients, and imitated them only in matters that would draw the least attention.

FABRIZIO: You have gallantly defended him, and you certainly speak the truth, but I was referring not so much to harsh ways of life as to the kind of humane ways of the ancients that could be adapted to our manner of living today. I believe these could easily be introduced by someone counted among the nobles of a city. In all my examples I shall stay with the Romans. If one considers their way of life and the institutions of their republic, one can see much that might be introduced into a society in which some good still remains.

COSIMO: What are the things having affinity with the ancient world that you would like to introduce?

FABRIZIO: Honoring and rewarding skill, not scorning poverty, esteeming the principles and institutions of military discipline, compelling citizens to love one another, living without factions, esteeming what is public more than what is private, and other such ideas that could easily be accommodated to our times. It would not be difficult to make these principles accepted if one thought the matter through and applied it in an adequate manner, because the truth in them would appear so clearly that the simplest mind would be capable of perceiving it. He who institutes these principles is planting trees beneath whose shade one can live with greater happiness and cheer.

COSIMO: I shall not respond to what you have said, but would like to leave judgment to the present company, who can judge easily. I shall address myself to your accusing those who are not imitators of the ancients in serious and important matters, as I believe that by doing so I will satisfy my intention better. I would therefore like to know how it is that on the one hand you condemn those who do not imitate the ancients in their actions, but on the other hand, in matters of war, which is your profession and in which you are considered to excel, one cannot see that you have made use of any ancient system or any similar system.

FABRIZIO: You have touched on the subject I expected you to, for what I said did not merit any other question, nor did I desire another. I could evade your question with a simple excuse, but nevertheless wish, for your greater satisfaction and mine, to enter into a much longer discussion, as the hour is still early. A man wishing to do something must first prepare himself with great application in order to be ready, if the opportunity presents itself, to accomplish what he has set out to do. When preparations are undertaken with circumspection they are unknown to others, and there can be no accusations of negligence unless the preparer is first caught out by the occasion. If he does not act once the opportunity presents itself, it is clear that he has either not prepared or not foreseen things. I have not had the opportunity to show the preparations I have made to draw the military back toward its ancient order, and if I have not done so I cannot be blamed by you or anybody else. I believe this excuse might suffice to counter your allegation.

COSIMO: It would suffice if I were certain that the opportunity had not presented itself.

FABRIZIO: I can understand your doubting whether the opportunity had in fact presented itself, and so, if you will not tire of listening, I wish to discuss at length which preparations must be made first, what occasion might arise, what difficulty might impede the preparations from succeeding and the occasion from arising, and how turning back toward the ancients is a thing at once most easy and most difficult, though this might seem a contradiction.

COSIMO: Nothing would delight me or the others more. If you do not find it disagreeable to speak at length, we will not tire of listening. As this discussion will inevitably be long, I turn, with your permission, to my friends, and ask on my and their behalf, that you not take umbrage should we occasionally interrupt you with an importunate question.

FABRIZIO: I will be very happy, Cosimo, if you and these young gentlemen ask me questions, for I believe that your youth will make you more accepting of military matters and more disposed to consider what I shall say. Men whose heads are wizened and whose blood is cold in their veins are either enemies of war or set in their ways. They are like those who believe that it is the times, and not bad government, that forces men to live in such a way. So I encourage you all to question me openly and without fear. This would be a pleasant diversion for me, and I will also be relieved not to leave any doubts in your minds.

I would like to begin with your question why I have not applied any of the ancient methods in war, which is my profession. My reply is that, as soldiery is a profession by which men cannot live honestly in both times of war and times of peace, it can be a profession only in a republic or a kingdom. And yet if a republic or a kingdom is well ordered, it will never allow any of its citizens or subjects to exercise soldiery as a profession. No good man ever adopted it as a profession, because a man will never be judged good who practices a profession in which, if he wants to do well both in times of war and times of peace, he must be rapacious, cunning, and violent, and have many other qualities that can only make him bad. Nor can men—great or small—who have soldiery as a profession act otherwise, for it is one that does not feed them in times of peace. Consequently these men are compelled either to find a way to fend off peace, or to gain such advantage for themselves in times of war that they can keep feeding themselves in times of peace. Whenever men entertain either of these thoughts they cannot be good, because it is from the need to provide for themselves in times of both war and peace that soldiers turn to the robbery, violence, and assassination that they inflict on both friends and enemies. Generals who do not want peace deceive the princes who hire them by drawing wars out; and even if peace does come, it frequently happens that the generals, deprived of their stipends and no longer able to live unencumbered by laws, raise the banner of the soldier of fortune, sacking a land without mercy.

Do we not see in your Florentine history the many soldiers throughout Italy finding themselves without pay once wars ended, gathering themselves into brigades called "companies," going around extorting money from cities, and plundering the land without anyone being able to do anything about it? Have you not read how the Carthaginian soldiers, after their first war with the Romans ended, rebelled and elected Mathos and Spendius as their leaders and waged a more dangerous war against the Carthaginians than they had just concluded with the Romans?[9] And in the time of our fathers, Francesco Sforza, in order to be able to live properly in times of peace, not only

9. Polybius in *Histories* (I, 69) identifies Mathos as a regular Libyan soldier in the Carthaginian army and Spendius as a runaway Roman slave, who through violence and intimidation incited the Carthaginian army to rebellion and had themselves appointed sole commanders. Machiavelli also mentions the incident in *The Prince,* chapter 12: "As for mercenary armies in ancient times, we have the example of the Carthaginians, who were almost overwhelmed by their mercenary soldiers after the first war with the Romans, even though the Carthaginians had their own citizens as generals."

deceived the Milanese in whose pay he was, but took away their liberty and became their prince.[10] All the other mercenaries of Italy who were professional soldiers were like Francesco Sforza, and though they might not have become dukes of Milan through evil deeds, they deserve all the more blame, for, if one looks at their lives, they all incurred the same guilt without, however, bringing as much benefit to a city. Muzio Attendolo Sforza, Francesco's father, forced Queen Giovanna to throw herself on the mercy of the King of Aragon, having quite suddenly abandoned her, leaving her disarmed and surrounded by her enemies, because of his ambition to extort a considerable sum from her or to seize her kingdom for himself.[11] Braccio[12] attempted to occupy the Kingdom of Naples by the same method, and would have succeeded had he not been defeated and killed at Aquilla. Such evils arise only from the existence of men who exercise the profession of mercenary. Do you not have a proverb that supports my argument, which says: "War creates robbers, and peace hangs them"? When men do not know how to live by any other profession, and are unable to find anyone who will pay them, and do not have the skill to come together and be honorably evil,[13] they are forced by necessity to become highwaymen, and justice is forced to eliminate them.

COSIMO: You have reduced the profession of soldiery to almost nothing, while I had supposed it to be the most excellent and honorable of professions. You must clarify this, because if it is as you say, how can one explain the glory of Caesar, Pompey, Scipio, Marcellus, and the many other Roman generals who are so famous they are celebrated as gods?

FABRIZIO: I have not yet finished discussing everything I proposed

10. Francesco Sforza (1401–66) had been a condottiere in the service of Duke Filippo Maria Visconti of Milan. In 1450 he blockaded the city, causing a rebellion by the starving inhabitants, until he finally marched in with his army as the new Duke of Milan.

11. Machiavelli uses almost the same words in *The Prince,* chapter 12: "Francesco Sforza's father, a mercenary to Queen Giovanna of Naples, left her defenseless, and she was forced to throw herself on the mercy of the King of Aragon so as not to lose her realm."

12. Braccio da Montone (1368–1424), a rival of Muzio Attendolo Sforza, was one of the greatest condottieri of his time, becoming Prince of Capua.

13. Machiavelli writes in *Discourses,* Book I, chapter 27: "Men often do not know how to be perfectly good or honorably evil, and when an evil deed has grandeur or is in some part generous, a man will often not know how to carry it off."

on two matters: first, that a good man cannot take up soldiery as his profession, and second, that a well-ordered republic or kingdom would never permit its subjects or citizens to exercise soldiery as a profession. As for the first matter, I have in fact told you everything that occurred to me, so it remains for me to speak of the second, with which I shall reply to your question concerning the Roman generals. Pompey and Caesar, and almost all the generals in Rome after the last Punic War, gained fame as valiant men, not as good men. Those who had lived before them, however, had acquired glory as valiant and good men, which happened because they did not take up the practice of war as their profession, while it was the profession of Pompey, Caesar, and the generals of their times. As long as the Roman Republic was uncorrupted, no great citizen ever attempted to gain power during times of peace through soldiery, breaking laws, despoiling provinces, imposing himself in every way, and usurping and tyrannizing his state. Nor did anyone of lower rank think of violating his oath to Rome, entering into conspiracies, and, without fear of the Senate, joining the ranks of someone seeking to be tyrant simply in order to be able to live by soldiery in peaceful times as well as in times of war. Those who were generals were content with triumph during wartime and very happy to return to private life, while those who were regular soldiers had a greater desire to lay down their arms than they had had to take them up. Everyone returned to the profession by which he made his living, and nobody hoped to live off plunder and the profession of war.

Marcus Attilius is an example of a great citizen of that kind. He was general of the Roman armies in Africa and on the point of defeating the Carthaginians when he asked the Senate for permission to return home to look after his estates, which were being ruined by his laborers. It is clear as day that if Marcus Attilius had practiced war as his profession, intending to profit from it—there being so many provinces he could plunder—he would not have asked permission to return home to take care of his fields. Every single day he was on the campaign he could have seized more than their entire value. But as these good men, who did not practice soldiery, expected nothing of war except hardship, danger, and glory, once they had sufficient glory, they wanted to return home and live by their professions. As for men of lower rank and the common soldiers, they too acted the same way. They gladly withdrew from warfare, for when they were not fighting they desired not to fight, and when they were fighting they wanted to be discharged. This can be verified in many ways, particularly as it was among the first privileges the Roman populace gave to a citizen, that he should not be constrained to fight against his will. Therefore while Rome was a well-ordered state, which it was up to the time of the Gracchi,[14] it did not have a single soldier who took up soldiery as a profession. Only a few soldiers were bad, and they were severely punished.

A well-ordered state should use military training in times of peace as an exercise, and in times of war as a necessity and for glory. The state alone should be allowed to use it as a profession, as Rome did. Any citizen who has other aims in using the military is not a good citizen, and any state that acts otherwise is not a well-ordered state.

COSIMO: I am very pleased and satisfied with what you have said up to now, and I like your conclusion. I believe that what you say is true when it comes to republics; but I am not certain if the same can be said of kings, because I believe a king would want to surround himself with men who have taken up soldiery as their profession.

FABRIZIO: A well-ordered kingdom must avoid the soldierly profession even more, since those men corrupt the king and are the ministers of tyranny. And do not counter what I say with an example of some kingdom from our times, because I cannot accept these as well-ordered kingdoms. A well-ordered kingdom does not grant its king absolute power, except over the army, because it is only for the army that quick decisions and hence absolute power are necessary. In other matters, the king should not be able to do anything without counsel, and those who advise him must fear that there might be a counselor close to him who desires war in times of peace because the counselor cannot live without it. But I would like to show some indulgence here, by seeking not a kingdom that is entirely good, but one like those that exist today, where the king has to fear those who make war their profession, because the backbone of every army is without doubt the infantry. If a king does not organize his army so that in a time of peace his infantrymen are happy to return home and live by practicing their

14. The reforms of Tiberius and Gaius Gracchus acted as a catalyst to end the Roman Republic, opening the way to imperial Rome.

own professions, the king will inevitably come to ruin, for no infantry is more dangerous than one composed of men who make war their profession. In the latter case, the king is forced either to make war continuously, or to pay his infantry continuously if he does not want to risk their seizing his kingdom from him. As it is impossible to wage war all the time, and also impossible to pay an infantry all the time, the king is faced with losing his kingdom.

As I have said, the Romans, while they were still wise and good, never permitted their citizens to take up soldiery as a profession, notwithstanding that they could have employed them continuously, as the Romans were continuously at war. They sought, however, to avoid the damage that the continuous practice of soldiery could do, and since the circumstances did not vary, they kept varying the men and continued temporizing, so that the legions were entirely renewed every fifteen years. Thus they made use of men in their prime, which is from the age of eighteen to thirty-five, during which time a man's eyes, hands, and legs work in unison. Nor did they wait for the soldiers' strength to diminish or their penchant for evil deeds to grow, as the Romans did later in corrupt times. Augustus and then Tiberius,[15] thinking more of their own power than of the public good, began to disarm the Roman populace in order to control them more easily, and kept the same armies continually at the frontiers of the empire. Since they believed that these armies would not hold the Roman populace and the Senate in check, they set up an army called the Praetorian Guard, which remained near the walls of Rome and acted like a fortress hovering over the city. The emperors began freely permitting men to practice soldiery as their profession, and this soon resulted in their becoming arrogant, dangerous to the Senate, and harmful to the emperor. As a result, many emperors were killed because of the armies' arrogance in giving and taking away power as they pleased, several armies creating a number of emperors simultaneously. This ultimately resulted in the division of the Roman Empire, and finally its ruin.

Therefore, if kings want to live securely, they must have an infantry composed of men who, when it is time for war, will willingly march

15. Augustus (63 BCE–14 CE), the first Roman emperor, and Tiberius (42 BCE–37 CE), the second Roman emperor.

forth out of love for the king, and afterward, when peace comes, even more willingly return home. This will always happen if the king selects men who know how to live by a profession other than soldiery. When peace comes, the king should expect his leaders to return to governing their people, his gentlemen to return to the cultivation of their possessions, and his infantry to their particular trades. The king must want them all to make war willingly in order to have peace, and not seek to break peace in order to have war.

COSIMO: Your reasoning strikes me as well considered. Nevertheless, as it is almost contrary to what I have believed until now, my mind is not yet purged of all doubt. I see many lords and gentlemen providing for themselves in times of peace through training for war, as do other condottieri like yourself who are funded by princes and states. I also see almost all cavalrymen retaining their stipends after a war, and I see many infantrymen remaining within the garrisons of cities and fortresses. So it does appear to me that there is a place for every soldier during times of peace.

FABRIZIO: I cannot imagine you would believe that all soldiers have a place in time of peace. The small number alone of men who remain in the garrisons and fortresses should suffice to remove any doubts you may have. What is the proportion of infantry needed in war to that needed in peace? A fortress and a city are guarded in times of peace, but much more so during times of war. Not to mention that the large number of soldiers kept in the field during wartime are all let go in times of peace. And as for the armed guards of the state, who are small in number, Pope Julius and you Florentines have proved to what extent one must fear men whose only profession is war. You Florentines have removed them from your garrisons because of their insolence and replaced them with the Swiss, who are born and raised under strict laws and selected by their communities in fair elections. So you must reconsider the idea that there really is a place in peacetime for every soldier. As for the cavalrymen who stay enlisted after a war, the problem seems more difficult; nevertheless, anyone considering the matter carefully will easily find the answer, for the method of retaining cavalrymen is corrupt and unsatisfactory. The reason is that they are men for whom soldiery is a profession, and this consequently gives rise to a thousand problems every day in the cities in which they are stationed, if they are backed up by sufficient numbers. But as they are few, and unable to gather into an army on their own, they usually cannot cause serious damage; but still they have done so many times, as I have said of professional soldiers such as Francesco Sforza and his father, and of Braccio da Montone. In short, I do not approve of the practice of keeping cavalrymen. It is corrupt and can cause great evils.

COSIMO: Would you prefer to do without them? Or if you were to keep them, how would you go about it?

FABRIZIO: I would use conscription. Not the way the King of France[16] does, because his cavalry is as dangerous and insolent as ours. I mean the kind of conscription practiced by the ancients, who created a cavalry from among their subjects, and in times of peace sent them back to their homes to live off their own professions, as I shall talk about at greater length before I finish this discussion. So if the cavalry can continue living by means of soldiery even when there is peace, it stems from corrupt institutions. As for the stipends granted to generals such as myself, I declare that this is just as corrupted, because a wise state will not grant a stipend to a professional general. It will use its own citizens as leaders in war, and in times of peace expect those citizens to return to their professions. Hence a wise king, too, will not grant stipends, or if he does, they ought to be either as a reward for some exceptional deed or because the king wishes to benefit from such a man in peacetime as well as in war. You have mentioned my case, and so I will propose myself as an example. First I would like to say that I have never practiced war as a profession, as my profession is to govern my subjects and to defend them.[17] For me to defend them, I must love peace and know how to make war. My king[18] does not reward and esteem me for my knowledge of war, but more importantly for my knowledge and counsel during peacetime. No wise king seeking to govern prudently should want someone next to him who is not of this kind, for the king will be led astray if he surrounds himself with too

16. See *The Prince*, chapter 13: "Louis XI's father, King Charles VII, who freed France from the English with the help of Fortune and his skill, recognized the importance of having his own army. He issued a decree in his kingdom to enlist an infantry and a cavalry. After him, his son Louis disbanded the infantry and began hiring Swiss mercenaries. This mistake, followed by others, has led, as we have seen, to the many dangers France has had to face."
17. Fabrizio Colonna, like many other Italian mercenary generals of the time, was also a feudal nobleman. He was Duke of Palliano and Marsi, and Count of Tagliacozzo and Celano.
18. Ferdinand the Catholic.

many lovers of peace or too many lovers of war. I cannot say more in this first discussion. Should this not suffice, you must seek someone else who might satisfy you. But I trust that you now see the many difficulties involved in introducing ancient methods into the wars of our times, the preparations a wise man must make, and what opportunities he can hope for to execute them.

•   •   •

BOOK II

[. . .] COSIMO: I would like you to tell me—if you have ever deliberated on the matter—what has caused the vileness, disorder, and laxity
in the armies of our times?

FABRIZIO: I will gladly tell you my thoughts on this. You know that
many men in Europe have been considered excellent in war, but few in
Africa, and even fewer in Asia. This is because Africa and Asia had one
or two principalities and only a few republics. Europe, on the other
hand, has had several kingdoms and an infinite number of republics.
Men become excellent and show their skill according to how their
prince, republic, or king makes use of them and gives them authority.
Where there are many rulers, there are many valiant figures, and
where there are few rulers, valiant figures are few. In Asia there were
Ninus, Cyrus, Artaxerxes, and Mithradates,[19] but there were not many
others in their league. The great warriors of Africa, if we leave aside
those of ancient Egypt, were Massinissa, Jugurtha,[20] and the generals

19. Ninus was a legendary king of Assyria and the founder of the city of Nineveh; Cyrus the
Great (d. c. 529 BCE), founder of the Persian Empire, is also discussed in *Discourses,* Book II,
chapter 13, and in *The Prince,* chapters 6, 14, and 26; Artaxerxes II (early fourth century) was
King of Persia and described in Plutarch's *Parallel Lives;* Mithradates the Great (d. 63 BCE)
was King of Pontus and a formidable enemy of Rome in Asia Minor.
20. Massinissa (d. 148 BCE) was an influential ruler of Numidia in North Africa and an ally of
Rome in the Second Punic War (218–201 BCE). Jugurtha (d. 104 BCE) was the grandson of
Massinissa and fought the Romans to end their rule in Numidia.

of the Carthaginian Republic. Compared to European warriors, they too were few in number, for in Europe there was an infinite number of excellent men, and there would have been many more were one to add those whose names have been extinguished by the ravages of time, for there has been more skill in the world when there have been more states that favored it, either from necessity or from some particular interest. Consequently, Asia created few exceptional men because it was ruled by a single kingdom: Much indolence resulted from its size, which hampered men who excelled in their vocation. The same is true of Africa, though the Carthaginian Republic gave rise to valiant men. More excellent men come from republics than from kingdoms because skill is usually honored in republics, while in kingdoms it is feared. As a result, republics encourage men of skill, while kingdoms destroy them.

Whoever, therefore, considers Europe will find it to have been full of republics and principalities which out of fear of one another were compelled to keep their military institutions alive and to honor those who rose to eminence within them. In Greece, besides the kingdom of the Macedonians, there were many republics, each producing excellent men. In Italy there were the Romans, the Samnites, the Etruscans, and the Cisalpine Gauls. France and Germany had many republics and principalities, as did Spain. And if besides the great Roman figures we hear of only a few heroes of these other peoples, it is because of the baseness of the historians who, in pursuit of Fortune, usually found it more to their advantage to praise the victors.[21] Would it not be reasonable to surmise that the Samnites and the Etruscans, who fought the Romans for a hundred and fifty years before being defeated, would have had many excellent warriors too? The same is true of France and Spain. And yet the greatness that historians will not praise in individual men they praise in a people as a whole, exalting to the heavens the single-mindedness with which they defended their liberty.

As it is true that more valiant men arise where there are more states, it follows of necessity that when those states are destroyed, valor and skill are also destroyed little by little, there being fewer reasons for men to become valiant. The Roman Empire grew, extinguishing all the

---

21. See the preface to *Discourses*, Book II, in which Machiavelli develops this theme: "Most historians bow to the fortunes of conquerors."

republics and principalities of Europe and Africa, and the greater part of those in Asia, and no other path to valor was left, except for Rome. The result was that valorous men began to be as few in Europe as they were in Asia, valor and skill ultimately falling into utter decline since it had all concentrated in Rome. But once Rome was corrupted, almost the whole world followed suit, and the Scythians were able to plunder Rome, which had extinguished the skill of others but did not know how to maintain its own. And even though the flood of barbarians caused the Roman Empire to split into several parts, the skill the empire had amassed did not resurge: first, because it is a long ordeal to rebuild institutions once they have been destroyed, and second because of the way of life today, where Christianity does not impose on man the necessity to fight and defend himself that existed in ancient times. In those times, men who were defeated in war either were slaughtered or remained slaves forever, living a life of misery.[22] Conquered states were either entirely devastated, or their inhabitants—their property seized—were driven out and scattered throughout the world. Those vanquished in war suffered extreme misery, and the ancients, terrified of this, kept their armies active, honoring those who excelled within them. But in our times this fear has for the most part been lost. Few of those defeated are slaughtered, and no one is kept prisoner for a long time, as prisoners can easily be freed. Cities might rebel a thousand times, but they are not destroyed, and their citizens are allowed to retain their property, so that the greatest evil they need fear is new levies. As a result, men do not want to subject themselves to military institutions and face continuous privation under them in order to escape dangers of which they have little fear. Furthermore, when compared to the past, the states of Europe exist under very few leaders, for all of France obeys a single king, all of Spain another, and Italy is divided into a few states. Hence weak cities defend themselves by allying themselves with victors, while the powerful states do not fear complete destruction, for the reasons I have just mentioned.

* * *

22. See also *Discourses,* Book II, chapter 2, in which Machiavelli discusses the weakening effect of Christianity from a different perspective: "Our religion glorifies men who are humble and contemplative rather than men of action. [...] If our religion does demand that you be strong, it is so that you will be able to bear suffering rather than carry out feats of strength."

. . .

BOOK VII

FABRIZIO: [...] I know that I have spoken to you of many things that
you could have understood yourselves. And yet I spoke of these matters, as I said earlier this afternoon, in order to demonstrate better
what kind of military training is best, and also to satisfy those (should
there be any) who do not understand these matters as readily as you
do. It seems to me that there is nothing left for me to say, other than to
give you some general rules which I am sure you will find familiar.[23]
They are:

What benefits the enemy will harm you, and what benefits you will
harm the enemy.

He who in war is more vigilant in scrutinizing the enemy's designs,
and more tireless in training his army, will face fewer dangers and have
greater hope for victory.

Never lead your soldiers into battle before you are certain of their
courage, that they are without fear, and that they are well ordered. Do
not engage your troops unless you can see that they hope for victory.

It is better to defeat the enemy with hunger than with steel, for in
victory with steel you will see Fortune playing a greater role than skill.

23. In the following, Machiavelli translates, adapts, and paraphrases maxims from *De re mili-
tari* by Flavius Vegetius Renatus (fourth century CE), a work that advocates and codifies the
arrangement of armies according to a classical Roman ideal. Machiavelli expands and adapts
Vegetius's Latin maxims and adds a few of his own.

The best strategy is that which remains concealed from the enemy until it has been carried out.

In war, knowing how to recognize and seize an opportunity is the most important ability.

Nature creates few brave men—diligence and training create many.

Discipline in war is more vital than fury.

Soldiers leaving the enemy's side to come to yours are an optimal acquisition if they are loyal, because the forces of your enemy diminish more with the loss of those who desert than with those who are slain, even though the word "deserter" wakes suspicion in new friends and hatred in old.

It is better when arranging your formations to set up considerable support behind the front line than to spread out your soldiers so that you can make the front line more imposing.

He who knows his forces and those of the enemy will be hard to vanquish.

The soldiers' skill is worth more than their number, and the site of a battle can sometimes be of greater benefit than skill.

What is new and unexpected will take an army aback, while the army looks down on what is customary and predictable. You will therefore give your army both practice and knowledge of a new enemy by engaging him in minor skirmishes before you face him in battle.

Whoever pursues a routed enemy in a disorderly manner is seeking to become a defeated victor.

Whoever does not prepare his provisions will be defeated without steel.

Whoever places more trust in cavalry than in infantry, or more in infantry than in cavalry, must accommodate himself to the site of battle.

If you want to ascertain whether a spy has entered your camp, have all men in the middle of the day return to their assigned quarters.

Change your battle plan when you see that your enemy has predicted it.

Seek the counsel of many on what you should do, but then confer with only a few on what you will do.

Soldiers are kept in their quarters by fear and punishment; when they are marched into battle, they are led by hope and reward.

Good generals never engage in battle unless necessity compels or opportunity beckons.

Make sure that your enemy does not know how you plan to order your ranks in battle, and in whatever way you order them, be certain that the first line can be absorbed by the second and third.

Never use a division in battle for another purpose than the one to which you assigned it, unless you want to cause disorder.

Sudden upsets are countered with difficulty, unless one can think on one's feet.

Men, steel, money, and bread are the backbone of war; but of these four the first two are more necessary, because men and steel can find money and bread, but money and bread cannot find men and steel.

The unarmed rich man is the prize of the poor soldier.

Accustom your soldiers to despise comfortable living and luxurious attire.

All this is what has generally occurred to me, though I know I could have told you many more things in our discussion: for example, in how many different ways the ancients organized their ranks, how they dressed, how they trained, and many other things. I could have brought up many other particulars, which I did not, however, judge necessary because you can read about them quite readily, and also because my intention was not to show exactly how the ancient army was created, but how an army should be organized in our times so that it might have more skill and ability than it does. Hence I felt it unnecessary to discuss ancient matters in greater depth beyond what I felt necessary as an introduction.

Selections from

FLORENTINE HISTORIES

Machiavelli's final major work was written in the last few years of his life. In 1520, after eight years of exclusion from politics and living in impoverishment on his farm, Machiavelli was offered the post of historiographer of Florence by Cardinal Giulio de' Medici, who in 1523 was to become Pope Clement VII. The contract Giulio de' Medici offered Machiavelli specified that it would be left up to Machiavelli to choose whether this work—"annalia et cronacas fiorentinas"*—would be written in Latin or the "Tuscan tongue." Machiavelli chose the elegant and modern Tuscan Italian in which he had written* The Prince, The Discourses, *and his graceful works of prose and poetry.*

In Florentine Histories, *Machiavelli, who for much of his life had been a sophisticated Florentine diplomat, could not refrain from producing a daring and at times highly critical rendition of Florence's history, much of which had been stamped by the Medici, who had been extremely hostile to him. But Giulio de' Medici—Pope Clement VII—to whom the book was dedicated, was a Renaissance prince and patron of the arts, and was pleased with this work.*

PREFACE

When I first decided to write down the deeds of the people of Florence within their city and without, it was my intention to begin my narration in the year of our Lord 1434, when the Medici family, through the qualities of Cosimo and his father Giovanni, achieved power beyond that of any other family in Florence. I resolved to begin in 1434 because two excellent historians, Messer Leonardo d'Arezzo and Messer Poggio,[1] had narrated in great detail all the events that took place before that date. I read their histories diligently in order to ascertain the modes and methods they followed, so that by imitating them my own histories would meet with greater acceptance among readers. I noted that in their descriptions of all the wars waged by the Florentines against foreign princes and peoples, Messer Leonardo d'Arezzo and Messer Poggio were most diligent, but when it came to civil disorders and internal enmities and the effects these had, they were either entirely silent or described them so briefly that readers could derive no use or pleasure from them. I surmise the reason for this could only have been that these historians judged these events to be so negligible

1. Leonardo Bruni (c. 1370–1444), also called Leonardo d'Arezzo as he was born in the city of Arezzo, was a scholar and historian who wrote *Historiarum Florentini populi libri XII* (*Twelve Books of the History of the Florentine People*). Gian Francesco Poggio Bracciolini (1380–1459) was one of the foremost scholars of the early Renaissance. From 1453 until his death in 1459 he was Chancellor of Florence, during which time he wrote his history of the city.

that they thought them unworthy of being recorded for posterity, or that they feared that the descendants of those they would have had to criticize in their narration might be offended. Both reasons, however, seem to me entirely unworthy of great men (may their souls rest in peace), for if anything in a history delights and instructs, it is that which is described in detail. If no other lesson is useful to citizens who govern republics, then it is the lesson that reveals the reasons for the hatreds and divisions within a city, so that the citizens who govern can gain wisdom from the perils of others and choose to remain united. If every example of the workings of a republic can affect readers, then readers encountering examples of the workings of their own republic will be affected even more and derive more benefit. And if divisions in any republic have been momentous, those in Florence were momentous indeed. Most republics of which we know were content with a single division which, depending on circumstances, either furthered or destroyed the republic; but Florence, not content with a single division, has had many. In Rome, as everybody knows, after the kings were expelled a division between the nobles and the plebeians ensued, and this division preserved Rome until its ruin.[2] The same was true of Athens and the other republics that flourished in the past. But in Florence there was first a division among the nobles themselves, then a division between the nobles and the populace, and finally a division between the populace and the plebeians. It often happened that whatever faction gained the upper hand proceeded to split in two. These divisions resulted in more citizens being killed and exiled, and more families destroyed, than in any other city in history. And truly, in my view no other example shows as effectively the power of Florence as the example of these divisions, which would have been powerful enough to destroy any other great and illustrious city.[3] But our city only seemed to become even greater, as the skill of the Florentines and the strength of their wit and spirit enabled them to make themselves and their city great, so that those who remained free from evil influence had more chance to exalt Florence than the dire circumstances the city faced had to diminish her and crush her. Should Florence,

2. With "ruin" Machiavelli is referring to the end of the Roman Republic. Machiavelli develops the idea of the destructive and regenerative qualities of divisiveness in a state in *Discourses,* Book I, chapters 4–6.
3. See *Florentine Histories,* Book III, chapter 1.

after freeing herself from the Holy Roman Empire, have been fortunate enough to adopt a form of government that would have maintained her united, I cannot think of a modern or ancient republic that
could have been superior to her;[4] she would have had a skill in productivity and arms beyond compare. Even after Florence had expelled the
Ghibellines in such numbers that Tuscany and Lombardy were filled
with them,[5] the Guelphs, along with those who remained in Florence,
still managed to draw from the city twelve hundred men at arms and
twelve thousand infantry in the war against Arezzo a year before the
Battle of Campaldino.[6] And in the war against Duke Filippo Visconti
of Milan, when Florence had to make use of her riches and not her
own weakened army, the Florentines spent three and a half million
florins in the five years that the war lasted. When that war was over, not
content with peace, the Florentines marched on Lucca to give more
evidence of their city's power.[7]

I cannot imagine why these divisions should not merit being described in detail. If our most noble historians refrained from such descriptions so as not to offend the memory of those whose actions they
had to assess, they were mistaken, and showed little understanding of
the ambition of men and their desire to perpetuate their own names
and those of their ancestors. It also escaped them that many who did
not have the opportunity to achieve fame through some laudable deed
strove to achieve it by contemptible means. Nor did they consider how
actions that have greatness in them, like the actions of governments
and states, however they are considered or whatever aim they have,
seem to bestow on men more honor than blame.

Having given thought to these matters, I changed my original plan
and decided to start my history from our city's beginnings. But as it is

4. After the Ghibelline faction, which supported the Holy Roman Emperor against the pope,
was expelled from Florence (see following footnote), the Guelph faction split into the feuding factions of the Neri (Black) and Bianchi (White).
5. In 1266 Carlo d'Anjou defeated King Manfred of Sicily, who had asserted himself in Tuscany and Lombardy as protector of the Ghibellines. The Florentine Guelphs then initiated
a mass expulsion of the Ghibellines from Florence.
6. The Battle of Campaldino (1289) between Florence, controlled by the Guelphs, and
Arezzo, controlled by the Ghibellines, marked the beginning of the supremacy of the Florentine Guelphs over Tuscany.
7. Florence's war with Duke Filippo Maria Visconti of Milan lasted from 1423 to 1428, and
that against Lucca from 1429 to 1433.

not my intention to tread where others have trod, I shall describe in detail only those incidents that occurred within the city up to 1434. Of incidents outside the city, I shall report only what is necessary for a better understanding of what occurred within it. Beyond 1434, I shall write in detail about both. Furthermore, so that this history can be better understood in all its periods, before I come to Florence I shall describe by what means Italy came to be under the powers that governed it in those times. [. . .]

* * *

BOOK II
25

Uguccione della Faggiuola became lord of Pisa and soon thereafter of Lucca, where he was installed by the Ghibelline faction.[8] With the backing of Pisa and Lucca he did serious harm to the neighboring cities, and to escape this threat the Florentines asked King Roberto to send his brother Piero to take command of their armies.[9] Uguccione, in the meantime, relentlessly continued to increase his power, and through force and deceit seized many fortresses in the Valdarno and the Val di Nievole. But when he besieged Montecatini, the Florentines concluded that they had to come to its aid, otherwise Uguccione's rage would wreak havoc on all their lands. They gathered a large army and entered the Val di Nievole, where they encountered Uguccione and were routed after a great battle. King Roberto's brother Piero was killed—his body was never recovered—and with him more than two thousand men perished. But the victory was not a happy one for Uguccione either, for one of his sons was slain, as were many of his commanders.

After this rout the Florentines fortified the towns of their territo-

8. Uguccione della Faggiuola (c. 1250–1319) was one of the most influential members of the Ghibelline faction of Tuscany. He had been elected chief magistrate of Pisa, then commander of the army, and in 1314, already in his late sixties, seized power and became tyrant of Pisa. The Ghibelline faction consisted for the most part of feudal aristocrats and their partisans, and supported the Holy Roman Emperor. The Guelph faction which supported the papacy was its longtime opponent.

9. Piero d'Anjou, the brother of King Roberto of Naples. See also *The Life of Castruccio Castracani*, p. 403.

ries, and King Roberto sent them as general for their army Count d'Andria, known as Count Novello.[10] Either because of the count's behavior, or because Florentines tend to find every government irksome and every incident divisive, the city, despite the war with Uguccione, split into friends and enemies of the king. The leaders of the king's enemies in Florence were Simone della Tosa, the Magalotti, and some other powerful men, members of the populace, in all outnumbering their opponents in government. They sent to France and then Germany to seek leaders and forces to drive out the count whom the king had appointed governor, but Fortune was against them. All the same, they did not abandon their enterprise, and though they did not find a leader in France or Germany they could look up to, they found one in Gubbio,[11] and, expelling Count Novello, brought Lando da Gubbio as chief magistrate to Florence and gave him absolute authority over her citizens.

Lando da Gubbio was a rapacious and cruel man who went about town with a large armed guard, putting this or that man to death at the will of those who had elected him. His arrogance reached such heights that he used the Florentine stamp to coin false money without anyone daring to oppose him: That was how powerful the discord in Florence had made him! A truly great and miserable city, which neither the memory of past divisions, nor the fear of Uguccione, nor the authority of a king could keep stable, Florence now found itself in a terrible state, plundered from without by Uguccione, and from within by Lando da Gubbio.

The friends of King Roberto and all who opposed Lando and his followers were Guelphs, mostly nobles and powerful men of the populace. Nevertheless, as their adversaries were in control of the state, they could not reveal themselves without putting themselves in grave danger. They were, however, determined to break free from Lando's reprehensible tyranny, and secretly wrote to King Roberto asking him to appoint Count Guido da Battifolle as his governor in Florence. The king immediately made the arrangements, and the enemy party, even

10. Bertrand de Baux, of the illustrious lords of Baux-en-Provence. He had married Beatrice d'Anjou, the sister of King Roberto, and had recently been given the title of Count d'Andria, hence his nickname "Novello"—"new" or "fresh."
11. A town in the province of Perugia in central Italy.

though the Signori[12] were against the king, did not dare oppose the count owing to his fine qualities. Nevertheless, he did not have much authority, because the Signori and the Gonfalonieri of the companies[13] favored Lando and his party.

While Florence was in the midst of these troubles, the daughter of King Albert of Germany arrived on her way to meet her husband Carlo, the son of King Roberto of Naples.[14] She was welcomed with great honor by supporters of King Roberto, who complained to her of the dire state Florence was in and of the tyranny of Lando and his partisans. Through her influence and the assistance of the king, the citizens united, and Lando was stripped of his office and sent back to Gubbio, weighed down with plunder and blood. With the change in government King Roberto kept sovereignty over the city for another three years, and as seven Signori of Lando's faction had already been elected, six more were elected from among the king's faction. There followed some magistracies made up of thirteen Signori, after which their number reverted back to seven, which it had always been previously.

26

It was during this time that Uguccione was stripped of the sovereignty of Lucca, and Pisa, and Castruccio Castracani, from being citizen of Lucca became lord of Lucca.[15] As Castruccio was young, bold, and fierce, and fortunate in his campaigns, in a very short time he became prince of the Ghibellines in Tuscany. The Florentines now put aside their civil discords for several years, and initially concentrated on how they might keep Castruccio's increasing power in check, and then, when his power increased despite their efforts, how they might best defend themselves. So that the Signori could deliberate with broader advice and carry out their decisions more efficiently, they appointed twelve citizens called *Buoni Uomini*—"Good Men"—without whose

12. The body of magistrates of Florence's supreme executive council.
13. The commanders of the people's militia, which originated in Florence in the 1250s.
14. Caterina, daughter of Albert of Habsburg, had married Duke Carlo of Calabria, oldest son of King Roberto of Naples, in 1316.
15. See *The Life of Castruccio Castracani*.

counsel and consent the Signori could not act on anything of importance.

The period of King Roberto's sovereignty over Florence ended, and the city became its own lord again. It reorganized itself with its customary rectors and magistrates, its great fear of Castruccio keeping it united. Castruccio, after his campaigns against the lords of Lunigiana, attacked Prato. Florence was determined to come to Prato's aid, and the Florentines closed their shops, armed the populace, and marched to Prato with twenty thousand foot soldiers and fifteen hundred horsemen. In order to reduce Castruccio's forces and enlarge their own, the Florentine Signori decreed that every exiled rebel of the Guelph faction who came to the aid of Prato would be allowed to return to Florence after the campaign. As a result, more than four thousand rebels came over to their side. This great army marched on Prato with such speed that Castruccio was alarmed enough to retreat to Lucca without putting Fortune to the test in battle. In the Florentine camp this sparked a dispute between the nobles and the populace, the latter wanting to pursue Castruccio and destroy him, while the nobles wanted to return home. They argued that it was enough that they had put Florence in peril in order to free Prato: They had been compelled by necessity to fight, but as that was no longer the case, it was not worth tempting Fortune when they stood to lose so much and gain so little. As the two factions were not able to agree, the judgment was referred to the Signori, who found the same disparity between the nobles and the populace in their council. This news spread through the city, drawing great crowds to the town squares, shouting such threats against the nobles that they yielded out of fear. As this resolution was adopted too late, and grudgingly by many, Castruccio had ample time to withdraw safely to Lucca.

27

This turmoil made the populace so indignant against the nobles that the Signori were now unwilling to honor the promise of repatriation they had made to the exiles at the nobles' suggestion. The exiles sensed this, and decided to preempt the Signori by marching at the head of the returning army, so that they would be the first to arrive at the gates of Florence. But as their action was foreseen, their plan did not succeed, and they were repulsed by those who had remained at home. The exiles now tried to obtain by negotiation what they had failed to obtain by force, and sent eight men as emissaries to remind the Signori of the promise that had been made to them and of the dangers they had submitted themselves to in the hope of the promised reward. The Florentine nobles felt bound by the promise which the Signori had made to the exiles and exerted themselves in favor of their repatriation, but the anger of the people was so great, since the campaign against Castruccio had not been won in the way they had wanted, that they refused to acquiesce. This resulted in humiliation and dishonor for the city. Many nobles were angered, and tried to obtain by force what had been denied by negotiation. They made arrangements with the exiles for them to enter Florence armed, and the faction of the nobles inside the city would take up arms to aid them. But the plot was discovered before the designated day, so that the exiles found the city armed against them, intending to halt the exiles outside and to intimidate their allies inside. Thus the idea of repatriation was abandoned, and the exiles left.

After their departure, it was decided to punish those responsible for bringing them to the city in the first place. Everyone knew who the culprits were, but no one dared name them, still less accuse them. It was therefore decided that the best method would be for everyone in the councils to write down the names of the culprits and present them secretly to the chief of the militia. Thus Amerigo Donati, Messer Teghiaio Frescobaldi, and Messer Lotteringo Gherardini were accused. But the judge sentencing them was more favorably disposed toward them than their offenses might have merited, and they were only given fines.

* * *

29

It was the year 1325. After occupying Pistoia, Castruccio had become so powerful that the Florentines, fearing his strength, were determined to attack and remove him from Pistoia before he could secure his position there. From their citizens and allies they gathered an army of twenty thousand foot soldiers and three thousand horsemen and besieged nearby Altopascio, with a view to occupying it and thus preventing it from coming to the aid of Pistoia. Once the Florentines had taken Altopascio, they marched on Lucca, laying waste to all the land, but did not make much progress because of their general's lack of prudence and even greater lack of loyalty.

The Florentine general was Messer Ramondo di Cardona. He had witnessed how quick the Florentines had been to relinquish their liberty, placing it first in the hands of the king of Naples, then of the legates, and then of men of inferior quality. He thought that if he put Florence in a difficult position, he might easily be made its prince. He in fact mentioned this frequently, and demanded that he be given the same authority over Florence that he had been given over the army; otherwise, he argued, he would not have the kind of obedience a general needed. But the Florentines did not consent, and he began wasting time while Castruccio gained it, as the latter was now able to receive the aid that Visconti and other tyrants of Lombardy had promised him. Messer Ramondo di Cardona had a superior army, but through lack of loyalty he did not know how to win, and through lack of prudence did not know how to escape. He proceeded slowly with his army, and Castruccio attacked him near Altopascio, defeating him after a great battle. Many Florentine citizens were killed or taken prisoner, among them Messer Ramondo, who received from Fortune the kind of punishment he would have deserved from the Florentines for his falseness and bad counsel.[16]

The harm that Castruccio wrought on the Florentines after his victorious battle, in plunder, prisoners, destruction, and fire, cannot be described. He rode through Florentine territory for many months, marauding without opposition. After such a defeat the Florentines were happy enough to save their city.

30

The Florentines, however, had not become so wretched that they were not able to raise large sums of money, hire soldiers, and send to their allies for help. But nothing they could do on their own would be suffi-

16. Ramondo di Cardona was captured and imprisoned in Lucca until Castracani's death in 1528.

cient to check an enemy as powerful as Castruccio, so they were forced to nominate as their lord Duke Carlo of Calabria, the son of King Roberto of Naples, if they wanted him to come to their defense: For as the d'Anjou family was accustomed to rule Florence, they preferred her obedience to her friendship. Duke Carlo, however, was engaged in the wars of Sicily and unable to assume control of the city. So he sent a Frenchman, Duke Walter of Athens,[17] who took possession of Florence as Carlo's governor, appointing the magistrates he liked. Contrary to his true nature his demeanor was modest, and hence he was liked by all.

When the wars of Sicily were over, Duke Carlo came to Florence with a thousand horsemen, riding into the city in July of the year 1326. His arrival finally prevented Castruccio from pillaging the Florentine countryside as he pleased, but the grand reputation Duke Carlo had acquired outside Florence was quickly lost within it, and whatever ravages the enemy had not wrought were now inflicted by friends, for the Signori could not do anything without the consent of the duke. Within a year he had drawn four hundred thousand florins from the city, even though the agreement had been that the sum would not exceed twenty thousand. So great were the burdens with which the duke or his father encumbered the city every day.

To these troubles were added new suspicions and new enemies, because the Ghibellines of Lombardy became so wary of Duke Carlo's presence in Tuscany that Galeazzo Visconti and the other Lombard tyrants turned to Louis of Bavaria, who had been elected Holy Roman Emperor against the wishes of the pope. With money and promises they persuaded Louis to come to Italy, and he entered Lombardy, from there proceeding to Tuscany, where, with the help of Castruccio, he took Pisa. Replenished with great sums of money, Louis then marched to Rome. At this, Duke Carlo, fearing for the Kingdom of Naples, left Florence, appointing Filippo da Saggineto as his governor.

After the departure of the Holy Roman Emperor, Castruccio took over Pisa, but the Florentines managed to negotiate a deal in which they took Pistoia from him. Castruccio then besieged Pistoia, and per-

---

17. Walter VI de la Brienne (c. 1304–56) was appointed governor of Florence for Carlo of Calabria, an office he held briefly in 1326. He returned to Florence in 1342 when the Florentine ruling classes called upon him to rule the city. Here he showed his "true nature," his despotic rule ending after only ten months.

sisted with such skill and obstinacy that even though the Florentines tried many times to aid Pistoia by attacking first his army and then his territories, they did not manage either by force or diligence to deter him: Such was Castruccio's passion to punish the Pistoians and to trounce the Florentines, until the Pistoians were forced to receive him as their lord. Though this campaign brought Castruccio immeasurable glory, it also utterly exhausted him, so that upon returning to Lucca he died. And as Fortune will almost invariably complement a good or an evil with another good or evil, Duke Carlo of Calabria, the lord of Florence, died in Naples, so that within a short time, beyond the Florentines' every expectation, they found themselves liberated from the control of the one and the terror of the other. Now that they were free, they reformed their city and annulled the system of the old councils, creating two new ones: one made up of three hundred citizens from the populace, the other of two hundred and fifty nobles and citizens from the populace. The first they called the Council of the People, the second the Council of the Commune.

BOOK III
1

The serious enmity between the populace and the nobles, which arises from the desire of the nobles to command and that of the populace not to obey, is the cause of all the evils that occur in a city.[18] It is this diversity of humors which feeds everything that throws republics into turmoil. It kept Rome disunited, and, if one may compare lesser things with greater, it is what kept Florence divided, even though the results were different in the two cities: In Rome the divisions that initially existed between the nobles and the populace were settled by debate, while in Florence they were settled by combat. The enmity between the two factions in Rome ended in new laws, while that in Florence

---

18. In *The Prince*, chapter 9, Machiavelli writes: "In every city there are two opposing humors. This arises from the fact that the nobles want to command and oppress the people, but the people do not want to be commanded or oppressed by the nobles." See also *Discourses*, Book I, chapter 5: "For without doubt, if one considers the respective aims of the nobles and the populace, one sees in the former a strong desire to dominate, and in the latter merely a desire not to be dominated."

ended in the banishment and death of many citizens. The enmity within Rome invariably increased her military skill, while that within Florence was crushed by its opposing factions. The divisions in Rome led from a state of equality among its citizens to a momentous inequality, those in Florence from a state of inequality to an admirable equality. This diversity of effects must have sprung from the different aims of the two peoples. While the populace of Rome strove to enjoy the supreme honors together with the nobles, the populace of Florence fought to govern Florence on its own without the participation of the nobles. As the desire of the Roman populace was more reasonable, the nobles came to see the populace's assaults as more bearable, and ceded easily, without taking up arms. Consequently, after some disputes and debates, populace and nobles came together to produce a law that satisfied the former and allowed the latter to keep their status. In contrast, the desires of the Florentine populace were harmful and unjust, so that the nobility prepared itself for its defense with greater forces, the result being bloodshed and the exile of citizens. The laws that were consequently enacted were not for the common good, but entirely in favor of the victor.

As a result of the victories of the populace, the city of Rome became more adept and expert. Because the populace could serve along with the nobles in the administration of the magistracies, the army, and the provinces, they could acquire the same skill as the nobles, and as the expertise of Rome grew, so did its might. But in Florence, when the populace was victorious, the nobility was deprived of magistracies, and if they wanted to regain them, it was necessary for the nobles not only to be like men of the populace in their behavior, spirit, and manner of living, but also to be seen to be like them. From this arose those changes in the coats of arms and the titles of families which the nobles adopted in order to seem part of the populace. Hence the military prowess and generosity of spirit that had resided in the nobility was extinguished, while it could not be rekindled in the populace since these qualities had never existed. So Florence became increasingly humble and wretched. But while in Rome the nobles' skill turned into arrogance, so that Rome reached a point where it could not exist without a prince, Florence was in a position where a wise lawgiver could institute any form of government.

• • •
BOOK VII
33

[. . .] Cola Montano was a man of letters and great ambition who taught Latin to the foremost youths of Milan. Either from hatred of the ways of Galeazzo Maria Sforza, Duke of Milan, or for some other reason, he was always arguing how detestable life was under a bad prince, and how lucky were those whom Nature and Fortune had granted the privilege of being born and living in a republic. He claimed that all famous men had been raised in republics, not in principalities, because republics reared skilled men while principalities destroyed them. Republics drew advantage from a man's skill, while principalities feared it.

The youths to whom Cola Montano was closest were Giovannandrea Lampognano, Carlo Visconti, and Girolamo Olgiato. He often discussed the duke's evil nature with them, and the misfortune of those who were under his rule, and his confidence in these young men's spirit and will grew so strong that he had them swear that once they were old enough, they would free their city from the tyranny of this prince. The young men were enthralled by the desire for freedom, which grew within them as the years passed. This desire was quickened by the duke's evil deeds and the harm he did the young men and their families, making them all the more resolved to carry out the conspiracy. Duke Galeazzo was profligate and cruel, and the ample evidence he had given of this inspired the hatred of all. Not content with corrupting noble ladies, he also took pleasure in humiliating them in public, nor was he content with murdering men unless he could do so in some cruel fashion. The rumor followed him that he had killed his own mother, for it was said that he did not consider himself a ruler as long as she was alive. He comported himself in such a way that she withdrew to her residence in Cremona, which had been part of her dowry, but on her way there she was seized by a sudden illness and died. Many subsequently claimed that her son had had her killed. Duke Galeazzo had dishonored the women of Carlo's and Girolamo's families, and had refused to give Giovannandrea possession of the abbey of Miramondo, as the pontiff had assigned it to one of the duke's close relatives instead.

These personal injuries fanned the young men's desire for vengeance and for delivering their city from so many evils, and they hoped that if they succeeded in killing the duke they would be supported by much of the nobility and the entire populace. Determined to proceed with their plot, they often met together, which, since they were all old friends, did not arouse any suspicion. They discussed the matter in great detail, and to strengthen their spirit for the deed practiced striking each other in the side and the chest with the sheaths of the daggers they were intending to use. They debated the best time and place for the deed: The castle did not seem safe, a hunting expedition was uncertain and dangerous, and the duke's strolls through the city seemed difficult, offering scant prospect for success, as did assassinating him at a banquet. The young men therefore decided to assassinate the duke at some public ceremony which he would definitely attend, and where they and their supporters could gather without arousing suspicion. They also decided that should one of them be seized or arrested for whatever reason, the others would draw their swords and kill the duke, even if they were surrounded by the duke's armed guard.

34

The year 1476 was drawing to a close and the Christmas feast was approaching. On Saint Stephen's Day the duke was accustomed to proceed with great pomp to the church of that martyred saint, and the conspirators decided that this would be the best moment to carry out their design. On the morning of the saint's day they armed some of their most trusted friends and servants, announcing that they were going to the assistance of Giovannandrea, who wanted to build an aqueduct leading onto his estate against the wishes of some of his neighbors. They led their armed men to the church, alleging that they wished to request permission from the prince before setting out. Under various pretexts they also gathered together other friends and kinsmen at the church, hoping that when the deed was done everyone would follow them in the rest of their enterprise. Their aim, after the duke's death, was to assemble their armed followers and march to those parts of the city where they believed they could easily incite the plebeians to take up arms against the duchess[19] and the leaders of the state. The starving populace, they believed, would readily follow them, as they planned to allow them to plunder the houses of Messer Cecco Simonetta, Giovanni Botti, and Francesco Lucani, all leaders of the state, and in this way secure themselves and restore liberty to the populace.

The young men's plan was fixed, and they were resolved to carry it out. Giovannandrea and the others went to the church early and heard Mass together, after which Giovannandrea turned to a statue of Saint Ambrose and said: "Patron of our city! You know our intention and what we are striving for with such great danger to ourselves. Favor our enterprise, and prove by your support of justice that you despise injustice!"

Meanwhile, as the duke was preparing to set out for the church, he encountered many omens of impending death. At daybreak, when he was dressing, he put on his cuirass as he often did, but then immediately took it off again, either because it was uncomfortable or because he did not like its appearance. He then decided to have Mass read at the castle instead, but found that his chaplain had left for the Church of Saint Stephen with all the sacral vessels. He then asked the Bishop of Como to celebrate the Mass instead, but the bishop was unable to. Consequently, it was almost as if the duke was being forced to go to the church. Before he left, he had his sons Giovangaleazzo and Ermes come to him, and embraced and kissed them many times, as if he could not part from them. But finally, having decided to go, he left the castle and walked to the church with the emissaries of Ferrara and Mantua on either side.

In the meantime, to excite less suspicion and escape the intense cold, the conspirators retired to the chamber of the archpriest, who was their friend, but on hearing the duke approach they returned to the church. Giovannandrea and Girolamo positioned themselves to the right of the entrance, Carlo to the left. Those preceding the duke had already entered and were then followed by the duke himself, who was surrounded by a great crowd, as was to be expected in a solemn ducal procession. The first to move were Lampognano and Girolamo,

19. Duke Galeazzo Maria Sforza's wife, Bona of Savoy.

pretending to clear the way for the duke. Once they were close enough, they grasped the short sharp knives hidden in their sleeves and struck at him. Lampognano inflicted two wounds, one in the belly, the other in the throat; Girolamo also struck the duke in the throat and in the chest. Carlo Visconti was standing closer to the door, and as the duke had already passed by when the others attacked, Visconti could not wound him in front, but with two blows pierced his back and shoulder. These six wounds were so rapid and sudden that the duke fell to the ground before anyone realized what was happening—nor could the duke do or say anything, except call out a single time to the Virgin Mary for help.

With the duke on the ground a great commotion broke out: Swords were drawn, and as happens at unforeseen events, some ran from the church and others ran blindly toward the uproar without anyone knowing what was happening. Nevertheless, those closest to the duke who had seen him slain recognized the murderers and pursued them. Giovannandrea tried to push his way out of the church through the large crowd of women who were sitting on the floor, as was their practice, but he became tangled in their dresses and was slain by a Moor, one of the duke's manservants. Carlo too was killed by the men around him. Girolamo Olgiato, on the other hand, managed to make his way through the crowd and out of the church. On seeing his companions dead, and not knowing where to flee, he ran home, where his father and brothers refused to receive him: Only his mother showed compassion, and entrusted Girolamo to a priest, an old family friend who disguised him in his robes and led him to his house. There Girolamo remained for two days, still hoping that some uprising in Milan might save him. But there was no uprising, so he tried to escape in disguise, afraid that sooner or later he would be discovered at the priest's house. But he was recognized and handed over to the magistrates, to whom he revealed all the details of the conspiracy. Girolamo was twenty-three years old, and he showed as much spirit at his death as he had during the conspiracy. Finding himself stripped before his executioner, who stood knife in hand, Girolamo, a man of letters, spoke the following words in Latin: *Mors acerba, fama perpetua, stabit vetus memoria facti.*[20]

The endeavor of these unfortunate young men was planned in secrecy and carried out with spirit, and they failed only when those who

20. "Death is bitter, fame perpetual, the memory of this fact will endure."

they expected would follow and defend them neither followed nor defended them. A prince should therefore learn to live in a manner that will make him loved and revered, so that no one who intends to assassinate him can hope to escape. Conspirators, on the other hand, should be aware of the futility of trusting the multitude, and of believing that even when malcontent the people will follow or join them in their perilous undertakings.[21] All Italy was alarmed by this event, but alarmed even more by the events in Florence that were soon to follow, events that ended a peace in Italy that had lasted for twelve years, as I shall show in the following book, which might have a sad and tearful ending, but will commence with bloodshed and terror.

BOOK VIII
1

The beginning of this eighth book falls between two conspiracies: one in Milan, which I have just described, and the other, which I will now describe, in Florence. Hence it would seem fitting, should I follow my usual practice, to discuss the nature of conspiracies and their significance. I would do this quite readily if I had not already discussed the matter elsewhere,[22] or if it were the kind of subject one could touch on briefly. But as the nature of conspiracies and their significance deserve extensive consideration and have already been discussed in another place, I leave them aside and move on.

The Medici had now crushed all the enemies who had challenged them openly, but in order for this family to wield exclusive power in Florence and distinguish themselves from other families in civic life, the Medici also needed to overcome enemies who were plotting against them secretly. When the Medici had been vying with other families of equal influence and standing, citizens who envied their power were able to oppose them openly without having to fear that they would be crushed at the first sign of opposition, since at that point the magistrates were independent and no faction had reason to be

---

21. Machiavelli analyzes "the dangers incurred after carrying out a conspiracy" in *Discourses*, Book III, chapter 6, and also in *The Prince*, chapter 19, where Machiavelli further develops why "it is difficult to attack or conspire against one who is greatly esteemed."
22. *Discourses*, Book III, chapter 6, titled "On Conspiracies."

afraid until they actually lost. But after the victory of 1466[23] the government was almost entirely in the hands of the Medici, who had acquired so much power that those who were dissatisfied either had to suffer in patience or, if they wanted to destroy the Medici's power, had to try doing so through secret means and conspiracy. But conspiracies barely ever succeed, more often than not bringing ruin to the conspirators and greatness to those they conspire against. As a result, when in such a conspiracy a prince is attacked and is not killed (the assassination of the Duke of Milan was a rare exception), the prince emerges with greater power, and frequently, even if he was a good man before the conspiracy, will turn evil. This happens because conspiracies give the prince reason to fear, and fear gives him reason to secure himself, and securing himself gives him reason to harm others, from which arises hatred and, often enough, the prince's ruin. Hence these conspiracies quickly crush those who conspire, while those who are conspired against will with time inevitably cause harm.

2

Italy was, as I have already shown, divided into two factions: Pope Sixtus IV and King Ferdinand on one side, and the Venetians, the duke, and the Florentines on the other. Though all-out war between the factions had not yet broken out, every day there were new grounds for such an event, the pope, particularly, endeavoring in all his enterprises to harm the government of Florence. Hence at the death of Filippo de' Medici, the Archbishop of Pisa, the pope bestowed the Archbishopric on Francesco Salviati, who he knew was an enemy of the Medici. The Signoria of Florence[24] was opposed to this and refused to grant Salviati accession to this office, which resulted in considerable turmoil between the pope and the Signoria. The pope also bestowed the greatest favors on the Pazzi in Rome, disfavoring the Medici at every opportunity.

In that era the Pazzi, through their wealth and nobility, were the foremost family of Florence. The head of the house of Pazzi was

---

23. In 1466, Piero di Cosimo de' Medici (the father of Lorenzo and Giuliano, whom Machiavelli discusses in this chapter) had crushed his opponent Luca Pitti.
24. The chief executive council of Florence.

Messer Iacopo, who had been made a *cavaliere* by the people on account of his wealth and nobility. He had no children except a natural daughter, but had many nephews born to his brothers Messers Piero and Antonio. The foremost of these were Guglielmo, Francesco, Rinato, and Giovanni, and after them in rank came Andrea, Niccolò, and Galeotto. Cosimo de' Medici, seeing their wealth and nobility, had given his niece Bianca in marriage to Guglielmo de' Pazzi in the hope that this alliance would bring the two houses closer, removing the enmity and hatred that is so often sparked by distrust.

However, our designs frequently tend to be uncertain and false, and this alliance brought unexpected consequences, for Lorenzo de' Medici's advisers drew his attention to how very dangerous and detrimental to his authority it was to unite wealth and status in a citizen. The result was that neither Messer Iacopo nor his nephews were given the ranks and honors they merited in relation to the other citizens. This sparked the first indignation in the Pazzi and the first fear in the Medici, and as one of these grew it gave fodder to the other to grow as well. Now whenever the Pazzi had a dispute with any citizen, the magistracy invariably ruled against the Pazzi. Once, when Francesco de' Pazzi was in Rome, the Council of Eight[25] forced him to return to Florence on some trivial matter without granting him the respect usually accorded to a dignitary, so that the Pazzi continuously complained with injurious and indignant words that increased people's suspicion of the Medici, and in turn increased the damage the Medici did to the Pazzi. Giovanni de' Pazzi had married the daughter of Giovanni Buonromei, a very wealthy man whose estate after his death came to his daughter, as he had no other children. Yet Giovanni Buonromei's nephew Carlo seized part of the estate, and when the matter was brought before the magistrates, Giovanni de' Pazzi's wife was stripped of her father's inheritance, which was granted to Carlo. The Pazzi saw this as the work of the Medici. In fact, Giuliano de' Medici often complained to his brother Lorenzo that he feared that should the Medici set their eyes on too much, they might well lose everything.

25. The purpose of the Council of Eight (*Otto di Guardia*) was to uncover conspiracies against the Florentine government.

3

But Lorenzo, flushed with power and youth, wanted to control everything and be the one to bestow or withhold all favors and honors. The Pazzi, with all their nobility and wealth, were unwilling to endure the many wrongs against them, and began to consider how they could avenge themselves against the Medici. Francesco de' Pazzi was the first to broach the subject. He was more spirited and fiery than the rest, so much so that he was intent on either gaining what he did not have, or losing all he did have. He so hated the rulers of Florence that he lived almost exclusively in Rome, where, as was customary with Florentine merchants, he worked with a great amount of capital. And as he was a close friend of Count Girolamo,[26] they frequently complained to each other about the Medici, and after much complaining came to the conclusion that it would be necessary, should the count wish to live securely on his estates and Francesco in Florence, to change the Florentine government. This, they believed, could not be done without the deaths of Giuliano and Lorenzo de' Medici. They were certain that the pope and King Ferdinand would readily consent to their plan once they saw how easily it could be accomplished.

Francesco de' Pazzi and Count Girolamo spoke of their plan to Francesco Salviati, the archbishop of Pisa, who was exceedingly ambitious and had recently been offended by the Medici.[27] He readily joined in the conspiracy, and they discussed among themselves what to do next. They decided to involve Iacopo de' Pazzi, without whom they believed they could not carry out their plan. The best tactic seemed for Francesco de' Pazzi to go to Florence while Archbishop Salviati and Count Girolamo remained in Rome so they would be close to the pope when the time came to approach him. Francesco de' Pazzi found Messer Iacopo de' Pazzi more cautious and inflexible than he would have liked, and on informing the others of this in Rome, it was decided that some greater authority would be necessary to draw him into the scheme. Consequently, the archbishop and the count approached Gio-

26. Count Girolamo Riario of Imola and Forlì (1443–88) was the nephew of Pope Sixtus IV. Machiavelli also mentions him in *Discourses,* Book III, chapter 6, titled "On Conspiracies."
27. Archbishop Salviati had aspired to the archbishopric of Florence and was successfully opposed by the Medici. When he was granted the archbishopric of Pisa in 1474, the Medici and their allies barred him from taking office for three years.

van Battista da Montesecco, an illustrious *condottiere* in the service of the pope, who was under obligation to both the pope and the count. Da Montesecco pointed out the difficulties and dangers of the scheme, but the archbishop strove to make light of them by calling attention to the backing of the pope and the king, the hatred of the citizens of Florence for the Medici, and the powerful houses of Salviati and Pazzi. The archbishop also noted the ease with which the Medici could be killed, as they went about town incautiously and without a guard, and how easily the government could be changed once the Medici were dead. Da Montesecco was not entirely convinced, as he had heard a quite different tale from many Florentines.

4

While they were engaged in these deliberations, Duke Carlo Manfredi of Faenza fell so ill that it was believed he was about to die. This offered the archbishop and the count the opportunity to send Giovan Battista da Montesecco to Florence and from there to the Romagna, under the pretext of retaking the territories that Duke Carlo had seized from Count Girolamo. The count commissioned da Montesecco to speak to Lorenzo de' Medici and to ask him on his behalf for advice on how to handle the matter of the Romagna, and then, together with Francesco de' Pazzi, to attempt to induce Messer Iacopo de' Pazzi to participate in the conspiracy. In order to impress Messer Iacopo with the authority of the pope, they asked da Montesecco before his departure to speak to the pontiff, who made the greatest offers he could in favor of the enterprise.[28]

On arriving in Florence, Giovan Battista approached Lorenzo de' Medici, who received him very warmly and offered him wise and gracious advice. Da Montesecco found himself filled with admiration for Lorenzo, who seemed a quite different man from what he had been led to expect. In fact da Montesecco thought him courteous, wise, and well disposed toward Count Girolamo. Nevertheless, da Montesecco was resolved to meet with Francesco de' Pazzi, but as Francesco had left for Lucca, he decided to speak to Messer Iacopo on his own, find-

28. The pope was in favor of the Medici being ousted from power, but was categorically against their assassination.

ing him initially quite averse to the conspiracy. All the same, before they parted company, da Montesecco saw that his invocation of the pope's authority seemed to have moved Messer Iacopo to some extent. Messer Iacopo told da Montesecco to go to the Romagna, and that by the time he returned Francesco would also have returned from Lucca, at which point they could discuss the matter in greater detail.

When da Montesecco returned to Florence from the Romagna he feigned further consultation with Lorenzo de' Medici about Count Girolamo's affairs, after which he and Messer Francesco met with Messer Iacopo and did not relent until he agreed to join the conspiracy. They then discussed how it was to be carried out. Messer Iacopo did not believe they would succeed if both Medici brothers were in Florence, and suggested they wait until Lorenzo went to Rome, a journey it was rumored that he was planning. Messer Francesco liked the idea, but suggested that in the event that Lorenzo did not go to Rome, both Medici brothers could be assassinated at a wedding, at a tournament, or in a church. As for assistance from outside, he felt that the pope could gather an army under the pretext of a campaign against the town of Montone, which the pope had every reason to seize from Count Carlo, who had caused the troubles in Siena and Perugia that I have already mentioned. Nevertheless, nothing was decided except that Francesco de' Pazzi and da Montesecco would go to Rome and arrange everything with Count Girolamo and the pope.

The matter was once more discussed in Rome, and it was finally decided that when the pope's expedition against Montone was over, Giovan Francesco da Tolentino, one of the pope's soldiers, would go to the Romagna, and that Messer Lorenzo da Castello[29] would go to Castello. The two men would gather troops provided by their territories and wait for an order from Archbishop Salviati and Francesco de' Pazzi, who had come to Florence with Giovan Battista da Montesecco, to see to any details necessary for the execution of the plan. King Ferdinand, too, promised through an emissary all the help he could.

Archbishop Salviati and Francesco de' Pazzi arrived in Florence and drew into the conspiracy Iacopo di Poggio,[30] a young man of letters who was, however, very ambitious and eager for change, and two

29. Lorenzo Giustini, the pope's governor of Castello.
30. The son of Gian Francesco Poggio Bracciolini, who was a foremost scholar and calligrapher of the Renaissance (see note 1 above).

Iacopo Salviatis, one a brother of Archbishop Salviati and the other a kinsman. They also involved Bernardo Bandini and Napoleone Franzesi, spirited young men indebted to the Pazzi family. As for men from outside Florence, beside those already mentioned, they also drew in Antonio da Volterra and a priest by the name of Stefano, who taught Latin to Iacopo de' Pazzi's daughter. Rinato de' Pazzi, a grave and prudent man who was quite aware of the dangers that can arise from such undertakings, was against the conspiracy; in fact he detested it, and tried to thwart it as best he could, short of endangering his family and friends.

5

The pope had sent Raffaello Riario, a nephew of Count Girolamo, to the University of Pisa to study canon law, and while he was still studying had advanced him to the rank of cardinal. The conspirators decided that they would invite the young cardinal to Florence, where his arrival would act as cover for the conspiracy. This way, any number of conspirators from outside Florence could be brought into the city concealed among his retinue.

The cardinal arrived in Florence and was received by Iacopo de' Pazzi at his villa Montughi outside the city. The conspirators also wanted to use the cardinal's arrival as pretext for a banquet where Lorenzo and Giuliano de' Medici could be assassinated. They therefore arranged for the Medici to invite the cardinal to their villa at Fiesole, but Giuliano de' Medici, either deliberately or by chance, did not attend. When this plan proved futile, the conspirators decided that if they invited the Medici to a banquet in Florence, both brothers would be compelled to attend, and they set Sunday, the twenty-sixth of April of the year 1478, for the feast.

The conspirators, intending to kill the Medici brothers during the dinner, met in the evening on Saturday to arrange what each would do on the following day. The next morning, however, Francesco was informed that Giuliano de' Medici would not be attending the feast, and the chief conspirators met again and decided that they could not defer carrying out the conspiracy, as it would be impossible with so many individuals now involved for the plot not to be exposed. They therefore decided to kill the Medici brothers in the Cathedral of Santa Reparata,

340 · The Essential Writings of Machiavelli

where it was their custom to go, and where the young cardinal would also be present. They wanted da Montesecco to carry out the murder of Lorenzo, while Francesco de' Pazzi and Bernardo Bandini would carry out that of Giuliano. But da Montesecco refused to undertake the murder, either because his meetings with Lorenzo had caused him to warm toward him or for some other reason, but he told the conspirators that he did not have the spirit to commit such a violent act in a church, adding sacrilege to betrayal.[31] This led to the ruin of the conspiracy, because as time was pressing, the conspirators were compelled to give the task to Antonio da Volterra and Stefano the priest, both utterly unsuited by nature and inclination to such a deed. For if there was ever a deed that demanded great courage and an unwavering spirit strengthened by much experience of life and death, it was an assassination such as this, where one might see even the courage of battle-scarred men falter.

Resolved to carry out the assassination, they chose as a signal the moment when the priest would take communion during High Mass. At that instant, Archbishop Salviati, along with his followers and Iacopo di Poggio, was to take possession of the Signoria, so that after the Medici brothers' death the magistrates would stand by the conspirators, either voluntarily or through force.

6

The conspirators now proceeded to the church, where the cardinal and Lorenzo de' Medici were already present. The church was crowded, and the divine service had commenced before Giuliano de' Medici arrived. Francesco de' Pazzi and Bernardo Bandini, who had been assigned to murder him, went to his house to find him, and enticed him to the church with much artistry. It is striking that Francesco and Bernardo were able to conceal so much hatred and violent intent with so much spirit and flinty courage, for as they led Giuliano de'

31. See also *Discourses*, Book III, chapter 6: "As a result, the conspirators quickly decided that they would do in the cathedral what they had intended to do in the Medici palace. This threw their entire plan into disarray, because Giovan Battista da Montesecco did not want any part in a murder committed in a church. Every action had to be reassigned to a different conspirator, who did not have time to steady his mind. In the end, the conspirators made so many mistakes that their plot was crushed."

Medici to the church they entertained him with jests and puerile banter. Francesco was quite willing, under the pretense of friendship, to throw his arms around Giuliano and press him close to see if he was wearing a protective cuirass or the like beneath his garments. The Medici knew the bitterness of the Pazzi toward them, and knew that the Pazzi wanted to undermine their power over the government; but they did not fear for their lives, as they believed that though the Pazzi would doubtless try to counter them, they would do so by means of civil authority and not through violence. Thus the young Medici, not fearing for their safety, were happy enough to join the Pazzi in their pretense of friendship.

The assassins were ready: some at the side of Lorenzo de' Medici, where they could stand easily and without raising suspicion on account of the large crowd in the church, the other assassins next to Giuliano. At the prearranged moment, Bernardo Bandini struck Giuliano in the chest with a dagger, Giuliano collapsing after a few steps. Francesco de' Pazzi then threw himself upon the body, stabbing it again and again, so blinded by rage that he severely wounded himself in the leg. Messer Antonio da Volterra and Stefano the priest attacked Lorenzo, but after repeated blows only wounded him with a slight cut on the neck, either because of their lack of skill or because of Lorenzo's spirit, for Lorenzo used his arms and the help of those around him to defend himself, rendering all the attempts of his attackers futile. They fled in terror and hid, though they were soon found and killed in a most humiliating manner, their bodies dragged through the city. Lorenzo, on the other hand, surrounded by his friends, locked himself in the sacristy of the church. Bernardo Bandini, seeing Giuliano de' Medici dead, also killed Francesco Nori, who was very close to the Medici, either out of longtime enmity or because Nori had tried to come to Giuliano's aid. Not content with these two murders, Bernardo Bandini ran in search of Lorenzo, intending to make up with his courage and speed for the ineffective attempts of the others. But finding that Lorenzo was hidden in the sacristy, he could do nothing. In the midst of these grave and violent events, which were so terrible that it seemed as if the church would come tumbling down, young Cardinal Riario clung to the altar, where the priests vied to protect him, until the Signoria, once the uproar died down, led him to their palace. There he remained in terror for his life until he was set free.

7

During that era there were in Florence a number of exiles from Perugia who had been driven from their homes by factional feuds, and the Pazzi secured their assistance by promising to help restore Perugia to their faction. Archbishop Salviati, who had set out with Iacopo di Poggio to seize the palace of the Signoria, had also taken with him his allies, his two Salviati kinsmen, and the exiles from Perugia. At the palace he left some of his men below, with orders that the moment they heard a noise they should immediately seize the gate. In the meantime, he and most of the Perugians went to the upper floors, where they found the magistrates of the Signoria at dinner, as the hour was late. Cesare Petrucci, the Gonfalonier of Justice,[32] asked him in, and he entered with only a few of his men, leaving the others outside, most of whom ended up locking themselves in the chancery because the doors were such that once they fell shut they could not be opened from either side without a key.

Archbishop Salviati stepped up to the Gonfalonier under the pretense of bringing him a message from the pope, but began talking with such faltering and jumbled words, and such a suspicious expression on his face, that the Gonfalonier ran shouting out of the chamber and, coming upon Iacopo di Poggio in the hall, grabbed him by the hair and dragged him to his sergeants. The gentlemen of the Signoria raised the alarm, and with whatever arms were at hand immediately killed or pushed out the windows all the men who had followed the archbishop into the palace, some of whom had been locked up, others overcome by terror. Archbishop Salviati, the two Iacopo Salviatis, and Iacopo di Poggio were hanged. But the men who had been left below in the palace had overcome the guards, taken control of the gate, and occupied all the lower floors, so that armed citizens who came running at the uproar could not offer their help to the Signoria, nor could unarmed citizens offer their support.

32. The Gonfalonier of Justice was an office instituted in the thirteenth century in Florence to protect the interests of the people against the powerful nobles and magnates. The Gonfalonier of Justice was also the most prominent member of the Signoria, Florence's supreme executive council.

8

Francesco de' Pazzi and Bernardo Bandini were gripped by fear, seeing Lorenzo de' Medici safe and Francesco himself, who bore the entire weight of the conspiracy, severely wounded. Bernardo was quick to apply the same frankness of spirit to his safety as he had to harming the Medici: Seeing that all was lost, he managed to escape unharmed. Francesco, on the other hand, returned wounded to his house and tried to mount his horse, as the plan had been that he would ride through the city with his armed men, rousing the populace to arms and liberty. But as his wound was too severe and he had lost too much blood, he could not get into the saddle. So he undressed and threw himself naked upon his bed, entreating Iacopo de' Pazzi to ride out in his stead.

Messer Iacopo, though old and unaccustomed to turmoil, mounted his horse in a final attempt to right their fortunes, and with about a hundred armed men assembled beforehand for the enterprise, rode out onto the piazza before the palace of the Signoria, calling out to the populace and to Liberty to come to his aid. But neither the one nor the other responded, for the populace had been rendered deaf by the fortune and munificence of the Medici, while Liberty was unknown in Florence. Only the gentlemen of the Signoria, who were masters of the upper floor of the palace, responded, greeting him with stones and attempting to intimidate him with threats. While Messer Iacopo wavered on the piazza, he was met by his brother-in-law Giovanni Serristori, who first reproached him for the mayhem he and his conspirators had unleashed, and then urged him to go home, assuring him that Liberty and the cause of the populace were as much in the hearts of other citizens as they were in his. But Messer Iacopo was deprived of all hope: The magistrates of the Signoria were hostile to his cause, Lorenzo de' Medici was alive, Francesco de' Pazzi was wounded, and no one was prepared to follow or support him. Not knowing what else to do, he decided to try to save himself by flight, and so rode out of Florence and headed to the Romagna with his company of armed men.

9

Meanwhile the whole city had erupted in turmoil, and Lorenzo de' Medici, accompanied by a crowd of armed men, had withdrawn to his house. The populace retook the palace of the Signoria, and all the conspirators who had occupied it were either taken prisoner or killed. All Florence called out the name of Medici in praise, and the limbs of the dead were speared on lances or dragged through the streets. The whole city pursued the Pazzi with words of rage and acts of cruelty. The populace seized their houses, and Francesco was dragged naked from his bed and led to the Signoria, where he was hanged next to Archbishop Salviati and the other conspirators. As Francesco was being dragged to the piazza, no amount of violent words or acts could induce him to say a single word—he only sighed quietly, fixing those around him with unwavering eyes.

Guglielmo de' Pazzi, Lorenzo de' Medici's brother-in-law, fled to Lorenzo's house, and escaped death through his innocence and the intercession of his wife, Bianca. All the citizens, armed and unarmed, came to Lorenzo during those trying days, and every one of them offered his support, so great were the fortune and grace the Medici had secured through prudence and bounty.

During these events, Rinato de' Pazzi had withdrawn to his villa. On hearing what had happened he attempted to escape in disguise, but was recognized, arrested, and taken back to Florence. Messer Iacopo de' Pazzi was also seized while crossing the Apennines, because the local people, having heard of the assassination and seeing him in flight, seized him and returned him to Florence. He kept begging his captors to kill him by the roadside, but to no avail. Messers Iacopo and Rinato were condemned to death within four days of the conspiracy, and despite the widespread slaughter and the streets filled with men's limbs, the only death lamented was that of Rinato de' Pazzi, for he was considered a wise and good man, and not known for the pride of which the rest of his family stood accused.

So that the incident would serve as a deterrent to future conspirators, Messer Iacopo, after having been buried in the tomb of his ancestors, was dragged out and buried by the city walls as if excommunicated, and then disinterred again and dragged naked through the city by the noose with which he had been hanged. Then, since no place could be found to bury him, his body was thrown into the Arno River, whose waters were very high. This is truly a great example of Fortune, to see a man of such riches and such favored position fall into utter misery, ruin, and degradation. It was said that Messer Iacopo had some vices, among them the kind of gambling and blasphemy that might befit many a lost man, but that he made up for these vices by great charity, giving generously to sanctuaries and the needy. One can also say in his favor that on the day before which Giuliano de' Medici's murder was planned, he paid all his debts and returned with exemplary solicitude whatever property of others he still held in customs or at his house, so that no one else would have to partake of his Fortune, should things go wrong.

Giovan Battista da Montesecco, after a long interrogation under torture, was beheaded. Napoleone Franzesi escaped punishment by flight. Guglielmo de' Pazzi was banished, while any cousins of his who were still alive were imprisoned in the dungeons of the fortress of Volterra.

Once the tumults were over and the conspirators punished, the funeral rites for Giuliano de' Medici were performed, accompanied by the laments of the whole of Florence, because Giuliano had exhibited all the kindness and bounty that could be wished for in a man of rank and fortune such as his. He left a natural son, born some months after his death and named Giulio, and who was graced with all the skill and fortune that in our present times is evident to the whole world, and of which, if God grants me life, I shall speak at length when I come to our own times.[33] The men who had gathered in support of the Pazzi under Lorenzo da Castello in the Val di Tavere, and under Giovan Francesco da Tolentino in the Romagna, marched on Florence, but retreated on hearing that the conspiracy had failed.

33. The *Florentine Histories* are dedicated to Giulio de' Medici, Pope Clement VII, but Machiavelli does not mention him again, the eighth book ending in 1492 at Lorenzo de' Medici's death.

POLITICAL
ESSAYS AND
TREATISES

These shorter pieces are a selection of discourses, legations, and notes that Machiavelli wrote in response to critical contemporary issues. They range from the "Discourse
on Pisa," which he wrote from his firsthand experience of
Florence's Pisan campaign in 1499, to "A Caution to the
Medici," written in 1512 after the return to power of the
Medici that signaled the end of Machiavelli's illustrious
political career and his ruin.

Discourse on Pisa

Pisa had belonged to Florence until 1494, when Piero de' Medici, the ruler of Florence, was compelled to cede Pisa and other territories to the French during Charles VIII's Italian campaign. Within a year, Pisa had declared independence from French rule. To Florence, however, Pisa provided access to a port and was thus absolutely vital, so the Florentines began an expensive military and diplomatic effort to regain it. Other Italian states initially came to Pisa's aid against Florence, but their support gradually fell away until Venice, its last ally and Florence's great commercial rival, engaged Florence in battle at Casentino. In April 1499 the Duke of Ferrara, who was asked to mediate, negotiated Venice's ceding Pisa to Florence for 180,000 florins. The Venetians retreated from Pisa, but without handing the city over to the Florentines. Machiavelli probably wrote this piece in May 1499, shortly after the Venetian withdrawal from Pisa.

As no one doubts that Florence must regain Pisa if it wants to maintain its independence, I do not feel I need argue the matter with other reasons than those we already know. I will examine only the ways that can or will lead to our regaining Pisa, which are either by force or by love. In other words, either we will besiege Pisa, or Pisa will willingly throw herself into our arms. As the course of love would be more secure, and consequently more desirable, I shall examine whether it is feasible. I propose that if Pisa should throw herself into our arms without our having to march into battle, then she will do so either of her own accord, handing herself over to us, or she will be handed over to us by someone who has taken control of her. Pisa's current predicament is reason enough to believe that she might want to return to our patronage, as she is alone and weak, lacking all defense, shunned by Milan, turned away by Genoa, frowned upon by the pope, and mistreated by Siena, doggedly waiting in a vain hope for weakness and disunion in Florence and others. Nor have the Pisans—this is how perfidious they are—ever been prepared to accept our emissaries or our slightest sign of goodwill. But though at present they are in such a dire state, they still will not bow their heads: hence we cannot believe that they will voluntarily submit themselves to our dominion. As for Pisa being handed over to us by someone who has managed to take possession of her, we must conjecture that such a man will have entered Pisa at their beckoning, or by force. If by force, we cannot reasonably expect him to hand Pisa over to us, because if he is powerful enough to occupy Pisa he will be powerful enough to defend and keep her for himself, as Pisa is not the kind of city to be voluntarily relinquished by whoever has become her lord. As for our entering Pisa through love, called in by the Pisans themselves—and I base my views on the recent Venetian example—I cannot believe that anyone would deceive Pisa and, under the guise of coming to her defense, betray her and hand her over as a prisoner. The only way another power's intervention would cause Pisa to come under our jurisdiction would be by that power abandoning Pisa and leaving her to us as prey, the way the Venetians did. For these reasons there does not seem to be any possibility of our reacquiring Pisa without force. As force is necessary, I believe we must now weigh whether it behooves us to use it in such times as these.

ON PISTOIAN MATTERS

Since the thirteenth century, Pistoia, a wealthy city eighteen miles northwest of Florence, had been under the rule of either the city of Lucca or the city of Florence, and was governed by tyrannical lords such as Uguccione della Faggiuola and Castruccio Castracani (see The Life of Castruccio Castracani *and* Florentine Histories, *chapters 29 and 30). In 1401 Pistoia finally came under Florentine rule, and as the city began to prosper in the early Renaissance, the clashes and skirmishes between the rivaling Panciatichi and Cancellieri factions grew. As Machiavelli pointed out in* The Prince, *chapter 20, "Our forefathers, and those we thought wise, used to say that Pistoia was to be held by factions and Pisa by fortresses." But while Florence put all its resources into attacking the "fortresses" of Pisa, it loosened its grip on Pistoia, and the discord between the two Pistoian factions grew into an all-out civil war. This resulted in the Cancellieri exiling from Pistoia the Panciatichi, who then established themselves in strongholds in the villages and hills surrounding the city. This was particularly dangerous for Florence because the factions had supporters and allies both in Florence and throughout northern Italy (the Panciatici, for instance, were pro-Medici, while the Cancellieri had allies in the Florentine anti-Medici faction).*

Machiavelli wrote this piece in mid-March 1502, titling it

in Latin De rebus pistoriensibus *("On Pistoian Matters")*.
Throughout this period, he had been sent to Pistoia on a number of
occasions to help negotiate peace and ensure Florence's reestablish-
ment of its dominion.

———

It is well known that in August of 1500 the Panciatichi family was expelled from Pistoia by the Cancellieri family, and that slaughter and
ruin ensued on both sides. The situation grew worse until our Signoria[1] lost all control over Pistoia and its territories, so that the Signori,[2]
in session last March or April, considered every possible remedy for
the situation, convinced that if the matter continued as it was, Pistoia
would go the way of Pisa.[3] The Signori convened numerous times with
the Collegio and the Otto,[4] and decided to send a commissioner with
substantial forces to take control of Pistoia and reestablish order. A
commissioner was sent last April, around the sixteenth, with a good
number of cavalry, a salaried infantry, and a considerable number of
regular soldiers, with six pieces of artillery and all the support needed
to exercise force if it should be necessary. The commissioner entered
the city with these forces and established his rule. The Signori of Florence decided to send two more commissioners with additional forces,
who also set out for Pistoia that April, around the twenty-third. The
Signoria had concluded and confirmed the particulars of the agreement according to which the commissioners were to act, and in order
to institute its provisions, a number of Panciatichi and Cancellieri
were brought to Florence and disarmed. The Panciatichi who wanted
to return to Pistoia from exile were allowed to do so, and things in Pistoia settled down for a few days. But then Cesare Borgia and his army
arrived at the gates of Florence, and the Signoria, no longer able to
concentrate on Pistoia, had to withdraw all the forces it had sent there.
As a result, the Panciatichi, their numbers already significantly diminished, either fled Pistoia of their own accord or were chased out, resulting in their renewed exile from the city. This was at the beginning
of last May. The commissioners then returned to Florence, Pistoia re-

1. The chief executive council of Florence.
2. The magistrates of the chief executive council of Florence.
3. Florence had lost Pisa in 1494.
4. The Collegio were a special council that convened in emergencies, and the Otto di
Pratica a council of eight responsible for Florence's external affairs.

maining with its two chancellors but without military backing. As a result of this, worse turmoil than before ensued, which gave rise to many grave incidents. The turmoil continued until July and August of 1501.

Then word reached the Signoria of Florence that the Cancellieri and Panciatichi factions were meeting secretly to reach an accord, excluding the Signori or the chancellors. The Signoria doubted that such negotiations would be in Florence's favor.[5] They ascertained who from both factions might be prepared to come to an agreement, and, finding them well disposed, assigned two of the magistrates of the Signoria and two members of the Collegio to oversee the matter. They sent an emissary to the Panciatichi who were stationed outside Pistoia, and another into the city, to ensure that neither party took any action on its own. Finally, after a long discussion by the committee, the articles of peace were agreed to and ratified on the twenty-first of August 1501. Florence then appointed new commissioners, who departed for Pistoia on the fifth of September, and from that day until the twentieth of October they worked on obtaining guarantees from the families and securing peace in accordance with the articles. This was done, and our Signori, wanting to conclude the peace and bring the Panciatichi back into Pistoia, sent a new commissioner with armed forces, and on the twentieth of October last they reinstated the Panciatichi in the city and established a guard, a measure deemed necessary to maintain the Panciatichi there. The situation remained thus until the twenty-third of February 1502.

The reason for the tumult breaking out again has been reported in different ways. It was dealt with in the following manner: The chancellors in Pistoia informed the Florentine Signoria of the outbreak of violence and urged them to send a commissioner. The Signori immediately appointed Tommaso Tosinghi. He left on the twenty-third of February, but in Pistoia he found that the Panciatichi had again been chased out, that there had been injuries, that two of the magistrates and the captain of the infantry had been killed (all three of whom had been of the Panciatichi faction), and certain houses looted and torched. The commissioners took every measure to ensure that the violence would not increase. Then the Signoria, wanting to settle things once and for

---

5. The Florentine Signoria would have appraised such secret meetings as an attempt by the two factions to join forces to oust Florence from Pistoia, gaining independence for the city.

all, called Tommaso Tosinghi back in order to consult with him. They concluded first that Florence had to take complete control of Pistoia, and after that they would see how to proceed. Consequently our Signori, without tarrying, ordered that by the seventeenth of this month an infantry of seven hundred men will have been gathered and sent to Pistoia along with ninety mounted crossbowmen. Pagolo da Parrano, who is currently in Pescia with forty mounted crossbowmen, has been sent moneys and directed to take orders from the commissioners of Pistoia. Our Signori have ordered all these forces to be ready by the seventeenth of this month, so that once the soldiers receive their pay they will take control of Pistoia, set up guards at strategic points, punish the delinquents, and force the leaders of the two factions to come to Florence. They would also destroy and dismantle all the fortifications, and take from both factions the artillery and as many weapons as they could. The commissioners, as they have the authority, have already accomplished this to a large extent. They have begun punishing the delinquents and have initiated proceedings against them. They have ordered the men from both factions to present themselves in Florence by the twenty-fifth of this month, and a good number of them have already complied. They have taken from the factions all their artillery and other weapons, and have dismantled fortifications.

It now remains for the Florentine Signoria to decide how we should proceed, particularly in the question of reforming the city of Pistoia. All this, as the commissioners have pointed out, is up to us, as none of the Panciatichi or the Cancellieri—more than 150 men, along with other rebels and troublemakers—are in Pistoia now. Hence it will not be difficult to implement any measures that the Signoria will decide upon.

On the Nature
of the French

Machiavelli's first diplomatic contact with the French was early in 1500 on the Pisan front when Florence, after its failed campaign against Pisa, sought the help of King Louis XII, who had come to Italy to conquer Milan and Naples. Later that year Machiavelli had his second diplomatic encounter with the French at the court of Louis XII in Lyons. This piece, titled originally in Latin De natura Gallorum, *is believed to be from that period. It reflects Florentine anti-French sentiment, for though Louis XII was prepared to support Florence's quest to regain its former territories, his help cost Florence a large sum of money and the exorbitant expense of provisioning and quartering the French army, which Louis used primarily for his own campaigns.*

———

The French are so intent on immediate advantage or injury that they have little memory of past wrongs or benefits, and little care for future good or evil.

For the French, first agreements are always best.

While they might not be able to do you a good turn, this does not hinder them from promising to do so. Yet if they are in a position to do you a good turn, they will do so only with great reluctance, or never.

The French are most humble in bad fortune, and most insolent in good.

They are miserly rather than cautious.

They weave their bad cloth with vigor and expertise.

They care little for what is said or written about them.

They are more eager for money than blood.

The French court is generous only at audiences.

A victorious Frenchman is constantly summoned into the presence of the king, he who loses a battle, rarely. Therefore, anyone who is about to embark on a campaign must first weigh whether he is likely to succeed or not, and whether or not this is likely to please the king. Cesare Borgia knew this well, which enabled him to march to Florence with his army.[6]

If a courtier and gentleman disobey the king in a matter concerning a third party, if he is in favor with the king he is not punished, but must show obedience in the future. If he is not in favor, he must stay away from the royal court for four months. This has twice cost us Pisa: once when Entragues held the citadel, and the second time when the French troops came to Pisa.[7]

He who wishes to conduct business at court must have money, great diligence, and good fortune.

If the French are asked to do a favor, they will first weigh the benefit it will bring them.

Unlike Italian gentlemen, they are usually not very particular about their honor. They were not overly concerned about losing face when they sent to Siena to demand the town of Montepulciano and were not obeyed.[8]

They are capricious and nonchalant.

6. Cesare Borgia, as head of the papal army, with assistance from Louis XII of France, marched through Florentine territory in 1501. (Machiavelli was one of the Florentine ambassadors attached to his camp.)

7. In 1496, Robert de Balzac, Comte d'Entragues, returned the occupied citadel of Pisa to the populace against the wishes of Charles VIII, and in 1500 the French army refused to help the Florentines recapture Pisa, despite a promise by Louis XII, Charles's successor, to do so.

8. Louis XII sent Francesco da Narni to Siena to ask Pandolfo Petrucci, Lord of Siena, that the town of Montepulciano be returned to Florence, which Petrucci refused to do, despite being an ally of Louis XII.

They have the arrogance of the victor.

They are enemies of the Latin language and of the glory of Rome.

Italians have a bad time at the French court, except for those whose ship is heading for the rocks and who have nothing more to lose.

ON HOW TO TREAT THE
POPULACE OF VALDICHIANA
AFTER THEIR REBELLION

In June 1502, as the Florentines were preparing a new expedition against Pisa and concentrating all their forces on that front, the city of Arezzo and the Valdichiana region to the south, in secret negotiations with Cesare Borgia, rebelled against Florentine authority. Borgia had already conquered the territories surrounding Florence, while Piero de' Medici, in the hope of returning to power in Florence, had made Arezzo his headquarters. Florence had a respite, as Borgia was busy confronting a major conspiracy among his generals, described in "How Duke Valentino [Cesare Borgia] Killed the Generals Who Conspired Against Him," which is also set in 1502. However, Borgia quickly and efficiently quelled the conspiracy and was again ready to turn his sights on Florence. This fragment of a discourse, written by Machiavelli in the summer of 1503, offers an important early example of how he looked to ancient Rome as a paradigm for solving contemporary problems.

[Appearing before the Senate, Lucius Furius Camillus spoke of]⁹ what should be done with the territories and cities of Latium. These are the

9. This is a conjectured beginning of the sentence, as the original manuscript began with the words *Quello che si dovesse fare* (what should be done). Lucius Furius Camillus (d. 365 BCE) was a heroic Roman general of the first Samnite War and a consul of Rome in 339 BCE. See also *Discourses*, Book I, chapter 8.

360 · *The Essential Writings of Machiavelli*

words he used, and the decision that the Senate reached, more or less verbatim, as Livy reports them:[10]

"Senators! What needed to be done in Latium with armies and wars has, by grace of the gods and the skill of our soldiers, been done. Slaughtered are the enemy armies at Pedum and Astura. All the lands and cities of Latium, and the city of Antium in the land of the Volsci, either were conquered or surrendered, and are now in your power. As they keep rebelling and putting Rome in peril, we must consult about how to secure ourselves, either by cruelty or by generously forgiving them. God has granted you the ability to deliberate whether Latium is to be maintained, and how to make it secure for us indefinitely. So consider whether you want to punish harshly those who have given themselves to you and want to ruin Latium entirely, turning into a desert a country that has often supplied you with auxiliary armies in dangerous times; or whether you intend to follow the example of our forefathers and enlarge the Roman Republic, forcing those conquered to live in Rome. This would give you the glorious opportunity of expanding Rome. All I have to say to you is this: The most enduring power is the state which has loyal subjects who love their prince.[11] But what must be deliberated must be deliberated swiftly, as you have many peoples hovering between hope and fear. You must free these peoples from their uncertainty and anticipate their every action, either with punishment or reward. My task was to ensure that this decision would be yours, and my task has been done. It is now for you to decide what is for the benefit of our republic."

The senators praised Furius Camillus's speech, and as the case in each rebellious city and territory was different, they agreed that it would be impossible to pass a general resolution, but that each instance would have to be considered separately. Furius Camillus specified the case of each of the territories, and the senators decided that the Lanuvians were to become Roman citizens, and that the sacred objects taken from them during the war were to be returned. They also made the Aricians, the Nomentians, and the people of Pedum Roman

10. Machiavelli is translating and paraphrasing Camillus's speech and the Senate's reaction to it from Livy's *History of Rome,* Book VIII, chapters 13 and 14.
11. Livy in fact says (Book VIII, chapter 1): "The most stable and long-standing empire is definitely that in which subjects take pleasure in obeying." Machiavelli adapts Livy's words, anticipating one of the ideas he develops in *The Prince.*

citizens, while the people of Tusculum were allowed to keep their privileges, their rebellion being blamed on a few individuals.[12] The people of Velitrae, however, were severely punished for having been Roman citizens who had revolted numerous times. Velitrae was destroyed, and all its citizens sent to live in Rome. To secure Antium the Romans sent new settlers, confiscated all the Antian ships, and prohibited the building of new ones.

It is clear from the judgment the Romans passed on these rebellious territories that they strove either to win their loyalty through benefits, or to treat the territories so harshly that they would never need fear them again. The Romans regarded any middle way as harmful. In their resolutions, they chose one extreme or the other: benefiting those with whom they saw hope for reconciliation, and, where there was no hope, making certain Rome could not be harmed again. The Romans carried this out in two ways: One was to destroy the city and bring the inhabitants to live in Rome; the second was either to strip the city of its inhabitants and send in new ones, or, leaving the former inhabitants in place, to send in so many new ones that the original inhabitants could never again conspire against the authority of Rome. The Romans used these two methods in the case of Latium, destroying Velitrae and providing Antium with new inhabitants.

I have heard it said that in our actions we should look to history as our teacher, which is particularly true for princes. The world has always been inhabited in the same way by men who have had the same passions: There have always been those who rule and those who serve, those who serve willingly and those who serve unwillingly, those who rebel and those who are punished. Should anyone doubt this, he has only to look at the incidents in Arezzo and the territories of Valdichiana last year,[13] where we saw a repetition of the example of the peoples of Latium. They had rebelled against Rome and Rome had reacquired their territories, as was recently the case with Florence reacquiring Arezzo and Valdichiana. Even though the particulars of the rebellion and reacquisition of these territories was quite different, the fact of the rebellion and the reacquisition are the same.

If it is true that in our actions we should look to history as our

---

12. Lanuvium, Aricia, Nomentum, Pedum, Tusculum, and Velitrae were cities of Latium within twenty-five miles of Rome.

13. There had been a rebellion against the Florentine occupation in 1502.

teacher, it would be good if those who will have to judge and punish the territories of Valdichiana would follow the example of those who once ruled the world, particularly in a case where the ancients teach us in no uncertain terms the best course of action. Just as the Romans judged each territory differently, as the offense of each people was different, so must we now strive to evaluate the difference in offense in each of our rebellious territories.

If you were to assert that this is precisely what we have done, I would reply that we have done so only to some extent, but that we have fallen short in important ways. It is good that we allowed Cortona, Castiglione, Borgo Sansepolcro, and Foiano to keep their assemblies, and that we indulged them, managing to reconquer them with benefits, because I equate them with the Lanuvians, Aricians, Nomentians, and the people of Tusculum and Pedum whom the Romans treated in a similar manner. But it is not good that the people of Arezzo, who acted in the same way as those of Velitrae and Antium, have not been treated the same way they were. If the judgment of the Romans merits commendation, our judgment merits criticism. The Romans believed that rebellious populaces had to be either benefited or destroyed, and that any other course of action was dangerous. From what I see with Arezzo, we have not adopted either of these two courses. One cannot claim that the Arezzans have benefited by having to come to Florence every day, their offices abolished, their possessions seized, their being disparaged publicly and having soldiers quartered in their homes. And yet one cannot claim, either, that we are securing ourselves against them by leaving their city walls intact and allowing five-sixths of their citizens to go on living there, not sending in new settlers who would keep them in check. In any future war that we might have to fight, we will have to face a greater expenditure in Arezzo than we will in fighting the enemy. Experience taught us this in 1498, before Arezzo rebelled or we began our cruel reprisals. For when the Venetian troops assaulted Bibbiena,[14] we had to send the forces of Duke Ludovico Sforza of Milan to Arezzo along with Count Rinuccio Marciano and his company in order to keep the city stable, instead of

14. A city eighteen miles from Arezzo, and thirty-five miles from Florence. The Venetians had attacked the Casentino Valley and occupied Bibbiena in 1498 in an attempt to aid Pisa in its fight to remain independent of Florence. See "Discourse on Pisa."

using those troops in Casentino against the enemy. Nor would we have had to pull Paolo Vitelli and his men from the Pisan front to send them to fight the Venetians in Casentino. Arezzo's disloyalty resulted in our having to face considerably more peril and expenditure than if it had remained loyal. Hence, putting together what one sees now and what one saw then, and the conditions we have imposed on the Arezzans, one can categorically conclude that if—God forbid!—we were to be invaded, Arezzo would either rebel or cause us so many problems as we tried to secure it that it would become an expenditure Florence would not be able to bear.

I do not want to neglect discussing the prospect of Florence's being invaded, and the inevitable designs any invader will have on Arezzo, as at the moment this is a central topic of discussion. Let us not concentrate on the danger we can expect from ultramontane princes,[15] but let us turn our sights on a peril closer at hand. Anyone who has observed Cesare Borgia's course of action will note that in his strategy for maintaining the states he has occupied, he never looks to Italian alliances, having little esteem for Venice and even less for Florence. One can only conjecture that he intends to create such a powerful state in Italy that he will be unassailable, making allegiance to him desirable for any ruler. Should this be his design, then he is clearly aspiring to possess all of Tuscany in order to form a greater kingdom with the states surrounding Tuscany that he already holds.[16] There is no doubt that these are his designs, because of what I have just mentioned, but also because of his boundless ambition, and the way he has drawn out negotiations with us without ever concluding any agreements. It now remains for us to see if the time is right for him to put his designs into practice. I remember hearing Cardinal Soderini[17] say that among the many reasons one could call Cesare Borgia and the pope[18] great is that they are experts at seeing an opportunity and seizing it. This view is proved by our experience of what they have carried out when they had the opportunity. If one were to debate whether now is an opportune

15. Primarily the King of France and the Holy Roman Emperor.
16. Romagna and Urbino.
17. Francesco Soderini, Bishop of Volterra, and brother of Piero Soderini, the Gonfalonier of Florence.
18. Pope Alexander VI, Cesare Borgia's father.

moment for them to assault Florence, I would say no. But one must consider that Cesare Borgia cannot wait for the kind of moment in which he can be assured of victory, as time is not on his side: His father the pope cannot be expected to live long,[19] and Cesare will have to grasp the first opportunity that presents itself and place his cause to a great extent in Fortune's hands.

19. Pope Alexander did in fact die a few months after Machiavelli wrote this discourse.

HOW DUKE VALENTINO KILLED THE GENERALS WHO CONSPIRED AGAINST HIM[20]

By the early 1500s, Cesare Borgia had become one of the most pow-
erful men in Italy. Since his father had been elected to the pontifi-
cate in 1492 as Pope Alexander VI, Cesare Borgia had been made
archbishop (at sixteen), cardinal (at seventeen), and finally Cap-
tain General of the Papal Armies. Although young Borgia was a
lackadaisical archbishop and cardinal, he filled the army post with
spectacular dexterity, fast expanding the papal territories. By late
1502, however, a number of his generals came together in a plot
against him. Borgia was caught entirely unawares, suddenly find-
ing himself stripped of most of his troops and having to fight defen-
sively within his own territories. But as Machiavelli shows in the
following piece, Borgia handled the matter with careful and ruthless
strategy.

Duke Valentino[21] had just returned from Lombardy, where he had
gone to justify himself before King Louis XII of France against the
many accusations the Florentines had leveled against him concerning

20. The first Italian publication of this piece in Rome in 1533 was titled *Il modo che tenne il duca Valentino per ammazar Vitellozo, Oliverotto da Fermo, il signor Pagolo et il duca di Gravina Orsini in Senigaglia* (The manner in which Duke Valentino killed Vitellozzo, Oliverotto da Fermo, Signor Pagolo, and Duke Orsini of Gravina in Senigaglia).
21. Cesare Borgia.

the revolt of Arezzo and other towns in the Valdichiana.[22] He had arrived in Imola, where he intended to stop with his troops while he prepared a campaign against the tyrant of Bologna, Giovanni Bentivoglio,[23] as Duke Valentino wanted to bring Bologna under his rule and make it the capital of his Duchy of Romagna. When the Vitelli and the Orsini and their followers heard of his plan, they began to worry that he was becoming too powerful. They feared that once he occupied Bologna, he would destroy them so that he would be the only leader with a powerful army in Italy.[24] They called a meeting in Perugia—the Diet of Magione.[25] Present were Cardinal Giambattista Orsini, Signor Paolo Orsini, Duke Francesco Orsini of Gravina, Vitellozzo Vitelli, Liverotto da Fermo, Giampaolo Baglioni, the tyrant of Perugia, and Antonio da Venafro, who had been sent by Pandolfo Petrucci, the ruler of Siena.[26] They discussed Duke Valentino's power and spirit, and how vital it was for them to check his hunger for supremacy before he ruined them all. They decided to stand by the Bolognese tyrant, Giovanni Bentivoglio, against Duke Valentino, and to seek to win over the Florentines. They sent emissaries to both Bologna and Florence, promising to help Bentivoglio and entreating the Florentines to join them in the fight against Duke Valentino, their common enemy.

News of this meeting immediately spread throughout Italy, and peoples unhappy under Duke Valentino's rule—among them the citizens of Urbino—gained hope that change was imminent. As a result,

22. Cesare Borgia had played a key role in inciting Arezzo and Valdichiana to rebel against Florentine rule. (Borgia was expanding his territories and had his sights set on Tuscany.) Both Florence and Borgia were, however, dependent on the King of France, who, displeased at Borgia's involvement in Florentine interests, had summoned him to France to explain himself. See "On How to Treat the Populace of Valdichiana After Their Rebellion" above.

23. Giovanni Bentivogli (1443–1508) had been Gonfalonier of Bologna until Pope Paolo II made him chief senator for life in 1466. Pope Julius II, however, excommunicated and ousted him from Bologna in 1506.

24. The Vitelli family were the lords of Città di Castello, a town east of Arezzo, and the Orsini were a powerful Roman family.

25. The place of the meeting, the castle of La Magione, belonged to the Cardinal Giambattista Orsini.

26. Cardinal Giambattista Orsini had been one of the cardinals who had voted for the election of Pope Alexander VI, Duke Valentino's father. Paolo Orsini, Francesco Orsini (the Duke of Gravina), and Liverotto da Fermo had been mercenary generals in the service of Duke Valentino. Giampaolo Baglioni had been Lord of Perugia until he was ousted by Cesare Borgia in 1502. Antonio da Venafro was a professor at the University of Siena.

spirits grew so heated that some men of Urbino decided to seize the Castle of San Leo, which was held by the duke. The castellan was having timber brought up to strengthen the castle's fortifications, and the conspirators lay in wait until the timber was being dragged across the drawbridge, preventing those inside from drawing it up. Seizing the opportunity, the armed men jumped onto the bridge and stormed the castle. Word of the capture spread, and the whole state of Urbino rebelled. The former duke was restored,[27] as the people had now taken hope, not so much from the occupation of the castle as from the Diet of Magione, which they were certain would come to their aid, and when the Diet of Magione heard of the rebellion in Urbino, its members were determined not to miss the opportunity. They set out to occupy all the towns belonging to Urbino that were still held by Duke Valentino. The Diet once more sent emissaries to Florence to entreat the republic to join them in crushing the common foe, arguing that the cause was already as good as won and that there would not be another such opportunity. But the Florentines, because of their hatred for the Vitelli and the Orsini, not only declined an allegiance but sent their minister Niccolò Machiavelli to offer duke Valentino shelter and aid against his new enemies. The Duke, in Imola, was in the grip of fear, for in a single stroke and against all expectations his former generals had become his enemies, and he found himself with a war on his doorstep. But he took courage from the Florentines' offer, and decided to forestall the war through peace negotiations, and in the meantime to marshal some help. He sent to the King of France for additional men, and hired all the cavalrymen he could find and anyone who had anything to do with horses.

Despite Duke Valentino's efforts his enemies advanced, reaching Fossombrone, where they encountered some of his soldiers, whom the Vitelli and the Orsini routed. As a result of this, the duke put all his resources into trying to stop this trouble through peace negotiations. As he was a great dissembler, he did not neglect to give every indication that the conspirators had taken up weapons against a man who had agreed to let them keep whatever territories they had acquired, and announced that he would be happy enough to keep the title of prince while they ruled the principality. Duke Valentino was so successful in

27. Duke Guidobaldo da Montefeltro had been ousted by Cesare Borgia in 1502.

his persuasion that the conspirators laid down their arms and sent Signor Paolo Orsini to him to negotiate a truce. In the meantime, Duke Valentino had continued building up his army, diligently strengthening his cavalry and infantry, and he distributed his men throughout the Romagna so that these preparations would not be noticed.

In the meantime, five hundred French lancers had also arrived, and though Duke Valentino was now strong enough to attack his enemies in open war, he nevertheless calculated that it would be safer and more useful to deceive them, so he continued his peace negotiations, orchestrating them so diligently that a truce was successfully concluded. He gave the conspirators back the old mercenary positions they had held in his army, made them a present of four thousand ducats, promised not to harm the Bentivoglio family, and even arranged an alliance through marriage with Giovanni Bentivoglio.[28] He also promised to order them into his presence only as often as they would allow. For their part, they promised to give him back the Duchy of Urbino and all the other territories they had occupied, to serve in all his campaigns, and not to make war on anyone or hire themselves out to anyone without his permission.

When this accord was completed, Duke Guidobaldo of Urbino once more fled to Venice, first destroying all the fortresses in his state: for he was certain that the populace was on his side, and he did not want his undefended fortresses to be occupied by the enemy, which would impair any action his supporters might attempt on his behalf. But Duke Valentino, having devised the accord and dispersed his own men and the French men-at-arms throughout the Romagna, set out for Imola at the end of November, stopping first at Cesena. There he stayed many days to negotiate with the envoys of the Vitelli and the Orsini, who had gathered with their men in the Duchy of Urbino, as to what campaign ought to be mounted next. Nothing was concluded, and so Liverotto da Fermo was sent to suggest that they would support a campaign against Tuscany if the duke wanted to mount one; if not, they could besiege Senigallia. To this the duke replied that as the Florentines were his allies, he did not want to wage war against Tuscany, but that he would support a march on Senigallia.

---

28. Cesare Borgia and Giovanni Bentivoglio agreed to the future marriage of Costanzo, Giovanni's nephew, with Angela Borgia-Lanzol, Borgia's niece. The wedding, however, never took place.

The result was that within a few days news came that Senigallia had surrendered, but that the castle would not yield because the castellan refused to give it up to anyone but Duke Valentino. They therefore urged him to come in person. The duke saw this as an excellent opportunity: He would be going to Senigallia not on his own initiative but because he was being implored to go, and thus no suspicions would be aroused. To reassure everyone even further, he dismissed all his French soldiers and sent them back to Lombardy, with the exception of a hundred lancers of the Comte de Candale, his brother-in-law.[29] He left Cesena in mid-December and went to Fano, where with all his shrewdness and sagacity he managed to persuade the Vitelli and the Orsini to wait for him in Senigallia. He made it plain that any show of distrust on their part would jeopardize the strength and duration of their new accord, and that he was a man who wanted to make use of the arms and the counsel of his friends. Vitellozzo Vitelli remained quite reluctant, because the death of his brother had taught him that one cannot first attack a prince and then trust him, but he nevertheless allowed himself to be persuaded by Paolo Orsini, whom the duke had bribed with gifts and promises, and so agreed to wait for the duke in Senigallia.

On the evening before his departure from Fano—the thirtieth of December 1502—Duke Valentino had revealed his secret plan to eight of his most trusted men, among them Don Michele and Monsignor d'Elna, who was later to become cardinal:[30] The moment Vitelozzo Vitelli, Paolo Orsini, Duke Francesco Orsini of Gravina, and Liverotto da Fermo approached, he wanted one man on either side of them, so that there would be two men consigned to each of them all the way to Senigallia, not allowing any of them to escape until they arrived at his quarters, where they would be seized. He then ordered all his soldiers, mounted and on foot—more than two thousand horsemen and ten thousand infantry—to gather at daybreak on the banks of the Metauro, a river about five miles from Fano, where they were to await his arrival. Then, finding himself there by the Metauro River with his men on the

29. The Comte de Candale had married Anne d'Albret, the sister of Cesare Borgia's wife, Charlotte d'Albret.
30. Don Michele, also known as Don Michelotto, was a mercenary and Cesare Borgia's feared henchman. Monsignor d'Elna, Francisco Galceran de Llori i de Borja, was a cousin of Cesare Borgia.

last day of December, he sent out in advance of his arrival a cavalcade of some two hundred horsemen, then all his infantry, after which he and his men-at-arms followed.

Fano and Senigallia are cities of La Marca on the shores of the Adriatic, situated about fifteen miles from one another. Whoever approaches Senigallia has on his right the mountains, with foothills that come so close to the sea that there is often only a narrow strip of land between them and the waves. Even in those places where the foothills are further inland, the strip is never more than two miles wide. Senigallia lies a bow's shot from these foothills, and less than a mile away from the shore. There is a little river by the city that washes the walls facing toward Fano. The road to Senigallia runs a good distance alongside the mountains, and when it reaches the river it turns left and goes along the riverbank for about a bow's shot until it reaches a bridge that crosses the river and almost meets the Senigallia city gate at an angle. Before one reaches the city gate there is a little village with a square, one side of which is formed by the river.

The Vitelli and the Orsini decided to wait for Duke Valentino and honor him personally, and had sent their men to a castle six miles away from Senigallia so that there would be room for the duke's men. Inside Senigallia they had kept only Liverotto da Fermo with his thousand foot soldiers and a hundred and fifty horsemen, who were quartered in the village outside the gates that I have just mentioned.

Duke Valentino approached Senigallia. When the vanguard of his cavalry arrived at the bridge, it did not cross, but stopped and formed two lines, one along the river, the other along the open country, leaving a path in the middle for the foot soldiers, who then marched straight into the town. Vitellozzo, Pagolo, and Duke Orsini of Gravina rode toward Duke Valentino on mules, accompanied by a handful of horsemen. Vitellozzo, unarmed and wearing a cape lined in green, seemed quite afflicted, as if he were aware of his impending death, which, in view of the prowess of the man and his former fortune, caused some amazement. And it is said that when he parted from his soldiers to go to Senigallia to meet the duke, it was as if he were saying a final farewell. He told his generals that he left his house and its fortunes in their hands, and cautioned his nephews that they should not remember the fortunes of their house, but the prowess of their fathers and uncles. When the three men arrived before the duke and greeted him with courtesy, they were received by him in a friendly manner and immediately escorted by the men who had been charged to keep an eye on them. The duke, however, saw that Liverotto was missing. He had remained back with his men in Senigallia and was waiting on the square in front of his quarters by the river, keeping them in order and exercising them. The duke winked at Don Michele, whom he had entrusted with the care of Liverotto, signaling that he see to it that Liverotto did not escape, at which Don Michele rode off to Liverotto and told him that this was not the time to have his men gathered outside their quarters, as they were to be occupied by the duke's men. He encouraged him to have them return to their quarters and come with him to meet the duke. Liverotto followed Duke Valentino's order and rode out to meet him, and the duke, seeing him, called out to him. Liverotto made his obeisance and joined the others.

They all rode into Senigallia and to the duke's quarters, where he led them into a secret chamber and had them taken prisoner. He then immediately mounted his horse and ordered that the soldiers of Liverotto and the Orsini be stripped of their arms and belongings. Liverotto's men were immediately plundered, as they were right there in Senigallia, but the men of the Orsini and the Vitelli, being at some distance and having a premonition of their masters' fate, had enough time to gather together, and, remembering the prowess and discipline of the House of Vitelli, stood their ground against the local people and the enemy soldiers, and saved themselves. But the soldiers of Duke Valentino, not content with merely plundering Liverotto da Fermo's men, began sacking Senigallia. And had the duke not put a stop to their audacity by putting many of them to death, they would have looted the town entirely.

When night came and the turmoil stopped, the duke felt that the time had come to kill Vitellozzo and Liverotto. He had them taken to a place together and strangled. Neither of them uttered any words worthy of their previous life: Vitellozzo begged that he might throw himself on the pope's mercy and plead for a full indulgence for his sins, while Liverotto, weeping, heaped all the blame for the harm done to Duke Valentino on Vitellozzo. The duke left Paolo Orsini and

Duke Orsini of Gravina alive until he heard from Rome that the pope[31] had seized Cardinal Orsino, Archbishop of Florence, and Messer Iacopo da Santa Croce. At this news, on the eighteenth of January, 1502, they too were strangled in the same fashion at the Castle of Pieve.

31. Pope Alexander VI, Duke Valentino's father.

Discourse on the
Affairs of Germany and
Its Emperor

In 1509, Gianvittorio Soderini and Piero Guicciardini sought Machiavelli's advice on the German emperor Maximilian, the Holy Roman Emperor, and his court before setting out from Florence on a diplomatic mission. To oppose Venice, Maximilian had entered into the League of Cambrai with France, Spain, and the pope in 1508. Now Venice had been defeated, and the powers were in negotiations about how to proceed.

———

When I returned from Germany last year [1508], I wrote a few things about the emperor of Germany and am not quite sure what else to add: so I shall say only some things about his character. The emperor is a spendthrift without equal, either in our times or in times past. Consequently he is always short of funds, and no sum of money can ever be sufficient, regardless of his situation or fortune. He is changeable: One day he will want something, the next day not. He confers with no one, but believes everyone. He wants all the things he cannot have, but turns his back on anything he can have. Therefore, he invariably reaches contradictory decisions. But he is also a man of military acumen: He keeps his army in excellent order, commands it with justice and discipline, bears fatigue as well as the most indefatigable man, and faces danger with courage, so that as commander he is second to none. He is forthcoming in the audiences that he grants, but will grant them only at his own initiative—nor does he like applications from ambassadors, unless he himself calls them into his presence. He is very secretive. He is in continuous agitation of body and mind, but will often undo in the evening what he has done in the morning. This makes legations to him difficult, because the most important duty of the envoy, whether sent by a prince or a republic, is to conjecture the future through negotiations and incidents. After all, the envoy who conjectures wisely and conveys his conjectures well to his government will assure his government the advantage, allowing it to take measures at an appropriate time. When the envoy conjectures well, this honors the envoy and his government, but if he conjectures badly he and his government are dishonored. To give you a better example, imagine yourself at a point where either going to war or negotiating is on the table. If you want to perform your duty well, you will have to say that existing opinion favors war as much as it does negotiation. War must be measured by the available forces, money, quality of government, and Fortune. And the side that has most of these is likely to be victorious. After evaluating who might be victorious, the ambassador must make his evaluation understood at home, so that he and his state can better deliberate.

There will now be several negotiations: those between the Venetians and the emperor, those between the emperor and France, those between the emperor and the pope, and those between the emperor and you. When it comes to your negotiations, you ought to have no difficulty making the right conjecture and weighing what the emperor's intentions are, what he really wants, which way his mind is turning, and what might make him move ahead or draw back. Once you have figured this out, you must judge whether it will be more to your advantage to be decisive or to play for time. It will be up to you to reach these decisions within the limits of your mission.

A Caution to the Medici

In 1512 the Medici returned to power in Florence, ousting and exiling Piero Soderini, who had been Machiavelli's patron, and whom Machiavelli had served in the highest political capacities. With the return of the Medici, Machiavelli was stripped of all his authority and influence and was forbidden to set foot in the Signoria. "A Caution to the Medici," first published in Italian in 1866 under the title Ai Palleschi *(To the Medici Faction), was a desperate attempt by Machiavelli to regain some of his standing. However, he was to face brief imprisonment and even torture for alleged conspiracy against the Medici, before being temporarily banished from the city.*

———

I wish to caution you against the counsel of those who argue that you would benefit by exposing Piero Soderini's shortcomings in order to blacken his name among the populace, and you would do well to look those individuals carefully in the eye and see what is motivating them. What you will see is that their motivation is not to benefit the new Medici government, but to strengthen their own faction. It does not seem to me that anything for which Piero Soderini might have been at fault would strengthen the position of the new Medici government in the eyes of the people, because the Medici government could easily be suspected and inculpated of the same things as Soderini. Hence, exposing Soderini's defects will not empower this government, but only those who were his enemies, who persistently countered him in Florentine politics.[32]

The current opinion of the people is that the faction in question wished Soderini ill so it could seize the government for itself. If, however, Soderini could be defamed to the Florentine people, they would say: "The enemies of Soderini were telling the truth! They are, after all, upright citizens who are blackening Soderini because he merits it! If things have turned as they have it is not because they planned it that way."

Consequently the new Medici government, by exposing Soderini, would destroy his reputation but not in any way strengthen its own position, only that of the individuals who were his enemies and who were badmouthing him. These enemies would then have more influence with the populace. This is in no way to the advantage of the Medici government, because it must find a way for this faction to be despised, not prized, by the people, so that the faction will be compelled to maintain its allegiance to the Medici, thus sharing the Medici's good or bad fortune.

If you look into who these people are, you will see that what I am saying is true. As they see it, their having been enemies of Soderini, their faction will have drawn the hatred of the populace upon themselves unless they can now prove that he was evil and deserved their enmity. The reason they want to free themselves of the populace's hatred is so that they can promote their own interests, not those of the Medici. The cause of the tensions between the populace and the Medici is not Soderini or his fall, but simply the change in government. So I repeat: Airing Soderini's defects does not raise the standing of the Medici government but that of Soderini's enemies, while the Medici government would only weaken itself by attacking a man who is in exile and cannot harm it, all the while strengthening individuals who are here in Florence and who have every opportunity to harm the Medici and incite Florence to rise up against their government.

In order to underline my conclusion, I shall say once more: It is not Piero Soderini who is the enemy of this government, but the old order. Therefore, it would benefit this government to assail the old order, not

32. Machiavelli is referring to the faction of aristocrats.

Soderini. Some individuals who pander both to the populace and the Medici are very hostile to Soderini and would welcome the opportunity to denigrate him so that they can cast off the burden they bear with the people for having been its enemy. But they are doing this for themselves, not for the Medici, nor for those who wish to stand by the Medici in good and bad fortune.

I also wish to clarify this matter in another way. There are some citizens who flock to the Medici because they are anxious for two things: not to be harmed by the Medici by distancing themselves from them, and that if the old order were to return with Piero Soderini in power, not to be exiled from Florence by him. Presenting Soderini as an evil man, so as to make him hated by the people, lessens their fear of him. These citizens hope to succeed to his position should the old order return. In this sense they have less need to support the Medici, and more to hope for by distancing themselves from them. How this is contrary to the benefit of the Medici is plain to see, because the Medici cannot remain in Florence should the old order return, with or without Soderini. Those individuals who want the old order restored would be exiled if Soderini returns, but if the old order is reestablished without Soderini, they will remain in Florence and thrive. This is why they wish to destroy Soderini's standing, so that they can strengthen their own faction, not that of the Medici. This is definitely not to the Medici's advantage. In fact, it is in every possible way most harmful and dangerous for both the House of Medici and its government, as it removes the muzzles from many mouths that will surely and most readily bite them.

LITERATURE

Today Machiavelli is considered a giant of political philosophy, his most widely read works being *The Prince* and *The Discourses,* neither of which had been published in his lifetime. In his day, however, Machiavelli was particularly appreciated as a writer of elegant prose and well-crafted tales, a successful playwright, and an original and accomplished poet. A great contemporary of Machiavelli, Mateo Bandello (who wrote the tale of Romeo and Juliet), remembers Giovanni de' Medici asking Machiavelli to entertain the company with one of his delightful "novelle." (Unfortunately, "Belfagor" is the only one that has come down to us). This section offers a glimpse of Machiavelli's literary range.

Rules for an
Elegant Social Circle

"Rules for an Elegant Social Circle" stands out among Machia-
velli's preserved works for its biting satire of Florentine mores of
the early sixteenth century. It is uncertain when Machiavelli wrote
this piece, but as Michelangelo's statue of David is mentioned in the
text, it would have been after 1504, which was the year the statue
was erected in the Piazza della Signoria.

———

A circle of ladies and gentlemen would gather for soirees where they
often did amusing things, but often dull things as well. They had not
found a way to make the amusing more amusing or the dull less te-
dious, for though they sometimes thought up little pranks, they never
made the effort to carry them out. Finally a quick-witted member of
the circle who had some experience in the ways of the world took it
upon himself to organize—or I should say codify—some rules for
these soirees, so that everyone could contrive this or that diversion for
the amusement of a lady, a gentleman, or perhaps even both, but then
also execute it. It was therefore decided that the circle would submit to
the following rules, which were agreed upon by common consent:

No gentleman under the age of thirty is to be admitted to the circle, though ladies of any age may attend.

The circle will have a leader—either a lady or a gentleman—who
will hold office for eight days. Gentlemen serve as leaders in descend-

ing order, from the gentleman with the longest nose to the one with the shortest, while ladies will serve in ascending order, from the lady with the smallest foot to the one with the largest.

Any gentleman or lady who does not within a day broadcast everything said or done at one of the soirees will be punished in the following manner: A lady transgressor will have her slippers nailed in a prominent place for all to see, with a note bearing her name; a gentleman transgressor will find his hose hung prominently inside out for all to observe.

Members of the circle must make a point of speaking badly of one another and revealing one another's sins to any and every stranger, trumpeting said transgressions without restraint.

No gentleman or lady of the circle may go to confession except during Holy Week. Should a lady transgress, she will be obliged to convey the leader of the circle to the confessional, and should a gentleman transgress, the leader of the circle will convey him there whenever he sees fit. (A blind confessor ought to be chosen, and if he is hard of hearing, too, even better.)

On no account must any member say a good word about another, otherwise he or she must submit to the above punishment.

If any of the gentlemen or ladies deem themselves uncommonly good-looking, and two witnesses can be found, the lady will be obliged to reveal her leg up to four finger widths above the knee, while the gentleman will have to reveal whether he is sporting a handkerchief or the like in his codpiece.

The ladies will be obliged to go to the church of the Friars of the Servi[1] at least four times a month, or at any other time members of the circle tell them to go. Should they fail to do so, they will have to go twice as often.

If a lady or gentleman launches into an anecdote and the other members of the circle do not interrupt them, these other members will be condemned to a punishment devised by the lady or gentleman who was not interrupted.

All decisions in the circle will be reached by a minority of votes. The smallest number of votes will always win.

---

1. In *Mandrake*, act III, scene 2, Lucrezia stopped going to the Friars of the Servi because she was molested by one of the friars.

If a member of the circle has been told a secret by a brother or close friend and has not revealed the secret to the ladies and gentlemen of the circle within two days, the transgressor will have to do everything backward without hope of ever being absolved from this punishment, directly or indirectly.

The members of the circle cannot and must not ever allow a moment of silence. The more a gentleman or lady chatters, the higher the commendation. The individual who is first to pause will be shunned by the rest of the company, so that he or she can ponder this transgression.

No member of the circle can or may render any kind of favor to anyone—but if compelled to do so, this favor must be executed in such a way that it will ultimately turn against the suppliant.

Each lady or gentleman shall be obliged to exhibit envy at any benefit enjoyed by another, and must act spitefully. Should any member of the circle not seize the opportunity to act with malice in such a situation, the transgressor will be punished at the pleasure of the circle's leader.

Should a lady or gentleman at any time or in any place encounter someone laughing or spitting or the like, they must imitate this action under pain of being compelled to do whatever is asked of them for a whole month.

So that all are content, every gentleman and every lady must undertake to sleep unencumbered by a husband or wife for fifteen days out of every month, under pain of having to sleep with said husband or wife every single night without respite for two months.

The lady or gentleman of the circle who can say the most while meaning the least will be held in highest esteem and honored above all others of the company.

Every lady and gentleman must attend every single feast, church fête, and pardoning in the city, as well as every afternoon gathering, soiree, spectacle, dinner, or other entertainment arranged in people's houses. A lady who fails to attend any of these must submit to being locked up with monks, and a gentleman in a nunnery.

The ladies of the circle will be compelled to spend three-quarters of their time standing by a window or a door—behind or in front, as they please—while the gentlemen of the company must parade before them at least twelve times a day.

No lady of the company may have a mother-in-law. Should one of

384 · The Essential Writings of Machiavelli

the ladies still be inconvenienced by one, said lady will have to dispose of her within six months by a purgative or some such means, which may also be used against a husband who does not fulfill his obligations.

The ladies of the circle may not wear crinolines or other such impeding undergarments, and the gentlemen must not lace and bind their underdrawers, which they must instead pin together, a practice strictly prohibited the ladies under pain of their having to inspect the David on the piazza through glasses.[2]

In order to appear in a better light, the ladies of the circle as well as the gentlemen will be forced to boast of things they do not own and do not do. Should any individual speak the truth about straitened circumstances and the like, they will be punished at the pleasure of the leader.

No one must show an inner state through any outward sign. In fact, quite the opposite: The lady or gentleman who can conceal true feeling best will deserve the highest commendation.

The greatest part of a lady or gentleman's time must be spent in dressing and preening. Any member of the circle who contravenes this rule will do so under pain of not being glanced at a single time.

A lady or gentleman who dreamily recounts what he or she did or said the day before will have to kneel with his or her bottom up for half an hour while everyone administers corrective measures.

Anyone attending Mass who does not keep looking around, or seat himself in a prominent position to be admired by all, will be punished for the sin of lèse-majesté.

No lady or gentleman, particularly those wishing to have children, must put a shoe on the right foot first under pain of having to walk barefoot for a month, or longer if the leader of the circle decrees it.

No one lying down to sleep will be allowed to close both eyes at the same time. The lady or gentleman must close one eye first and then the other—which is in fact the best method for conserving one's eyesight.

The ladies will have to walk in a way that will not show how much of their foot is revealed by their shoe.

No one may blow his nose while observed, except in an emergency.

The ladies and gentlemen of the circle will be obligated to scratch

2. Michelangelo's statue of David had recently been placed on the Piazza della Signoria in Florence.

when it itches, under pain of a fine to the Florentine Office of Finances.

Fingernails and toenails are to be cleaned every four days.

In order to appear taller, the ladies of the circle will be compelled to put something beneath them whenever they sit.

A doctor no older than the age of twenty-four must be chosen for the social circle, so that he will be able to administer first aid to all the members without succumbing to exhaustion.

THE PERSECUTION OF AFRICA

ON KING HUNERIC OF THE VANDALS, IN THE YEAR OF OUR LORD 500, COMPOSED BY SAINT VICTOR, BISHOP OF UTICA

In "The Persecution of Africa," Machiavelli paraphrases and recasts the opening chapters of Saint Victor of Utica's poignant three-volume Latin Historia persecutionis Africanae provinciae *(The History of the Persecution of the African Province), creating a compelling piece of literature. It describes the persecution of the Roman Catholics of the North African Roman provinces by the invading Vandal kings, Gaiseric and Huneric, fanatical Arian Christians who followed the teachings of the fourth-century Alexandrian presbyter Arius. The Church in Rome rejected the Arian Christians as heretics, but as Saint Victor demonstrates in his book, and Machiavelli reflects in this piece, the Christians of Africa saw the Vandals as brutal pagans: "Those churches the Vandals did not destroy [...] were transformed into temples of their religion."*

It is unclear when Machiavelli worked on this piece.

————

It has been sixty years since the cruel Vandal race entered the lands of Africa, crossing the straits that separate Africa from Spain. Short and tall, young and old, more than eight hundred thousand of them came, as they themselves asserted, so that our people, frightened by their number, would relinquish any thought of defending themselves. Finding Africa peaceful and calm, filled with riches and great abundance, the Vandals indulged in every violence, as much against men as against the earth. Wherever they trod they torched, ravaged, robbed, and slaughtered, taking men prisoner and forcing them to die in dungeons under every kind of torture. Nor did the Vandals withhold their cruelty from trees and plants. What was worse, they left neither church nor saint's tomb unscathed, torching and devastating them all. People tried to hide themselves and their possessions in valleys, forests, and caves, but to no avail, for wherever they hid they were found, robbed, and slaughtered. The Vandals attacked the churches of God and the houses of men with the greatest hatred and most fervent persecution, and wherever they found buildings locked, they hacked and hewed at them with axes as the oaks of the forest are felled, so that one could quote the verse from the Scriptures: "They behaved like men wielding axes to cut through a thicket of trees. They smashed all the carved paneling with their axes and hatchets. They burned your sanctuary to the ground."[1]

How many illustrious bishops and noble priests were tortured to death, unwilling to reveal where they kept their gold and silver! And if they relinquished what they had, this only convinced the Vandals that there was more they could give. The greater the riches the persecuted surrendered, the greater the torture. Some had foul-smelling mud poured down their throats, others were forced to drink seawater, still others were given vinegar, dung, the pungent dregs of wine, and other foul-smelling liquids. The merciless Vandals bloated their victims like wineskins, nor did they have pity on girls or women. They respected neither nobility nor learning and showed no reverence to the priesthood; in fact their spirits became more feral, and the Vandals unleashed their fury most, wherever they found nobility and rank. How many eminent men of the Church, how many illustrious gentlemen, were forced to carry burdens like camels and donkeys, driven on by the Vandals with goads and prods to quicken their pace, many dying under the strain. Neither youth nor age moved the Vandals to pity, and countless infants were torn from their mothers' breasts, sent into captivity, grabbed by their feet and dashed on the ground before their mothers' eyes, or were even held by their legs and sliced in half. This

1. Machiavelli quotes Psalm 74, lines 5–7, from the Vulgate in slightly altered Latin: *Quasi in silva lignorum securibus consciderunt* [Vulgate: *exciderunt*] *ianuas eius* [Machiavelli adds: *in id ipsum*], *in securi et ascia deiecerunt eam, incenderunt igni sanctuarium tuum.*

verse could have been cited at every instant: "You will kill their young
men with the sword, dash their little children to the ground, and rip
open their pregnant women."[2]

Buildings too immense to succumb to fire the Vandals ravaged and
defaced, so that today no trace remains of the ancient beauty of many
of our cities. Scores of towns are now inhabited by few, or are empty.
The theaters and churches of Carthage, Celestial Avenue, and many
fine buildings were destroyed, and those churches the Vandals did not
destroy, like the Basilica that holds the bodies of Saint Perpetua and
Saint Felicitas, were transformed into temples of their religion.[3]
Wherever they came upon a castle or fortress they could not besiege,
they slaughtered countless men from the surrounding areas and laid
them outside the walls, so that those inside were forced to surrender or
die of the stench.

Countless saintly priests were tortured and killed, among them the
venerable Papinianus, bishop of our city, who was scorched with burning blades of steel. Mansuetus was burned at the gates of Fornitana.
The city of Hippo was besieged, whose bishop was Saint Augustine,[4] a
man deserving the highest praise because the stream of his eloquence
flowed through all the fields of the church: but in those adverse times
that stream dried up and the sweetness of his speech turned into bitter
absinth. David's words proved true: *Cum consisteret peccator adversum me,
obmutui et humiliatus.*[5] Saint Augustine had written two hundred thirty-
two books, innumerable epistles, and a thorough exposition of the entire Book of Psalms and the Gospels, which are usually called
homilies, the number of which is vaster than the mind can grasp.

What more can I say? After much cruelty, Gaiseric[6] besieged and

---

2. Machiavelli quotes II Kings 8:12 in strongly altered Latin: *Dixit inimicis incendere se fines
meos, interficere infantes meos et parvulos meos elisurum ad terram.*

3. Saint Perpetua, a young Carthaginian noblewoman, and her slave Felicitas were martyred
in 203 CE during the Roman persecution of Christians and were among the foremost martyred saints of the North African Roman provinces. The Vandals were ardent Arian Christians (followers of the doctrines of the Alexandrian presbyter Arius), who differed in doctrinal
matters from the Roman Catholic Church, particularly regarding the divinity of Christ.

4. Saint Augustine (354–430 CE), one of the Latin Fathers of the Church and a leading Christian theologian, died during Gaiseric's siege of Hippo Regius (in today's Algeria).

5. Psalm 39:1 (Vulgate 38:2): "I will keep my mouth with a bridle while the wicked is before
me. I was mute with silence."

6. King Gaiseric of the Vandals (d. 477 CE) crossed the Straits of Gibraltar in 428 CE and conquered a large part of Roman North Africa.

conquered the great and beautiful city of Carthage, reducing to servitude its ancient liberty, so forthright and noble, and all its senators to slaves. Gaiseric decreed that the people had to bring him all their gold, precious stones, and rich vestments; in a short time he deprived them of all that their fathers and grandfathers had left them. Gaiseric divided the provinces among his generals, keeping the most important ones for himself. The emperor Valentinian managed to defend and hold on to some of the provinces, but Gaiseric seized them after Valentinian's death.[7] At that point Africa was his, as were the islands that lie between Africa and Italy—Sicily, Sardinia, Majorca, and Minorca—which he occupied and defended with his customary arrogance. Nevertheless, he later ceded Sicily to Odoacer, the king of Italy, in exchange for a tribute.[8]

As Gaiseric had power over Africa, he commanded that the Vandal chiefs expel all the bishops and noblemen from their territories. This order was carried out, and many distinguished men of the cloth and noblemen became Vandal slaves. Quotvultdeus, the bishop of Carthage, and a great number of men of the church were robbed of everything, put on ships, and sent away from Africa. By the mercy of God they made their way to Naples in Italy, while Gaiseric converted to his own religion the Restituta Cathedral, where their bishops had always officiated, plundering all the other churches inside and outside Carthage, particularly two beautiful cathedrals of Saint Cyprian the Martyr,[9] one where his blood was shed, the other where he was buried, in Mappalia. Who can remember without tears how that cruel tyrant ordered the bodies of our saints to be buried without solemn psalms? And while these things were being done, the men of the church who had not yet left for exile from the African provinces that he had divided among his generals decided to meet with King Gaiseric, to beg him to

---

7. Roman Emperor Valentinian III (419–55 CE). Saint Victor of Utica writes in *The History of the Persecution of the African Province*: "They then divided the conquered provinces among themselves, Gaiseric keeping Byzacena, Abaritana, as well as Gaetulia and part of Numidia, while he gave his army Zeugitana, or Proconsularis. Emperor Valentinian still held the other provinces that Gaiseric had tried to assail, but after Valentinian's death all of Africa was his."
8. King Odoacer (c. 433–93 CE) was the first barbarian king of Italy, the beginning of whose reign in 476 CE is considered the end of the Western Roman Empire.
9. Saint Cyprian (200–58 CE). As Bishop of Carthage he was a major spiritual leader during Rome's persecution of North African Christians. After his execution he became the first bishop-martyr of Africa.

show compassion. They gathered and went before the king, who was in the land of the Massyli,[10] and beseeched him to allow their Christian people to stay in Africa and eke out a living there. To this the king replied: "I am resolved not to leave a single man of your name and tribe in this land, and you have the impudence to beg for mercy?" He would have thrown them all immediately into the sea, but his barons pleaded that he refrain from such an evil act.

Despondent and miserable, the men of God retreated, and began secretly administering the divine rites whenever and wherever they had the opportunity.

10. A dominant Numidian tribe to which King Massinissa of Numidia had belonged.

BELFAGOR

Machiavelli's contemporaries prized him for his stories, but "Belfagor" is the only one that has come down to us. It is uncertain when it was written, but it is believed to have been composed between 1518 and 1520, after Machiavelli had completed The Prince *and* The Discourses. *The theme of "Belfagor" existed in medieval literature.*

———

One can read in the ancient chronicles of Florence and also hear tales told of a most saintly man whose life was extolled by all who lived in his times. Transported in prayer, he saw descend to Hell infinite souls of wretched mortals who had died in the displeasure of God, all these souls, or most of them, protesting that it was only because they had taken wives that they had been brought to such grief. Minos, Radamanthus, and the other judges of Hell were perplexed, unable to believe the accusations leveled at the fair sex, but the allegations grew with every passing day, until they saw themselves compelled to inform Pluto.

Pluto called together a council of infernal princes to examine and debate the matter so that pertinent action could be taken to reveal the falseness or truth of these claims, and stepping before the council he proclaimed: "Beloved friends! By celestial decree and the irrevocable course of destiny I am the ruler of this kingdom and thus cannot be bound by any judgment, earthly or celestial. Nevertheless, the wisest rulers are those who, though they have the greatest power, are keenest to submit themselves to the laws and are most inclined to respect the judgment of others. Therefore I have concluded that I would do well to be counseled by you on a matter that could bring shame to our reign. When all the souls of men who enter our kingdom proclaim that they have been driven here by their wives—a thing that seems impossible to me—I fear that if I should pass a judgment that is too severe, I might be accused of being too cruel, and if I should pass a judgment that is not severe enough, I might be accused of being too lenient, and not a lover of justice. The first sin is that of a frivolous ruler, the second of a ruler who is unjust. As I wish to avoid either charge but cannot find the means of doing so, I have called you together so that with your counsel you can offer assistance and be the reason that our kingdom will once again prevail without infamy!"

Each of the infernal princes saw that the case was very important and of the greatest consequence. They unanimously agreed that it was vital to discover the truth, but were divided on how this should be achieved. Some argued that one among their ranks ought to be sent up into the world, others that several should be sent, so that, adopting human form, they could discover the truth in person. Still others argued that this could be accomplished without so much inconvenience were they to compel various souls to reveal the truth through an array of torments. But as the greater part of the council advised that a single devil ought to be sent up into the world, this decision was finally adopted. None of the devils, however, was prepared to take on this expedition voluntarily, and so it was decided that one would be chosen by lot—a lot that happened to fall on Belfagor, an archdevil who had been an archangel before he fell from Heaven. Belfagor took on the duty with extreme reluctance, but compelled by Pluto's authority, declared himself willing to carry out the council's decree, and committed himself to the conditions that had been solemnly decided upon. The conditions were that the devil who was entrusted with this task would be provided with a hundred thousand ducats, with which he was to go into the world. There, in the guise of a man, he was to take a wife with whom he was to live for ten years, after which, feigning death, he would return to the netherworld, where he would report to his superiors concerning the burdens and afflictions of marriage. The council also declared that during his period in the world he would be subjected to every hardship and strife that beset mankind—poverty, prison, illness, and every other misfortune that men incur—unless he could free himself from these by means of deceit or trickery.

Belfagor entered the world with money and a human form. Provided by the tribe of devils with horses and attendants, he arrived in Florence with much pomp, having chosen that city above all others, as it struck him as the ideal place for a man wishing to employ his money in the arts of usury. He adopted the name Roderigo di Castiglia and took a house in the Borgo Ognissanti.[1] So that no one would discover his origins, he let it be known that he had left Spain for Syria as a boy and had made his fortune in Aleppo: He had now come to Italy with the intention of marrying and settling down, as Italy, being more humane and civilized, was more to his taste. Roderigo was quite a handsome man and looked to be about thirty years old, and having within a few days made a show of his great wealth and proven himself kind and generous, he was approached by many noble citizens who had an abundance of daughters but a scarcity of funds. Roderigo's choice fell upon a beautiful maiden by the name of Onesta, the daughter of Amerigo Donati, who had three other daughters who were almost of a marriageable age, and three grown sons. Amerigo Donati was of a noble family and was very highly regarded in Florence, but he was extremely poor in relation to his large brood of children and social position.

Roderigo had a magnificent wedding, not omitting any splendor that might be desired. The infernal council had decreed that he was now to be subjected to every human passion, and so he began taking delight in the honors and pomp of the world, and to value society's approbation. This cost him a significant amount of money. He had not lived long with Madonna Onesta before he fell in love with her beyond measure, and could not bear her being sad or displeased in any way. Along with her nobility and beauty, Madonna Onesta had brought into Roderigo's house a pride that outshone that of Lucifer. And Roderigo, who had had ample experience of both, had to admit that his wife's pride was far superior. But Madonna Onesta's pride grew by great

1. "The Quarter of All Saints," a street near the Arno River in Florence.

bounds the instant she perceived the love her husband bore her. She now felt that she could rule him in every way and began ordering him about without mercy or restraint, nor did she delay hurling harsh and hurtful words at him if he hesitated in fulfilling her every fancy. This caused Roderigo great distress. Nevertheless, his father-in-law, her brothers, her family, and the bonds of matrimony, and, above all, his great love for her, made him bear his plight with patience.

I shall pass over the vast expenditure he made in his attempts to appease her by dressing her in the latest fashions and styles that our city knows to vary with infinite resourcefulness. I will also pass over how Roderigo, in his quest for domestic peace, assisted his father-in-law in marrying off his other daughters, here too spending great amounts of money. To appease Madonna Onesta he was forced to send one of her brothers eastward with linen, another westward with silks, and set up her third brother as a gold beater in Florence, enterprises that depleted the greater part of his fortune. Then came the Carnival of San Giovanni, when by ancient custom the whole city revels and celebrates, and all the noblest and richest citizens make a great show with splendid banquets. Here Madonna Onesta would not be eclipsed by any other Florentine lady, and insisted that Roderigo's feasts outshine those of all the others.

Roderigo bore these trials for the reasons I have mentioned, and no expenditure, however vast, would have seemed excessive had it brought a measure of harmony to his house, giving him some peace of mind as he awaited his approaching ruin. But the opposite was the case, because the outlandish expenses and Madonna Onesta's insolent nature caused him infinite distress. No servant in the house could bear her ways for more than a few days. As a result Roderigo's dealings suffered, as he could not keep a single loyal servant who could see to his affairs. Even the devils he had brought with him as manservants preferred to return to Hell and roast in fire than live in the world under that woman's rule.

Roderigo, his life increasingly tumultuous and troubled, had soon consumed all his resources through immoderate spending, and now began to live in the hope that financial returns might be forthcoming from East and West. Roderigo still had good credit, and drew upon it so that he would not lose his standing in Florence. Soon there were so many of his promissory notes in circulation that the local creditors took note. His position was already precarious in the extreme when dire news arrived from East and West: One of Madonna Onesta's brothers had gambled away all of Roderigo's investment, while the other, sailing back to Florence entirely uninsured on a ship loaded with Roderigo's merchandise, had gone down with the ship and everything in it. No sooner did this become known than Roderigo's creditors met to confer. They were aware that he was ruined, but could not proceed against him as the time for repayment had not yet come. The creditors therefore concluded that they would watch him closely so that he would not attempt to escape behind their backs.

Roderigo could not see a way out of his predicament, and aware of the limits the infernal council had set upon him, was resolved to escape by fair means or foul. One morning he mounted a horse, and as he lived near the Porta al Prato, he rode out of Florence through it. No sooner did his departure become known, than a hue and cry arose among his creditors. They turned to the magistrates and set out after him with officers of the law and a crowd of townsmen. Roderigo was not more than a mile out of Florence when he heard the hubbub behind him. Realizing that the odds were against him, he decided that he would do better to leave the road and try his luck by escaping over the fields. He was, however, impeded from riding across the open country by many ditches, and so decided to continue his escape on foot. He left his mount by the roadside and made his way over fields covered in vines and cane brakes until he reached Peretola and the hut of Gianmatteo del Brica.

Gianmatteo was one of Giovanni del Bene's tenants, and Roderigo came upon him as he returned home to feed his cattle. He begged Gianmatteo to help him, promising great riches if he saved him from his enemies who were out to lock him up in a dungeon till the day he died. He would furnish him proof of the wealth that would be his, and should this not convince him, he could hand him over to his enemies. Gianmatteo, though a peasant, was a spirited man and quickly saw that he had nothing to lose by saving Roderigo. He pushed him into a pile of manure that lay in front of his hut, covering him with straw and chaff that he had raked together to burn. Roderigo had barely managed to hide when his pursuers arrived, and despite their threats they could not force Gianmatteo to admit that he had seen Roderigo. So they went on their way, looking for him in vain that day and the next, until they returned exhausted to Florence.

When all was quiet, Gianmatteo pulled Roderigo out from the manure heap and asked him to fulfill his promise.

"My brother," Roderigo said, "I am under great obligation to you and will in every way keep my pledge to you. And so that you will realize how capable I am of keeping my pledge, I shall tell you who I am." And Roderigo told him who he was, the conditions put upon him when he left Hell, and of the wife he had taken. He also told Gianmatteo how he intended to make him rich. News would come that a woman was possessed by a demon, and Gianmatteo should know that it was Roderigo who was possessing her, and that he would not leave her body until Gianmatteo came to perform an exorcism. He could then ask whatever sum he wished from her relatives.

Gianmatteo agreed, and Roderigo disappeared.

Only a few days later, word spread throughout Florence that the daughter of Messer Ambruogio Amidei who had married Bonaiuto Tebalducci was possessed by a demon. Her family was doing everything one did in such cases, placing the skull of Saint Zanobi on her head and covering her with the mantle of Saint Giovanni Gualberto, at all of which Roderigo thumbed his nose. To make it plain that the girl was possessed by a demon and not simply in the grip of some girlish fancy, he had her speak in Latin and debate on philosophical matters, and had her reveal the sins of many people, including a monk who for more than four years had kept a woman in his cell dressed as a novice. Everyone in Florence marveled at this. But her father, Messer Ambruogio, was not at all pleased. He had tried every remedy and had lost all hope of a cure when Gianmatteo stepped before him and promised that he would restore his daughter for a sum of five hundred florins, with which he intended to purchase a farm in Peretola. Messer Ambruogio agreed. Gianmatteo first had Masses sung and then went through some rituals to add color to the proceedings, after which he leaned down to the young woman's ear and said: "Roderigo, I have come so that you can keep your promise to me." To which Roderigo replied: "This has worked out well. But it will not be enough to make you rich. So I shall leave this young woman and enter the daughter of

King Carlo of Naples. I will refuse to leave her until you are summoned. King Carlo will reward you well, and you and I will be done." Having spoken these words, he left the young woman's body, to the delight and admiration of all Florence.

Soon word of the misfortune that had struck King Carlo's daughter spread throughout Italy. The king could find no cure, and, hearing of Gianmatteo, sent to Florence for him. Gianmatteo arrived in Naples and after a sham ceremony cured the princess. But Roderigo, before leaving, said: "As you see, Gianmatteo, I have kept my promise to make you rich. Now that I have fulfilled my obligation, I am no longer in your debt. You must never call upon me again, because if until now I have benefited you, in future I shall bring you harm."

Gianmatteo returned to Florence a wealthy man. The king had given him more than fifty thousand ducats, and he intended to enjoy his riches in peace, as he did not think that Roderigo would have cause to do him harm. But this thought was quickly dashed when news came that the daughter of Louis VII of France was possessed. Gianmatteo was distressed when he thought of the king's power on the one hand, and Roderigo's on the other. The king found no cure for his daughter, and having heard of Gianmatteo's skill, sent a messenger to find him. Gianmatteo resisted, alleging various difficulties, and the king turned to the Signoria of Florence,[2] which forced Gianmatteo to obey.

Gianmatteo arrived in Paris a miserable man. He informed the king that it was true enough that he had cured possessed women in the past, but that this did not mean that he could exorcise all demons, because some were so perfidious that they feared neither threat nor holy incantation. He promised to do his best, but if he did not succeed, he craved forgiveness and pardon. The king, vexed at these words, proclaimed that if Gianmatteo did not cure his daughter he would have him hanged. The poor man was distraught. Nevertheless he had the princess come to him, and, leaning down to her ear, humbly begged Roderigo to remember how he had helped him in his hour of need and how it would be great ingratitude on his part if he abandoned him now in such a dire circumstance. To this Roderigo replied: "Fie, cowardly traitor! You have the temerity to come before me again? Do you think

2. The chief executive council.

you can boast of having made yourself rich at my hands? I will prove to you and to everyone else that just as I can give, I can also take away. Before you leave this place, I shall see you hang."

Gianmatteo, in his distress, decided to try a different tactic. He had the possessed princess taken away and said to the king: "Sire, as I have informed you, there are many spirits that are so perfidious that one cannot hope for any good outcome. This spirit, unfortunately, is one of them. But I wish to try one final procedure. If it succeeds, Your Majesty and I will have achieved our aim. If it does not, I will be in Your Majesty's hands, and will hope for the mercy that my innocence merits. I request that Your Majesty set up a platform on the Place Notre Dame that will be large and strong enough to hold all the barons and clergy of Paris. The platform must be bedecked with drapes of silk and gold, and must have an altar in the middle. On Sunday morning, Your Majesty, the clergy, and all your princes and barons must congregate in rich vestments and royal splendor on this platform. First a solemn Mass must be sung and the possessed princess brought out onto the platform. I also require at least twenty men with trumpets, horns, tambours, bagpipes, drums, and cymbals, along with any other instrument that can make a din. When I raise my hat, the men must begin striking their instruments and blowing their horns as they march toward the platform. I believe that all this and certain other secret remedies will force the demon to depart."

The king had everything arranged. On Sunday morning, the noble personages crowded onto the platform and the populace of Paris crowded onto the square. A Mass was sung, and the possessed princess was led onto the platform by two bishops and a retinue of lords. Roderigo was amazed when he saw the multitude and the elaborate contrivances.

"I wonder what this cowardly sluggard is up to?" he said to himself. "Does he think he can frighten me with all this pomp? Does he not know that I have beheld all the splendors of Heaven and the furies of Hell? I will punish him."

When Gianmatteo approached the princess and asked Roderigo to leave, Roderigo said: "This is a fine idea you've had! What do you expect to achieve with these foolish contrivances? Do you think that you can either escape my power or the wrath of the king? I will see you hanged, you cowardly rogue!"

Gianmatteo begged, and the archdevil spewed abuse, until Gianmatteo realized that he had no more time to lose. He raised his hat, and the men who had been commissioned to make a great din began striking and blowing into their instruments, marching toward the platform with a clamor that rose to the heavens. Roderigo, greatly astonished, pricked up his ears, unable to fathom what all the noise might be. Perplexed, he asked Gianmatteo what was happening, to which Gianmatteo replied with great agitation: "Alas, Roderigo, it is your wife! She has come to get you!"

A miraculous change came upon Roderigo when he heard the word "wife." The change was so momentous that he gave no thought to whether it was even possible or a reasonable assumption that his wife could have come, and without another word, he fled in terror, releasing the young princess. He preferred to return to Hell and account for his deeds than ever again to face the trouble, spite, and dangers of the matrimonial yoke.

Thus Belfagor returned to Hell and bore witness to the ills that wives brought on a house, while Gianmatteo, who had outwitted the devil, traveled back home a cheerful man.

THE LIFE OF CASTRUCCIO CASTRACANI OF LUCCA

COMPOSED BY NICCOLÒ MACHIAVELLI AND SENT TO HIS DEAREST FRIENDS, ZANOBI BUONDELMONTI AND LUIGI ALAMANNI

In The Life of Castruccio Castracani of Lucca *Machiavelli blends biography, historical chronicle, and literary fiction to create a portrait of the ideal warrior prince. Since its first publication in 1533, it has traditionally been printed together with* The Prince *to provide an extension of Machiavelli's vision of the ideal ruler.*

Machiavelli relied on chronicles and accounts of Castracani's life for historical facts, but invented characters and situations and reshuffled and conflated historical events in order to enliven his narrative. Machiavelli wrote this piece at an important moment in his life: After eight years of exclusion from Florentine politics, he was sent to the city of Lucca as an official emissary in the bankruptcy case of Michele Guinigi, whose family name Machiavelli was to use in the story as that of Castracani's fictitious guardian.

Though Castruccio Castracani had been a dire enemy of Florence, causing untold damage to the city, Machiavelli did not allow this to affect his admiration for the self-made prince, who for a few years had turned the small town of Lucca into a foremost Italian power.

———

Those who have given the matter some thought, dearest Zanobi and Luigi, will marvel that most, if not all, men who have accomplished great deeds and excelled above all others of their era were of low birth and obscure origins, or were tormented beyond compare. They were exposed to wild beasts, or had such lowly fathers that in shame they declared themselves to be sons of Jove or some other god. It would be an onerous task and objectionable to the reader to list all these men, as they are well known, so I shall pass over them. I believe that the lowly origins of great men is Fortune's way of demonstrating that it is she and not Wisdom who makes men great. So that Fortune be acknowledged as supreme, she shows her powers very early in a man's life, well before Wisdom could hope to play a role.

Castruccio Castracani of Lucca was one of the men who, despite the times in which he lived and the city in which he was born, did great things. Like others who rose to great heights, he did not have a fortunate or distinguished birth, as will become clear in my description of the course of his life. I considered it useful to bring his life to wider attention, as I feel it demonstrates many instances of skill and Fortune that will provide a powerful example to others. I have decided to present this work to you, my friends, since you, more than anyone else I know, delight in valiant deeds.

The Castracani were among the noble families of Lucca, though since the wheel of Fortune turns, the Castracani of that era had fallen on hard times. A boy named Antonio had been born into the family and raised to become a man of the church, and soon became Lucca's canon of the order of San Michele. As a sign of honor, the people of Lucca addressed him as Messer Antonio. He had only one sister, who had been married to a Buonaccorso Cennami, but after she was widowed, not intending to remarry, she returned to live with him.

Behind Messer Antonio's house was a vineyard that was surrounded by gardens, and thus could be easily entered from many sides. One morning soon after sunrise, Madonna Dianora (that was the name of Messer Antonio's sister) was walking through the vineyard collecting herbs for the pantry, as women do. Suddenly there was a rustling beneath the branches of a vine. Madonna Dianora looked in that direction and heard what sounded like weeping. She walked toward the vine and saw the hands and face of a baby boy wrapped in leaves, who seemed to be calling out to her for help. Amazed and bewildered, but also filled with compassion and wonder, Madonna Dianora picked up the baby and carried him inside, where she washed him, wrapped him in white swaddling cloth, as was the custom, and presented him to Messer Antonio as soon as he came home. When he heard what had happened and saw the child, he was no less filled with amazement and compassion than she had been, and the two discussed what they should do. They decided to raise the child—Messer Antonio being a priest and she childless—so they hired a nurse, and brought up the child with as much love as if it were their own. They baptized the boy Castruccio, after their father.[1]

With every year Castruccio grew in charm and character, proving himself in all things an intelligent and clever boy. He studied under Messer Antonio, who hoped that he would become a priest, and who intended, when the time came, to leave him his canonry and his other worldly possessions. Messer Antonio tutored him with this in mind, but soon realized that Castruccio was unsuited for the priestly calling. By the time the boy was fourteen he began to stand up to Messer Antonio and no longer feared Madonna Dianora, and he set aside his ecclesiastical books to follow his interest in weapons. In fact, nothing pleased Castruccio more than handling weapons, running, jumping, and wrestling with other boys his age. Here he showed physical skill and courage far beyond that of his peers, and if he did pick up a book, then only one that told of wars and the feats of great men. Messer Antonio was deeply grieved.

There lived in Lucca a fine gentleman of the Guinigi family by the name of Messer Francesco, who was graced with skill and valor far surpassing that of any other gentleman of Lucca.[2] He was a condottiere who had fought for many years under the Visconti of Milan, and was one of the foremost partisans of the Ghibelline faction in Lucca.[3] Whenever he was in town, he would meet mornings and evenings with the other citizens beneath the balcony of the *podestà*, the chief magis-

1. This is a fictitious account. Castruccio Castracani was born in 1281 to Gerio Castracani of the wealthy and influential Antelminelli family that was exiled from Lucca in 1301 when Castruccio was twenty.
2. The Guinigi of Lucca were a prominent mercantile family. Machiavelli, however, invented Messer Francesco.
3. The Ghibellines, for the most part feudal aristocrats and their partisans, were supporters of the Holy Roman Emperor, and their opponents, the Guelphs, wealthy merchants, supported the papacy. Throughout the Middle Ages, the two factions vied for power in Italian cities. The Castracani were Ghibellines.

trate's palace, which is at the head of the Piazza di San Michele, Lucca's main square. There he often noticed Castruccio playing war games with the other boys, and saw that he surpassed them in skill and that he even had some sort of regal command over them for which the other boys seemed to love and respect him.

Messer Francesco desired to find out more about the boy, and when he was told the story of his background he resolved to take him under his wing. One day he called Castruccio into his presence and asked him where he would prefer to be, in the house of a gentleman who would teach him to ride and use weapons, or in the house of a priest where he would be taught nothing but services and Masses. It did not escape Messer Francesco that Castruccio brightened at the mention of horses and arms. The boy stood before him in modest silence, but when Messer Francesco encouraged him to speak, Castruccio replied that if Messer Antonio did not mind, nothing would make him happier than abandoning his priestly studies and taking up those of the soldier. Messer Francesco was pleased, and within a few days managed to persuade Messer Antonio, though it was in fact Castruccio's nature that had swayed the priest, since he knew he would not be able to keep him in check much longer.

Once young Castruccio moved from the house of Messer Antonio Castracani the priest to that of Messer Francesco Guinigi the condottiere, one can only marvel at the swiftness with which the boy mastered the skills and customs of a gentleman. He became an excellent horseman, able to handle the wildest horse with great dexterity. Though still a youth, he stood out above all others in jousts and tournaments, so that in every feat, whether of strength or skill, no man could surpass him. All the while, Castruccio's comportment was unfailingly modest. He never said or did anything that might displease: He was respectful to men stationed above him, modest with his equals, and pleasant to his inferiors. He was loved not only by the Guinigi family but by all of Lucca.

Castruccio had turned eighteen when the Ghibellines were ousted from Pavia by the Guelphs, and Messer Francesco Guinigi was sent by the Visconti of Milan to aid the Ghibellines. Castruccio went with him as captain of his company, and throughout the campaign showed so much prudence and courage that no other soldier acquired so much prestige. He became renowned and honored not only in Pavia, but in all of Lombardy.[4]

When Castruccio returned to Lucca he found that his standing had grown even more since he had joined the campaign, and he made sure to gain as many allies and supporters as he could, using all the methods necessary to win men over. Then Messer Francesco Guinigi died, leaving behind a thirteen-year-old son, Pagolo, with Castruccio as his guardian and the administrator of his estate. Before Messer Francesco died, he sent for Castruccio and entreated him to raise his son with the same devotion with which Messer Francesco had raised Castruccio, asking Castruccio to repay to his son the gratitude he owed him.

With Messer Francesco's death Castruccio became Pagolo's guardian, which further increased his standing and power. But some of the esteem in Lucca that had been his now turned into jealousy. Certain men of influence, suspecting that he had his mind set on tyranny, began slandering him. Foremost among them was Messer Giorgio degli Obizi,[5] the leader of the Guelph faction, who had hoped to become something like a prince of Lucca upon Messer Francesco's death. In Messer Giorgio's view, Castruccio was becoming the most influential man in Lucca on account of the admiration and prestige that his qualities inspired among the people, and so he began spreading rumors calculated to weaken Castruccio's standing. At first Castruccio looked on Messer Giorgio's efforts with contempt, but soon he began to worry that Messer Giorgio would not rest until he had blackened him in the eyes of the governor of King Roberto of Naples, and had him driven from Lucca.[6]

The ruler of neighboring Pisa in those days was Uguccione della Faggiuola of Arezzo. He had first been elected by the Pisans as their

4. Machiavelli's account is fictitious. In 1301 Castruccio and his family were banished from Lucca. On his father's death that year, Castruccio went to the court of King Edward I in England, after which he was said to have moved to Flanders before returning to Italy, where he worked as a mercenary captain.
5. The Obizi family had been instrumental in the exiling of the Castracani and the other Ghibelline families in 1301.
6. Lucca and other Tuscan cities had sought the protection of King Roberto I of Naples in 1311, when Henry VII of Germany marched against the Italian states in his mission to be crowned Holy Roman Emperor. The Guelph faction in Lucca were supporters of King Roberto, while Castruccio, a Ghibelline, supported the Holy Roman Emperor.

military commander, and afterward had made himself their prince.[7] In his entourage were a few men of the Ghibelline faction who had been banished from Lucca, with whom Castruccio communicated with the aim of bringing the Ghibellines back to power in Lucca with Uguccione's help. Castruccio revealed his designs to his allies in Lucca, who also resented the power of the Obizi family. They set up a plan, and Castruccio carefully began to fortify the tower of the Onesti family,[8] stocking it with munitions and provisions so that he could barricade himself in it for a few days if necessary.

On a night that Uguccione and Castruccio had agreed on, Uguccione rode out from Pisa with a large force and positioned his men on the plain between the mountains and Lucca. When Castruccio gave him a sign, Uguccione advanced on the Gate of San Piero and set fire to the portcullis, while inside, Castruccio called the populace to arms and forced open the gates so that Uguccione and his men could overrun the town and kill Messer Giorgio and all his family, friends, and partisans. The governor of Lucca was chased from the town, and Uguccione of Pisa rearranged the government to his liking, but at great cost to Lucca, for he banished more than a hundred families, some of whom fled to Florence, others to Pistoia, cities ruled by the Guelph faction, and so became enemies of Uguccione and the town of Lucca.

Florence and the other Guelph strongholds saw the Ghibelline faction as having gained too much power in Tuscany, and they forged an alliance to reinstate the banished Guelph families of Lucca. Gathering a large army, they marched on Val di Nievole, occupied Montecatini, and went on to Montecarlo to secure the mountain pass to Lucca.[9] In the meantime, Uguccione had enlisted many men from Pisa and Lucca, as well as German cavalrymen he brought in from Lombardy, and

---

7. Uguccione della Faggiuola (c. 1250–1319) was one of the most influential members of the Ghibelline faction of Tuscany. He had been elected chief magistrate of Pisa, then commander of the army, and in 1314, already in his late sixties, seized power and became tyrant of Pisa. Machiavelli is moving events back in time to fit the plot of his narration, as Castruccio was in fact in his mid-thirties and an experienced mercenary by the time of these events. See also *Florentine Histories*, Book II, chapter 25.
8. Giovanni Villani's *Nuova Cronaca* (New Chronicles), which Machiavelli used as a source, lists the Antelminelli (Castruccio's clan) joining with the Quartigiani, the Pogginghi, and the Onesti in this conspiracy.
9. Montecatini is a town eighteen miles northeast of Lucca, and Montecarlo seven miles.

marched on the Florentine encampment. When the Florentines heard of the enemy's approach they retreated from Montecarlo and posted themselves between Montecatini and Pescia. Uguccione took up position outside Montecarlo, some two miles from the enemy, but for a few days there were only light skirmishes between his cavalry and the Florentines, as Uguccione had fallen ill and did not want his soldiers to engage the enemy in all-out battle. Uguccione's health deteriorated and he was taken to Montecarlo to be treated, leaving Castruccio in charge of the army.[10] This led to the ruin of the Guelph army, for they took courage at the news that the enemy forces were without their commander. Castruccio was aware of this, and decided to reinforce this conviction by remaining inactive for a few days, feigning fear, and not allowing his forces to leave camp. At this the Guelphs' insolence grew, and they began parading every day in full battle formation before Castruccio's forces. Once Castruccio felt that he had studied their formation and emboldened them enough, he decided to engage them in battle, firing up his soldiers with a speech assuring them that victory would be theirs if they followed his command.

Castruccio had seen that the enemy had gathered all their power at the center of their formation, leaving the weaker men on the flanks; consequently he did the opposite, putting his most valiant men on his flanks, and those of lesser mettle in the center.[11] Castruccio's forces then marched out in this formation, and the moment he sighted the enemy, who with their usual insolence had come to find him, he ordered his weaker squadrons in the center to slow their step and the squadrons on the flanks to quicken theirs. In this way, when the two armies met, only their flanks would engage in battle, while the center battalions remained out of action. Castruccio's center forces stayed so far back that the enemy's powerful center could not reach them: thus Castruccio's most skilled soldiers fought the enemy's weakest, while the enemy's most valiant men could neither attack those who were out of reach in front of them, nor come to the aid of their weaker flank

10. Machiavelli invented Uguccione's illness and departure for Montecarlo in order to place Castruccio in the foreground of the action. Castruccio did participate in this battle, but not in the role of a military leader.
11. Though Villani's chronicles and other accounts of the battle describe the tactics Uguccione used, Machiavelli is describing the methods that Livy attributed to Scipio in his battle with Hannibal.

squadrons. As a result, Castruccio sent the two enemy flanks in headlong retreat, and the enemy's center forces, seeing their flanks exposed, turned and ran as well, robbed of the chance to demonstrate their prowess.

The rout and slaughter were great. More than ten thousand men were killed, among them many captains and prominent Guelph nobles from throughout Tuscany as well as princes who had rallied to aid them, such as King Roberto's brother Piero, the king's nephew Carlo, and Prince Filippo of Taranto.[12] Castruccio, on the other hand, lost only about three hundred men, among them Uguccione's young and valiant son Francesco, who was killed at the very beginning of the attack.

This victory brought Castruccio such prominence that Uguccione became jealous and suspicious, and was possessed by the idea of destroying him. Uguccione was convinced that the triumphant victory had not increased his own power but in fact had decreased it. Consumed by these thoughts, he waited for the opportunity to strike at Castruccio, which presented itself when Pier Agnolo Micheli, a man of great accomplishment and repute, was murdered in Lucca. His murderer fled to Castruccio's house, and when the officers came to arrest the murderer, Castruccio sent them away. The murderer managed to escape with his help. Uguccione, who was in Pisa, heard of the incident and saw the perfect chance to even the score with Castruccio.[13] He sent for his son Nieri, to whom he had given the rule of Lucca, and ordered him to invite Castruccio to a banquet in order to apprehend him there and put him to death.

Castruccio gladly accepted the invitation to Nieri's palace, not suspecting foul play, and was seized at the dinner. But Nieri feared that the people of Lucca would be outraged if he put Castruccio to death without justification, so he locked him in a dungeon and waited for his father to send word on what he should do next. Uguccione was furious at his son's wavering and cowardice, and set out from Pisa with four hundred horsemen to bring the matter to a conclusion. But he had not

12. Carlo d'Anjou and his father, Filippo d'Anjou, Prince of Taranto and Acaia.
13. This account is fictitious. Castruccio, outside his jurisdiction, had put to death some thirty men in Lunigiana, which historians believe Uguccione perceived as a challenge to his authority.

yet reached Bagni[14] when the Pisans took up arms, killed his deputy and all the members of Uguccione's family in Pisa, and made Count Gaddo della Gherardesca their new lord.[15]

Uguccione heard the news from Pisa before he arrived in Lucca, but he knew that it would be unwise to turn back and give Lucca the opportunity to imitate Pisa's example and close its gates to him too. However, the people of Lucca had also heard the news, and despite Uguccione's arrival seized the opportunity to try to free Castruccio. They flocked to the town squares to denounce Uguccione, took up arms, and began to stir up unrest, demanding that Castruccio be released. Uguccione, fearing the turn of events, freed him, upon which Castruccio immediately rejoined his allies. With the support of the populace, he attacked Uguccione, who was compelled to flee with his men, escaping to Lombardy to the domain of the Princes della Scala, where in due course he died in poverty.[16]

From being a prisoner, Castruccio now practically became prince of Lucca. With the help of his partisans and the populace's renewed favor, he was elected captain general of the army for a year. He was determined to increase his standing even further through war, and set out to win back for Lucca many of the towns that had revolted after Uguccione had been driven out. He marched on Sarzana with the backing of the Pisans, with whom Castruccio had formed an alliance, and during the siege built a fortress that was later walled in by the Florentines and is today known as Sarzanello.[17] Within two months he had conquered Sarzana, and then went on to occupy Massa, Carrara, and Lavenza. Soon all of Lunigiana was his, and to secure the mountain pass that led

14. Today San Giuliano Terme, about four miles from Pisa and five miles from Lucca. Machiavelli is closely following Giovanni Villani's *Nuova Cronaca* (IX, 78): "Uguccione had not yet reached the mountain of San Giuliano, when the populace of Pisa rose [. . .] and ransacked the building of the Signoria where Coscetto dal Colle was magistrate, and ran with arms and fire to the palace where Uguccione and his family lived, shouting 'Death to Uguccione the tyrant!' They robbed and killed his entire family."

15. Gaddo della Gherardesca, Count of Donoratico, also a prominent member of the Ghibelline faction, overthrew Uguccione in 1316.

16. Cangrande della Scala, Lord of Verona, was the leader of the Ghibelline League. Uguccione, however, did not die in poverty, but after an unsuccessful attempt to regain Pisa and Lucca, became chief magistrate of Vicenza, where he died in 1319.

17. Machiavelli is rearranging the sequence of events for effect. Castruccio built the Fortezza di Sarzanello in 1322 on the site of a tenth-century fortress.

from Lombardy to Lunigiana he stormed Pontremoli, driving out Messer Anastagio Palavisini, who was its prince. When Castruccio returned victorious to Lucca and was greeted by large crowds, he felt the time had come to make himself prince, and with the support of some of the foremost men of Lucca—Pazzino dal Poggio, Puccinello dal Portico, Francesco Boccansacchi, and Cecco Guinigi—all of whom he had bribed, he made himself lord of Lucca, and then in a solemn ceremony was elected prince by the people.[18]

When King Frederick of Bavaria, the Holy Roman Emperor, came to Italy to claim his imperial crown, Castruccio offered his allegiance. He rode out to meet him with a cavalry of five hundred, leaving Pagolo Guinigi, who was held in high esteem by the people in memory of his father, in charge of Lucca. Frederick received Castruccio with much ceremony, bestowing on him an array of privileges and making him his governor in Tuscany.[19] In the meantime, the Pisans had expelled Gaddo della Gherardesca,[20] and, fearing his retaliation, had turned to Frederick, who appointed Castruccio as prince of Pisa. The people of Pisa accepted Castruccio as their new ruler, as he was a Ghibelline who could keep them secure from the Guelph faction, and from the Florentines.

When Frederick returned to Germany, leaving a governor in Rome, all the Tuscan and Lombardian Ghibellines who were his followers turned to Castruccio for help, each promising to support him with their cities' forces if Castruccio would help them regain power. Among these were Matteo Guidi, Nardo Scolari, Lapo Uberti, Gerozzo Nardi, and Piero Buonaccorsi, all Ghibellines, and Florentine exiles. Castruccio's design was, by combining his forces with theirs, to become prince of all Tuscany. In order to strengthen his position even further, he allied himself with Matteo Visconti, the prince of Milan,[21] and began arming Lucca and its territories. As Lucca had five city gates, he divided its territories into five sections, which he armed and put under captains and banners so that he could swiftly and with ease bring to-

18. In April, 1320, Castruccio was elected Dominus Generalis of Lucca for life.
19. In 1320 Frederick III appointed Castruccio as his governor, or Imperial Vicar General of Lucca, Versilia, and Lunigiana.
20. Gaddo della Gherardesca, a moderate ruler who was an ally of Castruccio's, in fact died in 1320.
21. Matteo I the Great, 1250–1322.

gether twenty thousand men, not counting those he could call on from Pisa.

It was at this time that Matteo Visconti was attacked by the Guelphs of Piacenza, who had ousted the Ghibellines with the help of forces sent by Florence and King Roberto of Naples. Visconti asked Castruccio to attack Florence so that the Florentines, forced to defend their homes, would withdraw their army from Lombardy. Castruccio obliged, and marched on Valdarno with a large army, occupying Fucecchio and San Miniato,[22] causing great damage to the land and forcing the Florentines to withdraw their men from the battle with Visconti.

But as the Florentine army marched back toward Florence, an emergency forced Castruccio to return to Lucca. The Poggio family had been powerful enough to make Castruccio not only a great man, but prince. But now they felt that they had not been sufficiently rewarded, and joined with other families of Lucca to trigger a revolt to topple Castruccio. One morning they seized the opportunity, killed Castruccio's chief magistrate, and incited the populace to rise up. But Stefano di Poggio, an old and peaceable man who had not taken part in the conspiracy, stepped forward, and with his authority compelled the conspirators to lay down their arms, offering to act as mediator with Castruccio and to ensure that he would grant them what they demanded. The conspirators, however, laid down their arms with no greater prudence than they had taken them up in the first place, for when news of the conspiracy reached Castruccio, he immediately headed back to Lucca with some of his soldiers, leaving Pagolo Guinigi in charge of the rest. In Lucca, Castruccio was taken aback to find that the uprising had subsided, but still took the precaution of posting armed men throughout the city. Stefano di Poggio, who was certain that Castruccio would be obliged to him for his intercession, stepped before him, pleading clemency not for himself, as he felt he had nothing to fear, but for the other members of his family. He entreated Castruccio to pardon the recklessness of youth, and reminded him of the favors and friendship that the di Poggio family had accorded him. Castruccio replied with grace, reassuring the old man and

22. Valdarno is the Arno River valley, and Fucecchio and San Miniato important strategic castles on the Arno, approximately equidistant from Lucca, Florence, Pisa, and Pistoia. San Miniato had been the seat of the Holy Roman Emperors, and Frederick II had fortified the town extensively in the mid–thirteenth century.

declaring that he was happier at finding the uprising abated than he had been angry at hearing of its outbreak. He asked Stefano to have everyone come to him, affirming that he thanked God for the opportunity to demonstrate his clemency and charity. Assured by Stefano, they all came, and Castruccio had every one of them, including Stefano, seized and killed.[23]

The Florentines had in the meantime retaken San Miniato. But Castruccio felt he should put an end to the war, as he knew he could not venture far from Lucca until he had secured peace. He appealed to the Florentines for a truce and found them quite willing to accept, as they were exhausted and wanted to put an end to the expense. They agreed to a two-year peace and that each side could keep the territories it was then holding.

Freed from the burden of war, Castruccio set about ensuring that he would never again have to face the kind of dangers he had faced at home, and under various pretenses eliminated all those whose ambition might make them aspire to become prince. He spared no one, depriving his potential rivals of their citizenship and possessions, and those he managed to capture of their life. Experience, he avowed, had shown that he could not place any trust in their loyalty. So that he would be more secure he built a castle in Lucca, using the stones of the towers of those he had exiled and killed.[24]

During the period of peace with Florence, while Castruccio was building up his fortifications in Lucca, he did everything he could to increase his power short of going to war. He had his mind set on occupying Pistoia, knowing that once it was his he would almost have one foot in Florence. To this end he gathered supporters throughout the mountains.[25] As for the factions in Pistoia, Castruccio made certain that each placed its trust in him. The city was divided, as it has always been, between White and Black factions: The leader of the Whites was

23. Machiavelli has recast the incident. One of the junior members of the Poggio clan, Stefano di Poggio, had killed one of Castruccio's officials. Castruccio, on his immediate return to Lucca, invited the heads of the Poggio family to his house to discuss what should be done about Stefano. When they came, he had them seized and executed.

24. Giovanni Villani in *Nuova Cronaca* (IX) writes: "Fearing that the populace of Lucca would revolt, Castruccio ordered a wondrous castle to be built within the city, taking up almost a fifth part of the town facing Pisa. He reinforced the mighty walls with twenty-eighty towers."

25. Pistoia, surrounded by hills that form part of the Apennine Mountains, lies about eighteen miles northwest of Florence.

Bastiano di Possente, and the leader of the Blacks, Iacopo da Gia.[26] They both conducted secret talks with Castruccio, as each wanted to drive the other party out. The tensions between the White and Black partisans grew until finally they took up arms, Iacopo positioning his forces at Pistoia's Florentine Gate, Bastiano at the Lucca Gate. Both leaders trusted Castruccio more than they did the Florentines, considering him more resolute and ready to fight than the Florentines were, and so both covertly sent to him for help. Castruccio promised Iacopo that he would come in person, and Bastiano that he would send Pagolo Giunigi, and told them when to expect them. He sent Pagolo over the Pescia road, while he headed directly to Pistoia. At midnight both Castruccio and Pagolo arrived at Pistoia, and as allies they were allowed through the gates. Once inside, Castruccio gave Pagolo a sign, at which point Castruccio killed Iacopo da Gia, and Pagolo killed Bastiano di Possente, and then they slaughtered or took prisoner all their supporters. Castruccio and Pagolo occupied Pistoia without further opposition, expelling the magistrates from the Signoria, and Castruccio compelled the populace to show him obedience, annulling many old debts and making many promises. He did the same for all the territory around Pistoia, a good part of the people having come into the city to see the new prince. Everyone was impressed by Castruccio's qualities and filled with hope, so the people of Pistoia soon calmed down.[27]

In the meantime, the populace of Rome had become unruly because of rising costs triggered by the loss of the pope, who had moved to Avignon.[28] The Romans blamed the German governors for the disorder and daily murders. Enrico, the Holy Roman Emperor's governor,[29] found he was helpless, and feared that the Romans might turn to

26. The Whites (Bianchi) and Blacks (Neri) were feuding factions within the Guelph party that did much to destabilize Pistoia, and later Florence too. Machiavelli, however, invented the names of the faction leaders.

27. This account of Castruccio's seizing power in Pistoia is fictitious. Machiavelli closely follows a tale from Xenophon's *Cyropaedia* (7.4.4), in which Adusius, Cyrus's general, tricks two warring Carian factions and so takes over the city of Caria. "[Adusius] arranged a meeting with both factions for the same night, each without the other's knowledge. On the night in question he entered and took possession of the strongholds of both factions."

28. In 1309, when Pope Clement V moved the papal residence to Avignon in France, Rome suddenly lost its lucrative role as the center of the Catholic world and faced escalating turmoil triggered by the factional fighting of the Orsini and Colonna families.

29. According to Villani's *Nuova Cronaca*, Arrigo d'Ostericchi (Henry of Austria), the emperor's brother.

King Roberto of Naples and have him expelled from Rome and the pope reinstated. Having no closer ally than Castruccio to turn to, he sent him word beseeching him not only to send forces but to come to Rome in person. Castruccio realized that he had to act immediately, both to pay his debt to the emperor and also because if the emperor was expelled from Rome, his own position would be severely weakened.[30] He left Pagolo Guinigi in charge of Lucca and rode with six hundred horsemen to Rome, where he was received by Enrico with much pomp and ceremony. With Castruccio present, the emperor's cause quickly gained so much ground that peace was restored without bloodshed or violence: Castruccio had arranged for a large quantity of grain to be shipped from Pisa, thus removing the reason for much of the turmoil. Thus, partly reprimanding, partly punishing the leaders of Rome, Castruccio forced them to submit to Enrico's government. Castruccio was made senator of Rome and accorded many other honors by the Romans. He took office with much fanfare, wore a brocaded toga with the words "This is what God wants" embroidered on the front, and the words "And what God wants shall be" embroidered on the back.[31]

The Florentines were angry that Castruccio had taken over Pistoia after agreeing to a period of truce, and deliberated on how best to make the city rebel. They felt that this might be easy enough, seeing that Castruccio was away in Rome. Among the exiled Pistoians in Florence were Baldo Cecchi and Iacopo Baldini, both fearless men of authority. The two sent word to their friends in Pistoia, and with the help of the Florentines entered the city one night and chased out or killed all of Castruccio's supporters and officials, restoring liberty to Pistoia. This news greatly angered Castruccio. He took leave of Enrico and returned to Lucca in a relentless march. When the Florentines heard that Castruccio was back, they knew that he was bound to strike at them without delay, and decided to forestall him by entering the Val di

30. In 1320 the Holy Roman Emperor Frederick III had made Castruccio his "imperial vicar" of Lucca, Versilia, and Lunigiana. Four years later, Emperor Louis IV appointed Castruccio Duke of Lucca and Count of Latran. Beside this debt, which Castruccio felt he had to repay, it was strategically vital for him to keep Roberto of Naples, the champion of the Guelph cause and the enemy of the Holy Roman Emperor, out of Rome and Ghibelline territory.
31. Giovanni Villani describes Castruccio's pomp, commenting on the arrogant words of the toga: "And thus he himself prophesied the future judgment of God."

Nievole with their army before he could get there with his. They were aware that if they held the valley, they could hinder him from reaching and regaining Pistoia. Gathering a large army of Guelph supporters, they positioned themselves on the Pistoian plain, while Castruccio marched his army to Montecarlo. But he decided not to confront the Florentines on the plains of Pistoia, nor to wait for them on the plains of Pescia, but, if he could, to encounter them in the Pass of Serravalle, judging that victory would be his if his design succeeded. Castruccio knew that the Florentines had thirty thousand men to his twelve thousand, and though he had confidence in his skill and his men's valor, he did not want to risk being engulfed by the superior numbers of the enemy forces should he engage them in the open.

Serravalle is a castle town between Pescia and Pistoia, on a hill that blocks the Val di Nievole. It is not inside the pass itself, but about two bowshots above it. The pass is not steep, because it slopes up gently on both sides; but it is narrow, especially on the hill where the waters divide, so that twenty men standing side by side can hold it. This is where Castruccio wanted to meet the enemy: in part because his fewer men would have the advantage, but also because he did not want his troops to see the enemy forces before the battle, as he was worried that his men might be alarmed if they saw their great numbers. A German, Messer Manfredi, was the lord of Serravalle. Before Castruccio had become ruler of Pistoia, Messer Manfredi had been allowed to keep possession of the castle, even though it lay within the spheres of both Lucca and Pistoia. But as he promised to remain neutral, neither city moved to attack him. Furthermore, he was in a strong and secure location, and so was left alone. But now Castruccio wanted to occupy the castle of Serravalle. He had a good friend in Serravalle and made arrangements that on the night before he was to engage the Florentines in battle, his friend would allow four hundred of Castruccio's men through the castle gates and murder the castellan.

In order to encourage the Florentines to enter the pass, Castruccio did not move his army from Montecarlo, and the Florentines for their part wanted to move the battle from Pistoia to the Val di Nievole. So they set up camp beneath Serravalle with the intention of crossing the hill the following day. But Castruccio, having secretly seized the castle under cover of darkness, marched his troops out of Montecarlo in the middle of the night and furtively arrived at the foot of Serravalle at dawn. Thus Castruccio and the Florentines, each on their side of the pass, began climbing the slope at the same time. Castruccio had sent his infantry along the main road and four hundred cavalrymen along a path on the left toward the castle. The Florentines, on the other side of the hill, had sent some four hundred horsemen ahead, followed by their infantry and then their men at arms. They did not expect to find Castruccio up on the hill because they did not know that he had taken the castle. Hence the Florentine horsemen were utterly taken aback when they climbed the slope and came upon Castruccio's infantry. They found themselves so close to them that they barely had time to slip on their helmets. Unprepared soldiers were attacked by troops who were prepared and well ordered. Castruccio's spirited men pushed back the Florentines, who could barely stand up to them, though some did try. But as word spread through the rest of the Florentine army, confusion ensued: The cavalry was hemmed in by the infantry, and the infantry by the cavalry and the baggage train. The men in front, hindered by the narrowness of the pass, could go neither forward nor back, so that in all the confusion nobody knew what could or should be done. The Florentine cavalry, meanwhile, was fighting hand to hand with Castruccio's infantry and was being cut down and slaughtered, unable to defend itself because of the adverse terrain. The horsemen tried to stand their ground, more out of desperation than valor, because having the mountains on both sides, with their comrades behind them and the enemy in front, they found no road open for escape.

Castruccio saw that he did not have enough men to make the enemy retreat, and so sent a thousand infantry by way of the castle to join the four hundred horsemen he had positioned there. They struck the enemy's flank with such fury that the Florentine troops, unable to stand up to the onslaught, began to flee, defeated more by the terrain than by Castruccio's forces. The soldiers in the rear ran toward Pistoia, scattering over the plain, each man for himself.

The defeat was total and bloody. Many commanders were captured, among them Bandini de Rossi, Francesco Brunelleschi, and Giovanni della Tosa, all Florentine noblemen, as well as a number of Tuscans and Neapolitans sent by King Roberto to fight for the Florentines and the Guelph cause. When word of the rout reached the Pistoians, they immediately drove out the Guelph factions and surrendered to Castruccio, who then went on to occupy Prato[32] and all the castles of the plains on both sides of the Arno. He then set up camp with his men on the plains of Peretola, some two miles from Florence. He stayed there many days, distributing loot and celebrating the victory, mocking the Florentines by coining money and setting up races with horses, soldiers, and whores. He made efforts to bribe some influential Florentines to open the gates of Florence under cover of darkness, but the conspiracy was revealed, and Tommaso Lupacci and Lambertuccio Frescobaldi were arrested and beheaded.

The Florentines, alarmed by the defeat, were worried that they might have to forfeit their liberty to Castruccio, and to secure help they sent emissaries to King Roberto of Naples, offering him Florence and its dominions for his protection. The king accepted, not so much because of the honor the Florentines were according him but because he knew how vital it was for his own position that the Guelph faction keep the upper hand in Tuscany. He agreed that the Florentines would pay him a tribute of two hundred thousands florins a year, and sent his son Carlo to Florence with a cavalry of four thousand men.[33]

In the meantime, the Florentines were given a respite from Castruccio and his soldiers as he was forced to leave for Pisa to crush a conspiracy set up by Benedetto Lanfranchi, one of the foremost men of Pisa. Lanfranchi could not bear his city being enslaved by a man from Lucca, and plotted to occupy the citadel, drive out the guards, and kill Castruccio's supporters.[34] But in conspiracies, though it is good for secrecy to keep the number of conspirators to a few, these few will then not be enough to carry out the conspiracy. In his attempt to bring more men into it, Benedetto Lanfranchi involved one who revealed the plot to Castruccio. Nor did the plot's exposure occur without the help of Bonifacio Cerchi and Giovanni Guidi, two Florentines

32. A city eight miles northwest of Florence.
33. A cavalry of three hundred that King Roberto had sent in December 1325 had proved insufficient to curb the increasing raids of Castruccio's soldiers on the Florentine countryside. Carlo of Calabria, King Roberto's oldest son, was then officially proclaimed Lord of Florence for ten years in January 1326, though he did not serve the full term.
34. Machiavelli is transposing a Pisan plot that had occurred three years earlier, in 1323. Lanfranchi was in fact a supporter of Castruccio who was conspiring to kill Nieri della Gherardesca, the governor of Pisa. Lanfrachi was actually executed by della Gherardesca.

exiled in Pisa.[35] Castruccio captured Benedetto, killed him, and sent the rest of his family into exile, and had many other Pisans of the noble classes beheaded. Castruccio now felt that Pistoia and Pisa could not be trusted and set about to secure them with diligence and force. This gave the Florentines time to gather their strength and await the arrival of Prince Carlo. When he arrived they immediately assembled a huge force that mustered most of the Guelphs of Italy, creating a massive army of more than thirty thousand infantry and ten thousand cavalry. The Florentines conferred as to whether they ought to attack Pistoia first or Pisa and decided that Pisa was the better choice, since the recent conspiracy against Castruccio made success more certain. Pisa also seemed the better option, since the Florentines felt that once they had Pisa, Pistoia would surrender of its own accord.

The Florentines marched their army out in early May of 1328, immediately occupying Lastra, Signa, Montelupo, and Empoli, and marching all the way to San Miniato.[36] Castruccio was not alarmed at the news of the extensive forces mobilized against him, as he believed that Fortune would now grant him power over all of Tuscany. He felt that there was no reason for the enemy to cut a better figure in Pisa than they had in the Battle of Serravalle, and that this time they would not have any hope of regrouping. Having gathered twenty thousand foot soldiers and four thousand cavalrymen, Castruccio stationed himself at Fucecchio and sent Pagolo Guinigi with an infantry of five thousand to Pisa.

Fucecchio, standing quite high above the plain, halfway between the Gusciana stream and the Arno River, is in a more secure location than any other castle in the Pisan territories.[37] If the Florentines besieged Castruccio there, they could not block provisions coming in from Lucca or Pisa unless they split their forces in two; nor could they approach Fucecchio or Pisa without being at a disadvantage, because if they marched up to Fucecchio they would be caught between Castruccio's army and that of Pagolo Guinigi stationed in Pisa, and in order to march on Pisa they would have to cross the Arno, which, with

---

35. Bonifacio Cerchi and Giovanni Guidi, exiles from Florence, had been the co-conspirators who betrayed Lanfranchi's 1323 plot.
36. Castles and their communities near Florence along the Arno River. Machiavelli is combining elements from three major campaigns.
37. The castle, about twenty-five miles from Florence, stands on a two-hundred-foot hill.

the enemy at their back, they could do only at great risk. By not positioning himself with his army on the bank of the Arno but having his men line up along the castle walls, Castruccio encouraged the Florentines to choose the alternative of crossing the Arno, leaving considerable terrain between himself and the river.

Once the Florentines had occupied San Miniato, they knew that they had to either march on Pisa or face Castruccio at Fucecchio, and measuring one alternative against the other, decided to attack Castruccio. The Arno was shallow enough to be easily forded, though not without the infantry being submerged up to their shoulders and the horsemen to their saddles. On the morning of June 10, the Florentines assembled in battle formation and sent part of their cavalry and an infantry battalion of ten thousand into the river. Castruccio, ready and determined, attacked them with an infantry battalion of five thousand, and three thousand horsemen, and before the Florentines managed to emerge from the waters, Castruccio's forces set upon them. Then he sent a thousand infantrymen upstream along the riverbank and a thousand downstream. The Florentine infantry was weighed down by the waters and their weapons, and were struggling to climb the rocky banks. The horses that had managed to cross first had churned up the riverbed with their hooves, making the crossing harder for the rest, who were now stepping on unstable ground. Many horses toppled over onto their riders or became stuck in the mud. When the Florentine captains saw how difficult it was to cross at this part of the river, they moved their troops higher upstream to where the riverbed was not churned up and the banks were not as steep, but there they were met by the infantry Castruccio had sent upriver. These forces were lightly armed with bucklers and spears, and with loud battle cries plunged their blades into the foreheads and chests of the Florentine soldiers. The horses, alarmed by the shouting and carnage, balked and began falling and tumbling over each other.

The clash between Castruccio's men and the Florentines in the river was harsh and terrible. Many men fell on both sides, and both sides fought with all their might. Castruccio's men strove to drive the Florentines back into the river, while the Florentines strove to push ahead so that those emerging from the river behind them could fight. The captains on both sides exhorted their men, Castruccio reminding his soldiers that this was the same enemy they had vanquished at Serravalle not too long ago, while the Florentines rebuked their men for allowing Castruccio's small army to overcome their superior forces.

Castruccio saw that the battle was dragging on and that his men and the enemy were already exhausted, with many wounded and dead on both sides. So he sent forward a fresh infantry battalion of five thousand, positioning them behind the men who were fighting, and ordered the men in the fray to fan out, half retreating to the left, the other half to the right. This opened up the terrain for the Florentines, and they advanced, but when the battle-worn Florentine soldiers came upon Castruccio's rested men, they were easily pushed back into the river.

In the meantime, neither of the two cavalries had gained the upper hand because Castruccio, aware that his was the weaker, had ordered his captains to do no more than resist the enemy. He hoped to defeat the Florentine infantry first: Once the infantry was defeated, he could rout the cavalry with greater ease. And things went according to his plan. As the enemy infantry was driven back into the river, Castruccio unleashed the rest of his infantry on the enemy cavalry, wounding them with lances and spears, and then sent in his own cavalry with greater force, putting the enemy horsemen to flight. The rest of the Florentine foot soldiers fared no better: Once the Florentine captains had seen the difficulty their horsemen had in crossing the river, they had sent the rest of their foot soldiers to cross further downstream, with the design of attacking Castruccio's flanks. But this proved to be a mistake, for the banks there were steep and lined with enemy soldiers.

To the great honor and glory of Castruccio, the Florentine army was utterly routed. Of all the multitude of Florentine soldiers, less than one-third managed to escape. Many commanders were taken captive, while King Roberto of Naples's son Carlo and Michelagnolo Falconi and Taddeo degli Albizzi, the Florentine commissioners, fled to Empoli. As one can imagine in such a battle, the plunder was great and the slaughter even greater. The Florentine army lost 20,231 men, Castruccio 1,570.

But Fortune proved hostile to Castruccio's glory and took his life just when she ought to have nurtured it, cutting short the grand designs he had aimed to achieve for so many years, designs that nothing but death could hinder. Exhausted from the day-long battle, Castruccio stood above the castle gate of Fucecchio, breathless and covered in sweat, waiting for his men to return from their victory, to receive them and thank them in person. He also wanted to keep an eye out in case some of the enemy forces regrouped to attack. It was the duty of a good leader to be the first to mount his horse and the last to dismount. But standing above the gates, exposed to a wind that usually rises at midday over the Arno and is almost always pestiferous, Castruccio caught a chill. Accustomed to the rigors of battle, he paid little heed to this, but it proved the cause of his death. The following night he was seized by a strong fever that kept rising. As all the doctors judged it fatal, Castruccio called Pagolo Guinigi to him and spoke the following words:[38] "My son, had I believed that Fortune intended to cut me down midway to the glory I had seen was mine with so many successes, I would have tired myself less and left you a smaller state, fewer enemies, and less envy. I would have been content with ruling Lucca and Pisa and would not have subjugated the Pistoians and angered the Florentines with my many assaults. I would have made those cities my friends, and would have led my life, if not longer, then with greater tranquillity. I would have left you this state smaller, but doubtless more stable and secure. But Fortune, the arbitrator of all human affairs, did not give me sufficient judgment to understand this, nor enough time to be able to overcome what she had in store. Many have told you—and I have never denied it—that I came into your father's house as a boy, deprived of all the hopes that flourish in a young nobleman's heart, and how your father nurtured and loved me more than if I had been of his blood. Under his tutelage I became valiant and able to grasp the gifts of Fortune, which you yourself have seen and still see. When your father died, he placed you and all he possessed in my care, and I have raised you, bound as I was and still am by a love and loyalty that have increased that wealth for you. So that you would not only inherit what your father left, but also what Fortune and my skill have gained, I never took a wife. I did not want my love for my sons to hinder me from showing to your father's blood the gratitude I owe.[39] I leave you a

38. Machiavelli invented the speech, taking elements from Villani's *Nuova Cronaca,* in which Villani reports the advice and suggestions Castruccio gave to his actual son and heir Arrigo and to his closest supporters.
39. In fact Castruccio had a wife and nine children, four of whom were sons, which Machiavelli would have known from his sources.

great state, and of that I am pleased. But I am most unhappy that I leave it to you weak and unstable. You own the city of Lucca, which will never be content to live under your reign. You own Pisa, whose men are fickle and disloyal, and though over the years Pisa has been accustomed to subjugation, it will always scorn the rule of a lord from Lucca. You own Pistoia, which cannot be loyal, as it is divided and angry at your blood for the recent injuries we have inflicted on them. You have the Florentines for neighbors, whom we have offended and harmed in a thousand ways, though not destroyed. They will hear the news of my death with greater joy than if they had acquired all of Tuscany. And you cannot rely on the princes of Milan or the Emperor, as they are far away, sluggish, and slow to send help. You can only place your hopes in your own industry, in the memory of my skill and prowess, and in the standing that our present victory has afforded you. If you use it with prudence, it will bring you advantage in a treaty with the Florentines, who, alarmed at their defeat, will be eager to negotiate. Whereas I sought to make them my enemy, in the belief that such enmity would bring me power and glory, you must seek with all your strength to make them your friends, because their friendship will bring you security and benefit. In this world it is vital to know oneself, to know how to measure one's spirit and power. He who knows that he is unable to wage war must strive to reign through the art of peace, and my counsel to you is that you would do well to master this art, and so enjoy what my toil and peril have gained. It should be easy for you to accomplish this, if you esteem what I am telling you as true. And you will be indebted to me in two ways: first, for having left you this realm, and second for having taught you how to keep it."

Then Castruccio called to his side the men of Lucca, Pisa, and Pistoia who had fought under him, and presented Pagolo Guinigi to them. Castruccio made them swear obedience to Pagolo, and died. All who knew him and were his friends had happy memories of him, and he was mourned like no other prince. His funeral was celebrated with the greatest honors, and he was buried in the church of San Francesco in Lucca. But skill and Fortune were not as forthcoming for Pagolo Guinigi as they had been for Castruccio. He was soon to lose Pistoia and then Pisa, and with difficulty held on to power in Lucca, which remained under his family's rule until the reign of his great-great-grandson Pagolo.[40]

As I have demonstrated, Castruccio was a rare man not only in his era, but in all eras that had come before. He was taller than average, each limb in perfect harmony with the others. His features were so handsome, and he received everyone with such grace, that none who left his presence ever spoke badly of him. His hair had a reddish tint, and he wore it short above the ears, and always and in all weather—in rain or snow—he left his head uncovered.

He was kind to his friends, ruthless to his enemies, fair to those under his rule, and unfair to those who were not. If he could win through deception, he never sought to win through force. "Victory brings glory" was his motto—it mattered little how victory was achieved.

No man was bolder in encountering dangers, nor more cautious in emerging from them. He used to say that man must attempt everything and fear nothing, and that God loved strong men because one could see that God always punished the weak through the strong.

Castruccio was also admirable with his quick answers and retorts, which at times could be pointed or elegant, and because he had no misgivings about directing his wit at anyone, he also was not angered when wit was directed at him. So we know of many witticisms that he uttered, and many that he heard good-naturedly.

· Castruccio had once bought a partridge for a ducat, and when a friend rebuked him at the expense, Castruccio asked him: "Why, you mean you would not have given more than a brass coin for it?" When his friend said no, Castruccio replied: "A ducat is worth far less to me."[41]

Once he had spat at a flatterer in derision, upon which the flatterer

---

40. Castruccio's empire in fact fell apart within a few weeks of his death on September 3, 1328. After the people of Lucca revolted on October 7, Holy Roman Emperor Ludwig IV removed Arrigo Castracani from office. According to Giovanni Villani's *Nuova Cronaca* (X, 104): "Castruccio's sons were deprived of their ducal title and were exiled to Pontremoli with their mother."

41. Machiavelli took or adapted most of the sayings in this section from Diogenes Laertius, *Lives of Eminent Philosophers* (c. third or fourth century CE). This saying comes from "Aristippus" (Book 2:66): "It is said that Aristippus ordered a partridge to be bought for fifty drachmas. When he was admonished, he asked: 'Would you yourself not have bought the partridge for an obol?' When the man who had reproached him said that he would, Aristippus replied: 'Well, fifty drachmas are no more to me.'"

said: "A fisherman will let the waves of the sea wash over him to catch a tiny fish. I, on the other hand, will gladly let myself be wetted by a little spit to catch a whale."[42] Castruccio not only heard him good-naturedly, but rewarded him.

He was told by someone that his extravagant way of life was evil, to which he replied: "If that were a vice, then we should not dine so lavishly on the feast days of our saints."[43]

Walking down the street, Castruccio saw a young man coming out of a prostitute's house, the young man blushing with shame at being seen. But Castruccio said: "There is no need to be ashamed when you come out of there, only when you go in."[44]

A friend handed him a complicated knot to untie, to which Castruccio said: "You fool, do you think I wish to untie something that gives me so much trouble tied?"[45]

Castruccio said to a man whose trade was philosophy: "You are made of the stuff that dogs are, always following behind those who feed them." The philosopher replied: "In fact, we are more like doctors who go to the houses of those who need us most."[46]

On his way by ship from Pisa to Livorno there was a sudden tempest that made Castruccio quite anxious. A man in his entourage reproved him for his faintheartedness, saying that he himself feared nothing, to which Castruccio replied that he was not surprised, as every man valued his soul at what it was worth.[47]

---

42. From Diogenes Laertius (Book 2:67): "Dionysius once spat at Aristippus, without Aristippus reacting with a single word. When Aristippus was reproached for his silence he replied, 'Fishermen are patient at being sprayed by the sea in order to catch a tiny gudgeon, so why should I not endure being sprayed with a little wine to catch a whale.'"

43. From Diogenes Laertius (Book 2:68): "Upbraided for living extravagantly, Aristippus said: 'If extravagance were bad, we wouldn't have so much of it during the feasts of the gods.'"

44. From Diogenes Laertius (Book 2:69): "Aristippus once entered the house of a hetaera. When one of the young men accompanying him blushed, Aristippus said, 'It is not going into such a house that is bad, but not being able to leave.'"

45. From Diogenes Laertius (Book 2:70): "Someone asked Aristippus to solve a riddle, to which Aristippus replied: 'You fool, why would you have me unknot something that vexes us so much even when it is safely tied up?'"

46. From Diogenes Laertius (Book 2:70): "When someone said that he always saw philosophers at the doors of the rich, he replied: 'One also always sees physicians at the doors of the sick. And yet nobody would choose to be a sick man above being a physician.'"

47. From Diogenes Laertius (Book 2:71): "Aristippus was once sailing to Corinth when a violent storm arose and he became perturbed. Somebody said, 'We simple folk are not afraid,

Castruccio was once asked by a man what he should do to gain respect, and he replied: "When you go to a banquet, be sure that one block of wood is not sitting on another."[48]

A man prided himself for having read much, to which Castruccio said: "It would be better to pride yourself if your mind had retained much."[49]

A man expressed pride at being able to drink a great deal without becoming drunk, to which Castruccio said: "An ox can do the same."[50]

Castruccio was living with a young woman and was reproached by a friend who told him that it was bad to be taken in by her. "You are mistaken," Castruccio replied, "I have taken her, not she me."[51]

Someone blamed him for eating food that was too sumptuous, to which Castruccio replied: "So you do not spend as much as I do?" The man replied that this was true. "Then," Castruccio said, "you are more miserly than I am gluttonous."[52]

Castruccio was invited to dinner by Taddeo Bernardi of Lucca, a very rich and ostentatious man. When Castruccio arrived at his house, Taddeo showed him a room beautifully draped, its floor composed of elegant stones interwoven in an array of colors representing flowers, leaves, and foliage. Suddenly Castruccio cleared his throat and spat in Taddeo's face, and seeing that Taddeo was taken aback, said: "I was not sure where my spitting would offend you less."[53]

---

but you philosophers tremble.' To which Aristippus replied: 'That is because we are not trembling over the same kind of soul.' "

48. From Diogenes Laertius (Book 2:72): "When a man asked him in what way his son would be better once he had completed his education, he replied: 'If nothing else, he won't sit at the theater like one stone on another.' "

49. From Diogenes Laertius (Book 2:71): "Seeing a man who prided himself on the extent of his erudition, he said, 'Those who eat and exercise without limit are in no better health than those who do so within limits. Likewise, it is not those who read much, but those who read what is useful who excel.' "

50. From Diogenes Laertius (Book 2:73): "A man boasted of being able to drink a great deal without becoming drunk, to which Aristippus said: 'A mule can do the same.' "

51. From Diogenes Laertius (Book 2:74): "Reproached for living with a hetaera, he said, 'Does it make a difference whether one chooses a house where many have lived or one where no one has lived before?' "

52. From Diogenes Laertius (Book 2:75): "When someone reproached him for buying expensive food, he asked, 'Wouldn't you have bought all this for three obols?' The other said that he would, to which Aristippus replied: 'In that case, I am not as much of a glutton as you are a miser.' "

53. From Diogenes Laertius (Book 2:75): "One day Dionysius's steward Simos, a Phrygian and a contemptuous fellow, showed Aristippus a lavish house paved with mosaics. Suddenly

Asked how Caesar died, Castruccio remarked: "God wanted me to die as he did!"[54]

One night, Castruccio was at the house of one of the gentlemen of his entourage where many ladies had gathered for a ball. There he danced and amused himself more than was seemly for a man of his position, and when a friend called him to account, he replied: "He who is considered wise during the day will never be considered foolish at night."[55]

A man came to ask Castruccio for a favor, and when Castruccio pretended not to hear, the man threw himself on his knees. When Castruccio reproved him, the man answered: "You are the reason why I am kneeling, as your ears are in your feet." At this, Castruccio granted him twice the favor he asked.[56]

Castruccio used to say that the path to hell was easy, since you went downward with your eyes shut.[57]

A man was bothering Castruccio for a favor with a stream of words, to which Castruccio said: "The next time you want something from me, send someone else."[58]

A similar man, having annoyed Castruccio with a long speech, concluded by saying: "I have perhaps tired you with speaking too much." "Not at all," Castruccio replied. "I haven't listened to a word you said."[59]

Castruccio used to say about a handsome man who had been a

Aristippus cleared his throat and spat in Simos's face. Simos was outraged, but Aristippus said: 'I couldn't find a more suitable place to spit.' "

54. From Diogenes Laertius (Book 2:76): "Asked how Socrates died, he said, 'The way I hope that I shall die.' "

55. This is a conflation of two different anecdotes. The opening line is from Diogenes Laertius (Book 2:76).

56. From Diogenes Laertius (Book 2:79): "He was once asked a favor of Dionysius for a friend, but as Dionysius would not listen, he fell at his feet. When someone made fun of him for this, he replied: 'It's Dionysius's fault I am doing this, as his ears are in his feet.' "

57. From Diogenes Laertius (Book 4:49): "Bion used to say that the road to Hades is an easy one. One goes downhill with one's eyes shut."

58. From Diogenes Laertius (Book 4:50): "To an idle prattler harrying him for aid, Bion said: 'I will do what I can for you, as long as you send mediators instead of coming yourself.' "

59. From Diogenes Laertius (Book 5:20): "An idle prattler who had poured a stream of words over him asked Aristotle: 'I hope I haven't been boring you.' To which Aristotle replied, 'By Zeus you haven't, I wasn't even listening.' "

handsome boy that he was quite destructive, having first taken husbands from their wives, and then wives from their husbands.[60]

To an envious man who laughed, he said, "Are you laughing because you are doing well, or because someone else is doing badly?"[61]

While he was still in the care of Messer Francesco Guinigi, one of his companions said to him: "What can I give you in exchange for letting me give you a blow on the nose?" "A helmet with a visor," Castruccio replied.[62]

Castruccio put to death a citizen of Lucca who had been instrumental in his rise to greatness. When people said that he had done a bad thing in killing an old friend, he replied that they were wrong, as he had put to death a new enemy.

Castruccio greatly praised men who chose a bride but then did not marry her, as he praised those who prepared to go on a sea voyage but then did not go.

Castruccio expressed surprise that a man who bought a clay or glass pot would tap it first to see if it was good, but in taking a wife was content just to look at her.

As Castruccio was dying, someone asked him how he wished to be buried, to which he replied: "Face down, as I know that once I am dead everything in this land will be upside down."[63]

When asked if he had ever thought of taking up the cloth to save his soul, he replied that he had not, because it seemed strange to him that Brother Lazarus should go to Heaven while Uguccione della Faggiuola should go to Hell.[64]

---

60. From Diogenes Laertius (Book 4:49): "Bion used to reproach Alcibiades, saying that as a boy he had taken husbands from their wives, and as a young man wives from their husbands."

61. From Diogenes Laertius (Book 4:51): "Bion said to a despondent envious man: 'I do not know whether you are sad because something bad has happened to you, or because something good has happened to someone else.'"

62. From Diogenes Laertius (Book 6:54): "When Diogenes was asked what he would take in exchange for a blow on the head, he replied: 'A helmet.'" The sources of the three anecdotes that follow are unidentified.

63. From Diogenes Laertius (Book 6:31): "When Xeniades asked Diogenes how he wanted to be buried, he replied, 'On my face.' When asked why, he said, 'Because soon enough everything will be turned upside down.'"

64. From Diogenes Laertius (Book 6:39): "When the Athenians asked him why he would not become initiated, as those initiated were accorded the best place in Hades, he replied: 'It would be ridiculous if Agesilaus and Epaminondas remain in the mud, while men of no im-

When he was asked at what time it was best for a man's health to eat, he replied: "If you are rich, eat when you are hungry. If you are poor, eat when you can."[65]

When he saw a gentleman in his retinue have one of his servants button him up, he said, "I hope to God that you also have him feed you."

Once he saw that someone had written above a door in Latin: "May God preserve this house from the wicked," to which he said: "In that case, the head of that household had better not go in."[66]

Walking down the street, he saw a small house with a big door, to which he said: "That house will escape through its own door."[67]

On being told that a certain foreigner had ruined a boy, he said: "That man must be from Perugia."[68]

When asked which city was renowned for cheaters and frauds, he replied: "Lucca, where all men are cheaters and frauds, except for Bonturo."[69]

Castruccio was in discussion with an emissary of the King of Naples concerning the property of some exiles, and voices were raised. At which the ambassador said: "But are you not afraid of the king?" Castruccio replied: "Is this king of yours good or bad?" When the

---

portance, just because they are initiated, will live on the Isles of the Blessed.'" Machiavelli juxtaposes Lazarus the beggar at the rich man's banquet from the New Testament, who receives his reward in Paradise, to the heroic but unreligious Uguccione della Faggiuola.

65. From Diogenes Laertius (Book 6:40): "Asked when it was the best time for a man to eat, he replied, 'For a rich man, whenever he wants to; for a poor man, whenever he can.'" The source of the anecdote that follows is unidentified.

66. From Diogenes Laertius (Book 6:39): "An odious eunuch had written above his door: 'Let no evil enter.' To which Diogenes said: 'But then how will the master of house get inside?'"

67. From Diogenes Laertius (Book 6:57): "Arriving at Myndus, where he saw large gates but a small city, he said: 'Men of Myndus, shut your gates or your city will escape through them.'"

68. From Diogenes Laertius (Book 6:61): "He was once asked where a certain depraved boy was from, to which he replied: 'He is from Tegea'" (a pun on the city of Tegea and *tegos,* "brothel"). In Boccaccio's *Decameron* (Fifth Day), Pietro, a man from Perugia, catches his wife with a youth, whom he then seduces.

69. A witty reference to Dante's *Inferno* (Canto XXI) which Machiavelli's readers would have recognized, where a devil says that Lucca is well furnished with sinners, as "Every man is a fraud, except Bonturo." Merchant and demagogue Bonturo Dati had in fact gone down in history as a politician who was particularly corrupt.

emissary replied that he was good, Castruccio said, "Then why do you think that I should be afraid of a good man?"[70]

I could relate many other things that Castruccio said—both witty and serious things—but I think these are a sufficient testimony to his great qualities. He lived for forty-four years and remained a great prince in good and bad fortune. Since much has been said about his good fortune, I have wanted to present as well moments when his fortune was bad. The manacles with which he was chained in prison can still be seen today in the tower of his home, where he had them put so they would always bear witness to his adversity. In his life he was in no way inferior to Philip of Macedon, Alexander's father, nor Scipio of Rome, and he died at the same age they did. Had he not been born in Lucca, but in Macedonia or Rome, he would doubtless have surpassed both of them.

70. From Diogenes Laertius (6:68): "Alexander once stopped Diogenes and asked, 'Are you not afraid of me?' To which Diogenes replied: 'Are you good or evil?' 'I am good,' Alexander replied. To which Diogenes said: 'So why should anyone fear what is good?'"

THE MANDRAKE

The Mandrake *is the foremost play of the Italian Renaissance and the one most performed today. It is Machiavelli's literary masterpiece, a comedy in prose in five acts. Machiavelli wrote it sometime around 1518, during his exile from Florence. He was already an established and successful playwright: his audience would have known* The Woman of Andros, *a paraphrase of Terence's play, and perhaps his lost plays* Eunuchus *(also an adaptation of Terence),* Aulularia *(an adaptation of Plautus), and* Le Maschere *(The Masks).*

The Mandrake *was an instant success; the audience was exhilarated by its well-crafted elegance and scandal. The increasing double entendres as the play progresses (most of them explicitly sexual) kept audiences laughing, as did the farcical situations. Word of the play quickly spread to the Vatican. Pope Leo X, formerly Giovanni de' Medici, was intrigued, and in 1520 commanded a performance in Rome. He was very impressed.*

———

CHARACTERS

Callimaco—a wealthy young Florentine merchant
Siro—his servant

Ligurio—a former matchmaker
Messer Nicia—a wealthy, middle-aged Florentine lawyer
Lucrezia—his beautiful wife
Sostrata—Lucrezia's mother
Friar Timoteo
A Woman

PROLOGUE

God bless you, gracious audience, though I imagine your graciousness will depend on our pleasing you. Please be silent now, and we will acquaint you with a strange and novel event that took place in our city. Look at this stage that is now being set up before you: it's Florence, but it could just as well be Rome or Pisa.

This door on my right leads into the house of a certain lawyer, who learned all about law from Boo . . . Boo . . . Boethius. That street at the corner is the Street of Love, where he who *falls* will never *rise* again. And as for that church, if you sit still and do not leave our theater too soon, you will see what kind of man of cloth it houses by his outer garb.

There, behind that door to the left, lives Callimaco Guadagni, a young man fresh from Paris. Of all the fashionable young men in town, he shows at first glance every sign of upright gentleness and worth. He has fallen passionately in love with a wise young woman, which is why she was tricked, as you shall see—and I sincerely wish that all of you might be tricked as she was.

This play is called *The Mandrake*, and I trust you shall see why as the plot unfolds. The playwright is not of any great renown, but he will stand you a glass of wine if he cannot make you laugh. He has gathered together a miserable lover, a lawyer of little sense, a friar with wicked ways, and a sponger who is the darling of malice, for your entertainment today.

And if this material, slight as it is, does not prove worthy of a playwright who wishes to appear wise and grave, excuse him with this: that he is trying his utmost to lighten his misery, for he has nowhere else to turn, barred as he is from demonstrating his skills and abilities through worthier tasks, his labor no longer prized. The only prize he can expect is to be sneered at and maligned. And, believe me, this is the reason why ancient skill and craft have degenerated in our century. When a man sees that everything he does is maligned, he will prefer not to toil and strain to accomplish with a thousand hardships a work that an ill wind will topple or clouds will obscure.

But if anyone believes that in speaking badly he can grab the playwright by the hair and intimidate him or make him recant, I shall caution him that the playwright too knows how to malign, as he has proven in an earlier work.[1] I will have you know that he values no one in all the lands where *sí* means "yes," even though he might bow and scrape to those who sport a better cloak than he. But let all those who wish to do so cast aspersions, and let us turn to the matter at hand, so that the play does not run too much beyond its time, for we must not pay heed to mere words nor hold in high regard some fool who knows not whether he is coming or going.

Callimaco has come out of his house along with Siro, his servant, and will shed some light on matters. Watch carefully, for you will not get another explanation.

---

1. This is thought to be a reference to Machiavelli's lost play *Le Maschere*, which was said to lampoon many distinguished Florentines of the time.

ACT I

Callimaco and Siro.

CALLIMACO: Siro, don't go. I want to tell you something.

SIRO: Here I am.

CALLIMACO: I imagine you must have been quite surprised by my sudden departure from Paris, and wondering that I have been a whole month here without doing a thing.

SIRO: That is true.

CALLIMACO: If I haven't told you before now what I am about to tell you, it's not because I don't trust you, but because in my view it is better for a man not to discuss the things he doesn't want known unless he has to. But I think I might need your help, so I will tell you everything.

SIRO: I am your servant, and servants should never ask their masters anything or peek into their private affairs. But when the master speaks of his own accord, a servant must serve loyally. That is what I've always done and what I will always do.

CALLIMACO: I know, I know. You must have heard me say this a thousand times, but it won't matter if you hear it a thousand and first time: When I was ten and my mother and father died, my guardians sent me to Paris, where I lived for twenty years. I had been there just ten years when King Charles marched on Italy and the Italian wars began, which ravaged the whole country. I decided to stay in Paris and never return to Italy, as I felt I could live more safely there than here.

SIRO: So it is.

CALLIMACO: And having from Paris commissioned someone to sell all my property in Florence except for my house, I settled down in France and continued living there most happily for another ten years...

SIRO: I know.

CALLIMACO: ... dividing my time among studies, pleasure, and business, always striving that no activity should encumber the others. As you know, I lived a calm life, being of use to everyone and doing my best not to harm anyone, so that from what I could tell I was liked by townspeople and gentlemen, foreigners and locals, rich and poor.

SIRO: This is true.

CALLIMACO: But Fortune deemed that I was having too good a time, and sent a certain Cammillo Calfucci to Paris.

SIRO: I am beginning to guess what your trouble is.

CALLIMACO: I often invited him to my house, as I invited many other Florentines in Paris. Then one day, as we were conversing, we began to debate which were more beautiful, the women of Italy or the women of France. As I could not evaluate Italian women, since I was young when I left, another Florentine who was present debated for France, and Cammillo for Italy. After many arguments presented by both sides, Cammillo, almost irate, proclaimed that even if all Italian women were monsters, there was one lady of his family who could single-handedly win back their honor.

SIRO: Now I see what you mean.

CALLIMACO: And he named Madonna Lucrezia, the wife of Messer Nicia Calfucci. He so praised her beauty and grace that he left the rest of us stupefied. He sparked such a desire in me to see her that without further ado, and without giving a thought to war or peace in Italy, I set out for Florence. Here I found to my amazement that Madonna Lucrezia's beauty far outshines its fame, which so rarely happens. I have been seized by such a desire to be with her that I shall go mad.

SIRO: Had you told me about this in Paris, I'd have known how to advise you. But now I don't know what I can say.

CALLIMACO: I'm not telling you this so you can advise me, but to get it off my chest, and also to have you prepare yourself to help me should the need arise.

SIRO: I am ready and willing, but what hopes do you have?

CALLIMACO: Alas, none—or few, if any.

SIRO: Oh, why is that?

CALLIMACO: I'll tell you. First of all, her nature wages war on me, for she is most virtuous and a stranger to matters of love. Then, she has a husband who is extremely rich and who allows her to rule him in every way, and though he is not prodigiously young, he is not prodigiously old either, from what I can tell. She has no relatives or neighbors with whom she could go to a soiree or a ball, nor does she involve herself in any of the entertainments in which the young delight. No tradesmen ever visit her house. All her maids and servants tremble before her, so there is no possibility of bribery.

SIRO: So what do you think you might be able to do?

CALLIMACO: No circumstance is ever so desperate that one cannot nurture some spark of hope. And even if this spark is weak and futile, man is blinded by his will and desire to achieve his goal.

SIRO: So what is it that gives you hope?

CALLIMACO: Two things: One is the foolishness of Messer Nicia, who, though a doctor of law, is the simplest and most foolish man in all of Florence, and the second is his desire to have children. They have been married for six years and have not had any yet, but as they are so rich, they do not wish to die childless. There is also a third thing that gives me hope: Her mother used to enjoy going out on the town a bit, but now she is rich and I'm not sure how she is to be approached.

SIRO: Have you tried anything yet?

CALLIMACO: Yes, I have, but nothing substantial.

SIRO: What do you mean?

CALLIMACO: You know Ligurio, who's always coming around to dine here? He used to be a matchmaker, but now he's taken to scrounging lunches and dinners. He is a charming man, and he and Messer Nicia have become quite inseparable. Ligurio is swindling him for all he can. Messer Nicia never asks him to dinner, but sometimes lends him money. I've befriended Ligurio and told him about my love, and he's promised to help me body and soul.

SIRO: You must be careful he doesn't trick you. Such villains aren't known for their loyalty.

CALLIMACO: True. But when a man will gain from a deal, and you make certain he knows it, he will serve you loyally. I have promised him a good sum of money if he succeeds. And if he doesn't, he'll get a lunch and a dinner out of it: That way at least I won't have to dine alone.

SIRO: What has he promised to do so far?

CALLIMACO: He has promised to talk Messer Nicia into taking his wife to a spa this May.

SIRO: What good will that do you?

CALLIMACO: What good? A spa might change her nature. In such places all people do is enjoy themselves, and I'd go there and instigate all the fun I could, missing no occasion for extravagance. I would befriend her, her husband . . . You never know. One thing leads to another, and time has a habit of steering things.

SIRO: That's not a bad scheme.

CALLIMACO: Ligurio left me this morning saying he'd have a word with Messer Nicia and would let me know.

SIRO: Ah, I see them coming toward us.

CALLIMACO: I shall step a little to the side so I'll be in time to talk to Ligurio once he has gotten rid of Messer Nicia. In the meantime, go back inside and continue what you were doing. I'll let you know if I want you to do something for me.

SCENE TWO

Messer Nicia and Ligurio.

NICIA: That was very good advice you gave me. I had a word with my wife, and she told me she'd let me know today. But to tell you the truth, I can't say I'm champing at the bit.

LIGURIO: You're not?

NICIA: Home is home, and I don't like crawling out of my cave. Not to mention having to drag wife, servants, and cartloads of knickknacks across open fields. That's not my idea of fun. Also, I spoke to all kinds of doctors yesterday: One tells me to go to San Filippo, another to Porretta, another to Villa. They're all a bunch of frauds! Those damn doctors couldn't find your gizzard if you dangled it before their eyes.

LIGURIO: It's the idea of leaving Florence that's putting you on edge. You're just not used to losing sight of the great cupola.

NICIA: You're wrong there. When I was younger I was a great vagabond. I was always the first to stroll over to Prato whenever they had a fair, and there's not a castle within walking distance of Florence that I haven't been to! And I'll have you know that I've often taken a stroll over the hill to Pisa or to Livorno, so there!

LIGURIO: You must have seen the Gleaming Tower of Pisa.

NICIA: You mean the Leaning Tower?

LIGURIO: Oh, yes, the one that leans. And did you manage to see the sea at Livorno?

NICIA: Of course I did.

LIGURIO: How much bigger than our Arno River is it?

NICIA: How much bigger? Four times bigger! Maybe even six, maybe seven times. You wouldn't believe it, but all you see is water, water, water!

LIGURIO: I'm surprised that having sown your seed in every corner of the earth you would make such a hullabaloo about going to one of the spas just outside town.

NICIA: What a milksop you are! Do you think it's a trifle to pack up a whole house? But I'm so eager to have children that I'm ready to do anything. Go have a talk with those doctors and see which of the spas that they suggest would be best for me to go to. I'll be with my wife in the meantime. I will see you later.

LIGURIO: That is a good idea.

SCENE THREE

Ligurio and Callimaco.

LIGURIO [*aside*]: I cannot believe you'll find a more foolish man in all the world! And yet how Fortune has favored him: He is rich, and he has a beautiful wife who is wise, has every grace, and is fit to rule a kingdom. People say about marriage, "Like meets like," but if you ask me, that is rarely the case. You often see a man of substance married to a beast of a woman, or a wise woman on the arm of a fool. But Callimaco has something to hope for from this man's foolishness. [*Enter Callimaco*] Ah, there he is. Hello, have you been lingering in the shadows?

CALLIMACO: I saw you with Messer Nicia and was waiting for you to get rid of him so you can tell me what you've accomplished.

LIGURIO: You know what kind of man he is: of very little wisdom and even less spirit. He resists leaving Florence, but I've warmed him up to the idea, and he has finally agreed to everything. I believe he will follow our lead should we decide on that plan. Only I'm not sure we can reach our goal that way.

CALLIMACO: Why not?

LIGURIO: Well, you know all kinds of people go to those spas, and some man might show up who will find Madonna Lucrezia as appealing as you do, a man richer than you and of a more pleasing countenance, so that you run the risk of exerting yourself only for the benefit of others; or else the large number of competitors will make her more reticent, or once you have overcome her reticence, she will favor someone else, not you.

CALLIMACO: I know what you are saying is true. But what can I do? What path can I choose? Where can I turn? I must try something, be it momentous, be it dangerous, harmful, underhanded! It is better to die than to live like this. If I could sleep at night, if I could eat, if I could converse, if I could take pleasure in anything at all, I would be more patient and wait for the right moment. But there is no remedy, and if I cannot be kept in hope by some scheme, I shall die! Hence, if I am bound to die, I don't see why I should be afraid of anything! I'm even ready to throw myself into a scheme that is wild, cruel, abominable!

LIGURIO: Don't say such things! Restrain such impulses!

CALLIMACO: You know well enough that it is in order to restrain these impulses that I am entertaining such thoughts. Therefore we must either pursue sending him to a spa, or set out on some other path that will give me hope—some false hope at least—so that I can sustain a thought that will at least help assuage my suffering.

LIGURIO: You're right, and I'll be the one to help you.

CALLIMACO: I believe you will, even though I know you make a profession of duping people. Anyway, I don't believe that I will be one of your dupes, because if you try to hoodwink me I will take revenge, and you will lose the use of my house and any hope of getting all that I have promised you.

LIGURIO: You mustn't doubt my loyalty: Even if there were not the profit you mentioned, and which I am hoping for, I feel that your temperament mirrors mine, and I am quite as eager for you to fulfill your desire as you are yourself. But let us leave all that aside. Messer Nicia has commissioned me to find a doctor to see which spa would be best for him to go to. What I suggest is this: You will tell him that you have studied medicine, and that you have had ample experience in Paris. It will be easy to convince him, fool that he is, and as you are a man of letters, you will be able to spout a few words of Latin at him.

CALLIMACO: Where will that get us?

LIGURIO: It will get him to the spa that we choose, and will help me put into effect another scheme I've thought up, one that will be quicker, more certain, and quite possibly more successful than the spa.

CALLIMACO: What do you mean?

LIGURIO: What I mean is that if you have courage and put your trust in me, by this time tomorrow I shall present you with a fait accompli. Then, even if Messer Nicia were a clever enough man—which he isn't—to realize that you are not really a doctor, our fast action will ensure either that he will not have time to weigh the matter, or, if he does, that he won't have time to interfere with our plan.

CALLIMACO: Your words fill me with life! This is too great a promise, and gives me too great a hope. How do you intend to do it?

LIGURIO: You will find out when the time is ripe. For now there is no need for me to tell you, for we barely have time to put things into action, let alone discuss them. Go back home and wait for me there. I shall go find Messer Nicia. If I bring him to you, I want you to follow my lead and play along with anything I say.

CALLIMACO: I will do it, even though you're filling me with hopes that I fear might end up drifting away like smoke.

ACT II

SCENE ONE

Ligurio, Messer Nicia, and Siro.

LIGURIO: As I have told you, I believe God has sent us this doctor so you can fulfill your desire! He has had endless experience in Paris, and you mustn't wonder at his not practicing here in Florence: First of all, he is rich, and second, he's planning to return to Paris any day now.

NICIA: He's planning to return to Paris? I don't want him to get me all tied up in a tangle and leave me dangling!

LIGURIO: Don't worry about that. What we need to worry about is whether he will agree to take you on. If he does, he will see you all the way through.

NICIA: As far as that goes, I shall place myself in your hands; but as for his medical knowledge, I'll tell you after I've spoken to him whether he's a man of learning or a charlatan quack.

LIGURIO: It is because I know you well that I'm taking you to him so you can talk to him. And if his presence, learning, and discourse do not strike you as those of a man in whose lap you could lay your head, then you may say that I am not I, but someone else entirely!

NICIA: So be it, by the Archangel in Heaven! Let's go. But where are his lodgings?

LIGURIO: He lives on this square. That's his door, the one right in front of us.

NICIA: I pray that all this comes to some good! You knock.

LIGURIO: Here I go.

SIRO: Who's there?

LIGURIO: Is Callimaco home?

SIRO: Yes, he is.

NICIA: How is it that you don't ask for *Doctor* Callimaco?

LIGURIO: He does not care for such trifles.

NICIA: Still, you must address him correctly, and if he doesn't like it he can drop his pants and you know what.

SCENE TWO

Callimaco, Messer Nicia, and Ligurio.

CALLIMACO: Who is asking for me?

NICIA: *Bona dies, domine magister.*

CALLIMACO: *Et vobis bona, domine.*[2]

LIGURIO [*aside to Nicia*]: What do you think?

NICIA [*aside to Ligurio*]: First-rate, by the Holy Gospels!

LIGURIO: But if you want me to stay, you'd better drop the Latin and speak so I can understand too, otherwise we'll be stoking two fires to spit a single roast.

CALLIMACO: How may I be of service?

NICIA: It's a long story. I suppose I'm looking for the two things from which another man might run as from a burning house. It's trouble I'm looking for, both for myself and for others. In short, I have no brats but want some. So you could say I've come to trouble you to make some trouble for myself.

CALLIMACO: Being of service to you or any gentleman of quality and standing like yourself can hardly be considered trouble. The only reason I toiled away in Paris all those many years, studying so hard, was to be of service to gentlemen like yourself.

NICIA: I thank you most prodigiously. And should you ever need my legal services, I will be most happy to oblige. But *ad rem nostram.*[3]

2. Latin: "Good day, Doctor." "And to you, Sir."
3. Latin: "To the matter at hand."

Have you given thought to which spa I should take my wife to so that she might conceive? I know Ligurio has spoken to you on this matter.

CALLIMACO: Yes, he has. But in order for you to fulfill your desire we must find the cause of your wife's sterility. You see, there can be many reasons: *nam cause sterilitatis sunt: aut in semine, aut in matrice, aut in instrumentis seminariis, aut in virga, aut in causa extrinseca.*[4]

NICIA [*aside*]: We could not have found a worthier doctor!

CALLIMACO: Then again, if you are impotent, you yourself could be the cause of the sterility. If that is the case, then I can offer no cure.

NICIA: Me, impotent? You make me laugh! You will not find a more stalwart and virile man than myself in all of Florence!

CALLIMACO: If that is so, then I can assure you we shall find a cure.

NICIA: Might there not be another remedy than the spa? You see, I'm not too happy about the inconvenience of going there, and my wife is not too happy about leaving Florence.

LIGURIO: There is another remedy, if I may be so bold—the doctor is circumspect to a fault, so I shall permit myself to speak on his behalf. [*To Callimaco*] Did you not mention that you can concoct a certain potion that unfailingly leads to pregnancy?

CALLIMACO: Yes, I did. But I am usually reticent about mentioning that among people I do not know well, as I would not want them to think me a quack.

NICIA: Do not worry about me! You have already amazed me with the extent of your learning: there's nothing I would not believe or do at your bidding.

LIGURIO [*to Callimaco*]: I believe you need to see a specimen from Madonna Lucrezia.

CALLIMACO: Yes, definitely, I must see a specimen!

LIGURIO [*aside to Callimaco*]: Call Siro and have him accompany Nicia to his house to get a specimen and bring it here. We'll wait inside.

CALLIMACO [*calling into the house*]: Siro, I want you to accompany that gentleman. [*To Nicia*] And if it please you, Messer Nicia, I

---

4. Latin: "For the causes of sterility are: either in the seed, or in the uterus, or in the testicles, or in the penis, or in some extrinsic cause."

would be grateful if you would come back here as soon as possible, so that we might initiate matters.

NICIA: If it please me? I shall be back in a flash! I have more faith in you than a wild Hungarian has in his spade. [*Callimaco and Ligurio go back into the house*]

SCENE THREE

Messer Nicia and Siro.

NICIA: This master of yours is a very capable man.

SIRO: More than you imagine.

NICIA: The King of France must regard him highly.

SIRO: Very highly.

NICIA: That is why I suppose he wants to live in France.

SIRO: I believe so.

NICIA: He does well to want to stay there. This place is full of brick-shitters with no appreciation for a man's skill and accomplishment. If he stayed here, there wouldn't be a man who'd look him in the eye. You wouldn't believe what I had to go through: I had to shit my guts out to learn a word or two of Latin, and if I had to earn my living off that, I'd be out in the cold, let me tell you!

SIRO: Surely you earn at least a hundred ducats a year?

NICIA: Not even a hundred lire, or a hundred *grossi*, I'll have you know! And the reason is that here in Florence, if you're not in with the ruling party and don't have good connections, you can't even get a dog to bark at you. All you can do is lounge about at funerals and weddings and loaf all day on a bench on the Via del Proconsolo. But I don't give a damn! See if I care! And that goes for those worse off than me, too! But don't repeat any of this, as I don't want to end up being slapped with a fine or having a leek shoved up my ass.

SIRO: I won't say a word.

NICIA: Here we are, this is my house. Wait for me here, I'll be right back.

SIRO: Go ahead.

SCENE FOUR

Siro alone.

SIRO: If all learned men were like him, we'd all be tipping rocks into our stoves.[5] One thing that's certain is that that crook Ligurio and my besotted master will lead Messer Nicia to shame. And that's fine by me, as long as word doesn't get around, because if it does my life will be in danger, not to mention the danger to my master's life and property. He's suddenly turned himself into a doctor: I don't know what plan they're hatching and where their deception is heading. But here comes Messer Nicia with a chamber pot! How can anyone help laughing at such a dupe?

SCENE FIVE

Messer Nicia and Siro.

NICIA [*talking through the door to Lucrezia*]: I've always done things your way, but this time I want you to do things my way. If I'd believed I wasn't going to have children, I'd rather have taken a peasant wench than you! [*To Siro, handing him the chamber pot*] Here you are, Siro. Follow me. You wouldn't believe what I went through to squeeze this damn sample out of that wife of mine! I'm not saying she's not eager to have children—she grieves about it even more than I do—but the moment I want to do something about it, that's another story.

SIRO: A little patience should do the trick. "Whisper a woman a sweet word or two, and she'll be happy enough to follow you."

NICIA: A sweet word or two after she's rattled me to the bone? Hurry and tell the doctor and Ligurio that I've arrived.

SIRO: Here they are: They're coming out.

5. Machiavelli's creativity in creating colorful idioms in *The Mandrake* had baffled Francesco Guicciardini, who asked for an explanation of some of the expressions. In a letter from October 1525, Machiavelli explains that "if we were all like Messer Nicia, we would be tipping rocks into our stoves, in other words doing things that only a madman would do."

SCENE SIX

Ligurio, Callimaco, Messer Nicia, and Siro.

LIGURIO [*aside to Callimaco*]: Messer Nicia will be easy enough to sway—the hard part will be convincing his wife. But there's no lack of means.

CALLIMACO [*to Messer Nicia*]: Do you have the sample?

NICIA: Siro has it there, covered up.

CALLIMACO [*to Siro*]: May I have it? [*He examines the sample*] Aha, this sample reveals a weakness of the kidneys.

NICIA: It does seem a little cloudy, though she produced it only a few minutes ago.

CALLIMACO: You must not be surprised. *Nam mulieris urine sunt semper maioris grossitiei et albedinis, et minoris pulchritudinis, quam virorum. Huius autem, inter caetera, causa est amplitudo canalium, mixtio eorum quae ex matrice exeunt cum urinis.*[6]

NICIA [*aside*]: By Saint Puccio's pussy! That man is so refined he could trickle through your clenched fist! How wonderfully he explains things!

CALLIMACO: I fear she might be lying exposed at night, hence the impurity of her urine.

NICIA: She's got an excellent blanket, but insists on kneeling by the bed for hours at a time every night, rattling off the Lord's Prayer over and over before she climbs in. That woman can outlast the sturdiest heifer in the cold.

CALLIMACO: Well, Messer Nicia, the question is whether you have faith in me or not, and whether I shall offer you a certain remedy—or not. I do have a remedy to offer you, and if you believe in me, you can have it. And if within a year from today your wife is not cradling her very own child in her arms, I shall give you two thousand ducats.

NICIA: Your word is my command! I shall follow you blindly and trust you more than my father confessor.

CALLIMACO: It is a fact that nothing is more certain to make a woman conceive than to give her a potion made from mandrake. I have

---

6. Latin: "For a woman's urine is always of greater thickness and whiteness, and of lesser beauty, than a man's. This is because, among other things, of the width of the canal and the mixture of matters that flow out of the matrix with the urine."

tried it out half a dozen times, and have found it to work every time. If it wasn't for this potion, the queen of France would be barren, as would countless other French princesses.

NICIA: Can that be?

CALLIMACO: It is just as I say. Fortune has smiled upon you, for I have brought with me all the ingredients that go into the potion, so you can have it at your pleasure.

NICIA: When would she have to take it?

CALLIMACO: This evening after dinner. The moon is favorably positioned, and the time could not be more propitious.

NICIA: There is no problem, then. You mix it and I'll get her to drink it.

CALLIMACO: There is one thing you need to be cognizant of, however: The first man to have intimate relations with her after she has drunk the potion will die within eight days. Nothing in the world can save him.

NICIA: Well, I'll shit my guts out! In that case I want nothing to do with that nasty pigs will! You're trying to put one over on me!

CALLIMACO: Calm yourself, there is a remedy.

NICIA: What remedy?

CALLIMACO: You must have another man sleep with her for one night, drawing all the mandrake's poison out of her. Then you can lie with her without putting yourself in peril.

NICIA: I will have nothing to do with this!

CALLIMACO: Why not?

NICIA: I'm not going to turn my wife into a whore and me into a cuckold!

CALLIMACO: My dear Messer Nicia, I took you for a wiser man. What can I say if you hesitate to do what the King of France and so many gentlemen there have done?

NICIA: Who can you find who would take part in such a harebrained scheme? If I tell the man he will die within a week, he won't want to do it, and if I don't tell him, I'll be breaking the law, and I'll end up being dragged before the High Council of Justice. It'll be my neck in the noose!

CALLIMACO: If that is all that is worrying you, leave it to me.

NICIA: What will you do?

CALLIMACO: I'll tell you: I shall hand you the potion this evening after dinner. You will have your wife drink it and then have her immediately go to bed. That should be around nine o'clock. Then you, Ligurio, Siro, and I shall disguise ourselves and scour the New Market and the Old Market, and we will gag the first young fellow we come across strolling about and march him back to your house and into your bedchamber in the dark. There we'll put him in the bed and tell him what he has to do—I doubt he'll cause any problems. In the morning you'll send him off before dawn, have your wife washed, and then you can lie with her at your leisure without any danger at all.

NICIA: I like the idea, since you tell me that princes and gentlemen have followed that path. But above all, word must not leak out, for the love of the High Council of Justice!

CALLIMACO: Who would say a word?

NICIA: There's only one hurdle left, a considerable one.

CALLIMACO: What hurdle?

NICIA: Getting my good lady to play along—I don't think she'd ever agree.

CALLIMACO: I can see that is a problem. I just don't know how one can marry a woman before one tames her to do as one bids.

LIGURIO: I have a solution.

NICIA: You do?

LIGURIO: Her confessor.

CALLIMACO: And who is going to sway her confessor—you?

LIGURIO: I, money, our roguery—and that of the confessor.

NICIA: I'm worried that she'll dig in her heels about going to her confessor if I command her to go see him.

LIGURIO: There's a solution for that too.

CALLIMACO: Yes?

LIGURIO: We can have her mother take her.

NICIA: Yes, yes, she trusts her!

LIGURIO: And I know for a fact that her mother sees things as we do. Off we go! Time is not on our side. Callimaco, you go on a walk, and make sure we'll find you at home with the potion ready by four. Messer Nicia and I shall go to her mother's house and prepare her, as I know her well. Then we will go to the friar, at which point we will inform you of what we've achieved.

CALLIMACO [*aside to Ligurio*]: I say, you're not leaving me alone, are you?

LIGURIO [*aside to Callimaco*]: You look as if you're at the end of your tether!

CALLIMACO [*aside to Ligurio*]: Where am I supposed to go now?

LIGURIO [*aside to Callimaco*]: Here, there, along that street, along the other: Florence is a big city.

CALLIMACO [*in a low voice*]: I'm at my wits' end.

ACT III

SCENE ONE

Sostrata, Messer Nicia, and Ligurio.

SOSTRATA: People always say that a wise man must choose the lesser of two evils. If this is the only solution for having children, you must take it, so long as it does not weigh too heavily on your conscience.

NICIA: I agree with you.

LIGURIO: If you go get your daughter, Messer Nicia and I shall go find her confessor, Friar Timoteo, so we can inform him of the matter. That way you won't have to tell him yourself. Let's see what he'll say.

SOSTRATA: That should work. You go that way, and I shall go find Lucrezia and see to it that she speaks to the friar.

SCENE TWO

Messer Nicia and Ligurio.

NICIA: I suppose, Ligurio, you're taken aback that we've had to go through all that folderol to get my wife to see her confessor. But if you knew the half of it, you wouldn't be the least bit surprised.

LIGURIO: I suppose it's because all women have suspicious minds.

454 · *The Essential Writings of Machiavelli*

NICIA: No, no, that's not it. She was the sweetest woman in the world and the most pliable. But then one of the neighborhood wives told her that if she made a solemn vow to go forty times in a row to matins at the Friars of the Servites, she would conceive. She went for twenty mornings or so, and then, wouldn't you know, one of those damn friars crept up behind her, after which she refused to go. It's terrible that those who ought to be setting us a good example are of that ilk. Isn't that true?

LIGURIO: The devil if it isn't!

NICIA: Ever since that day she's been as jumpy as a hare. And the moment you tell her something, she rattles off a thousand objections.

LIGURIO: I'm not surprised. But what about her solemn vow to attend the forty matins in a row?

NICIA: We purchased a dispensation.

LIGURIO: That's good. But give me twenty-five ducats, if you happen to have them on you. It's the amount one needs in a case like ours if one wants to befriend a friar quickly and with ease, as long as one can convince him there's more to come.

NICIA: Here, take them, I don't mind, I'll find a way to cut back elsewhere.

LIGURIO: These friars are cunning and shrewd, which is to be expected, since they know our sins as well as their own. Anyone who isn't accustomed to their ways is easily hoodwinked, and quickly finds he's getting nowhere with them. But we don't want you to start talking and ruining everything, because a man like you who spends all day in his study might know his way around books, but is not wise in the ways of the world. [*Aside*] This man is such a fool that I'm afraid he'll ruin everything.

NICIA: Tell me what you want me to do.

LIGURIO: Let me do the talking, and don't say a word unless I give you a sign.

NICIA: That's fine by me. What sign?

LIGURIO: I shall close one eye and bite my lip . . . No, no, we'll do it differently. How long has it been since you last spoke to the friar?

NICIA: More than ten years now.

LIGURIO: That's good, I'll tell him you've gone deaf. And don't answer or say a thing unless we talk loudly to you.

NICIA: Agreed.

LIGURIO: You must also not be alarmed if I say something that doesn't tally with anything, because, as you will see, in the end everything will turn out the way we want.

NICIA: Well, good luck to us.

LIGURIO: Ah, I see the friar talking to a woman. Let's wait till he gets rid of her.

SCENE THREE

Friar Timoteo and a woman.

FRIAR: If you'd like to confess, I will be pleased to oblige.

WOMAN: Not today, thank you. I'm expected, and just wanted to pop by to get a few things quickly off my chest. Have you said those Masses for Our Lady?

FRIAR: I have.

WOMAN: Here's a florin for you to say a requiem for my dead husband's soul every Monday for the next two months. He was a rough brute of a man, but my flesh is weak and I can't help feeling all aflutter whenever I think of him. Do you believe he's in Purgatory?

FRIAR: He definitely is.

WOMAN: I am not so sure myself. You remember what he used to do to me from time to time. Oh, how often I came running to you about that! I used to try and get away from him, but he always managed to corner me! Ah, God in Heaven!

FRIAR: Have no fear, the Lord's mercy is boundless. As long as man has the desire to repent, there is always ample time to do so.

WOMAN: Speaking of which, do you think the Turks will invade Italy this year?

FRIAR: They will if you do not say your prayers!

WOMAN: Heaven forbid! God save us from their devilish ways! My hair stands on end when I think about all that impaling they do. But I see a woman here in church who's got some of my cloth: I need to have a word with her. I wish you a good day.

FRIAR: Bless you.

SCENE FOUR

Friar Timoteo, Ligurio, and Messer Nicia.

FRIAR [*aside*]: Women are the most charitable creatures, and the most troublesome. He who shuns women passes up the trouble, but also the benefits. He who puts up with them gains the benefits, but also the trouble. As the saying goes, there's no honey without bees. [*To Ligurio and Messer Nicia*] What brings you here, my good gentlemen? Is that Messer Nicia I see?

LIGURIO: Speak louder, as he's grown so deaf he can barely hear a word.

FRIAR: Welcome, gentlemen!

LIGURIO: Louder!

FRIAR: Welcome!

NICIA: Greetings, Friar!

FRIAR: What brings you here?

NICIA: I'm doing quite well, thank you.

LIGURIO: It is better that you speak to me, Friar, because if you want him to understand what you are saying, you'll have the whole square running for cover.

FRIAR: How can I help you?

LIGURIO: Messer Nicia here, and another gentleman of standing, wish to distribute several hundred ducats to charity.

NICIA: Well, I'll shit my guts out!

LIGURIO [*to Nicia in a low voice*]: Be quiet, damn it! It won't be that much! [*Turning back to the friar*] You mustn't be surprised at the things he says, Friar. He might be deaf, but he has the impression he can hear, and then he says things that don't make the slightest bit of sense.

FRIAR: Go on, and let him say whatever he likes.

LIGURIO: I have some of the money here with me. The gentlemen would like you to be the one to distribute it.

FRIAR: With pleasure.

LIGURIO: But before this charity is provided, we must ask your help in a strange matter that has befallen Messer Nicia, a matter in which only you can be of assistance. The honor of his house is at stake.

FRIAR: How can I help?

LIGURIO: I'm not sure if you know Cammillo Calfucci, Messer Nicia's nephew.

FRIAR: Yes, I do.

LIGURIO: He went to France on business a year ago, and as he is a widower, he left his marriageable daughter in the care of a certain convent.

FRIAR: And what happened?

LIGURIO: What happened was that through either negligence on the nuns' part or the girl's frivolity she is now four months pregnant, so that if the matter is not handled with prudence we shall see Messer Nicia, the nuns, the girl, Cammillo, and the whole house of Calfucci disgraced. Messer Nicia is so apprehensive about this shame that he has vowed to give three hundred ducats for the love of God if the matter is dealt with.

NICIA [*aside*]: That'll be the day!

LIGURIO [*to Nicia in a low voice*]: Will you be quiet! [*Turning back to the friar*] And he wants the donation to pass through your hands. You and the abbess are his only hope.

FRIAR: How can I be of assistance?

LIGURIO: You must persuade the abbess to have the girl drink a potion that will make her miscarry.

FRIAR: I will have to give the matter some thought.

LIGURIO: Why do you need to? Look at how many benefits will arise from this: You will maintain the honor of the convent, the girl, and the family; you will give a father his daughter back, please Messer Nicia and all his relatives, and do as much charitable work as the three hundred ducats will allow; and all the while you will harm nothing but a bit of unborn, unfeeling flesh that could be eliminated in a thousand ways. I believe that that is good which does the greatest amount of good and makes the greatest number of people happy.

FRIAR: So be it, in the name of God! I shall do as you propose. Let it all be done for God and charity! Tell me the name of the convent, give me the potion, and, if you like, the money too, so that we can start doing some good.

LIGURIO: Now I can see that you are the kind of friar I believed you were. Take this portion of the money. The convent is . . . Ah, one moment please, I see a woman waving to me from the church. I'll be right back. Please stay here with Messer Nicia, I need to have a word with her.

SCENE FIVE

Friar Timoteo and Messer Nicia.

FRIAR: The girl, how old is she?

NICIA: I am stunned.

FRIAR: I said, how old is the girl?

NICIA: God curse the day!

FRIAR: Why?

NICIA: Because he'll get it!

FRIAR: I see I have crawled into the lion's den. I'm tangled up with a madman and a deaf coot. One suddenly runs off, the other can't hear a word. Yet if these coins are real, I can make much better use of them than they can. But here comes Ligurio once more.

SCENE SIX

Ligurio, Friar Timoteo, and Messer Nicia.

LIGURIO [*to Nicia in a low voice*]: Be quiet, Messer Nicia. [*To the friar*] I have great news, Friar!

FRIAR: You do?

LIGURIO: That woman I spoke with has informed me that the girl miscarried on her own.

FRIAR [*aside*]: Well, great! There goes all that money!

LIGURIO: What did you say?

FRIAR: I said that there is now a greater reason for you to make the donation.

LIGURIO: The donation will still be made—but there is one more thing you need to do to help Messer Nicia.

FRIAR: What would that be?

LIGURIO: A minor thing that is much less shameful, much more acceptable to us, and much more useful to you.

FRIAR: What thing? I feel you and I are kindred spirits, and now such good friends that there is nothing I wouldn't do for you.

LIGURIO: I'll tell you in confidence what this minor thing is inside the church, while Messer Nicia will wait out here and let me speak on his behalf. [*Loudly to Nicia*] Wait here, we will be back right away!

NICIA [*aside*]: Said the toad to the harrow.[7]

FRIAR: Let's go into the church.

SCENE SEVEN

Messer Nicia alone.

NICIA: Is it day or night? Am I awake or dreaming? I'm not drunk—I haven't had a drop all day—but I ought to be drunk if I am to put up with this load of crap. We set out to tell the friar one tale and end up telling him an entirely different one! Then I am supposed to play deaf, though I'd have done well to plug up my ears like Prince Uggieri of Denmark so I wouldn't hear those crazed things he said for God knows what reason! I'm already twenty-five ducats poorer, and the matter at hand has not even been mentioned yet. And now they make me stand here like a dough puff on a skewer. But I see they're coming back. There will be hell to pay if they have not discussed my affair.

SCENE EIGHT

Friar Timoteo, Ligurio, and Messer Nicia.

FRIAR: Have the ladies come to me. I know exactly what to do. If my authority is worth anything we will set up the union by this evening.

LIGURIO: Messer Nicia! Friar Timoteo has agreed to everything. We must see to it that the ladies come.

NICIA: I am a new man! Will it be a boy?

LIGURIO: It will be a boy.

NICIA: I am shedding tears of joy.

---

7. Machiavelli explains this curious saying in his letter of October 1525 to Francesco Guicciardini: "A peasant was harrowing the earth one day when a toad, not used to such a great commotion, craned its neck in wonderment to see what was happening. Suddenly the harrow reached it and grazed its back [...], at which point the toad said to the harrow: 'Don't bother coming back!' This gave rise to the adage 'Said the toad to the harrow' when one doesn't want someone to return."

FRIAR: You two go into the church while I await the ladies. Stay there so that they do not see you. The instant they are gone I shall tell you what they said.

SCENE NINE

Friar Timoteo alone.

FRIAR: I'm not sure who is tricking whom here. That crook Ligurio told me that first tall story only to test the waters: If I hadn't agreed to his offer, he wouldn't have confided in me his real designs so as not to reveal them needlessly. Since the first matter he and Nicia disclosed to me was false, they weren't worried for themselves if I hadn't played along. Well, I've been duped. But it must be said, I have been duped to my advantage. Messer Nicia and Callimaco are rich, and I can get plenty out of them both in different ways. And I need not fear anything, for this is the kind of matter that absolutely must remain secret. It's as little to their advantage as to mine to spread the word. Be that as it may, I have no qualms. I do fear, however, that as Madonna Lucrezia is upright and good there will be difficulties. Nevertheless it is through her goodness that I will get at her. In the end, all women have little sense—the instant you find a woman who can put two words together, you throw your hands up to Heaven and cry "Hallelujah!" because in the land of the blind the one-eyed man is king. But here she comes with her mother, who does not have any morals worth mentioning. She'll be a great help in making Lucrezia follow my lead.

SCENE TEN

Sostrata and Lucrezia.

SOSTRATA: You know very well, dear daughter, that I value your honor and well-being more than anyone else in the world, and that I would not advise you to undertake anything that is not proper. I have told you time and time again that if Friar Timoteo tells you that this need not weigh on your conscience, you can go ahead without giving the matter a second thought.

LUCREZIA: I have always worried that Messer Nicia's desire to have children would lead us into trouble. That's why, whenever he brings up a plan, I become concerned and apprehensive—especially after what happened when I went to those friars at Servi. But of all the things we have tried, this seems to me the strangest, to have to submit my body to such shame and then to be the cause of a man's dying for my disgrace! I think if I were the last woman in the world—if all humanity depended on me for its regeneration—I would not agree to such a scheme!

SOSTRATA: I'm not the one to discuss such matters with, my daughter. Speak to the friar, see what he says, and then do what he, we, and everyone who loves you advise you to do.

LUCREZIA: I'm racked by despair!

SCENE ELEVEN

Friar Timoteo, Lucrezia, and Sostrata.

FRIAR: Welcome, welcome. I know why you have come—Messer Nicia has already spoken to me. As God is my witness, I have been sitting over my books for a good two hours studying this case, and after much careful scrutiny I have found many particulars that both specifically and generally are in our favor.

LUCREZIA: Are you speaking the truth, or are you poking fun at me?

FRIAR: Ah, Madonna Lucrezia! Are these matters of fun? It is not as if you are meeting me now for the first time!

LUCREZIA: No, it isn't, Friar. But this seems to me the strangest scheme I have ever heard.

FRIAR: I believe you, Madonna Lucrezia, but you must stop worrying. There are many things that from a distance strike one as terrible, unbearable, and strange, but the moment one steps closer they turn out to be human, bearable, and familiar. This is why people say that fear of evil is greater than the evil itself, and our case is just one of those.

LUCREZIA: May God in Heaven will that it is so!

FRIAR: I would like to return to what I was saying before. When it comes to your conscience, you must take it as a general rule that when there is a good that is certain and an evil that is uncertain, one must never turn one's back on what is good out of fear of what is evil. Here we have a good that is certain: your becoming pregnant and providing another soul for our Lord God in Heaven. The uncertain evil is that he who will lie with you after you have drunk the potion will die. But then again there have been men who have not died. Yet as there is a certain uncertainty about the matter, it is better that Messer Nicia not run the risk. As for the act itself being sinful, that is pure nonsense, because it is the will that is sinning, not the body. A sinful thing would displease a husband, while in our case you will be pleasing him; a sinful thing would be enjoyable, while you, in our case, will not enjoy this. Furthermore, one must never forget to look at the aim of a matter: Your aim is to occupy a seat in Paradise and to please your husband! The Bible says that the daughters of Lot, believing they were the last women on the earth, lay with their father. As their intention was good, they did not sin.

LUCREZIA: What are you trying to talk me into?

SOSTRATA: Let yourself be persuaded, my daughter. Don't you understand that a woman who has no children has no house? If her husband dies, she ends up like a discarded animal, abandoned by all.

FRIAR: I swear to you, Madonna Lucrezia, by my monastic heart, that obeying your husband in this matter need not prey more on your conscience than eating meat on a Wednesday, a sin that can be sprinkled away with a little holy water.

LUCREZIA: What are you telling me to do, Friar?

FRIAR: I am telling you to do something for which you will always have reason to thank God. And you will see how happy you'll be a year from now.

SOSTRATA: She will do as you say, Friar. I'll put her to bed myself tonight. [*To Lucrezia*] What are you frightened of, you silly goose? I can think of at least fifty women in this town who'd throw up their hands in thankfulness to the Lord.

LUCREZIA: I will do as you say, but I do not believe I shall live through the night.

FRIAR: Have no fear, my child. I shall pray to the Lord on your behalf, and will direct a prayer to the Archangel Raphael himself that he may stand by your side. Go with my blessing and prepare yourself for this evening's rite.

SOSTRATA: Peace be with you, Friar.

LUCREZIA: May God intercede, and our Holy Virgin too, so that I do not come to harm.

SCENE TWELVE

Friar Timoteo, Ligurio, and Messer Nicia.

FRIAR: Ah, Ligurio, come here.

LIGURIO: How did things go?

FRIAR: They went well. Lucrezia and her mother returned home prepared to do as we say. We won't run into any difficulties, because her mother will stay with her—she'll put her to bed herself.

NICIA: Can this be true?

FRIAR: Well, well! So you are cured of your deafness?

LIGURIO: Saint Clement has wrought a miracle!

FRIAR: Yes, and you'd do well to purchase a grand votive offering for the church so we can spread the word about this miracle.

NICIA: Let us stick to the matter at hand. Is my wife going to create any problems about what I'm asking her to do?

FRIAR: I tell you she won't.

NICIA: I am the happiest man on earth!

FRIAR: I believe you. You'll get yourself a baby boy, for which many men would gladly give their eyeteeth.

LIGURIO: Off to your prayers, Friar, and if we need anything else, we'll come look for you. Messer Nicia, go to your wife's side and make sure her mind does not waver, and I shall go find Doctor Callimaco to see that he sends you the potion. But be sure we meet at six so we can see to everything that has to be done by nine.

NICIA: Good idea! Good-bye.

FRIAR: Go with God.

ACT IV

SCENE ONE

Callimaco alone.

CALLIMACO: I wish I knew what they've managed to do. Will I ever see Ligurio again? Four o'clock has come and gone—it's five already. Oh, the anguish! How true it is that Fortune and Nature keep their books balanced: They never send good your way without sending evil too. The more my hope has grown, the more my fear has grown as well. Woe is me! How can I live in so much pain, racked by these fears and hopes? I am a ship whipped by two opposing winds, which it need fear all the more as it approaches its haven. Messer Nicia's foolishness fills me with hope—Lucrezia's prudence and steadfastness fill me with fear. Alas, wherever I turn there is no respite. At times I try to get hold of myself, chastise myself for this passion, ask myself: "What are you doing? Have you gone mad? Once you have obtained her, what then? You will see your error, and repent all your exertions and thoughts. Don't you know how little good ultimately turns up in what man desires, as opposed to what he hoped to find? On the other hand, the worst that can happen is that you will die and go to Hell; but so many have died, and there are so many men of quality in Hell—is there any reason why you should be ashamed to join them? Look Fate in the eye! Escape evil, or if you cannot escape it, then at least bear it like a man. Don't bow your head before it, and don't lower yourself like a woman." Here I am bolstering myself. But my spirits are bolstered only for a little while. I am assaulted from all sides by such a desire to be with her just once that I am racked from head to toe: legs shaking, innards rattled, my heart trying to break out of my chest, my arms at a loss, my tongue gone mute, eyes blinded, head spinning. If only I could find Ligurio, I could let off some steam. —But here he is, hurrying toward me! His news will give me life or kill me altogether.

SCENE TWO

Ligurio and Callimaco.

LIGURIO [*aside*]: I've never been so eager to find Callimaco, nor have I ever had such a hard time doing so. If I had been the bearer of bad news, you can be sure I'd have run into him right away. I've been to his house, the piazza, the market, the Pancone delli Spini, the Loggia de' Tornaquinci, and haven't managed to find him. Men in love have quicksilver in their feet, and cannot stay still.

CALLIMACO [*aside*]: Why do I refrain from calling out to him? But he strikes me as quite happy. Hey, Ligurio! Ligurio!

LIGURIO: Ah, Callimaco! Where have you been?

CALLIMACO: What news, Ligurio?

LIGURIO: Good news.

CALLIMACO: Truly good news?

LIGURIO: The best.

CALLIMACO: Lucrezia is agreeable?

LIGURIO: She is.

CALLIMACO: The friar has set things up?

LIGURIO: He has.

CALLIMACO: O blessed friar! I shall forever pray to the Lord on his behalf!

LIGURIO: Ha, ha, I like that! As if God bestows his grace for evil as well as good! The friar will want more than your prayers.

CALLIMACO: What will he want?

LIGURIO: Money.

CALLIMACO: I'll give him some. How much did you promise him?

LIGURIO: Three hundred ducats.

CALLIMACO: You did well.

LIGURIO: Messer Nicia has already coughed up twenty-five.

CALLIMACO: What?

LIGURIO: He paid up: Why ask questions?

CALLIMACO: What about Lucrezia's mother, what did she do?

LIGURIO: What didn't she do? No sooner did she hear that her daughter could have a fun night without its being a sin, she begged, cajoled, and reassured Lucrezia until she finally agreed to see the friar. Then she saw to it that her daughter would agree.

CALLIMACO: Lord in Heaven! What have I done to deserve so much grace? I could die of happiness!

LIGURIO [*aside*]: What kind of man is this? First he wants to die of sorrow, now he wants to die of happiness. [*To Callimaco*] Is the potion ready?

CALLIMACO: Yes, it is.

LIGURIO: What are you sending Messer Nicia?

CALLIMACO: A goblet of elegant spiced wine, just the thing to settle one's stomach and invigorate the mind . . . Oh no, oh no! I am ruined!

LIGURIO: What is it? What happened?

CALLIMACO: All is lost!

LIGURIO: What the devil's happened?

CALLIMACO: Nothing has happened, nor is anything likely to happen! I've dug a hole and fallen into it!

LIGURIO: Why? Tell me what you mean! Take your hands from your face.

CALLIMACO: Do you remember I told Messer Nicia that you, he, Siro, and I would grab some fellow and push him into bed with his wife?

LIGURIO: Well?

CALLIMACO: What do you mean, "well"? If I am with you, how am I supposed to be the man who will be grabbed? And if I'm not with you, Messer Nicia will catch on to our trick.

LIGURIO: You have a point there. But isn't there a way out?

CALLIMACO: Not that I can see.

LIGURIO: There must be!

CALLIMACO: Like what?

LIGURIO: I need a moment to think.

CALLIMACO: Oh, that's great! All is lost if you have to start thinking now!

LIGURIO: I have an idea!

CALLIMACO: You do?

LIGURIO: I'll have the friar, who's helped us up to now, do the rest.

CALLIMACO: How?

LIGURIO: We'll all be in disguise. I'll disguise the friar, who will change his voice, his face, and his clothes, and I'll tell Messer Nicia that he is you. He'll have no reason to doubt it.

CALLIMACO: I like the idea. But what am I going to do?

LIGURIO: Well, you could wear one of those rakish mantles and come strolling along past his house, sporting a lute and singing some little ditty.

CALLIMACO: What, with my face uncovered?

LIGURIO: Yes, because if you were wearing a mask you'd rouse suspicion.

CALLIMACO: But he'll recognize me.

LIGURIO: No, he won't. You'll have to twist up your face: Hold your mouth open, or try pouting, or perhaps scowling—close one of your eyes. Go on, try.

CALLIMACO: You mean like this?

LIGURIO: No.

CALLIMACO: Like this?

LIGURIO: No, that's not enough.

CALLIMACO: How about this?

LIGURIO: Yes, yes, remember that one. I have a false nose at home: I want you to stick it on.

CALLIMACO: Fair enough. And then?

LIGURIO: We'll be here as you come around the corner. We'll grab your lute, seize you, lead you to the house, and shove you into bed. The rest you will have to do yourself.

CALLIMACO: As long as I get that far.

LIGURIO: You will get that far. But getting back will be entirely up to you.

CALLIMACO: What do you mean?

LIGURIO: You'll have to win her over tonight. Before you leave, you must tell her who you are, reveal the trick, profess your love, tell her how dearly you hold her, and how she can be your friend without the slightest touch of scandal, or your enemy with a blazing scandal. It's impossible that she won't reach some kind of agreement with you, and refuse a second encounter.

CALLIMACO: Do you think so?

LIGURIO: I am certain of it. But let's not lose any more time. It's already past seven o'clock. Call Siro, send the potion to Messer Nicia, and wait for me in your house. I shall go find the friar. I'll have him put on a disguise and then I'll bring him here. After that we'll go get Messer Nicia and see to everything.

CALLIMACO: That's a good idea. Off you go!

SCENE THREE

Callimaco and Siro.

CALLIMACO: Hey, Siro!

SIRO: Yes, sir?

CALLIMACO: Come here.

SIRO: Here I am.

CALLIMACO: Go get the silver goblet in my bedroom cabinet. Cover it with a cloth and bring it to me. Make sure you don't spill anything along the way.

SIRO: I'll be right back. [*Siro exits*]

CALLIMACO: He's been with me ten years and has always served me loyally. I think I'll find him loyal in this matter too. I haven't revealed the trick to him, but I'm sure he's guessed what we're up to, as he's enough of a rascal—and from what I can see, he's playing along.

SIRO [*reentering*]: Here it is.

CALLIMACO: Good! Quick, go to Messer Nicia's house and tell him that this is the medicine that his wife must take immediately after dinner—and the sooner she dines, the better. We'll be waiting around the corner at the appointed time, so tell him to meet us there. Hurry!

SIRO: I'm on my way.

CALLIMACO: Listen. If he wants you to wait, then do so and come back here with him. If he doesn't want you to wait, then come back as soon as you've given him the medicine and the message. Do you understand?

SIRO: Yes, sir.

SCENE FOUR

Callimaco alone.

CALLIMACO: I'm waiting for Ligurio to return with the friar. Whoever said that waiting is the hardest part was speaking the truth. I'm losing ten pounds an hour thinking where I am and where I could be two hours from now, frightened that something might come up to ruin my plan. If that happens, this will be the last night of my life, because I will throw myself into the River Arno, or hang myself, or hurl myself out one of the windows, or plunge a knife into my heart on her doorstep. I will end my life somehow! But is that Ligurio I see? Yes, that's him! And he has someone with him all hunchbacked and limping. That must be the friar in disguise. Those friars! You've seen one, you've seen them all. But who's that other fellow? That must be Siro, who will have given the message to Messer Nicia. Yes, that's him. I'll wait for them here, so we can join forces.

SCENE FIVE

Friar Timoteo in disguise, Siro, Ligurio, and Callimaco.

SIRO: Who's that with you, Ligurio?

LIGURIO: A worthy gentleman.

SIRO: Is he really lame, or is it part of his disguise?

LIGURIO: Mind your own business.

SIRO: He has the face of the Devil himself!

LIGURIO: Hold your tongue! You're rattling me! Where's Callimaco?

CALLIMACO: Here I am, welcome.

LIGURIO: Callimaco, you need to have a word with this clown! Every time he opens his mouth . . .

CALLIMACO: Listen, Siro, tonight you must do exactly as Ligurio says. When he tells you to do something, I want you to jump to it, as if the order came from me. Whatever you see or hear must be kept in strictest secrecy, if you value my property, my honor, my life, and what's good for you.

SIRO: I shall do exactly as you say.

CALLIMACO: Did you give Messer Nicia the goblet?

SIRO: Yes, sir.

CALLIMACO: What did he say?

SIRO: That he will do everything as planned.

FRIAR: Is this Callimaco?

CALLIMACO: At your service. Let us settle the conditions: I put my-self and my entire fortune at your disposal.

FRIAR: I humbly accept, and take you at your word. I have done things for you I would not have done for anyone else in the world.

CALLIMACO: Your efforts will not go unrewarded.

FRIAR: Your kindness toward me is sufficient reward.

LIGURIO: Let's drop the ceremonies. Siro and I will go disguise our-selves. You, Callimaco, come with us so you can get ready too. The friar will wait for us here: We'll be right back, and then we can go off to get Messer Nicia.

CALLIMACO: Great, let's go.

FRIAR: I'll be waiting for you here.

SCENE SIX

Friar Timoteo in disguise.

FRIAR: How right are those who say that bad company will lead a man to the gallows! And a man will come to such an end as much from being too good and too easily swayed as from being too much of a villain. God is my witness that I have never intended to harm any-one: I kept to my cell, preached my sermons, attended to my flock. But suddenly that devil Ligurio appeared and made me dip my fin-ger in sin, into which I then plunged my whole hand until I fell in all the way, body and soul, and who knows how deep I still have to sink! One saving grace is that when many people are involved, many have to share the burden. —But here come Ligurio and that servant.

SCENE SEVEN

Friar Timoteo, Ligurio, and Siro, all in disguise.

FRIAR: Welcome back.

LIGURIO: Do we look good?

FRIAR: Very good indeed.

LIGURIO: All we need now is Messer Nicia, and we'll be ready. Let's go over to his house, it's already past eight! Off we go!

SIRO: Who's that at his door? Is it him or a servant?

LIGURIO: No, it's him. Ha, ha, ha, ha!

SIRO: What are you laughing at?

LIGURIO: How can I help laughing? He's donned a cape that's so short, his bottom's uncovered. And what the devil is he wearing on his head? It looks like one of those monk's hoods, and he's got a little sword too. Ha, ha! And he's muttering something. Let's conceal ourselves here so we can hear how his wife's been raking him over the coals.

SCENE EIGHT

Messer Nicia in disguise.

NICIA: The trouble that fool of a woman is making! She's sent her maids to her mother's house and my servant out to the country. A wonderful idea, of course. But what's not so wonderful is all the moaning and groaning I had to put up with before she got into bed—"No, I can't go through with this!" "Oh, this'll be the end of me!" "What are you making me do?" "Angels in Heaven!" "Woe is me!" If her mother hadn't sworn she'd give her a good hiding, she'd never have got into that bed. A pox upon her! I don't mind a feisty woman, but there's a limit to everything! She's driven me up and over the wall, the rabid little shrew. If I were to say, "Find me one levelheaded woman in all of Florence and I'll hang myself!" her reply would be, "Why, what have I done to deserve this?" As sure as Pasquino entered Arezzo through the back gate, I'll make sure she's good and ready in that bed before the evening's done. But I must say I cut a splendid figure in this outfit: No one would ever recognize me. It makes me a good deal taller, younger, and slimmer—there's not a bawd in all of Florence who'd have me pay to bed her. But where is everyone?

SCENE NINE

Ligurio, Messer Nicia, Friar Timoteo, and Siro.

LIGURIO: Good evening, sir.

NICIA: Oh, ah, I say!

LIGURIO: Don't be afraid, it's only us.

NICIA: Oh, so you are all here? If I hadn't recognized you in the nick of time, I'd have plunged my sword into you, good and hard. Is that you, Ligurio? And is that you, Siro? And the other one here, is that Doctor Callimaco?

LIGURIO: Yes, Messer Nicia.

NICIA: Let me take a look at him! Oh, he has disguised himself excellently, his own grandmother wouldn't recognize him.

LIGURIO: I've had him put two nuts in his mouth so his voice won't give him away.

NICIA: You fool!

LIGURIO: Why?

NICIA: You should have told me! Then I'd also have put two nuts in my mouth, if it's that important for our voices be disguised too!

LIGURIO: Here, you can put this in your mouth.

NICIA: What is it?

LIGURIO: A ball of wax.

NICIA: Let me try . . . yuck, ugh, ooh, what, yuck, ooh, ugh, ooh! A dropsy upon you, you damn rascal!

LIGURIO: Forgive me, I gave you the wrong one by mistake.

NICIA: Yuck, yuck, ugh, ooh . . . What, what w-w-was it?

LIGURIO: Just a little purgative resin.

NICIA: A curse upon you! Yuck, ugh! Doctor, aren't you going to say something?

FRIAR: I'm outraged that Ligurio gave you that!

NICIA: I say, you are doing a splendid job of disguising your voice!

LIGURIO: Let's not waste any more time. I shall assume the role of captain, and will set up our forces for the coming battle. Callimaco will be on the right flank, I shall be on the left, and Messer Nicia will be in between. Siro will bring up the rear to bolster any flank that might flag. The battle cry will be "Saint Cuckoldino"!

NICIA: Who is Saint Cuckoldino?

LIGURIO: The most honored of all the saints in France. Forward, march! Let's set up our ambush here at this corner. Listen! I hear a lute.

NICIA: Yes, it's a lute! What shall we do?

LIGURIO: We must send out a scout to see who he is and then act according to what he reports back.

NICIA: Who will go?

LIGURIO: Siro, you go. You know what you have to do. Observe, examine, return swiftly, report!

SIRO: Yes, sir! [*Siro exits*]

NICIA: I don't want us to slip up and grab some old doddard who can barely stand up, or we'll have to go through this whole rigmarole again tomorrow.

LIGURIO: Rest assured—Siro's a good man. Ah, he's back. What did you find?

SIRO [*reentering*]: He's the handsomest young fellow you've ever seen. He can't be a day over twenty-five. He's alone, and he's coming this way wearing one of those stylish mantles and playing a lute.

NICIA: If what you say is true, then he's just what we're looking for. If he's not, believe me, you will end up with more than egg on your face.

SIRO: Have no fear, he's just as I say.

LIGURIO: Let's wait till he gets to this corner, and we'll jump him.

NICIA: Come over here, doctor. You strike me as a man of steel. Here he is!

CALLIMACO [*enters, singing*]: "The Devil might come to lie with you, while I'm far across the oceans blue."

LIGURIO [*seizing Callimaco*]: Fear not, sir! Give me that lute!

CALLIMACO: Alas! Leave me be! What have I done to you?

NICIA: You'll see! Cover his head and gag him.

LIGURIO: Turn him around.

NICIA: Turn him again—and again! Take him into the house!

FRIAR: Messer Nicia, I shall retire, as I have a most prodigious headache. If I am not needed, I shall not return until tomorrow.

NICIA: Indeed, we will not need you this evening, Doctor. We're quite able to handle this on our own.

SCENE TEN

Friar Timoteo in disguise.

FRIAR: They are nicely tucked up in the house, so I shall now return to my monastery, and you, dear audience, do not blame us: For if we were not to move on to the next act, then neither you nor I nor anyone here would get any sleep tonight. Before the next act, I shall have given a sermon, Ligurio and Siro will have dined, as they haven't eaten all day, and Messer Nicia will have left his bedchamber for his living room, as too many cooks spoil the broth. Callimaco and Madonna Lucrezia will not sleep a wink, because I know that if I were he and you were she, you and I wouldn't sleep a wink either.

Act V

SCENE ONE

Friar Timoteo alone.

FRIAR: I didn't close an eye all night, such is my fervor to hear how Callimaco and the others fared. I tried to pass the time in various ways: I said matins, read the *Lives of the Holy Fathers*, went over to the church and lit a lamp that had gone out, changed a veil on one of the statues of Our Lady that has wrought miracles. How many times have I told those brother friars of mine to keep her clean! And then they wonder why the votive offerings don't keep coming! I remember the days when we had five hundred offerings—now you'd be hard put to find twenty! But I'll tell you one thing: It's our fault! We've not done a good job of keeping the church's reputation going. In the old days we used to walk in solemn processions after the evening service, we had hymns sung every Saturday. We would have the congregation pledge solemn vows so that there'd always be a stream of votive offerings. Yes, back then we always got both men and women to make vows and purchase offerings! Now none of that's being done. And then we're surprised when business is down? My brother friars have nothing but air in their heads! But I hear a great ruckus coming from Messer Nicia's house! Here he comes, by my faith! They're sending out the prisoner. I've come just in time.

They've squeezed out the last drop, and dawn is breaking. I shall step aside to hear what they are saying.

SCENE TWO

Messer Nicia, Callimaco, Ligurio, and Siro, all in disguise.

NICIA: You grab him from that side, and I'll grab him from here, and you, Siro, hold on to his mantle from behind.

CALLIMACO: Don't hurt me!

LIGURIO: Don't be frightened, just get a move on.

NICIA: Let's not go any farther.

LIGURIO: Good idea. We can free him here: Whirl him around twice so he doesn't know which way he came from. Whirl him, Siro!

SIRO: Here we go.

NICIA: Again!

SIRO: Here we go again.

CALLIMACO: What about my lute?

LIGURIO: Away with you, you rascal! One more word and I'll chop your head off!

NICIA: He's run away. Let's go get out of these clothes: We'd do well to go out early this morning so it doesn't look as if we've been up all night.

LIGURIO: That is a splendid idea.

NICIA: Ligurio and Siro, go and find Doctor Callimaco and tell him that everything went well.

LIGURIO: What do you expect us to tell him? We don't know anything. After all, once we were inside your house, we went into the cellar to have some wine. It was your mother-in-law and you who stayed with them, and we didn't see you again until now, when you called us to help you kick him out of the house.

NICIA: You're right. Ha, do I have some funny things to tell you! There was my wife in bed in the dark. Sostrata was waiting for me by the fire. So I took the young rake upstairs, and so that I could get a good look at what's what, I pushed him into a storeroom off the hallway where there's enough light to see, but not enough for him to get a good look at my face.

LIGURIO: Very clever.

NICIA: I told him undress, but he dug in his heels. Then I went at him like a rabid dog, and he ripped off his clothes as if they were on fire. So there he stood stark naked. His face was quite ugly—what a nose, and his mouth all twisted!—but I'd never seen a handsomer body! White, smooth, soft. As for his other . . . um . . . charms . . . I shall say no more.

LIGURIO: The less said the better, I think. But why did you need to see all that?

NICIA: Why did I need to see all that? I'd already poked my finger into the pie, so there was no reason not to check the filling. I also wanted to see if he was healthy: If he had the pox, where would I be now? You hadn't thought of that, had you?

LIGURIO: You're right, I hadn't!

NICIA: Once I assured myself that he was healthy, I dragged him out of the storeroom and into the chamber, where I pushed him into the bed. And before I left I poked my hand under the blanket to see if the fellow was rising to the occasion. I'm the kind of man who grabs a bull by the horns.

LIGURIO: I marvel at the wisdom with which you handled this matter!

NICIA: Once I made sure everything was coming up roses, I left the bedchamber, locked the door, and went to sit with my mother-in-law by the fire, where we stayed up all night waiting and talking.

LIGURIO: What did you talk about?

NICIA: About how foolish Lucrezia is, and how she'd have done better to give in right away, without all the back-and-forth. Then we talked about the baby that I can already see in my arms, the chubby-cheeked little rascal! Until I heard the bells strike six. Worried that dawn was about to break, I went into the bedchamber. And would you believe it, there was no waking that scoundrel!

LIGURIO: I believe it.

NICIA: He was lying there like a roast pig in its own juice, but I got him up, summoned you, and we took him outside.

LIGURIO: So things went very well.

NICIA: But would you believe it, I feel bad.

LIGURIO: You do?

NICIA: I feel bad that that poor fellow will have to die so soon, and that this night will cost him so dearly.

LIGURIO: Ah, is that all you're worried about? Well, let that be his problem.

NICIA: You're right. —But it's taking an eternity to find Doctor Callimaco, I want to tell him the good news!

LIGURIO: He'll be out within the hour. Ah, the sun's come up already.
We'll go and change. What about you?

NICIA: I'll go home as well and dress. I'll see to it that my wife gets up,
and I'll have her come to church with me to have her purified. I'd
like Callimaco to be there too, so we can see the friar to thank him
and reward him for everything he has done.

LIGURIO: That's a splendid idea. Go with God.

SCENE THREE

Friar Timoteo alone.

FRIAR: I have heard what Messer Nicia said and am well pleased, considering what a fool that man is. But his final words please me no
end! As they are all coming to see me, I don't want to dally here, but
will go and wait for them in church, where my merchandise is
worth more. But who is that coming out of that house over there?
It's Ligurio, if I'm not mistaken, and the man with him must be Callimaco. I don't want them to see me here, for the reason I've just
mentioned. After all, even if they don't find me in church, I can always go look for them.

SCENE FOUR

Callimaco and Ligurio.

CALLIMACO: As I've already told you, Ligurio, I felt quite uneasy
until two in the morning. Though it was such a pleasure, it didn't
seem right. But then I revealed to her who I was and told her of my
love for her, and how easily we could live happily without a breath
of scandal, her husband being such a fool. I promised that should
God ever whisk him off, I would take her as my wife. These were all
sound enough reasons, but once she experienced the difference between my technique and that of Messer Nicia, and between the
kisses of a young lover and those of an elderly husband, she sighed
a few times and said: "Your shrewdness, my husband's foolishness,
my mother's silliness, and my confessor's wickedness have led me to
do what I would never have done of my own accord; therefore I ac-

cept that it was the will of Heaven for things to be this way. And as it is not for me to question the will of Heaven, I submit. I shall take you as my lord, master, and guide. You will be my father, you will be my champion, I want you to be my idol of goodness. And what my husband wished for a single night, I want to be forever. Be a brother to him, come to the church tomorrow morning, and then come back home to dine with us. From then on, you will be able to come and go at will, and you and I will be able to be together whenever we desire without scandal." I melted at the sweetness of her words, and was unable to say even a fraction of what I wanted to say. I am the happiest and most delighted man in all the world! And if this happiness does not elude me through death or the passing of time, I shall be more blessed than the blessed, more saintly than the saints.

LIGURIO: I am overjoyed at anything good that befalls you, and pleased that everything has turned out exactly as I predicted. What shall we do now?

CALLIMACO: Let us go to the church, for I promised to be there when she, her mother, and Messer Nicia arrive.

LIGURIO: I hear their door opening: it's them! They're coming out with Messer Nicia in tow.

CALLIMACO: Let us go to the church and wait for them there.

SCENE FIVE

Messer Nicia, Lucrezia, and Sostrata.

NICIA: Lucrezia, I think it would be good to do things fearing God, and not in just any old way.

LUCREZIA: Oh, do we still have to do more?

NICIA: Ha, she's become quite feisty.

SOSTRATA: Don't be surprised—she's a changed woman.

LUCREZIA: What do you mean by "doing things fearing God"?

NICIA: I mean that it would be good for me to go on ahead and talk to the friar and tell him to meet you on the steps of the church so he can lead you in to the purification ceremony, because this morning it truly is as if you were reborn.

LUCREZIA: So go ahead.

NICIA: You are really feisty this morning! And yesterday evening you seemed more dead than alive.

LUCREZIA: I have you to thank.

SOSTRATA: Go find the friar. Oh, but you needn't—I see him in front of the church.

NICIA: Yes, there he is.

SCENE SIX

Friar Timoteo, Messer Nicia, Lucrezia, Callimaco, Ligurio, and Sostrata.

FRIAR [*to himself*]: The only reason I'm coming out is because Callimaco and Ligurio told me that Messer Nicia and the ladies are coming to the church. And here they are.

NICIA: *Bona dies,*[8] Father.

FRIAR: Welcome, welcome. May all this augur well, Madonna Lucrezia, and God send you a nice baby boy.

LUCREZIA: May God will it!

FRIAR: God will most definitely will it.

NICIA: Do I see Ligurio and Doctor Callimaco inside the church?

FRIAR: Yes, sir.

NICIA: Wave them over.

FRIAR [*to Callimaco and Ligurio*]: Come here!

CALLIMACO: The Lord be with you.

NICIA: Doctor, take hold of my wife's hand.

CALLIMACO: Gladly.

NICIA: Lucrezia, this man is the reason we will have a staff to lean on in our declining years.

LUCREZIA: I am most grateful, and would be happy if he would be our friend.

NICIA: Bless you, Lucrezia! I would like him and Ligurio to come dine with us today.

LUCREZIA: Most definitely.

NICIA: And I shall give them the key to the room above the arcade so that they can come whenever they like, as they do not have women at home to attend to them.

CALLIMACO: That is very kind. I will gladly make good use of it from time to time.

FRIAR: Am I to receive some money for charitable purposes?

8. Latin: "Good day."

NICIA: You certainly will, Friar. It will be sent you today.

LIGURIO: Will anyone see to Siro?

NICIA: Let him come to me: What is mine is his for the asking. Lucrezia, how many coins do you have on you for the Friar's purification ceremony?

LUCREZIA: I don't quite remember.

NICIA: Well, how many?

LUCREZIA: Let's give him ten *grossi*.

NICIA: Well, I'll be hanged!

FRIAR: And you, Madonna Sostrata, it seems, have made a robust new stalk shoot up in place of the old.

SOSTRATA: That's reason enough to rejoice, wouldn't you say?

FRIAR: Let us all go inside the church, where we can say our prayers. Then, after the sermon, you can go back home and dine at leisure. —As for you, dear spectators, do not wait for us to come back out: The service will be long, and afterward I shall stay inside the church, while they will use a side exit to go home. Farewell.

LETTERS

This selection from Machiavelli's correspondence ranges from one of the earliest of his letters that has come down to us—a fascinating firsthand account of Savonarola's final desperate sermons before his execution—to one of Machiavelli's last letters, full of warmth and hope, written to his teenage son a few months before his death. The letters are elegant and informative, and they are carefully crafted, as they were written to be shown and read to friends and influential patrons. Machiavelli, forthright and outspoken in all his works, is even more at ease expressing his opinions in his correspondence, and we find in his letters some of his most creative, original, and inspired writings.

TO RICCARDO BECCHI

FLORENCE, MARCH 9, 1498

Machiavelli composed this letter during a crucial and tumultuous period of change in Florence. Over the previous few years, Girolamo Savonarola had attained unprecedented political power in Florence, gaining an ever-larger fanatical following through eloquent sermons, in which he attacked the vice and worldliness of Florence, as well as through his predictions, such as that of the death date of Pope Innocent VIII. He arranged massive bonfires of the vanities in which citizens were pushed to burn worldly items ranging from clothing to books and paintings. Now, at the beginning of 1498, Savonarola was about to succumb to his opponents.

This letter is addressed to Riccardo Becchi, Florence's emissary to the court of Pope Alexander VI in Rome, and describes what were to be Savonarola's last sermons. (He was executed two months later.) As Florence's negotiator in Rome, it was important for Becchi to be apprised of the situation in Florence, and Machiavelli was eager to find out from Becchi the stratagems of the pope, Savonarola's most formidable enemy. In The Prince, *chapter 6, Machiavelli gives his assessment of Savonarola's failure as a leader: "Savonarola did not have a system for holding on to those who had believed in him, nor did he have a system for making those believe who did not. Therefore, rulers like Savonarola have great difficulty*

> *in proceeding; their path is strewn with difficulties that they must overcome through prowess. Once they overcome these difficulties, the populace begin to venerate them. And once these rulers have eliminated those who resent their achievement, they remain powerful, secure, honored, and content."*

———

So that I may give you a full report of matters here in Florence concerning the Friar, as you requested, you must know that after the two sermons he delivered[1]—of which you have received copies—he gave another on Carnival Sunday. He preached at length, after which he invited all his followers to take communion on Carnival Day at the Monastery of San Marco, saying that he would pray to God to send a clear sign in the event that the things he had predicted had not come down from Him.[2] The Friar did this in order to unite his supporters, some say, and to reinforce them in his defense, as he was certain that the new Signoria, who had already been elected but whose identity had not yet been made public, would be opposed to him.[3] When the members of the Signoria were announced on Monday (I assume you are aware of their names), the Friar determined that more than two-thirds of the new Signori would be hostile to him, not to mention that the pontiff had sent a papal brief summoning him to Rome under pain of interdiction. As the Friar felt certain that the Signoria would want him to obey the papal order, he decided, either by his own counsel or on the advice of others, not to preach in the Cathedral of Santa Reparata, but to retire to the safety of the Monastery of San Marco. On Thursday morning, however, when the new Signoria came into office, he announced—at Santa Reparata—that he would comply with the papal order so as to avoid turmoil and to serve the honor of God. The men of his congregation were to come to hear his sermon at San Marco, and the women were to go to Fra Domenico at the Cathedral

1. Savonarola had given two sermons in Santa Reparata after the pope's threat to interdict all Florence.
2. Savonarola was prior of the Monastery of San Marco. He had summoned up his followers to pray to God that the instant he raised the sacrament, God would send a "clear sign" in the form of fire from Heaven that would drag him down into Hell.
3. The body of magistrates of Florence's Signoria, or supreme executive council, were elected for two-month periods, to ensure that no group or individual could gain control of the state.

of San Lorenzo.[4] If you had heard the audacity with which our Friar, finding himself in his own sanctuary, began his sermon, and the audacity with which he continued, your admiration would have been boundless. He was now greatly afraid for himself, and believing that the new Signoria would not hesitate to harm him, he had decided to bolster himself with as many citizens who would go down to ruin with him as he could. And so he began his sermon by instilling great fear and alarm, using reasoning that seemed sound enough to anyone not weighing it too carefully. His followers, he proclaimed, were the very best of men and his adversaries the very worst, and he summoned up every argument that might weaken the opposing party and reinforce his own—a sermon that, as I was present, I shall briefly describe.

The subject of his first sermon at San Marco was the following text from Exodus: "The more they oppressed them, the more they were multiplied and increased."[5] But before he began expounding on these words, he justified at some length his having given in to the pope's command, saying: "Prudence is the right knowledge about what is to be done."[6] All men, he declared, have and have had an aim, but different aims: The aim of the Christians is Christ, while the aims of other men, past and present, depended on their religion. As we are Christians, our aim is Christ, and we must strive toward this aim and serve the honor of Christ with utmost prudence and according to the times. If the times demand that we endanger our life for Christ, then we must endanger it. If the times demand that we hide ourselves, then we must hide, as we have read of Christ and Saint Paul. That, the Friar added, is what we must do, and that is what we have done: For when the time came to stand up to the furor and turmoil, we did so, as we did

4. The men and women of Savonarola's congregation were segregated, since the entire congregation was too large to assemble in the courtyard of the monastery. Fra Domenico da Pescia was one of Savonarola's closest adherents.

5. Machiavelli, probably quoting from memory, presents a slightly altered quotation from the Vulgate, Exodus 1:12.

6. *Prudentia est recta cognitio agibilium,* an altered quote from Thomas Aquinas, *Summa Theologica,* in which the actual words are *Prudentia est recta ratio agibilium* (Prudence is the right reasoning about what is to be done). Savonarola had studied Aquinus's works in depth and quoted him extensively.

on the Day of Ascension,[7] because the situation demanded it, as did the honor of God. Now that the honor of God demands that we cede to wrath, we shall do so.

Having made this brief speech, he described two groups: one that fought under God, which comprised himself and his followers, and the other that fought under the Devil, which comprised the factions opposing him. After expounding on this at some length, he began an interpretation of the words he had quoted from Exodus, saying that tribulations made good men grow in two ways: in spirit and in number. Man grows in spirit, he explained, because when adversity descends on him, he draws closer to God, becoming stronger for being nearer his agent, just as hot water when it is brought closer to fire becomes scalding from being nearer its agent. And man grows in number because there are three types of man: the good man, in other words, he who follows me; the perverse and obstinate men, who are my adversaries; and a third type, who leads a dissolute life dedicated to pleasure, but who is neither obstinate in evil deed nor inclined to do good, because he cannot distinguish between evil and good. The moment there is an actual conflict between the two—"Opposites when placed next to each other come better to light"[8]—the malice of the evil and the candor of the good become clear, and man flees the former and draws close to the latter, because by nature man flees evil and readily follows good. Hence in times of adversity the evil ones become fewer while the good multiply, "and therefore they grow so much more, etc."[9]

I am discussing this only briefly, because the confines of a letter do not encourage lengthy narration. The Friar then entered into various discourses, as is his habit, and then, in order to deal his adversaries a hefty blow and lay the groundwork for his next sermon, announced that our discords and turmoil would engender a tyrant who would de-

7. In April 1497 a Signoria was elected with a majority that was against Savonarola. He initially remained within the safety of the Convent of San Marco, but came out to preach at great risk on the Day of Ascension on May 4, despite the interdiction and excommunication by Pope Alexander VI. A tumult broke out and there was an attempt on Savonarola's life, but he managed to escape with an armed guard to the safety of the Monastery of San Marco.
8. Machiavelli quotes in Latin from Thomas Aquinas's *Commentary on the Book of Job: Quia opposita iuxta se posita magis elucescunt.*
9. Quoted in Latin: *Ideo quanto magis,* etc. A reference to Savonarola's initial quote from Exodus 1:12.

stroy our houses and ravage our land. This, he said, did not contradict what he had already preached—that Florence would prosper and rule all Italy—because the tyrant would prevail for only a short time in Florence before he was chased from the city. With this he completed his sermon.

The following morning, still expounding on Exodus, he came to the line where it says that Moses killed an Egyptian.[10] The Egyptian, he explained, stood for evil men, and Moses stood for the preacher who slew them by uncovering their vices. "O Egyptian, I shall stab you!" the Friar proclaimed, and began leafing through the books of priests, treating the men of cloth so vilely that even dogs would shun them. Then he added—and this is what he had been intending all along—that he wanted to inflict a second and greater wound on the Egyptian, announcing that God had told him that there was a man in Florence who had his sights set on becoming tyrant and was already pulling strings to accomplish his scheme, and that anyone wanting to oust the Friar, excommunicate the Friar, persecute the Friar, was simply aiming to become tyrant of Florence. But the laws, the Friar proclaimed, had to be observed. He continued about this at such length that in the course of the day people began publicly speculating about the intentions of a certain individual, who is as close to becoming tyrant as you are to being whisked up to the heavens. But then the Signoria responded to the papal brief in support of Savonarola, who suddenly felt he need no longer fear his adversaries in Florence. Where before he sought to unite only his own followers in hatred of his opponents and the fear of the word "tyrant," now, seeing that he no longer needed them, he has changed masks and incites them to the union that had been initiated, and no longer mentions an impending tyrant or his evil ways. He now seeks to set them against the supreme pontiff, turning to the pontiff and his attacks, and what he says about the pontiff is what one might say about the most wicked of men. As I surmise, the Friar is adapting to the times and shifting his lies accordingly.

I shall leave it to you and your wisdom to judge what the common people are saying, what their hopes and fears might be, because you can judge that better than I, as you know the humors of our city and the quality of the times. And as you are in Rome, you also know the

10. Exodus 2:11–12.

pontiff's mind better than I. I beg only this of you: If it has not been too onerous a task to read these words of mine, then I pray that it will not be too onerous a task for you to reply and give me your judgment of the disposition of the times and the people's stance as to what is happening in Florence. Farewell.

Yours,
Niccolò di M. Bernardo Machiavelli

To Giovan Batista Soderini

Machiavelli's letter to Giovan Batista Soderini, the twenty-two-year-old nephew of the Gonfalonier of Florence, for whose government Machiavelli was working, opens with a witty response to the young man's short letter of September 12, 1506, and segues into a lengthy discourse on Fortune. The ideas Machiavelli expounds in this letter are mirrored (in some cases almost verbatim) in chapter 25 of The Prince, *which it is believed Machiavelli worked on some seven years later. In the letter Giovan Batista Soderini had sent to Machiavelli, he had written: "If my affection for you did not lead me to doing many things without purpose, I would beg your pardon for writing you, or would find some pretext or excuse. But I do not have anything to tell you, nor do I want you to write back to me. [. . .] I cannot tell you how much Filippo di Banco and I want to go to Piombino [to meet King Ferdinand the Catholic], but if one of us is impeded by the stars, the other is impeded by the sun."*

A disguised letter of yours reached me, but I recognized your hand within ten words. Knowing you, I believe you will manage to get to Piombino, though I am also certain of your impediments and Filippo's, one of you challenged by too little light, the other by too much.[11] I do

---

11. A pun on Soderini's mention in his letter that the stars and the sun were impeding them.

not mind returning in January, though I know by February I'll be sinking with all hands. I am sorry about Filippo's misgivings, and await the outcome with suspense.[12] Your letter was short, but I made it longer by rereading it. I was grateful, because it gave me the opportunity to do what I might not have done and which you suggested I not do[13]—that was the only part of your letter I found without purpose. This would have surprised me, had Fate not shown me so many and varied things that I am rarely astonished and can seldom confess that I have not savored—through reading or experience—the deeds of men or their manner of behaving. I know you and the compass of your navigation, and how it might be blamed, though in fact it cannot be, nor would I blame it, considering what ports it has steered you to and what hope it can nurture in you (hence I do not think from your perspective, where one can see only wisdom, but from the perspective of the multitude where one sees the ends and not the means). One can see that various kinds of action achieve the same outcome, and acting in different ways the same result.[14] If this idea was untested, the actions of our pope and their results have proved it true.[15]

Hannibal and Scipio excelled equally in their military approach, but Hannibal kept his army in Italy united by means of cruelty, deceit, and unscrupulousness, attracting the admiration of the people who rebelled against the Romans in order to follow him, while in Spain, Scipio achieved the same admiration through kindness, loyalty, and scrupulousness. Both achieved countless victories. But as we have a tendency to ignore Roman examples,[16] let me provide some from our times: Lorenzo de' Medici disarmed the populace in order to hold Florence, while Messer Giovanni Bentivogli armed it in order to hold

---

12. Soderini mentions in his letter to Machiavelli that Filippo "is expecting any moment now a verdict against him."

13. Soderini's letter gave Machiavelli the opportunity to respond (which he would perhaps not have done), despite Soderini's having written that Machiavelli need not bother responding.

14. See *The Prince,* chapter 25: "Hence two men operating differently can obtain the same result, while when two men operate in the same way, one might achieve his goal, the other not."

15. Machiavelli is referring to Pope Julius's victory over Giampaolo Baglioni, the particularly ruthless tyrant of Perugia. *Discourses,* Book I, chapter 27: "[Pope Julius II], escorted only by his personal entourage, and driven by the rage with which he conducted all his affairs, put himself in the hands of his enemy Giampaolo, who then meekly followed him out of the city."

16. *Discourses,* Preface: "The most skillful actions that the histories show us [. . .] are admired rather than imitated—or, I should say, they are avoided in every way."

Bologna; Vitelli of Città di Castello and the current duke of Urbino destroyed their fortresses in order to hold on to their states, while Count Francesco [Sforza] in Milan and many others built fortresses in order to secure their states.[17] Emperor Titus believed he would lose his state the day he did not do something good for someone, while another might believe he would lose his the day he did something good. Many achieve their aims by measuring and pondering over every matter; but our current pope, who has neither scales nor yardstick in his house, with a flick of the wrist achieved, unarmed as he was, what he would have been hard put to obtain through organization and arms.[18] We see in all the examples I have cited, and in countless other examples I could give, that you acquire states, are subjugated, or are chased out of them depending on the turn of events. Often the same approach that was praised when you conquered the state is condemned when you lose it, and sometimes, when you lose a state after a long period of prosperity, you will not blame your own actions but accuse Heaven and Fate.[19] I do not know why different courses of action sometimes succeed and sometimes fail, though I would like to. So in order to hear your opinion on this I shall presume to tell you mine. I believe that just as Nature has given man different faces, she has also given him different kinds of intelligence and imagination. The result is that everyone comports himself according to his own intelligence and imagination. But on the other hand, because the times and the order of things vary, some men's aims succeed according to their wishes: He who conforms his course of action to the times will fare well, and conversely, he whose actions go against the times and the order of things will fare badly.[20]

17. Niccolò Viteli and Guido Ubaldo da Montefeltro, the last of his family to rule Urbino. Machiavelli makes the same argument in *The Prince*, chapter 20: "And yet in our own times Niccolò Vitelli tore down two fortresses in Città di Castello in order to hold on to that state, while Guido Ubaldo, the Duke of Urbino, when he returned to his dominions from which Cesare Borgia had driven him, razed all the fortresses of that province to the ground, judging that he would be less likely to lose his state a second time without them. [...] The Castle of Milan built by Francesco Sforza has done and will do more harm to the house of Sforza than any turmoil in that state."

18. Machiavelli is again referring to Pope Julius's capture of Giampaolo Baglioni, the tyrant of Perugia.

19. Machiavelli develops this idea in *The Prince*, chapter 25, titled "On the Extent to Which Fortune Wields Power in the Affairs of Men, and on How This Is to Be Resisted."

20. This line appears almost verbatim in *The Prince*, chapter 25: "In my view, he who conforms his course of action to the quality of the times will fare well, and conversely he whose course of action clashes with the times will fare badly."

Hence it can come about that two men acting differently might achieve the same result, because each man can conform to what he encounters, there being as many orders of things as there are states and countries. Times and events change often, both in general and in particular, and yet men's imagination and behavior do not change, and so it comes about that one man at one time has good fortune while another has bad. In fact, he who is so wise that he understands the times and the order of things and can adapt to them will always have good fortune or guard himself against bad, and would learn that it is true that wise men can control the stars and the fates. But because one cannot find such wise men, as man tends to be shortsighted and unable to control his nature, we see that changing Fortune controls men and keeps them under her yoke.[21]

I would like the examples I have offered to suffice as proof of my view. I have based it on them and hope that they will sustain each other. Cruelty, deceit, and unscrupulousness do much to give standing to a new ruler in a land where kindness, loyalty, and scrupulousness have thrived for a long time, just as kindness, loyalty, and scrupulousness give standing where cruelty, deceit, and unscrupulousness have reigned for a time. Just as bitter things perturb the taste and sweet things cloy, men become weary of the good and are irked by the bad. It was this, among other things, that opened up Italy to Hannibal and Spain to Scipio, both men adapting their course of action to the situation and the times. Someone like Scipio would not have been able to achieve Hannibal's success in Italy during that era, just as someone like Hannibal would have been unable to achieve Scipio's success in Spain.

21. This idea is also reflected in *The Prince*, chapter 25: "One cannot find a man prudent enough to be capable of adapting to these changes, because man cannot deviate from that to which nature inclines him."

To Alamanno Salviati

FLORENCE, 28 SEPTEMBER 1509

In 1509 Pisa capitulated to Florence after more than ten years of war and siege.[22] (The city's surrender on June 4 had been signed by Florence's First Secretary and Machiavelli.) The following letter to Florence's new governor of Pisa, Alamanno Salviati, demonstrates Machiavelli's lucid tactical analysis as he informs the governor of the immediate details of the progress of Emperor Maximilian I's invasion of Padua and the dangers this presents to Florence. Maximilian had entered into the League of Cambrai with Pope Julius II, France, and Spain, their aim being to conquer and destroy the Republic of Venice and partition its territories (to which Padua belonged). Thirty years later, Francesco Guicciardini, the foremost historian of the Renaissance, confirmed in his book The History of Italy *many of the details of Machiavelli's firsthand evaluation of the siege.*

———

Honored Sir. Since I do not believe I can offer you a more welcome gift than to inform you of the matters of Padua and the emperor, I shall write you about the circumstances and what evaluation is made and could be made of their aim and outcome. Should my opinion seem in

22. See also "Discourse on Pisa."

any way presumptuous, I crave Your Magnificence's forgiveness, and beg you to take for granted that I speak with utter frankness.

On the tenth of this month, the emperor and his army were in Sancta Croce, about a mile from Padua, but he sought to move his forces to a position both more favorable for striking Padua and suitable for blocking any supplies that might come from Venice. He therefore had to make a large arc around the city in order to avoid the marshes. He finally set up camp at Bovolento on the river Bacchiglione, seven miles from Padua, where his army plundered and slaughtered many peasants who had taken refuge there with their livestock.

He then set up another camp at Stra, an estate four miles from Padua where the Bacchiglione and Brenta rivers meet. From there he approached the city and began battering it on the 21st.

He positioned his army from the gates of Portello to the gates leading to Treviso, which I hear is a stretch of about three miles, and in width his men have taken up a mile. They say his army has thirty thousand foot soldiers, of which seventeen thousand are German, the rest having been sent to him by Ferrara, the pope, and France. The word is that every day new German infantrymen arrive, their only pay being present plunder and the hope for more. There are in addition twelve thousand or so horsemen, half Burgundians and Germans, the rest all Italian and French, and forty pieces of heavy artillery and up to a hundred pieces of medium and light artillery.

Our Florentine emissaries arrived in the field on the 21st, and their letters are from the 24th. They inform us that the emperor has set up the majority of his artillery during this time, that he has already demolished Padua's wall from Sancto Stefano to Mercato Nuovo, and that some of his heaviest artillery has shot three hundred pounds of iron. They make admirable strikes and no defense can resist them, and those who have managed to flee Padua have reported that many people have been killed, among them, they say, Il Zitolo[23] and Messer Perecto Corso.

Our emissaries report that the emperor is resolved to conquer Padua and excel as a military man and general, and that his army is thoroughly united and extremely well-provisioned.

23. Il Zitolo was a renowned general from Perugia who had come with his army to Padua's defense. Francesco Guicciardini in his *History of Italy* (Book VIII, chapter 11) writes: "The fortification of the moat was impressive, as was the prowess of the defenders (among whom Il Zitolo of Perugia, fighting most gloriously, was gravely injured)."

Our emissaries write nothing of the goings-on inside Padua, except that their army is continually firing at the emperor's camp and has caused much damage, and that Messer Lucio Malvezzo went to Venice for funds with a good escort and returned to Padua without much hindrance.[24]

That is what our emissaries have reported. We have also been apprised of the city's military setup and defenses by a friar who came from Padua eight days ago. He informs us that they first filled the moats surrounding the city with water, and have erected fortifications by the walls to defend the moats and the outer walls. Then there are the inside walls, which they have bolstered with logs that are six feet from the walls and linked to each other with beams and girders, creating a barrier. The space beyond this barrier is heaped with earth that they have pummeled as flat as they can. Furthermore, they have dug a deep moat—also on the inside—the way the French do, about 22 feet deep, beyond which they have raised a twelve-foot barrier above the moat. On the inside this barrier is leveled in such a way that horses can gallop on top. Behind this barrier they have set up wide spaces for grouping the horses.

The friar reports that there is a swarm of munitions and artillery spread out over the ramparts and the defenses of the moats I have mentioned. He says that there is a paid infantry of ten thousand, four thousand horses, ten thousand men brought in from Venice, and more than four thousand peasants, all united and set on defending Padua, showing every confidence in the preparations and in the weather, which is turning bad for the siege.

This is how things stand, while here in Florence the argument is first whether Padua should be lost or not, and then, in either event, whether one need fear that the emperor will now bring turmoil to Tuscany and Rome.

I shall pass over what is said for and against the loss of Padua, because I do not see anyone informed discussing it—everyone talks about it according to his opinion—but propose that we consider only whether one ought to fear either outcome.

---

24. A general and nobleman from Bologna who had also been involved in the Pisan campaign. Guicciardini in *History of Italy* (Book VIII, chapter 11) seconds Machiavelli: "Lucio Malvezzo also rode out of Padua with many horsemen in order to collect forty thousand ducats sent by Venice. Though on his return his rearguard was assaulted by the enemy, he brought back the ducats safely despite losing a number of his horsemen."

First, most people here in Florence are extremely worried about the emperor's conquering Padua, but they are also worried about his not managing to conquer it. They believe that if he is successful, his standing will increase to such an extent that France will side with him and he will be given the Holy Roman crown by the pope without hindrance,[25] and we and the rest of Italy will be at his disposal. If, on the other hand, he does not manage to conquer Padua, he might reach an agreement with Venice to our detriment with the same result: Because he is so well armed, no one will be able to stand up to him should he unite his army with that of Venice.

But I am of the opposite opinion, and do not fear the emperor whether he conquers Padua or not. Let me say to begin with that if he does not take Padua, he must do one of three things: return to Germany and leave Italian matters in the hands of others; retreat to Vicenza and Verona, shedding to a large extent the expense of the infantry and expecting instead with the aid of the French to wage a sustainable war with the Venetians during the winter; or, indeed, to enter into a treaty with the Venetians.

In the first two cases there is no need to fear him. As for the third— his entering into a treaty with the Venetians—this would have to be done either with the consent of his allies or against the will of all or some of his allies. In the first case there is not much to fear, because his allies will hold him back and will want to secure themselves entirely and their protectorates at least in part. If he reaches an agreement with Venice against the will of his allies, I cannot see what harm that could do us, nor do I see how such an agreement could be reached that would be in his and Venice's interest, because wanting to see if a treaty should ensue, one must examine first what motives move the parties and then, if there are such motives, to believe them.

The motives that would move the emperor are honor and profit. Those that would move the Venetians are the opportunity to gain time, temporarily sidestepping the dangers that shadow their liberty, and also the opportunity to lighten their expenses.

I cannot see at this stage what kind of treaty could be entered into against the wishes of the emperor's allies that would be of advantage to

25. Maximilian I had not actually been crowned Holy Roman Emperor, as Venice would not allow his progression to Rome. Officially, he held only the title Emperor Elect, bestowed on him with the consent of Pope Julius II the previous year (1508).

the emperor and to Venice, or that would serve the motives of either side. First, for the emperor to have his profit and honor, the Venetians must give him Padua, or at least so much money that he and his army would make the kind of profit that would correspond to the campaign for Padua he will have renounced. In either of these two cases it seems to me that the Venetians gain neither time nor money, because while right now they have only a single enemy on their backs, they will then have three—France, Spain, and the pope—who have all but sheathed their swords, but will be very quick to unsheath them. Hence, such an accord between the emperor and Venice will alleviate neither danger nor expense but will in fact double both, because besides the great amount of money the Venetians would have to give the emperor, they would also have to continue paying the army they have now, in order not to find themselves at the mercy of someone they cannot trust.

Consequently, I do not know how or why Venice would enter into a treaty with an emperor who cannot conquer Padua, only to double their expenditure and end up in a greater war than before. Hence, in conclusion, I do not see how this treaty could be made against the wishes of his allies, and, even if it were to be made, I cannot see that it should be feared. Nor can I see either how it could be reached with the consent of only a part of his allies, since for the emperor to achieve greatness in Italy is not to the advantage of France, Spain, or the pope, for reasons so obvious that I need not mention them. Thus, if the emperor does not conquer Padua we need not fear him, regardless of whether or not he enters into a treaty with Venice.

Nor is he to be feared if he does conquer Padua, because should he do so, he will have to undertake one of two things: either conform to the treaty entered at Cambrai, or break the treaty.

If he abides by the treaty, he will have to be in agreement with the members of the league[26] on what is to be done with the Venetians, and must put an end to the war with Venice either through a treaty with them or through their total destruction. Their destruction, however, seems difficult: first, because some of the emperor's allies want Venice to remain as it is, particularly Spain and the pope, who see Venice as an opportune thorn in the emperor's side and in that of France. The

26. Principally Pope Julius II, Louis XII of France, and Ferdinand II of Aragon, but also Mantua and Ferrara.

other problem is the season, which poses difficulties for the provision of water. This could lead to the dissolution of the army, with the result that the allies will have to opt for an agreement that the Venetians remain there and live under their own laws. In that case, the emperor might turn his thoughts to collecting his crown, which, once it is settled, is not to be feared much, as I have already pointed out.

If the emperor does not want to keep to the agreement of Cambrai, he will find himself suddenly lacking a third of his forces, because if you look at his army, as he has been given so many soldiers by France, the pope, and Ferrara, a third is not his. Should he seize Padua, these foreign soldiers will immediately draw together, as the rulers who sent them will be wary of his new eminence in Italy, which, as I have already pointed out, would not be to the advantage of any of them. And the French, one can say, are well armed indeed, as they are extensively equipped with soldiers and money and have the Swiss at hand, so that the emperor would have much to counter before he could come down to Tuscany at his leisure. Much time would pass before he could consider doing this, because I cannot see how he can move beyond Padua, should he occupy it, without having first settled things there; and settling things by force takes time and much expenditure. And if the emperor found himself alone and without the financial support of allies, he would doubtless be made to wait by whoever was in a position to fund him. In the shortest time he would find himself without an army, which has happened to him often enough in his campaigns. And I would laugh were someone to suggest that the Venetians might fund him, because their wound has already bled so much that whenever it begins to staunch they are in such a weakened condition that they would not dare reopen it (and we can presume that their wounds hurt them in the same way they would hurt anyone else).

That is how I see these matters, and while all these princes are alive I am not particularly afraid, even though that goes against the common opinion.

I was driven to write to you by my desire to hear your opinion, but also to amuse you with this whimsical trifle.

Farewell. From Florence. On the 28th day of September 1509.

Your servant, Niccolò Machiavelli, secretary.

To Luigi Guicciardini

Verona, 8 December 1509

Luigi Guicciardini was the older brother of Francesco Guicciardini, Renaissance Italy's foremost historian. Luigi Guicciardini had written Machiavelli a letter describing a wonderful amorous adventure and how he yearned to encounter the lady again, to which Machiavelli sent the following scabrously satirical reply.

———

Well, I'll be hanged, Luigi! It is amazing how in the same situation Fortune can lead men to such different results! You fucked that girl you met and are ready for another go. I, on the other hand, having been here for a few days and driven mad by the lack of matrimonial bliss, happened to run into the old woman who has been washing my shirts. She lives in a hovel, really more of a cellar; the only light that enters it comes through the door. So there I was, walking past one day, when she recognized me and made quite a fuss. She asked if I wouldn't mind stepping inside, as she wanted to show me some nice shirts that I might like to buy. Innocent dupe that I am, I fell for her ruse. I followed her inside and saw a woman cowering in the dim light, covering her face with a towel in a great show of modesty. The old bawd took me by the hand, led me over to her, and said: "Here is the shirt I am selling. Wouldn't you like to try it on before you buy?" Timid man that I am, fear gripped me. But to cut a long story short, as I found myself alone with the girl in the dark (the old woman having quickly left, shutting the door behind her), I went ahead and fucked her. Her thighs were flabby, her cunt soggy, and her breath somewhat ripe, but as my lust was rampant I did the deed. Having had my way with her, I thought that I might as well view the merchandise, and so took a burning ember from the hearth and lit the lamp that was hanging above it. No sooner was it lit than it nearly fell from my hands. Woe and strife! The woman was so ugly that I was almost struck dead. The first thing I saw was a clump of hair wavering between white and black—in other words, gray—and, though she was hairless on top, her baldness revealing a procession of lice marching over her scalp, the few strands of hair she did have were tangled with whiskers sprouting all the way to her eyebrows. On top of her small wrinkled head was a burn scar that gave her the air of having been branded at the market. Her eyebrows were a clump of bristles filled with louse eggs; one eye pointed up, the other down—one eye very much larger than the other, her eyelids mangy. Though her nose hung low, it managed to curl upward, one nostril open and clogged with snot. Her mouth bore a great resemblance to that of Lorenzo de' Medici—but it was twisted to one side, and slobber was bubbling out of it, since she had no teeth that might keep the saliva in. Her upper lip had a long but sparse mustache, and her chin jutted out sharply with a slight upward twist, folds of skin dangling from it to the base of her neck. I stood before this monster dumbfounded. Noticing my bewilderment she attempted to say "What is the matter, Signore?" but she could not because of her stammer. But the moment she opened her mouth, a surge of putrid breath hit my nose and mouth, the gateways to my two most offended senses. The surge assaulted my stomach and I, unable to fend off the attack, heaved and gagged and retched all over her. Having paid her with the coin she deserved, I went on my way.

And by the Heaven I hope will one day receive me, I do not believe that my lust will return while I am here in Lombardy. But you must thank God that you have the hope of having more such pleasure, as I thank God that I have lost the fear of ever again experiencing such displeasure.

I am hoping that I will have some money from this journey, and I would like to do some business once I am back in Florence. I've been thinking of setting up a small poultry farm, but I would have to find a man to manage it for me. I hear Piero di Martino might be good. I'd like you to sound him out. If he's interested in the job, let me know, because if he is not, I'll try to dig up someone else.

Giovanni will fill you in on any other news from here. Greetings to Jacopo and give my best to him, and do not forget Marco.

In Verona, on the eighth day of December 1509.

I am awaiting a reply from Gualtieri about my bit of doggerel.

Niccolò Machiavelli

TO FRANCESCO VETTORI

FLORENCE, 13 MARCH 1513

Machiavelli's high position in Florentine politics came to an abrupt end in 1512, when the Gonfalonier, Piero Soderini, was deposed and the Medici returned to power in Florence. Not only did Machiavelli find himself stripped of his office and forbidden to set foot in the Signoria, Florence's executive council, but in early 1513 his name appeared on a list drawn up by anti-Medici conspirators. He was thrown into prison, maintaining his innocence despite rigorous torture. Through the intercession of Francesco Vettori, Florence's ambassador to the newly elected Medici pope, Leo X, Machiavelli was pardoned. The day after his release, Machiavelli wrote the following letter to Francesco Vettori.

———

Honored Sir. As you will have heard from your brother Pagolo, I have been released from prison amid universal rejoicing in the city.[27] I did indeed have every hope of being freed through your and Pagolo's kind intervention, and am extremely grateful for it. I will not repeat the long story of my humiliation, but will only say that Fate has done its

27. The election of Pope Leo X, Giovanni de' Medici (the older brother of Giuliano de' Medici, who now held the first place in the Florentine Republic), unleashed euphoria and celebration in the streets of Florence. The populace was aware that with a Florentine Medici as the pope, Florence could expect unprecedented favors, benefits, and prominence in Italy and the world.

utmost to harm me. I thank God, however, that all this is over, and I have every hope that I shall not meet with such reversals again. I will be more careful henceforth, and the times are bound to be more liberal and not so replete with suspicion.

You are aware of the plight of our Messer Totto,[28] and I must turn to you and Pagolo for help. Messer Totto and I desire only one thing: that he be placed at the court of the pope, and so entered in the pontiff's scroll and provided with official credentials. We beg you for this.

Remind His Holiness about me so that if possible I might prove useful to Him or His entourage, for I believe I could bring you much honor as well as much benefit to myself.

> *On the 13th day of March 1512 [1513]*
> *Yours,*
> *Niccolò Machiavelli, in Florence.*

---

28. Machiavelli's brother.

To Francesco Vettori

FLORENCE, 10 DECEMBER, 1513

This letter begins with Machiavelli's witty response to Vettori's description of his elegant and world-weary life as Florence's ambassador to the pope's court. Vettori wrote of getting up late in the morning, of sauntering over to the pope's palace every other day "to speak twenty words with the pope, ten with Cardinal de' Medici, and six with Giuliano the Magnificent," of stylish card games, Roman gardens, and horseback riding. Machiavelli counters with a witty description of an inelegant rural existence in exile: "I have been catching thrushes with my bare hands. I would get up before daybreak, prepare the bird lime, and set off with a stack of cages loaded on my back." Vettori interacts with the foremost men of the day, while Machiavelli's companions are cantankerous woodcutters, "a butcher, a miller, and two kiln tenders."

This is one of Machiavelli's most celebrated letters, containing a lyrical passage in which he describes his discourse with the ancient philosophers and working on The Prince.

Most honored Ambassador. "Divine favors were never late."[29] I say this because it seemed to me that I had not lost your favor but merely mis-

---

29. A slightly altered quotation from Petrarch's poem "Triumph of Eternity" (line 13): *Ma tarde non fur mai grazie divine* (But divine favors were never too late). Machiavelli writes: *Tarde non furon mai grazie divine.*

laid it, for when you had not written to me for such a long time and I wondered what the cause might be, I paid little heed to all the reasons that filled my mind except for the one that made me believe you might have refrained from writing because someone had informed you that I was not a good custodian of your letters.[30] I knew that I had not shown them to anyone except Filippo [Casavecchia] and Pagolo [Vettori]. But your recent letter of the 23rd of last month reassured me: I am very pleased to see how calmly and methodically you are exercising your public duties. I encourage you to continue in this fashion, because he who abandons his advantages for those of others only loses his own without receiving anyone's gratitude. As Fortune insists on doing everything, she also insists that we leave her to her own devices and not interfere, biding our time until she allows us to do something: That is the moment for one to exert oneself and keep a closer eye on matters, and the moment for me to leave my farm and say: "Here I am!"

In the meantime, as I would like to repay you in kind, I want to tell you in this letter only what my life is like, and should you decide you would like to trade your life for mine, I will be happy to oblige.

I am on my farm, and since my recent problems I have not been twenty days in Florence.[31] I have been catching thrushes with my bare hands. I would get up before daybreak, prepare the bird lime, and set off with a bundle of cages stacked on my back, much like Geta returning from the harbor laden with the books of Amphitrion.[32] I'd catch at least two thrushes, at most six. I spent the whole of November in this way. Then to my regret this little amusement, though irksome and strange, came to an end. I shall tell you what my life is. I rise in the morning with the sun and head over to some woods I am having cut down, where I stay two hours surveying the work done the day before and to spend some time with the woodcutters, who are always in the middle of some dispute, either among themselves or with their neighbors. I could tell you a thousand amusing things about these woods that have happened to me, with Frosino da Panzano and others who wanted the timber. Frosino in particular. He sent for some stacks of

---

30. In the sense of having shown them to the wrong people.
31. Machiavelli is referring to his falling out of grace with the new government of the Medici, and his imprisonment and torture in March of that year.
32. A reference to *Geta e Birria*, a Renaissance adaptation of the twelfth-century Latin elegiac comedy of Vitale di Blois.

wood without telling me anything, and when it came time to pay he wanted to withhold ten lire that he says I owe him from a card game at Antonio Guicciardini's some four years back. I raised hell. I was about to accuse the carter who came to collect the timber of being a thief. But Giovanni Machiavelli finally stepped in and made us reach an agreement. Batista Guicciardini, Filippo Ginori, Tommaso del Bene, and certain other citizens each ordered a stack of wood from me when the north wind was blowing.[33] I promised to send them all. I sent one stack to Tommaso, which turned up in Florence half its original size, because he brought along his wife, the children, and his sons to lash the logs—they looked like Gaburra on Thursdays when he and his men cudgel an ox.[34] So, seeing who was profiting, I told the others I didn't have any more timber, and they were all angry, especially Batista, who includes this among other disasters of Prato.[35]

Leaving the woods I go to a spring, and from there to one of my bird traps. I have a book under my arm, either Dante, Petrarch, or one of the minor poets, Tibullus, Ovid, or the like. I read of their amorous passions and their loves, remember mine, and take pleasure for a while in these thoughts. Then I walk down the road to the tavern, speak to passersby, ask them news of their villages, learn various things, and note various tastes and thoughts of man. Meanwhile it is lunchtime, and with my family I eat the food that this poor farm and paltry patrimony bring. Having eaten, I return to the inn, where I find the innkeeper, and usually a butcher, a miller, and two kiln tenders. With these men I dawdle all day playing cards and backgammon, which results in a thousand quarrels with streams of spiteful and wounding words. Most of the time we battle over brass coins, and can be heard shouting all the way to San Casciano. Immersed among these lice I wipe from my mind all the mold and vent the malignity of Fate, happy to be trampled on in this way to see if Fate will be ashamed for what she has done to me.

33. Some scholars believe this is a veiled reference to political matters concerning the Medici and the opposition to them, others that Machiavelli is simply describing friends ordering timber from him.
34. It is thought that Gaburra must have been a well-known butcher in Florence.
35. Batista Guicciardini (b. 1468) had been the chief magistrate of Prato when it was sacked just before the Medici's takeover of Florence. Machiavelli is saying that Batista lists Machiavelli's refusal of timber among the disasters of Prato.

When evening comes I return home and go into my study. At the door I take off my everyday clothes, covered with mud and dirt, and don garments of court and palace. Now garbed fittingly I step into the ancient courts of men of antiquity, where, received kindly, I partake of food that is for me alone and for which I was born, where I am not ashamed to converse with them and ask them the reasons for their actions. And they in their full humanity answer me. For four hours I feel no tedium and forget every anguish, not afraid of poverty, not terrified by death. I lose myself in them entirely. And because Dante says, "Having heard without retaining is not knowledge,"[36] I have noted down how I have profited from their conversation and composed *De principatibus,* a little study in which I probe as deeply as I can into deliberations on this subject, exploring what a principality is, its genus, how it is acquired, how it is maintained, and why it is lost. If you have liked any of my previous caprices, then I am certain you will not dislike this one. It ought to be received with pleasure by a prince, particularly a new prince. Therefore I am dedicating it to His Magnificence Giuliano [de' Medici]. Filippo da Casavecchia has looked at it and will be able to fill you in on the work and its context, and of the discussions he and I have had, though I am still filling it out and filing it down.

Most Honored Ambassador, you wish me to abandon my life here and come to enjoy yours with you. I shall definitely do so, but am kept here by matters that I will have settled within six weeks. What makes me hesitate is that the Soderini are in Rome,[37] and if I came I would be pressed to visit and converse with them. I am also afraid that on my return from Rome I would not dismount at home but at the Bargello prison, because even though the current government has very strong foundations and great security, it is also new, and therefore suspicious, nor is there a lack of arrogant men, who, like Pagolo Bertini, would make others pay but still leave me with the bill. I beg you to relieve me of this fear, and then I shall definitely come at the said time to visit you.

I have discussed with Filippo whether it would be a good idea for me to present this little study [to Giuliano] or if that would not be

---

36. A quote from Dante's *Paradiso,* Canto V, lines 41–42.
37. Piero Soderini, the former Gonfalonier of Florence for whom Machiavelli had worked and who had been ousted by the Medici, had subsequently been brought to Rome by Pope Leo X (Giovanni de' Medici), who employed him as an adviser. Cardinal Francesco Soderini, his brother, was also in Rome.

such a good idea, and if I am to present it, whether it would be good to do so in person, or have it presented to him by you. What argues against presenting it to Giuliano are my doubts that he will even read it and that that fellow Ardinghelli[38] will take the credit for this most recent of my efforts. What argues for it is the neediness that is hounding me, because I am wasting away and cannot remain like this much longer without becoming contemptible in my poverty, not to mention my desire that the Medici princes begin putting me to use, even if at first only to roll a stone.[39] If I could not win them over then, I would have only myself to blame. As for *De principatibus*, anyone who reads it will clearly see that in the fifteen years during which I applied myself to the study of government, I was neither nodding off nor wasting time, and I would think that anyone would be keen to put to use someone so replete with experience at the expense of others.[40] My loyalty should be beyond doubt, because as I have always been most loyal, I would hardly now learn to change my ways, for whoever has been loyal for a good forty-three years—which I have been—is not able to change his nature. And my poverty stands witness to my loyalty and goodness.

I would be grateful if you wrote me your thoughts on this matter. I put myself in your hands. I wish you happiness.

On the tenth day of December 1513.

Niccolò Machiavelli, in Florence

---

38. Piero Ardinghelli was a courtier close to the Medici who was hostile to Machiavelli.
39. A reference to Sisyphus, who was punished in Hades by constantly having to roll a huge stone up a hill, only to have the stone roll down again once he reached the top.
40. Having gathered so much experience at the service of the previous government.

To Francesco Vettori

Florence, 3 August 1514

In Machiavelli's elegant and correct correspondence this letter stands out for its remarkable exuberance. Machiavelli is in love, and he shares his high spirits with his old friend Francesco Vettori. It is unclear who the "creature so gentle, delicate, and noble" is, but Machiavelli's biographers Ridolfi and Viroli propose that it might be his friend Niccolò Tafani's sister, who had been abandoned by her husband. The evidence they present is that on December 4, a few months after Machiavelli wrote this letter, he sent Niccolò Tafani to Vettori in Rome with a formal letter to him in Latin, asking him to intercede as ambassador to the pope, in order to compel Tafani's renegade brother-in-law to either return to his wife or give back her dowry and accede to an annulment of the marriage.

———

Dear friend, you have kept me cheerful and merry with your dispatches about your Roman love affair, and swept countless cares from my mind as I read and mused about your pleasure and vexation, for the one does not come without the other. But Fortune has granted that I can render you equal recompense, because here in the country I have met a creature so gentle, delicate, and noble—both in nature and circumstances—that I could never praise or love her as much as she merits. I ought to tell you, as you have told me, the beginnings of this love, in what nets it entangled me, where love cast these nets, and of

514 · *The Essential Writings of Machiavelli*

what kind they were; you would see that they were nets of gold woven by Venus and cast among flowers, so delicate and gentle that though an unfeeling heart could have torn them, I did not want to, and for a while basked within these nets until their tender threads grew firm and locked with the tightest knots. Do not think that Cupid used ordinary means to ensnare me, for, knowing that these would not suffice, he resorted to uncommon methods unknown to me and against which I did not know how to shield myself. Let me just say that although I am approaching fifty,[41] the sun's rays do not vex me, nor rough roads tire me, nor does the darkness of night frighten me. Everything now seems effortless, and I adapt myself to all her whims, no matter how contrary they might be to my disposition. Even though I sense I am courting great trouble I feel such sweetness, because of how her rare and gracious countenance transports me, and because it has cast aside all thoughts of my many predicaments, so that I would not want to free myself for anything in the world, even if I could. I have left behind thoughts of great and serious subjects. I no longer delight in reading of ancient matters or discussing those of our own times. All that has changed into sweet musings, for which I thank Venus and all of Cyprus.[42] Hence, write me anything you wish concerning your lady, but discuss all other matters with those who value and understand them better than I do, for I have found nothing but harm in them, while in matters of love I have always found goodness and pleasure.

Greetings. From Florence, on the third day of August 1514.

Your Niccolò Machiavelli.

---

41. Machiavelli was in fact forty-five.
42. Homer called Venus (Aphrodite) "Cyprian" after the island of Cyprus, where according to myth she was born from sea foam.

TO GUIDO MACHIAVELLI

IMOLA, 2 APRIL 1527

On the day Machiavelli wrote this warm and seemingly carefree letter to his teenage son Guido, he also sent a dire missive to Florence warning the city to fortify itself against the Holy Roman Emperor, Charles V, who was marching against the Medici pope Clement VII and his allies. Florence, Machiavelli warned, should not attempt to pay the emperor off: "It is better to spend ten florins so we can categorically remain free than forty florins that will fetter and destroy us."

Machiavelli ends this letter to his son asking him to reassure his mother that he will be back "before any trouble comes." This was, however, among Machiavelli's last letters, as he fell ill after returning to Florence and died on June 21, 1527.

—

Guido, my dearest son, I received a letter from you that has made me very happy, above all because you write that you are now recovered. What good news! If God grants you life, and me as well, I believe I can make you a man of standing, as long as you are prepared to do your part. Among the great friendships I have I can count a new one with Cardinal Cybo,[43] a friendship that is so close that I myself am aston-

---

43. Cardinal Innocenzo Cybo (1491–1549) was the son of Francesco, the illegitimate son of Pope Innocent VIII and Maddalena de' Medici. In 1521 he had come close to being elected to the pontificate himself. Machiavelli had stayed at his palazzo in Bologna the previous month.

ished. This will be to your advantage. But you must study and, as you no longer have your illness as an excuse, exert yourself learning literature and music, since you can see how much honor my few accomplishments have secured for me. Thus, my dear boy, if you want to make me happy and bring advantage and honor to yourself, you must study, do well, and learn. Everyone will help you if you help yourself.

Since the little mule has gone mad, it must be handled in the opposite way one would treat a man who has gone insane. A madman might be tied up, but I want you to untie the animal. Give it to Vangelo and tell him to take it to Montepugliano, remove its bridle and halter, and let it roam wherever it wants, making its own way to free itself of its madness. The village is big and the beast is small. It will not do anybody any harm. So without having to worry ourselves in any way we shall see what it wants to do, and we can always catch it again should it come to its senses. As for the horses, do whatever Ludovico[44] has told you to do. Thank God he is cured and has sold them. I am certain he has made a good profit, as he sent some money, but I am surprised and saddened that he has not written.

Greet Madonna Marietta[45] and tell her that I have been hoping to leave any day now, and am still hoping. I have never wished to be in Florence more than now, but I have no choice. Just tell her that regardless of what she hears she should be of good cheer, since I will be there before any trouble comes. Kiss Baccina, Piero, and Totto,[46] if he is there—I very much want to know if his eyes are well again. Live cheerfully and spend as little as you can. And remind Bernardo to mend his ways: I have written him two letters in the past two weeks and have not received a reply. May Christ watch over you all.

On the second day of April 1527

Niccolò Machiavelli
in Imola

---

44. Machiavelli's son Ludovico was in Constantinople.
45. Machiavelli's wife.
46. Machiavelli's daughter and sons. The infant, Totto, was away with his wet nurse.

ABOUT THE TRANSLATOR

PETER CONSTANTINE was awarded the 1998 PEN
Translation Prize for *Six Early Stories* by Thomas Mann,
and the 1999 National Translation Award for *The Un-
discovered Chekhov*. His widely acclaimed translation of
the complete works of Isaac Babel received the Koret
Jewish Literature Award and a National Jewish Book
Award citation. His translation from the Greek of a poetry collection by Stylianos Harkianakis received the
Hellenic Association of Translators of Literature Prize
(2005). Peter Constantine has translated Gogol's *Taras
Bulba*, Tolstoy's *The Cossacks*, and Voltaire's *Candide* for
the Modern Library. He was one of the editors for *A
Century of Greek Poetry* (2004) and is currently co-editing
an anthology of Greek poetry since Homer for W. W.
Norton. He is also a senior editor of *Conjunctions*. His
translations of fiction and poetry have appeared in many
publications, including *The New Yorker*, *Harper's*, and *The
Paris Review*. He lives in New York City.

A NOTE ON THE TYPE

The principal text of this Modern Library edition
was set in a digitized version of Janson, a typeface that
dates from about 1690 and was cut by Nicholas Kis,
a Hungarian working in Amsterdam. The original matrices have
survived and are held by the Stempel foundry in Germany.
Hermann Zapf redesigned some of the weights and sizes for
Stempel, basing his revisions on the original design.

MODERN LIBRARY IS ONLINE AT WWW.MODERNLIBRARY.COM

MODERN LIBRARY ONLINE IS YOUR GUIDE TO CLASSIC LITERATURE ON THE WEB

THE MODERN LIBRARY E-NEWSLETTER

Our free e-mail newsletter is sent to subscribers, and features sample chapters, interviews with and essays by our authors, upcoming books, special promotions, announcements, and news. To subscribe to the Modern Library e-newsletter, visit **www.modernlibrary.com**

THE MODERN LIBRARY WEBSITE

Check out the Modern Library website at
www.modernlibrary.com for:

- The Modern Library e-newsletter
- A list of our current and upcoming titles and series
- Reading Group Guides and exclusive author spotlights
- Special features with information on the classics and
  other paperback series
- Excerpts from new releases and other titles
- A list of our e-books and information on where to buy them
- The Modern Library Editorial Board's 100 Best Novels and
  100 Best Nonfiction Books of the Twentieth Century written in
  the English language
- News and announcements

Questions? E-mail us at **modernlibrary@randomhouse.com**.
For questions about examination or desk copies, please visit
the Random House Academic Resources site at
www.randomhouse.com/academic.